THE
AMERICAN EXPRESS
POCKET GUIDE TO
VENICE

Sheila Hale

PRENTICE HALL PRESS
NEW YORK

The Author
Sheila Hale is also the author of the *The American Express Pocket Guide to Florence and Tuscany*. She was born in New York, but has lived in Italy and England since 1962. A writer and journalist, she contributes to a number of newspapers and magazines, including *Connoisseur*, the *New York Times* and the London *Observer*.

Contributors
John Julius Norwich (Venice Restored)
Burton Anderson (The wines of northeast Italy)
Paul Holberton (Art and architecture)

Acknowledgments
The author and publishers would like to thank the following for their invaluable help and advice: Sir Ashley and Lady Clarke, Elspeth Collins, John Hale, Liselotte Hoehs, Charles Hope, Italian State Tourist Department, Peter Lauritzen, Sarah Quill, Baroness Maria Theresa Rubin. And for the revised edition: Robert Morgan, Tom Pocock.

Quotations
The author and publishers are grateful to those listed below for their kind permission to reprint the following extracts: the quotation from *Remembrance of Things Past* by Marcel Proust (page 80), translated by C.K. Scott Moncrieff © 1925, Chatto & Windus (UK) and Random House Inc. (USA); the quotation from *The Innocents Abroad* by Mark Twain (page 104), The New English Library (UK) and The New American Library Inc. (USA); the quotation from *Pictures from Italy* by Charles Dickens (page 108), Andre Deutsch (UK, USA).

Few travel books are without errors, and no guidebook can ever be completely up to date, for telephone numbers and opening hours change without warning, and hotels and restaurants come under new management, which can affect standards. While every effort has been made to ensure that all information is accurate at the time of going to press, the publishers will be glad to receive any corrections and suggestions for improvements which can be incorporated in the next edition, but cannot accept any consequences arising from the use of the book, or from the information contained herein. Price information is accurate at the time of going to press, but prices and currency exchange rates do fluctuate. Dollar amounts relate to exchange rates in effect in mid-1987.

Series Editor David Townsend Jones
Editor (first edition 1984) Carole McGlynn
Editor (second edition 1988) Alison Franks
Art Editor Eric Drewery
Designer Nigel O'Gorman
Illustrators Jeremy Ford (David Lewis Artists), Illustrated Arts, Rodney Paull
Map Editor David Haslam
Production Barbara Hind

Edited and designed by
Mitchell Beazley International Limited,
Artists House, 14-15 Manette Street,
London W1V 5LB
© American Express Publishing
Corporation Inc. 1984, reprinted 1986
New revised edition © American Express
Publishing Corporation Inc. 1988
All rights reserved including the right of
reproduction in whole or in part in any form
Published by Prentice Hall Press
A Division of Simon & Schuster, Inc.
Gulf & Western Building
One Gulf & Western Plaza
New York, New York 10023
PRENTICE HALL PRESS is a trademark
of Simon & Schuster, Inc.
Maps in 4-color by Clyde Surveys Ltd, Maidenhead, England
Typeset by Bookworm Typesetting, Manchester, England
Printed and bound in Great Britain by Purnell Book Production Ltd,
a member of the BPCC Group

Library of Congress Cataloging-
in-Publication Data
Hale, Sheila.
    The American Express pocket guide to
Venice / Sheila Hale. — Rev. ed.
    p. cm.
    Includes index.
    ISBN 0-13-025149-6
    1. Venice (Italy)—Description—1981-
—Guide-books. I. American Express
Company. II. Title.
DG672.H24 1988
914.5'31—dc19   87-21898
                                          CIP

Contents

How to use this book

The American Express Pocket Guide to Venice is an encyclopedia of travel information, organized in the sections listed on the previous page. There is also a comprehensive index and gazetteer (pages 200-208), and there are full-color maps at the end of the book.

For easy reference, all major sections (Sights and places of interest, Hotels, Restaurants) and other sections as far as possible are arranged alphabetically. For the organization of the book as a whole, see *Contents*. For places that do not have individual entries in *Sights and places of interest,* see the *Index.*

Abbreviations

As far as possible only standard abbreviations have been used. These include days of the week and months, points of the compass, San, Sant', Santa or Santo (S.), Santi or Santissima (SS.), Saint (St), rooms (rms), C for century, and measurements.

Floors

To conform with European usage, 'first floor' is used throughout the book to refer to the floor above the ground floor, 'second floor' to the floor above that, and so on. In Venice the *piano nobile* is the main floor of a palace, usually found above the ground-floor level.

Cross-references

Whenever a place or section title is printed in *sans serif italics* (for example, *San Marco* or *Basic information*) in the text, you can turn to the appropriate heading in the book for fuller information. Cross-references in this typeface refer either to sections in the book — *Basic information* or *Planning*, for example — or to individual entries in the *A-Z* of Sights and places of interest, such as *Doges' Palace* or *San Marco*. For easy reference, use the running heads printed at the top corner of the page (see, for example, *Basic information* on pages 9-10, *Doges'*

How entries are organized

Accademia ★
Map 14E2. Campo della Carità, Dorsoduro ☎ *5222247* ■
Open Mon-Sat 9am-7pm; Sun, hols 9am-1pm. Water bus 1 ___
or 2 to Accademia.

The Accademia houses the most complete collection of Venetian paintings in existence. Even the most shamelessly rushed tourists – will wish to visit it for the sake of Giorgione's *Tempest*, Carpaccio's *St Ursula Cycle*, Titian's *Presentation of the Virgin*, and the outstanding works by Bellini, Veronese and Tintoretto. Be warned though. The gallery suffers from acute staffing problems and often the most popular sections are closed without warning.

If you are approaching the galleries across the **Accademia Bridge** you may be detained at its summit by an irresistible view of the *Grand Canal*, as far as the *Salute* and Bacino di San Marco on your left and the bend of the canal at Palazzo Balbi on your right. The wooden bridge was built as a temporary structure in 1932 by Eugenio Miozzi, but has become as much a permanent landmark as if it were made of stone.

The galleries and the Accademia di Belle Arti (Academy of Fine Arts) occupy the former church, monastery and *scuola* of the Carità. The original appearance of the buildings from the San Marco side, now much altered, was lovingly recorded by Canaletto

---

Palace on pages 62-68, or *San Marco* on pages 106-114).

Bold type is used in the text mainly for emphasis, to draw attention to something of special interest or importance. At the same time it picks out places — churches or minor museums, for example — that do not have separate descriptions of their own.

Map references

Each of the full-color maps at the end of the book is divided into a grid of squares, identified vertically by letters (A, B, C, D, etc.) and horizontally by numbers (1, 2, 3, 4, etc.). A map reference identifies the page and square in which the street or place can be found — thus *San Marco* is located in Map **15D5**.

Price categories

Price categories for hotels and restaurants are denoted by the symbols □ ▫ ▪ ▪▪ and ▪▪▪ which signify cheap, inexpensive, moderately priced, expensive and very expensive, respectively. In Venice these correspond approximately with the following actual prices, which give a guideline at the time of printing. Although actual prices will inevitably increase, in most cases the relative price category — for example expensive or cheap — is likely to remain more or less the same.

Prices on the mainland are usually much lower, sometimes by as much as 50 percent.

Price categories	Corresponding to approximate prices:	
	for **hotels**	for **restaurants**
	double room with bath (single rooms are not much cheaper)	*meal for one with service, tax and house wine*
□ cheap	under $40	under $12
▫ inexpensive	$40-75	$12-25
▪ moderate	$75-150	$25-40
▪▪ expensive	$150-300	$40-60
▪▪▪ very expensive	$300-500	over $60

Bold blue type for entry headings

Blue italics for address, practical information and symbols. For list of symbols see page 6 or back flap of jacket.

Black text for description.

Bold type used for emphasis.

Sans serif italics used for cross-references to other entries or sections.

Entries for hotels, restaurants, shops, etc. follow the same organization, and are sometimes printed across a half column. In hotels, symbols indicating special facilities appear at the end of the entry, in black.

Gritti Palace 🏨 🏛
Map 14E3. San Marco 2467, Campo Santa Maria del Giglio
🕿 *794611* ☎ *410125* ▪▪▪ *92 rms*
▤ *92* 🖩 ♿ ⚏ *AE* ⑤ ⑥ VISA
Landing stage: Santa Maria del Gigli.

The Gritti is one of the most distinguished luxury hotels in Europe, with a deserved reputation for comfort and cordial management. The terrace bar on the Grand Canal is a fashionable rendezvous and the restaurant **Terrazza del Doge** serves above-average hotel food. Service apartments in a separate section of the hotel may be rented for a minimum of one week.
🛏 ⚑ ♿ ⚏ ⊡ 🔌 ♨ 👥 ⚲

5

Key to symbols

☎ Telephone

☺ Telex

★ Not to be missed

☆ Worth a visit

♣ Good value (in its class)

i Tourist information

🚗 Parking

🏛 Building of architectural interest

† Church or cathedral

📷 Free entrance

📷 Entrance fee payable

📷 Entrance expensive

📷 Photography forbidden

𝄡 Guided tour available

🍽 Cafeteria

👶 Special interest for children

🏨 Hotel

🏠 Simple hotel

🏩 Luxury hotel

□ Cheap

▯ Inexpensive

▮ Moderately priced

▮ Expensive

▮ Very expensive

🛏 Rooms with private bathroom

❄ Air conditioning

🏠 Residential terms available

🅰🅴 American Express

🅲🅱 Carte Blanche

🅳 Diners Club

🅼 MasterCard/Eurocard

🆅 Visa

🚗 Secure garage

🍴 Meal obligatory

☽ Quiet hotel

⬆ Elevator

♿ Facilities for disabled people

📺 TV in each room

☎ Telephone in each room

🐕 Dogs not allowed

🌳 Garden

⋘ Outstanding views

🏊 Swimming pool

🏖 Good beach nearby

🎾 Tennis court(s)

⛳ Golf

🏇 Riding

🎣 Fishing

👥 Conference facilities

🍴 Restaurant

🍴 Simple (restaurant)

△ Luxury (restaurant)

🍽 A la carte available

📋 Set (fixed price) menu available

🍷 Good for wines

🍽 Open-air dining available

🍸 Bar

● Disco dancing

🎰 Casino/gambling

♪ Live music

💃 Dancing

An introduction to Venice

Venice is the most bewitching of cities, but the spell it casts is not simple, nor is it altogether benign. It is impossible to feel indifferent about the place. Indeed, many reasonable people loathe it at first sight. They go away grumbling, echoing Gibbon's complaint about 'stinking ditches dignified with the pompous denomination of Canals,' muttering also about high prices, crowds and the vulgarity of Murano glass.

But other people — be warned — fall unexpectedly, obsessively in love with Venice; and they find that whatever else Venice may be, she is not an easy mistress.

Venice-lovers tend to be worldly, lonely wanderers. The city can induce violent swings of mood in the most even-tempered of them; but it also soothes their restlessness. They know that no place on earth is more exotic, that there is no more richly concentrated blend of cultures. As capital of a precocious and extensive empire stretching from Cyprus to the Lombard plain, the city's character was determined from the start by Orient and Occident and remains a unique fusion of both — floating improbably and precariously in the middle of the sea, as uncompromisingly urban as New York, as softly insinuating as a seraglio. It is a cosmopolitan city, visited sooner or later by everyone who is anyone, not to mention a million and a half foreigners each year; it is also a cozy, gossipy village which you can walk across in less than an hour — a *salotto città*, Venetians call it, a city like a drawing room.

Like the most intriguing of courtesans, Venice offers more than merely physical pleasure. It challenges the imagination. It insists upon itself, commanding total attention. And yet it seems ultimately unknowable. Its dense labyrinthine topography baffles the sense of direction. The buildings and bridges are dissolved and reassembled by the light, their proportions altered by the ebb and flow of the tides. Even after years of intimate acquaintance, you may be delighted in the course of an aimless walk by some undiscovered detail: a minor relief carving, an archway or wellhead.

There are, of course, crystalline winter days when you can see as far as the Dolomites; on such days Venice holds no secrets, is as crisp and colorful as a postcard. But there are other days when a dazzling explosion of golden morning light will modulate through a silvery haze of the tilting purple shadows of evening: Turner into Guardi into Monet. Then there are the evenings when all color and dimension is drained away with the setting sun and the city becomes a black and white engraving of itself.

In such a changeable, complex and famous city it is impossible not to feel sometimes bewildered and self-conscious. Venice has been so often described, painted, photographed and filmed that we can only sigh, with Henry James, that 'There is nothing new to be said about her . . . originality of attitude is completely impossible.' This, as he added, is annoying; it is also muddling, because inevitably everyone's perception of Venice is veiled by layer upon layer of other people's interpretations. The facts about the city's past and present, even about its arts, become unfocused.

There is certainly no lack of hard factual information about Venice. The State Archives are unusually rich in sources of information. But the myths are more compelling than the facts. If you are in love with the city, at first it scarcely seems to matter which is the Bridge of Sighs and which the Rialto and whether Giorgone painted four or four hundred pictures. You are inclined to believe the less reliable guidebooks when they tell you that

Venice rose from the water like her namesake Venus, or that this was Desdemona's house and that was Othello's. Then, slowly, you come to realize that you have been beguiled by mythmakers who were themselves beguiled by other mythmakers. The character of Venice as we see it is an invention imposed upon it over the centuries by alien imaginations.

One of the more macabre myths, for instance, is perpetuated by modern novelists and movie-makers, who persist in associating Venice with the uncanny, the morbid, and with death. This myth goes back to the early 17thC when Venice was regarded, particularly by the English, as the most successful but also the most corrupt and sinister of Italian cities. The myth persists in the face of the truth, which is that Venice is one of the safest and healthiest of all cities, with a very low crime rate and a high record of longevity.

Nor is there anything new about the *Schadenfreude* with which journalists attack the question, 'Is Venice sinking?' Submersion was predicted by many Romantic writers including Shelley, Byron and Ruskin. It was, and still is, a good metaphor for moral decay. In fact, the sinking has abated since the construction of aqueducts, obviating the need to draw water from the subsoil. And movable flood barriers will be installed between the *lidi* by the end of this century.

Meanwhile, Venice faces more complex problems. The decline of the port has led to an excessive reliance on tourism. In summer and during Carnival the narrow streets are clogged with short-term visitors. Cynics compare this loveliest of old cities to Disneyland and suggest charging an entrance fee from the mainland. Monuments are restored, crowd-drawing art exhibitions are mounted; but the ecological balance of the lagoon is neglected and the canals stagnate for lack of dredging. Housing is scarce and expensive. Since the 1950s more than half the native population has emigrated to the mainland. Depopulation is a more imminent danger than drowning, but perhaps not glamorous enough to compete for our attention with the romantically chilling Byronic convention of palaces crumbling to the shore.

A peculiar aspect of the image of Venice as depraved and decaying is that it co-existed for so many centuries with an exactly opposite idea of the city. From the middle of the 15thC until quite recently, the constitution of the Venetian Republic, an elaborate system of checks and balances, was widely regarded by political thinkers as the perfect form of government. Apparently impervious to hostile forces from within or without, it placed the pursuit of justice above personal ambition and allowed the social classes to co-exist in productive harmony. The Venetian Utopia was cited by James Harrington in his seminal work *Oceana* (1656); it influenced the philosophy of, among many others, John Locke.

Historians now tell us that this ideal of Venice was an exaggeration, that a close examination of events under the thousand-year life of the Republic reveals flaws and weaknesses in the Venetian constitution, remarkable an instrument though it undoubtedly was.

Nevertheless, this myth of Venice was to have far-reaching consequences. When the founding fathers of the newly independent United States of America drew up a constitution, they looked to the Venetian model of checks and balances. Republican government in Venice itself was by then nearly finished. Venice, in the Age of Enlightenment, was wholly despised. But the myth persisted — and myths, as all Venice-lovers know, are often more powerful than reality.

Before you go

Documents required

For citizens of the USA, EEC and British Commonwealth, a
passport is the only document required for visits not exceeding
three months. For some other nationals, a visa must be obtained in
advance in the country of departure. Vaccination certificates are
not normally required, but if you are traveling from the Middle
East, Far East, South America or Africa, check when buying your
ticket.

To drive a car in Italy, you must have a valid national driver's
license accompanied by a translation into Italian, available from
Italian State Tourist Offices abroad and most automobile clubs.
You must carry the vehicle registration document (logbook) and an
international green card or other insurance certificate, and display
a national identity sticker.

Travel and medical insurance

It is advisable to travel with an insurance policy that covers loss of
deposits paid to airlines, hotels and tour operators, and the cost of
dealing with emergency requirements such as special tickets home
and extra nights in a hotel, as well as a medical insurance policy.

The IAMAT (International Association for Medical Assistance
to Travelers) has a list of English-speaking doctors who will call for
a fee, as well as having member hospitals and clinics in Italy.
Membership of IAMAT is free.

For information and a directory of doctors and hospitals that are
members, write to: IAMAT, 736 Center St., Lewiston, NY 14092.

Money

The monetary unit is the lira (plural lire). There are coins for 50,
100, 200, and 500 lire, and notes for 500, 1,000, 2,000, 5,000,
10,000, 20,000, 50,000 and 100,000 lire. You may not take more
than 200,000 lire in or out of the country without official clearance,
but check with your bank before departure. If you intend
exporting more than 200,000 lire's worth of any other currency,
complete form V2 at customs on entry. It is a good idea to carry
cash in small amounts only.

Travelers cheques issued by American Express, Thomas Cook,
Barclays and Citibank are widely recognized. Make sure you read
the instructions included with your travelers cheques. It is
important to note separately the serial numbers of your cheques
and the telephone number to call in case of loss. Specialty travelers
cheque companies such as American Express provide extensive
local refund facilities through their own offices or agents.

Readily accepted charge and credit cards are American Express,
Diners Club, MasterCard (Eurocard) and Visa. Personal checks
supported by a Eurocheque Encashment Card can be cashed at
major banks by American citizens who also bank in Europe.

Customs

Any item clearly intended for personal or professional use may be
bought into the country free of charge. In the following list of
duty-free allowances, figures in brackets show the increased
allowances for goods obtained duty and tax paid in the EEC.
Tobacco If you are coming from an EEC country, you are
allowed 300 cigarettes *or* 150 cigarillos *or* 75 cigars *or* 400g tobacco.
If you are coming from outside Europe, you are allowed 400
cigarettes *or* 200 cigarillos *or* 100 cigars *or* 500g (1.1lbs) tobacco;
however, if you are coming from a non-EEC European country

you are allowed half these amounts.

Alcoholic drinks   (1.5) liters spirits (over 22% alcohol by volume) *or* 2 (3) liters alcoholic drinks of 22% alcohol or less; *plus* 2 (4) liters still wines.

Other goods   Goods (excluding personal possessions) to the value of $500.

When leaving the country, you may export up to 1,000,000 lire's worth of goods. The export of works of art is restricted and an application must be made to the Export Department of the Italian Ministry of Education.

When passing through customs, you must have dated receipts for any valuable items such as cameras or you may be charged duty on them.

Getting there

By air   Marco Polo airport, on the N edge of the lagoon near Tessera, serves European and domestic flights, and handles considerable charter traffic in summer. It is about 13km (9 miles) by road from Venice (Piazzale Roma). Some domestic and charter flights arrive at the smaller San Nicolò Airport on the N end of the Lido. Passengers from outside Europe will usually have to make a transfer stop at Milan or Rome.

By train   Santa Lucia railroad station is linked to the major Italian cities, with mainline trains from Milan, Rome and Trieste. There are also regular scheduled direct services from Vienna, Lausanne, Munich, Belgrade and Paris. In summer only there is a through train from Calais. The most luxurious way to arrive is by the Venice Simplon Orient-Express which runs between London and Venice with stops at Paris and Milan.

By bus   **Euroways** (☎*(01)278-0831*) run a luxury bus service to Venice from London via Turin, Genoa and Milan.

By car   The main highway (autostrada) serving Venice is the A4, running E from Turin to Trieste. The A13 link at Padua brings in traffic from central and southern Italy, and there is a short A27 link from Vittorio Veneto in the N.

As Venice is traffic-free, visitors must leave their vehicles outside the center. There are multistory parking lots at Piazzale Roma, but they are expensive and fill up quickly in peak tourist seasons. Alternative, cheaper parking lots are at Isola del Tronchetto, San Giuliano, Fusina and Mestre.

By boat   Various companies operate ferries linking Venice with other Adriatic and some Mediterranean and Aegean ports.

Climate

Venice has a variable although rarely extreme climate. The temperature ranges from a chilly average of 14°C (39°F) in January to a muggy 24°C (75°F) in July-Aug. High humidity can intensify the discomfort of both the hottest and coldest days as can two nasty winds, the piercingly cold *bora* which blows from the NE in winter and the *scirocco* which often brings oppressively sticky weather. Snow is rare but it can rain for prolonged periods in Mar-Apr and Nov-Dec. There are fine sunny days throughout the year and the climate is often idyllic, especially in May and Oct. The major nuisance is flooding (*acqua alta*), most likely in Nov and Dec.

Clothes

Since walking is both a necessity and a pleasure in Venice, be sure to pack comfortable shoes. The lightweight clothing suitable for summer should be supplemented by a sweater or light coat and umbrella in spring and fall. In winter you will need a heavy coat and sturdy shoes or boots.

Although informal day clothes are perfectly acceptable in most situations, including the opera and elegant restaurants, so is the most formal or fantastic dress. Venetians tend to dress up for the street more than other Italians.

Older Italian men tend to wear ties, but they are seldom obligatory. Women must wear clothes that cover thighs and shoulders when visiting churches.

General delivery

Correspondence marked *Fermo Posta* and addressed to Ufficio Postale, Fondaco dei Tedeschi, 80100 Venezia, will be held for collection at the central post office near the Rialto. Passports must be shown when collecting mail, and a small fee is payable. American Express Travel Service will also hold post for their card and travelers cheque holders at their office at San Marco 1471, near San Moisè (☎*5200844*).

Getting around

From the airports to the city

The most thrilling — and most expensive — way to get from Marco Polo airport to the center is by water. Public motor launches, approximately scheduled to meet incoming flights, take passengers across the lagoon to San Marco in about 30mins. (The schedule for the round trip is posted in major airline offices and hotels.) Private water taxis tout for business at the airport and cost about five times as much. If you wish to be taken directly to your hotel (most of the larger hotels have water entrances), you must pay the price of a taxi. San Nicolò airport on the Lido is served both by motor launches and by the cheaper vaporetti.

Land buses from Marco Polo to the city terminal at Piazzale Roma are very inexpensive. They leave hourly from 6.10am through to 12.10am and take about 20mins. Land taxis are much more reasonably priced than water taxis.

Porters

Porters (*facchino, -i*) are usually available at San Marco, Piazzale Roma and other main vaporetto stops. If you wish to book a porter, ask the information office at the airport to do so or ring the porters' stand (*stazio portabagagli* — ☎*5232385/5200545 for San Marco* ☎*5203070/5223590 for Piazzale Roma* ☎*715272 for the station*). Porters' charges are controlled by an official tariff.

Getting around within Venice
Water buses (*vaporetti*)

The water bus network is shown on the map on pages 30-31. An 'accelerato' is, confusingly, the slowest; a '*diretto*' is a slimmer, faster craft which makes fewer stops; a '*motoscafo*' is the smallest and fastest boat. The main internal lines are the *accelerato* no.1, which stops at every landing stage on the Grand Canal, and the *diretto* no.2, which is often very crowded but is the fastest way from the station and Piazzale Roma to the Rialto and San Marco. No.4, a summer-season-only service, roughly follows the course of water bus no.2. The circle line, the *motoscafo* no.5, travels in both directions around the periphery of Venice and to San Michele and Murano; it is, incidentally, a magnificent ride in itself and an inexpensive way of seeing the outer areas of the city from the

water. Bus no.12 for Murano-Burano-Torcello departs from the
Fondamenta Nuove. Boats for the Lido (nos. 6 and 11) leave from
the Riva degli Schiavoni.

There is an extra charge for each large suitcase taken on board
vaporetti. A tourist ticket entitling the holder to 24hrs' unlimited
travel on the vaporetti may be purchased at some landing stages
and tobacconists.

Gondola ferries (traghetti)

The Grand Canal may be crossed at many points by inexpensive
public gondola ferries rowed by pairs of professional gondoliers.
Some *traghetti* operate daily from morning to evening, others
mornings only. Landing stages are indicated on the map on p.32.

Gondolas

The privately-rented gondola remains the most delightful, if
extravagant, way of admiring Venice as it was built to be admired
— from the water. Gondoliers form a special class within Venetian
society and their licenses, skill and knowledge of the city are
passed on from one generation to another.

Although their prices are very high they are controlled by an
official tariff which is published in the weekly tourist magazine *Un
Ospite di Venezia*.

Water taxis

Water taxis are readily available but very expensive, although the
prices are regulated by tariffs. A radio taxi operates throughout the
city (☎5232326/5222303).

Walking

Venice is so small — scarcely an hour on foot from end to end —
that nothing is beyond reasonable walking distance. The major
hazard is losing one's way. If you are not in a hurry, this can be a
pleasure and in any case Venetians are extremely helpful about
giving directions. Streets are designated in a variety of ways listed
under *Words and phrases* in *Special information*.

Getting around on the mainland
Railroad services

Santa Lucia station is well connected with the rest of Italy
(*information desk open 7am-10.40pm* ☎715555).

Italian State Railways offer a wide choice of services at
reasonable prices. There are various special reduced-rate tickets
available, for specific periods of time, or passes for certain
distances. Trains are classified as follows:

Super-Rapido: Luxury, first-class-only trains running between
the major Italian cities. A supplement is payable, and seats must be
reserved.

Rapido: Fast trains serving major towns, some carrying only
first-class coaches. A supplement is payable, and seat reservation is
obligatory.

Espresso: Long-distance express trains stopping only at main
stations, with both first- and second-class coaches.

Diretto and *Locale*: Trains stopping at most, or all, stations; both
classes.

Buses

Buses leave for the mainland from Piazzale Roma; the service is
cheap and efficient. Tourist offices will advise about lines and
schedules from Venice, and the ACTV Information Center at
Piazzale Roma will tell you about mainland buses.

Getting around by car

Traveling by car is a very pleasant way to see the Venetian
mainland. Tolls are payable on the autostrada (highway) but this is

partly compensated for by their high standard and the time that can be saved.

Maximum speed limits are 50kph (32mph) in built-up areas, 110kph (70mph) on country roads and 140kph (85mph) on highways. Heavy, on-the-spot fines are strictly enforced for breaking these limits. Gasoline is expensive but tourists who take their car to Italy are entitled to a reduction on the normal price of gas and on highway tolls. Gasoline coupons may be purchased at the border at any ACI (Automobile Club of Italy) or ENIT office upon entering Italy. Payment for coupons must be made in foreign currency and they are available only to tourists driving their own cars with a non-Italian registration. Rental cars are not available for this reduction. Gas stations often close between noon-3pm and after 7pm.

The ACI (Automobile Club of Italy) will give free assistance to members of touring clubs such as the AA, RAC, or AAA to which it is affiliated.

Renting a car

Cars can be rented on the spot at Marco Polo airport or Piazzale Roma, or reserved in advance along with airline or rail tickets.

Domestic airlines

Alitalia operates direct daily flights to Rome and Milan.

On-the-spot information

Public holidays

New Year's Day; Easter Monday; Liberation Day, Apr 25; Labor Day (*Festa del Lavoro*), May 1; Assumption of the Virgin (*Ferragosto*), Aug 15; All Saints' Day (*Ognissanti*), Nov 1; Immaculate Conception (*Immacolata*), Dec 8; Dec 25 and 26. Shops, banks and offices close on these days.

Feast days are not official bank holidays, but many stores close in Venice on Nov 21 (*Festa della Salute*).

Time zones

Italy is 6hrs ahead of EST most of the year.

Banks and currency exchange

Banks are open Mon-Fri 8.30am-1.20pm. Bureaux de change (*cambio*) are open during normal shopping hours. They are plentiful in the center, less crowded than banks, and usually give the same rate. American Express Travel Service (*San Marco 1471*) also has an exchange desk. Hotels will cash travelers cheques but the rate is usually less favorable than in banks.

See *Money* for further details in *Before you go*.

Shopping hours

Shops are normally open 9am-1pm and 3.30 or 4-7 or 7.30pm. Many big stores close on Monday mornings. Certain large items are exempt from IVA (Value Added Tax) if they are exported direct to a country outside the EEC.

Post and telephone services

You can buy stamps at tobacconists (marked with a black 'T' outside) as well as post offices. The main post office in Venice is at

Fondaco dei Tedeschi, near the Rialto. There are various special services available, such as express or recorded delivery — ask for details. Mail boxes are red and marked *Post* or *Lettre*.

The telegram office at the central post office is open daily for 24hrs. Telegrams can be sent from post offices or by telephone ☎186. For international telegrams, ring Italcable ☎170.

Public telephones are to be found on some streets in the center, also at post offices, the station and some tobacconists and bars. Tokens (*gettone*) are decreasingly used but when required can usually be purchased at bars and newsstands as well as at post offices. The ringing signal is a single repeated tone, the busy signal a series of rapid pips. Long-distance calls can be made from telephone booths marked *interurbano*.

Telephone numbers: Most Venetian telephone numbers have seven digits beginning with 52. The exceptions are those beginning with 71-79, which retain six digits. The Venice code, for calls from outside, is 041.

Public rest rooms

There are public rest rooms at the Accademia and in the Albergo Diurnale, or day hotel, behind the w wing of Piazza San Marco as well as others at Rialto (Campo San Bartolomeo), Piazzale Roma and the railroad station, but they are few and far between and may well be closed. Most large bars have rest rooms which may be used in exchange for the price of a coffee. *Signori* means 'men' and *Signore* 'women.'

Electric current

Electricity in most places is 220V AC. The standard two-pin plugs or adaptors can be purchased in most countries.

Laws and regulations

Visitors are required to register with the police within three days of entering Italy. If you are staying at a hotel this will be done for you. Otherwise, you are responsible for registering yourself. Ask at the police information office ☎5203222.

Customs and etiquette

When visiting churches, it is important to remember that they are not museums, and it is offensive to interrupt a service.

Children are welcome even in the smartest restaurants; indeed they often get better service than adults.

Tipping

High prices and service charges mean that Italians tip less freely than is usual in some other countries. In restaurants, if service is not included in the bill, leave 15%; if service is included, a small note per person is an adequate supplement. If a sacristan or custodian does you any special favor, such as opening parts of a church or museum which are normally closed to the public, you should be more generous.

Disabled travelers

Unfortunately, Italian legislation regarding premises for the disabled is not enlightened and Venice, with its many bridges, can be inconvenient for those with crutches or in wheelchairs. The Italian State Tourist Office publishes an *Annuario Alberghi D'Italia*, which marks with the wheelchair symbol hotels suitable for disabled visitors.

Access to the World: A Travel Guide for the Handicapped (Chatham

Square Press, Inc., 401 Broadway, New York, NY 10013) will
also prove useful.

Local and foreign publications
The daily newspapers of Venice are *La Nuova Venezia* and *Il
Gazzettino*. The weekly magazine *Un Ospite di Venezia/A Guest in
Venice* is issued free by tourist offices and many hotels. It is written
in Italian and English and contains much practical local
information as well as articles about cultural events. The
Assessorato al Turismo has information sheets and an almanac of
events. Most major European newspapers are available on the
afternoon of issue, as is the *International Herald Tribune*, published
in Paris.

Useful addresses

Tourist information
Ente Provinciale per il Turismo (*71C Piazza San Marco*
☎*5226356, Piazzale Roma* ☎*5227402 and Santa Lucia station*
☎*715016*), for information about the city and province of
Venice.

Assessorato al Turismo, Ca'Giustinian (*San Marco 1364*
☎*5224842*), for information about the city's cultural events.

Ente per le Ville Venete (*Piazza San Marco 63* ☎*5230783*), for
information about villas in the Veneto open to the public.

American Express Travel Service (*San Marco 1471, near San
Moisè* ☎*5200844*) is a valuable source of information for any
traveler in need of help, advice or emergency services.

Main post office
Fondaco dei Tedeschi 80100, near the Rialto ☎5286212/5204143

Telephone services
Time ☎161
Weather ☎191
Sailing bulletin ☎196

Airlines and airports
Alitalia   San Marco 1463, near San Moisè ☎5200355/5225428
British Airways   Castello 4191, Riva degli Schiavoni
☎5285026/5205699
TWA   San Marco 1475, near San Moisè ☎5203219/5203220
Marco Polo airport   ☎661111
San Nicolò airport   ☎765427

Tour operators
American Express   San Marco 1471, near San Moisè ☎5200844
CIT   San Marco 4850 ☎5285480
Wagons-Lits/Cook   San Marco 289, Piazzetta Leoncini
☎5223405

Hotel information
Associazione Veneziana Albergatori   San Marco 2475 ☎5228004

Tourist guides
Guide Turistiche Associazione   Castello 5267 ☎5209038
Ritrovo Gruppo San Marco   Castello 6118 ☎5236100

Basic information

Automobile club
Automobile Club d'Italia (ACI)   Santa Croce 518 ☎5200300

Major public libraries
Correr   San Marco 52 ☎5225625/5222185
Marciana   San Marco 7 ☎5208788
Querini-Stampalia   Castello 4778 (near S.M. Formosa) ☎ 5225235

Lost property
Santa Lucia station   ☎716122 (ext.3238)
ACTV (for property lost on vaporetti)   ☎780310
Municipio (town hall)   ☎5208844

Major places of worship
Roman Catholic Mass is held daily in most churches, and High
Mass with music only on Sunday. Other churches include:
Church of England   St George's, Campo San Vio ☎5229195
Christian Evangelical/Baptist   Via Canetti ☎5220704
Greek Orthodox   Ponte dei Greci ☎5225446
Methodist   Campo Santa Maria Formosa ☎5227549
Synagogues   Ghetto Vecchio ☎715012

Consulates
Austria   Piazzale Roma 416 ☎5200459
Belgium   San Marco 2632 ☎5224124
Denmark   San Polo 2347   ☎796511
Finland   San Giuliano, Mestre ☎5259912
France   Dorsoduro 1397 ☎5222392/5224319
Germany, West   San Marco 2888 ☎5225100
Greece   San Polo 720, near Rialto ☎5237260
Netherlands   San Marco 423 ☎5225544
Norway   Lung Rotondo 12/7 Garibaldi, Mestre ☎962050
Spain   San Marco 2442 ☎5204510
Sweden   Santa Croce 499, Piazzale Roma ☎791611
Switzerland   Dorsoduro 810, near Accademia ☎5225996
UK   Dorsoduro 1051, near Accademia ☎5227207
   Australia, Canada, Ireland (Eire), Japan, New Zealand, South
Africa and the USA are countries not represented in Venice; for
help and information contact the appropriate consulate in Rome.

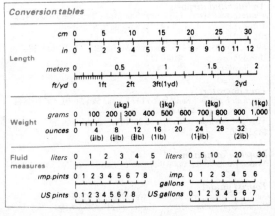

Emergency information

Emergency services

Police	☎ 113 (free from any telephone)
Ambulance }	You will be asked which service
Fire	you require.

Hospitals with casualty departments

Civili Riuniti di Venezia   Campo Santi Giovanni e Paolo
☎ 5205622/5207556
Ospedale al Mare   Lungomare d'Annunzio, Lido
☎ 761750

Other medical emergencies

Consult the telephone directory Yellow Pages to find a
doctor or dentist. The *Unità Sanitaria Locale* keeps a register
(*Dorsoduro 3493* ☎ *5208811; Castello 2689* ☎ *5236132*).

Late-night pharmacies

Pharmacies operate a rota for late-night opening. A notice in
the door or window of any pharmacy will give details, as will
local newspapers. Alternatively ☎ 192.

Help lines

Local police (Carabinieri) ☎ 5232222.
Police headquarters (Questura) ☎ 5203222.

Automobile accidents

— Call the police immediately.
— Do not admit liability or incriminate yourself.
— Ask any witness(es) to stay and give a statement.
— Exchange names, addresses, car and insurance company
  details with other involved parties.
— Remain to give your statement to the police.
— Report the accident to your insurance company.

Car breakdowns

— Put on hazard warning lights and place a portable warning
  triangle 50m (55yds) behind your car.
— ☎ 116 and give the operator your location, car
  registration and make. The ACI will bring assistance.

Lost passport

Contact the police, then your consulate (see opposite page)
for emergency travel documents.

Lost travelers cheques

Notify the local police immediately then follow the
instructions provided with your travelers cheques, or
contact the nearest office of the issuing company. Contact
your consulate or American Express (☎ 5200844) if you are
stranded with no money.

Lost property

Report your loss to the police immediately.

Emergency phrases

Help!   *Aiuto!*
There has been an accident.   *C'è stato un incidente.*
Where is the nearest telephone/hospital?   *Dov'è*
  il telefono/l'ospedale più vicino?
Call a doctor/ambulance.   *Chiamate un dottore/un'ambulanza.*
Call the police.   *Chiamate la polizia.*

Time chart

452	Destruction of Aquilea by Attila the Hun. Refugees from the mainland settle in the Venetian lagoon.
489	Lagoon communities governed by Ostrogoths of Ravenna.
539	Ostrogoth kingdom, including Venetian islands, conquered by Byzantine general Belisarius.
568	Lombard invasion of Italy, followed by mass migration from the mainland and settlement of Torcello, Grado, Caorle and Malamocco.
639	Bishop of Altino founds cathedral on Torcello.
726	Venice declares its independence from Byzantium and elects Orso Ipeto as first 'Dux' — or Doge.
775	Bishopric founded on the Island of Castello.
811-14	Under the *Pax Nicephori* between Charlemagne and the Byzantine emperor, Venice becomes a semi-independent province of Byzantium.
*c.*828	The body of St Mark, stolen from his tomb in Alexandria by two Venetian merchants, is brought to Venice, and the first church of San Marco is built as his shrine.
1000	Venice, now in control of the coasts of Dalmatia and Croatia, attains a new peak of prosperity.
1032	First steps toward oligarchic government taken when Doge Domenico Flabanico abolishes the ducal privilege of nominating colleagues and successors.
1109	Venice joins the Crusades.
1110	Second expedition to the Holy Land, motivated by commercial rivalry with Pisa and Genoa.
1124	Siege of Tire, first conquest of the overseas Empire.
1171	Venice divided into six districts of *sestieri* to facilitate raising of taxes for war against Byzantium.
1172	Power of the doge further weakened by establishment of self-electing Great Council.
1200-70	Venice emerges as a world power as the Empires of the East and West decline.
1202-4	Venice joins the Fourth Crusade, led by the blind Doge Enrico Dandolo. Sack of Byzantium: Constantinople is captured and many of its artistic treasures, including the four bronze horses, brought to Venice.
1284	The first of many Papal interdicts served on Venice. The first golden ducat coined, its weight in gold to be maintained until the collapse of the Republic.
1294	Unsuccessful war with Genoa over trading rights in the Black Sea.
1297	The *Serrata*. Membership of the Great Council closed to nonpatricians.
1325	The names of members of the hereditary ruling patrician class inscribed in the *Libro d'Oro*.
1349	First recorded use of naval artillery in battle between Venice and Genoa off Sardinia.
1355	The Council of Ten established as safeguard against bids for absolute power after Doge Falier attempts to overthrow the aristocracy.
1379-80	The War of Chioggia against the Genoese is followed by a new wave of imperial expansion.
15thC	The Venetian mainland empire extends as far w as Bergamo and Crema and E through the Friuli and Istrian peninsula.
1406	Angelo Correr is the first Venetian patrician to be elected

	Pope (as Gregory XII).
1416	First battle against the Turks at Negropont (modern Euboea). The Venetian fleet is victorious, but the expansionist Ottoman Empire becomes a threat.
1453-54	Fall of Constantinople to the Turks. Venice loses territorial and commercial rights in Byzantium and signs trade agreement with the Turkish Sultan.
1454	Peace of Lodi. Peace settlement between Venice and Milan and establishment of defensive alliance of Venice, Milan and Florence and later of Naples and Pope Nicholas V.
1470s	Turks capture Negropont and Scutori and invade the Friuli, but a treaty negotiated with the Sultan in 1479 heralds a period of peace and prosperity.
1489	Cyprus ceded to Venice by Queen Caterina Cornaro.
1495	Venice allies with Duke of Naples, Emperor Maximilian and Pope Alexander VI against invasion of Italy by Charles VIII of France.
1497	Vasco da Gama's voyage threatens Venetian monopoly of the spice trade.
1508-17	League of Cambrai. Pope Julius II, Louis XII of France, Ferdinand of Aragon and the Emperor Maximilian join forces against Venice to carve up its mainland empire. Venice divides the League by diplomatic means and keeps its dominions intact.
1514	Fire destroys the Rialto.
1527	Sack of Rome. Venice becomes a haven for artists, writers and religious reformers.
1570	Loss of Cyprus to the Turks.
1571	Battle of Lepanto. Resounding naval victory against the Turks, fought outside the Gulf of Corinth. But the balance of power remains unchanged and Venice fails to regain Cyprus.
1606	Venetian Republic excommunicated by Pope Paul V.
1630	The worst plague in the history of Venice.
1669	Loss of Crete, the last major Venetian possession outside the Adriatic, to the Turks.
1718	Congress of Passarowitz, under which Venice is forced to surrender the Morea to the Turks, marks end of Venetian power in the eastern Mediterranean.
1797	The Venetian Republic falls to Napoleon. The Veneto is placed under Austrian rule.
1805-14	Veneto made part of Napoleon's Kingdom of Italy.
1814	Venice under the Austro-Hungarian Empire.
1846	Railroad bridge connects Venice to the mainland.
1848	Daniele Manin leads doomed uprising against the Austrians.
1866	Venice annexed to United Kingdom of Italy.
1920s-30s	Construction of a petro-chemical port and factory complex at Marghera, on the edge of the lagoon, provides employment for Venice's population but introduces industrial pollution.
1950s	Residential expansion of nearby Mestre and gradual depopulation of Venice.
1966	Nov 4. Worst flood in Venice's history leads to the setting up of international funds to aid in the restoration of its buildings and works of art.
1970s	The Special Law for Venice: Italian government raises an international loan for pollution and flood control. Revival of Carnival increases winter tourism.

Art and architecture

Venice was founded on the cusp between antiquity and the Middle Ages and grew to power in the divide between East and West. These unique circumstances conditioned her art through and through. At first she was drawn naturally toward the East, as the stronger culture, then, with the decline and eclipse of Byzantium and the acquisition by Venice of extensive mainland territory, toward the West. But the Western Renaissance inevitably presented something of a paradox for Venetians, because on the one hand, unlike the rest of Italy, they had no Roman past to recover, and on the other, again unlike the rest of Italy, they had preserved their blood and traditions intact from Early Christian times, unsullied by 'barbarian' invasions. As a result the Venetian Renaissance was not so much a rebirth as a graft that fruited with some of the fairest produce in the whole garden of Italian art.

Byzantine Venice

At first Venice was merely a satellite in the orbit of Byzantine art. The purest survivals from her early Middle Ages are on the outlying islands of Torcello and Murano. Although the cathedral on Torcello and Santi Maria e Donato on Murano are in their present form 11th-12thC, the most obvious point of comparison for them is the group of rather grander 6thC Byzantine-built Early Christian basilicas at Ravenna. They are plain, airy, barnlike buildings in brick, their chief glory being their decoration — the lonely, courtly mosaic of the *Madonna* at Torcello and at Santi Maria e Donato the magnificent mosaic floor.

Likewise the most important Byzantine monument in Venice, the Basilica of San Marco (then the doges' private chapel) is nothing if not decorated. Essentially an 11thC rebuilding on a 9thC core, it represents a specifically Byzantine type of church, the 'apostolic' type. Structures dedicated to apostles were built in symmetrical Greek-cross layout, with one central dome and four surrounding ones, all of equal size. However, the symmetry of San Marco has been slightly squeezed, to move it closer to the Western pattern of a nave and transept, or Latin cross. Once the difficult construction of the brick domes had been completed in the 11thC, the marble and mosaic decoration of the interior began, to continue virtually until the end of the Venetian Republic. The interior glitters and glows with a specifically Venetian modulation, even if the overall effect of the church — with its atmosphere like a veil, a dark matrix shot through with light — derives from Greek Orthodox practice. The unique exterior is essentially 13thC, that is, dates from after the Sack of Byzantium by the Fourth Crusade in 1204, when Venice may be said to have come of age.

Gothic Venice

Next door to the Doges' Chapel of San Marco, the Doges' Palace was substantially rebuilt in the 14thC and completed in the 15thC. Its elevations are topsy-turvy — the second story is much larger than the first-floor loggia or the ground-floor arcade — and yet the unknown architect achieved a miraculous balance and splendor.

The rebuilding of the Doges' Palace was undertaken during a momentous period for the rest of Italian art. But although Giotto was painting nearby in the Scrovegni Chapel in Padua, this proto-Renaissance style did not reach Venice until the Paduan artist Guariento came to paint the throne wall of the Great Council Hall in 1365-68. Before Guariento, Venetian painting had been dominated by Paolo Veneziano (active 1321-62). Paolo enlivened and varied a fundamentally Byzantine outlook; like his Sienese contemporary, Duccio, he was influenced by Gothic line and he began to use color to help in telling the story. Paolo's follower Lorenzo Veneziano (active 1356-72), however, moved closer to the style of the mainland in adopting a tighter, harder technique.

The influence of Guariento can be traced in the work of some interesting painters of the early 15thC — especially Jacobello del Fiore (active 1401-39) and Michele Giambono (active 1420-62). But Guariento's influence was overlaid by an even more powerful one. This was International Gothic, with its leaping linear rhythms and curlicue drapery. In 1409 the greatest practitioner of International Gothic in Italy, Gentile da Fabriano, is recorded as painting in the Doges' Palace in Venice. Although those frescoes are lost, marks of his supremely elegant and yet always meltingly human style can be seen above all in the work of Giambono.

International Gothic also made its presence felt in sculpture and in architectural decoration: in the work of the dalle Masegne brothers, for instance, who made the screen (1391-94) with its lissom marble figures for San Marco, as well as one of the earliest doges' tombs in Santi Giovanni e Paolo, and the window on the waterfront side of the Doges' Palace with its fluid tracery and graceful ogee frame. Similar Gothic ornament can be seen on the facade of San Marco, and in the decorative stonework, especially of windows and wellheads, of palaces throughout the city.

Venice is a predominantly Gothic city. It is rare, however, that Gothic — or what passes in the rest of Italy for Gothic — appears in its pure form. Two great exceptions are the Dominican church of Santi Giovanni e Paolo and the Franciscan Frari, built after the pattern of their equivalents in Florence and elsewhere. Otherwise, Gothic is blended with a Byzantine base, seasoned often by Islamic influence — for in the Gothic period the bulk of Venice's trade was with the Levant. Venetian Gothic is in fact a style *sui generis* and a telling example are the great key-like columns of the Doges' Palace loggia, unparalleled except by their descendants on private palaces (such as the Ca' d'Oro) on the Grand Canal and elsewhere.

Above The 7thC **Torcello Cathedral** was rebuilt in the 11thC.

Below The 11thC **Basilica of San Marco**, whose gothic roofline is 13th-15thC.

Above The **Doges' Palace**, the seat of government, was rebuilt in the 14th-15thC.

Early Renaissance Venice

Early Renaissance painting in Venice was dominated by two families, the Bellini and the Vivarini. Founder of the Bellini clan was Jacopo (*c*.1400-70), who stands somewhat unclassifiably between International Gothic and a true Renaissance style. Jacopo worked not only in Venice but also on the mainland, notably in Ferrara, where he is reported to have won a portrait-painting contest with Pisanello. Other paintings and his famous sketchbook demonstrate a significant interest in landscape. Founder-member of the Vivarini was Antonio (*c*.1419-76), originator of a robust but luminous style, and painter of the earliest *sacra conversazione* in Venice (1446; in the Accademia). Antonio's style has a gawkiness which is also typical of early Renaissance sculpture in Venice; no sculptor emerged who could achieve convincing classical proportions until Tullio Lombardo at the end of the century.

Although the Florentine Castagno, whose frescoes survive in San Zaccaria, had brought an authentic Renaissance style to Venice in 1441-42, the decisive event was the marriage of Jacopo Bellini's daughter Nicolosia in 1453 to Mantegna, the most classical artist in all Italy. Jacopo's elder son Gentile (*c*.1429-1507), however, did little more than abandon his father's linear mannerisms and improve his perspective. He became the semi-official archivist to the Venetian Republic; his *Procession in the Piazza* in the Accademia is justifiably his most famous work.

The first, most powerful influence on Giovanni Bellini (*c*.1430-1516), Jacopo's younger son, was his brother-in-law Mantegna: Giovanni adopted the latter's figure-style, a process of translating sculptural mass into linear form. This linear tendency is exaggerated toward the wiry, expressive style of the Paduan school in Giovanni's *St Vincent Ferrer* altarpiece in Santi Giovanni e Paolo. The next important influence was Piero della Francesca's lucid perspective, his still, deep figures and clear, absolute light. In the second half of the 1470s the impact of the Sicilian Antonello da Messina was crucial: Antonello not only brought the use of the oil medium, but also demonstrated that objects could sometimes be modeled in it entirely without the use of line, but simply in terms of abutting and modulating colors. In the 1480s and 1490s Giovanni gradually explored the possibilities of this technique, but retained a minute, very carefully shadowed finish — as can be seen in the San Giobbe altarpiece and the bust-length *Madonna and Two Saints* against a black background, both in the Accademia.

Bellini's painting in the 16thC was an independent development. Painting now without modeling in line, he achieved effects of form and, even more importantly, of space, in terms of color alone. In his greatest late works (the best examples in Venice are the *Pietà* with a landscape background in the Accademia and the San Zaccaria altarpiece), he conveys a feeling of air and light, and at the same time makes the picture echo with the harmony of colors. Running through all Giovanni's work is an extraordinary ability to express emotion, from the sometimes violently poignant *Pietàs* of his youth to the miraculous mellow trance of these late works.

Meanwhile Antonio Vivarini was joined and then succeeded by his brother Bartolomeo (*c*.1432-99), an essentially derivative but charming painter at his peak in the 1470s, as his two altarpieces in the important church of the Frari show. Antonio's son Alvise (*c*.1445-1505) was the only painter who at least attempted to rival Giovanni Bellini: a letter survives in which he proffered himself as worthy to paint beside him in the Doges' Palace, and he won the commission. (The Doges' Palace decorations of the 15th and 16thC were destroyed by fire in 1577 — the biggest missing piece in the history of Venetian art.) Alvise practiced a more sculptural, more intensely modeled and less attractive style than Giovanni Bellini.

There was a similar development in architecture from International Gothic through a period of hesitant or awkward assimilation to a fully-fledged Renaissance style. The International Gothic masterpiece is the Ca' d'Oro, with its ostentatious display of gloriously idiosyncratic ornament; the use of colored marble is a typical hangover from the Byzantine past, and the elaborate Gothic tracery, obviously dependent on the Doges' Palace loggia, still has a flavor of the seraglio. Subsequent Grand Canal palaces show the invasion of classical ornament — notably the precocious rusticated fragment of the Ca' del Duca.

The first Venetian who successfully assimilated Tuscan Renaissance architecture was Mauro Codussi (c.1440-1504), whose most important works are San Michele in Isola, Santa Maria Formosa, San Zaccaria and the Palazzo Vendramin Calergi. Codussi, however, adapted mainland principles to Venetian needs and taste. A good example is the arch crowning the glistening, uncluttered stone facade on San Michele: this recalls Alberti's Tempio Malatestiano at Rimini, and Roman triumphal arches, but it brings to mind even more strongly those above the portals of San Marco. Again, Santa Maria Formosa is a classical church, but composed on the old Byzantine Greek-cross plan. Codussi's final masterpiece, edging into the 16thC, was the Palazzo Loredan (now Vendramin Calergi), where he brilliantly converted the traditional Venetian Gothic facade into an acceptable Renaissance equivalent.

Santa Maria dei Miracoli, by contrast, dresses out in Renaissance guise the taste of the Ca' d'Oro. This jewel-box of a church was designed by Pietro Lombardo (c.1435-1515), with the help of his sons Tullio and Antonio. The influence of Tullio is that of a sculptor: he refined his father Pietro's rather stiff style into an almost pernickety, highly polished, small-boned one.

Two nowadays very popular painters belong stylistically to the Early Renaissance although their careers carried well into the 16thC: Vittore Carpaccio (c.1460/5-1523/6) and Cima da Conegliano (c.1459-1518). Carpaccio was a successor to Gentile Bellini in narrative commissions for the Venetian *scuole*. But his light is flusher than Gentile's, and his settings are grander. Later, he painted some bleak *Pietàs* and a highly unpleasant *Martyrdom* in the Accademia: this gory side, however, has already been seen in the dragon scene in his *St George* in San Giorgio degli Schiavoni.

Cima's 15thC painting tends toward waxen-like modeling; his later pictures are sweetened versions of Giovanni Bellini's late style.

San Michele in Isola (1469-77), built by Codussi, was the first Renaissance church in Venice.

Codussi's **Palazzo Vendramin Calergi**, begun c.1510, is the supreme Venetian Renaissance building.

23

High Renaissance Venice

The High Renaissance, terminated in Rome by the Sack of 1527, continued in Venice without a perceptible break into the second half of the 16thC. Indeed Venice benefited from the Sack of Rome by receiving the refugees Jacopo Sansovino and Pietro Aretino, who formed with Titian a 'triumvirate' of taste. By the mid-16thC Titian, painter to the Holy Roman Emperor and then to Philip II of Spain, painter to the Pope, painter to whomsoever he pleased, was acknowledged throughout Europe, and Palladio had entered on his mature career. In the last third of the century the Venetian school, with Veronese, Tintoretto and Jacopo Bassano, was the healthiest in Italy; and although the 17thC is something of a trough in Venetian art, Titian and Palladio were the two most important single models for the new Baroque style that was forged elsewhere.

The High Renaissance had hardly begun in Venice when in 1510 its first luminary, Giorgione (born *c*.1475), died. Vasari, in his *Lives of the Artists*, brilliantly characterized Giorgione's importance when he told the story (for which there is no other evidence) of how Giorgione died for love. He was the first Romantic painter in the modern sense. His few surviving works consist most importantly of artfully constructed pastorals, including the *Tempest*, now in the Accademia. In these the main themes are love and transience (the ruin behind the soldier in the *Tempest* suggests the wrack of time). Remarkably, Giorgione often made the natural phenomenon of light part of the subject of his paintings, evolving a wonderfully soft, edgeless style, making minimal use of preliminary drawing and composing directly onto the panel.

Giorgione had two 'creatures,' as Vasari called them — Titian (*died* 1576) and Sebastiano del Piombo (*died* 1547). The three formed into a team to decorate Andrea Loredan's new palace built by Codussi in 1509 (although this work is now lost or sold). On Giorgione's death Sebastiano chose to try his luck in Rome; his last and finest work in Venice was the altarpiece still in San Giovanni Crisostomo. Titian stayed behind, developing rapidly beyond Giorgione: although Titian imitated Giorgione's mood and themes, there was little technique that Giorgione could teach him (rather the reverse); however, Titian undoubtedly was also influenced by the aged Bellini to a crucial extent.

In a way that modern chemistry is slowly enabling art historians to unravel, Titian evolved a method of building up his modeling in layers of color to give an extraordinary vivacity to flesh or to drapery. It was sensuous, extrovert, exhilarating; bold, grand and confident; communicative, expressive and human. And it was wholly unprecedented. In sheer beauty of form, painters from other parts of Italy could rival Titian; in color, other Venetian painters could be almost as gorgeous; but Titian had one extra string to his bow: he could make this brighter-than-life illusionism work at a distance. The 1519 altarpiece of the *Assumption* in the Frari, which commands the spectator's attention from the entrance to the choir, made Titian's international reputation.

The *Pesaro Madonna*, completed in 1526 for the same church, reveals further qualities of the mature Titian. He was a brilliant designer: the composition, with its diagonals and asymmetry, achieves a dynamic equilibrium. He also managed to achieve an entirely satisfactory approximation to Roman classical form — in Venetian color. And he has provided for the donors lively, glamorous and affecting portraits; it was Titian's portraiture that won him the patronage of Charles V, and greatly influenced the Baroque style. He could not merely achieve a likeness but also project an image, usually one that was singularly appropriate. It was flattering, of course, but always realistic and convincing.

Titian's clientele was soon international; comparatively few of his middle- and late-period works were destined for Venice, and even fewer have stayed there. Not only many of the portraits but also his famous mythological *poesie* were for export. The religious work that is most plentiful ranges from the highly sculptural, monumental *St John the Baptist* (*c*.1530) with a sparkling landscape background (now in the Accademia) to the violent drama, torment and turmoil of the *Martyrdom of St Lawrence* in the Gesuiti. In the *St Lawrence*, which dates from the 1550s, the surface quality is different, for the colors are much reduced and the light and shade are in urgent movement. The tendency that runs throughout Titian's work, to flatten out the figures or unroll them across canvas, becomes stronger, as if he were released from the orthodox of mainland perspective and foreshortening; St Lawrence, as a result, seems to grasp at the air and flail his limbs with more immediacy.

Although the darkling vision of Titian's old age did not until the very end oust a much more colorful one, the surface quality changes irreversibly after about 1560, becoming increasingly vibrant. The forms take shape in strokes and swathes and patches from a highly charged colored mist. The *Pietà* in the Accademia, which was finished after his death by Palma il Giovane, shows Titian's last style applied hauntingly to a lugubrious subject.

The most individual artist active at this time was Lorenzo Lotto, who returned to metropolitan Venice from the mainland in 1525 and executed some marvelous patrician portraits, including the haunting *Young Man in his Study* in the Accademia. The altarpieces found less favor in Venice and he turned elsewhere for commissions from the 1530s onward. In the late 1530s even Titian had to look to his laurels when the Veneto artist Pordenone introduced a striking, if crude, heavyweight version of Michelangelo's *terribilità*.

Pordenone (*c*.1483-1539) heralded a period of turmoil in Venetian painting, which was suddenly exposed to Central Italian Mannerism when Vasari, Salviati and the architect Serlio came to visit in the early 1540s. At the same time Andrea Schiavone (*c*.1522-63) and the young Tintoretto (1518-94) emerged on the scene. Schiavone, influenced particularly by the prints of Parmigianino, developed a style of etiolated figures swiftly 'impasto'd' in streaks of color — a Venetian equivalent to the freedom of Tuscan sketching, just then beginning to be appreciated by connoisseurs. Tintoretto took from Central Italy the use of vertiginous perspective for expressive effect and the influence of Michelangelo, although increasingly he broke up Michelangelo's striving forms in a dramatic light and shade. Titian was not unaffected by all this, as his ceiling paintings now in the Salute show.

Vasari strongly disapproved both of Schiavone and of Tintoretto for their distortion of form and lack of 'finish'; but he praised the moderation and classicism of Paolo Veronese (1528-88). Looking at a painting by Veronese is rather like taking a pill: you have to wait for it to work. His grand, bland forms are seldom insistent, although the distinctive perspective of his ceiling paintings often has a highly dramatic effect. Veronese used color to convey a mood or to give emphasis in a story in a studied, subtle way, quite the opposite of Tintoretto's aggressive approach, with its rushing and swooning forms and 'snail's trail' brush work.

While Veronese won the accolade of the Establishment for his ceiling paintings in Sansovino's new Marciana Library in 1557, it was Tintoretto who obtained the commission to decorate the non-patrician Scuola Grande di San Rocco in 1564 — reputedly by unfair means. Veronese darkened his palette and painted more atmospherically later in his career — perhaps to keep up with Tintoretto, although this was a general tendency in Venetian painting, as Titian's late work shows.

The painter who (briefly) came closest to Titian's late style was Jacopo Bassano (1510-92), who developed from an exaggeratedly gawky mannerism to a more mellow and more painterly approach, achieving a beautiful and distinctive tonality of silvery phosphorus. His sons perpetuated his popular genre of dusky biblical idylls and also painted true night-scenes, although they never approached the pyrotechnics of Tintoretto's later works, such as the *Last Supper* in San Giorgio Maggiore.

San Giorgio Maggiore is the greatest of Andrea Palladio's churches and one of the supreme accomplishments of the Renaissance in Italy. Its bold, grand and perfectly correct and coherent classicism is distinctly more spare than that of the Marciana Library (and its continuation around the Piazza) by Jacopo Sansovino (c.1486-1570). The latter building has rich swags and rippling, shadow-catching colonnades; the *loggetta* beneath the Campanile shows a similar lively and imposing classicism — in lighter mood — and also bears Sansovino's figures. These again are typical of the taste of the Sansovino-Titian-Aretino triumvirate. Just as Titian could not abide Tintoretto, so Sansovino could not abide his successor in sculpture, Alessandro Vittoria (1525-1608), who was again a Michelangelist. But Sansovino's *Neptune and Mars* on the ceremonial staircase in the Doges' Palace show him to be quite capable of the grand and monumental.

In architecture his impact can be gauged by comparing his Marciana Library with the flat, pedestrian Procuratie Vecchie across the Piazza, begun in 1513. Sansovino's only rival before Palladio was Michele Sanmicheli (c.1484-1559), whose Palazzo Grimani on the Grand Canal is more severe and gridlike than Sansovino's relaxed and ample Palazzo Corner (Ca' Grande) and Palazzo Dolfin-Manin.

Although his villas on the mainland are famous, Andrea Palladio (1508-80) built no palaces in Venice and, unlike Sansovino, who was also of course a foreigner, he made few concessions to Venetian taste in his churches. Sansovino gave their almost final form to the twin hearts of the city, the Piazza San Marco and the Rialto, while Palladio's great works stand isolated on its outskirts. San Giorgio, so full of white light in the interior, so dazzlingly shadowless and pure on the exterior, is descended from Alberti's church of Sant' Andrea at Mantua, and achieves with consummate and rigorous mastery what Alberti had attempted there — a Christian church founded on classical principles and divine geometry. Palladio's spaces are perfectly ordered around the dome, the proportions are systematized throughout the building, and, on the facade, a temple front is reconciled with the profile made by nave and aisles. And so again in Palladio's last building in Venice, the church of the Redentore on the Guidecca, which shows perhaps even better Palladio's sense of theater.

Baroque and Rococo Venice

Venetian painters of the 17th and 18thC studied the achievements of the Venetian High Renaissance in the context of the international Baroque movement. Seeing Titian according to the interpretation of Rubens, they developed a style of showy brushwork and color, layering a sparkling surface over a design rather than kindling form out of color elements in a truly 'colorist'

Left Sansovino's **loggetta** (1540) was inspired by Roman triumphal arches.

Below Palladio's **San Giorgio Maggiore**, begun in 1565, is a masterpiece of the classical Renaissance. Its facade is composed of two overlapping Roman temple fronts.

Above **Ca' Rezzonico** was begun in 1667 by the great Baroque architect Longhena.

Above The **Marciana Library** (1588) by Sansovino.

manner. Immigrants such as Jan Liss demonstrated a creamy, succulent brushwork with rather more inspiration than native painters, until the arrival in 1685 of Luca Giordano, the leading painter of the late Baroque in Italy. Giordano came to paint in Santa Maria della Salute, the new church by Baldassare Longhena (1598-1682) which is the leading monument of the Baroque in Venice. The Salute is somewhat cold inside and its spaces do not flow together, but from the outside it makes a splendid white merry-go-round with its series of giant volutes, amd may have been directly inspired by the theatrical traditions of Venice's great festivals. Longhena also designed Ca' Rezzonico and Ca' Pesaro, the last worthy successors to the Grand Canal palaces of Codussi, Sansovino and Sanmicheli.

Luca Giordano seems to have catalyzed the art of Sebastiano Ricci (1659-1734), whose career typifies that of the 18thC Venetian school. With the exception of Giovanni Battista Piazzetta (1683-1754), first president of the Venetian Academy, and Francesco Guardi, who made a poor living from mostly local patrons, the painters of this school can be divided into two classes: those who painted primarily for the English and those who also appealed to the Rococo taste of the Continent. All exported under the Venetian trademarks of decorative brushwork and striking vistas extending into space, whether or not these were views of the lagoon. Sebastiano and his nephew Marco worked for the British, painting a series of imaginary tombs for English lords that are important examples of the new fashion for *vedute* and *capricci* —

27

straightforward views and views shuffled together. Otherwise Sebastiano emulated the pomp and circumstance of Veronese, but his sharp, clashing colors utterly opposed Veronese's harmony.

The greatest master of *vedute* and *capricci* was Canaletto (1697-1768), who painted almost exclusively for the English, moving from an early liking for bold angle-shots to detailed, dotted panoramas bathed in a mild sun. Francesco Guardi (1712-93), by contrast, painted scuddy, wispy vistas or seedy, backstreet scenes in an exciting, blistery sort of brushwork.

Leader of the Rococo school and the greatest painter of 18thC Venice was Giambattista Tiepolo (1696-1770), for whom the melancholy but sympathetic figure of Piazzetta was an important predecessor. Piazzetta's altarpieces and genre scenes introduced a Caravaggesque weight into the more usual Venetian atmospherics, and his ceiling painting in Santi Giovanni e Paolo was also influential. Thus Tiepolo achieved a greater solidity by his airborne forms than did his fellow interior decorators such as Pellegrini or Amigoni, and he could temper the graceful, operatic posturing typical of the Rococo school with an Olympian grandeur.

His son Giandomenico (1727-1804) closely followed his style, but could give a sinister edge to his frivolous subjects — to his mountebanks in Ca' Rezzonico, for instance. Such an edge is markedly lacking in the genre scenes of Pietro Longhi (1702-85), which can also be seen in Ca' Rezzonico. And so Venetian art ended, in Longhi's small-talk and Guardi's romanticized image of decay.

Venice Restored

A remarkable number of organizations, both public and private from almost all the major countries of the Western world have been working for the past 20 years to restore the buildings of Venice and its art treasures. This international effort, unique in its scope and ambition, has come about as a result of the threefold attack the city faces: from the sea, from the land and from the air.

The danger from the sea is essentially that of flooding. The Venetian lagoon is almost landlocked, being cut off from the open Adriatic by a line of long, low sandbanks — the *lidi* — which is broken only by three relatively narrow channels. Over the centuries these sandbanks have usually afforded adequate protection. However, the slow but steady rise in the mean level of the Mediterranean has left the lagoon increasingly vulnerable to a number of dangers. The tide is obviously one. The wind, rather less obviously, is another, since the frequent southeasterly *scirocco*, if it blows for any length of time up the axis of the Adriatic, and particularly if it then chances to coincide with a build-up of low atmospheric pressure in the area, has the effect of piling up the waters at the northwestern end, from which there is no natural outlet. The consequence is the *acqua alta* — high water — which manifests itself not as an inrushing wave but as a slow, deadly welling up of water around the city's buildings.

Every few years, the greater part of the city is inundated to a depth of several feet. This occurred as recently as February 1986; before that there had been another, graver still, in December 1979. But the most disastrous flood of all came on Saturday, November 4 1966, when the waters rose more than six feet (1.8m) above the mean sea level and much of the city was submerged, not only in water but in every sort of detritus: garbage, sewage and — most damaging of all — fuel oil.

The second attack that Venice has to face is from the land: in a word, subsidence. Some of the 117 interconnected islands on which the city is built may be stronger and firmer than others, but all are essentially composed of the sand and mud of the lagoon, and it is one of the many miracles of Venice that her immense marble churches and palaces have not centuries ago crumbled into the canals. The local technique of building on a foundation of countless wooden piles driven deep into the lagoon bed is primarily responsible for their survival; but a glance at many of the *campanili* (those of *Santo Stefano* and *San Giorgio dei Greci* are perhaps the best examples) will be enough to show that even this has not always been entirely successful.

Here again, there has been a serious aggravation of the problem in recent years, due this time to the activities of the huge industrial zone at Mestre and Porto Marghera on the mainland shore. Founded after World War I but trebled in size after World War II, this undertaking has had a highly beneficial effect on the Venetian economy, but a disastrous one on Venice itself. Thus the table of fresh water that lies beneath the lagoon and that had been more than sufficient to meet the domestic needs of the city soon proved hopelessly inadequate for the new industries. As they pumped out more and more, so the bed of the lagoon began to sink, and Venice with it. With the construction by the Italian Government of two immense aqueducts, which now supply both city and industries with water from the mainland, subsidence has returned to its former acceptable levels; but much damage has already been done.

Lastly, there is the attack from the air. Venice is not the only city to suffer from atmospheric pollution, but its unique location greatly intensifies the problem. It is surrounded, and to a large extent permeated, not just by water but by salt water; and the sulfur dioxide issuing from the industries of Mestre (and, until they were all converted to gas, from the oil-fired central heating systems in the city itself) combined with these exceptional degrees of humidity and salinity has proved quite terrifyingly corrosive. Fortunately, the prevailing southeast wind carries most of the pollution in the other direction, across the mainland. But sometimes, particularly on summer nights, the wind changes and blows it for a few hours over the city, enough for it to eat its way into the whole fabric of Venice. Stone, marble, brick, even bronze: nothing is safe.

The Italian Government, realizing after the great flood of 1966 that the problem was far too wide-ranged and urgent to be tackled by itself alone, appealed to UNESCO. In its turn, UNESCO appealed to its constituent members, an impressive number of whom responded at once. Simultaneously, an even greater number of private organizations from both Italy and abroad — charities, educational foundations, and several individual funds established specially for the purpose — proclaimed their readiness to contribute. By the time that UNESCO published its *Report on Venice* in 1969, the international campaign to save the city was under way.

What, then, is being done, and how much has been achieved in the past 20 years? There is only one long-term answer to the threat from the sea: some means must be found of controlling the water level within the lagoon, regardless of wind or weather. To this end, the Italian Government in 1969 set up, in the Palazzo Papadopoli on the *Grand Canal*, a highly sophisticated research laboratory that for the first time has succeeded in making a proper analysis of the dynamics of the lagoon. In consequence there has now been set up a consortium known as the *Consorzio Venezia Nuova*, to whom the whole future of the lagoon has been effectively entrusted. The first task of this body will be to open up the lagoon to its maximum extent: this will mean the return of all the land reclaimed for the foundations of the so-called Third Industrial Zone (which was never built) and, wherever possible, the reopening of those sections closed off for fish farming. Later, it is proposed to build gates across the three openings to the Adriatic.

The problem of subsidence is largely a thing of the past since the construction of the two aqueducts; and it is worth mentioning that Venice has proved a fertile field for experimentation in the raising of buildings by concrete injection and other methods. The problem of atmospheric pollution, on the other hand, appears less immediately tractable. Thanks to heavy expenditure by Montedison and several other major companies on new plant and purification systems, the position is slowly improving; but there is still a long way to go.

The private international funds are directed primarily toward the restoration of buildings damaged in the past. By the late 1960s there were literally hundreds of buildings in desperate need of attention and fast deteriorating. A system was accordingly evolved by which each private fund would 'adopt' one or more buildings and make itself responsible for its restoration; not only the architecture but also the contents would be restored, for Venetian churches and *scuole* are quite astonishingly rich in paintings and sculptures, a large proportion of the latter forming part of the exterior decoration and being therefore totally unprotected from atmospheric pollution. Special laboratories for this vast body of work have been set up, for paintings in the now redundant church of San Gregorio, for sculptures in the Abbazia della Misericordia. All the restoration is, of course, carried out with the approval and under the supervision of the Italian Government authorities — The Superintendent of Works of Art and the Superintendent of Monuments — in Venice. All restoration work is carried out by local artisans and, with few exceptions, under the direction of Italian experts. It ranges in technical complexity from the cleaning and consolidation of stone (the major part of many restoration projects) to the meticulous repair and restoration of works of art.

An enormous amount of useful work has been carried out in the years since 1966, when the Italian Government first turned to UNESCO for assistance. Some of the more important restorations — notably the mosaics in the cathedral of *Torcello* (see *The lagoon*) — are joint undertakings by a group of organizations working together; but the majority are the work of individual private funds. The representatives of all these funds, Italian and foreign, meet every 18 months or so, under the auspices of UNESCO, at the Cini Foundation on San Giorgio Maggiore for consultations and meetings with government officials at municipal, regional and national levels.

It should be emphasized that the entire international effort, impressive as it is, is by no means the whole story. No article of this kind would be complete without mention of the work of the Italian Government itself, which makes a large annual contribution to Venice, as to all the other historic cities in Italy. To quote just two examples, it has been responsible for the restoration of the *Ca' d'Oro* — recently opened as a museum — and is now working on the immense Palazzo Grimani at *Santa Maria Formosa* to which, it is hoped, the outstanding collection of classical sculpture amassed by the Grimani family in the 16thC (and at present in the *Archeological Museum*) will eventually return.

Suggestions for further reading

Guidebooks
There are probably more guidebooks to Venice than to any other city. The first, by Francesco Sansovino, was published in 1581 and is still available.

Blue Guide, Venice (latest edition 1986). Reliable, topical, ubiquitous.

The Companion Guide to Venice by Hugh Honor (1965, second edition 1977). Written with lightly worn erudition.

Venice for Pleasure by J.G. Links (1966, revised edition 1979). An engaging, personal and deeply informed guide to walking — and stopping for coffee — in Venice.

Venezia e il suo estuario by Guilio Lorenzetti (1926, English translation 1975). One of the most detailed and lovingly compiled guides to any city; but an oddly organized index makes the English edition difficult to use for reference.

Venezia, Touring Club Italiano (1985).

Art, architecture and history
The most readable and authoritative short summary of the history is still Horatio Brown's article first published in the 1911 edition of the *Encyclopedia Britannica*.

Palladio by James S. Ackerman (1966).

The Architectural History of Venice by Deborah Howard (1980).

Venice, A Thousand Years of Culture and Civilisation by Peter Lauritzen (1978). The art and its historic background.

Renaissance Architecture in Venice 1450-1540 by Ralph Lieberman (1982). Brilliant photographs; clear, analytical descriptions.

Venice, the Rise to Empire (1977) and *Venice, the Greatness and the Fall* (1981), both by John Julius Norwich. Recent and valuable.

The Stones of Venice by John Ruskin (1853). Although Ruskin passionately hated many of the buildings we most admire, his long, magnificent, often ecstatic account remains a classic, especially admired for the section on 'The Nature of the Gothic.' The many abridged editions begin with Ruskin's own *Travelers Edition* (1877, now out of print) and include those of J.G. Links (1960) and Jan Morris (1981).

A Concise History of Venetian Painting by John Steer (1979). A brief survey of Venetian painting from the 14th-18thC.

Impressions and memoirs
Italian Hours by Henry James (1909).

The Quest for Corvo by A.J.A. Symons (1934).

Memoirs by Jaques Casanova (first published 1826-38).

Venetian Life by William Dean Howells (1866).

Venice by James Morris (revised edition 1983).

Venice Observed by Mary McCarthy (1956).

Novels
Eustace and Hilda by L.P. Hartley (1947).

Those who Walk Away by Patricia Highsmith (1967).

The Aspern Papers (1888) and *The Wings of the Dove (1902), both by Henry James.*

Serenissima by Erica Jong (1987).

Death in Venice by Thomas Mann (1912).

The Comfort of Strangers by Ian McEwan (1981).

Temporary Kings by Anthony Powell (1973).

Remembrance of Things Past: 'The Sweet Cheat Gone (Albertine Disparue)' by Marcel Proust (1925).

The Desire and Pursuit of the Whole by Frederick Rolfe (1953).

Territorial Rights by Muriel Spark (1979).

The Criminal Comedy of the Contented Couple by Julian Symons (1985).

The Stone Virgin by Barry Unsworth (1985).

Orientation map

N

⑤

S. Alvise
5

Ponte Tre Archi
5

Madonna
dell'Orto
5

11

CANNAREGIO

Ponte
Guglie
5

S. Marcuola
1, 2

⑤

⑤

⑳

⑩

Riva di Biasio
1

S. Stae
1

4

Ca' d'Oro
1

Ferrovia
1, 2, 4, 5

S. CROCE

Piazzale Roma
1, 2, 4, 5, 10, 20

S. POLO

8

S. Silvestro
1

Rialto
1, 2, 4

Grand Canal

S. Tomà
1, 4

②

S. Angelo
1

DORSODURO

S. Samuele
2

S. MARCO

3

6

Ca' Rezzonico
1

S.M. del Giglio
1

San Marco
1, 2, 4

S. Basilio
5

Accademia
1, 2, 4

1

Salute
1

14

Zattere
5

⑤

9

Sacca Fisola
5

⑤

⑨

S. Eufemia
5

Giudecca
9

GIUDECCA

Redentore
5, 8

13

----- District (Sestieri) boundaries

② Water bus services

• Ferry services
(across the Grand Canal)

S. Eufemia
5   Landing stage (indicating major
routes calling at this pier)

| 0 | 250 | 500 | 750 metres |
| 0 | 250 | 500 | 750 yds |

Malam
and Ch

Murano

Burano, Torcello

S. Michele
5

(12)

(5)

ondamenta
uove
12

Ospedale
Civile
5

(5)

(16)

Celestia
5

(18)

CASTELLO

S. Zaccaria/Riva Schiavoni
1, 2, 4, 5, 6, 11, 10 (20)

Campo della
Tana
5

Arsenale
1

(5)

S. Giorgio
5

(11)

(15)

Giardini
1, 2, 4

(1)

(6)

(4)

(2)

S. Elena
1, 2, 4

telle

(1)

(11)

(20)

(10)

(11)
bis

(1)

(2)

San Lazzaro

Chioggia (11) bis

LIDO

Lido
1, 2, 4, 6, 11

Important sights

1   Accademia
2   Arsenale
3   Carmini
4   Ca' d'Oro
5   Ca' Pesaro
6   Ca' Rezzonico
7   Doges' Palace
8   Frari
9   Gesuati
10 Gesuiti
11 Madonna dell'Orto
12 Marciana Library
13 Redentore
14 Salute
15 San Giorgio Maggiore
16 Santi Giovanni e Paolo
17 San Marco
18 Santa Maria Formosa
19 San Michele in Isola

Calendar of events

Nothing about Venice is ever entirely certain. Even the major events are sometimes shifted or cancelled, while each year seems to bring new festivals and entertainments. Two useful sources of information are the weekly magazine *Un Ospite di Venezia* and the monthly almanac *Venezia Almanacco*.

Winter: December, January, February

Week before Lent (Feb). *Carnevale*. Officially revived by the Mayor in the late 1970s, Carnival is once again a time of riotous entertainment in Venice. Masks and costumes are worn day and night. There are masked balls and every kind of theatrical entertainment. The preparations, which begin in early Jan, are if anything more fun than the main events.

Spring: March, April, May

Apr–June is a good season for concerts and recitals at the Fenice, Malibran and many other venues (see *Nightlife*).

Ascension Sunday (first Sun after Ascension Day). *La Vogalonga*. The 'long row' into the Venetian lagoon was started in 1975 and is now the most popular event of the spring season. Anyone may take part (including foreigners) in any kind of oar-powered craft, and thousands do. It is not a race, but a marathon regatta. Participants set off at 9.30am from the Bacino di San Marco. The 32km (20-mile) course takes them around Sant'Elena, into the lagoon as far as Burano and San Francesco del Deserto, re-entering Venice by the Cannaregio Canal, joining the Grand Canal and finishing at the Customs House Point. You can watch the boats returning from about 11am–3pm.

From the year 1000 until the fall of the Republic, Ascension Sunday was the day on which the doge rowed out to the Lido in his ceremonial barge, the *Bucintoro*, and cast a ring into the Adriatic, symbolizing the marriage of Venice with the sea. A paler version of this ceremony is still conducted on the morning of the Vogalonga by the Mayor and Patriarch.

Summer: June, July, August

June–Oct. *Biennale*. Held in even years, and still, despite recent political upheavals, the largest modern art show in the world. There are 30 permanent pavilions next to the Giardini Pubblici, and parallel exhibitions take place in the Magazzini del Sale (the salt

warehouses) and Cantieri Navali (former shipyards), both on the Zattere. Founded in 1895, the *Biennale* is now a powerful cultural institution responsible for other major events, including the International Film Festival and Carnival, and for the exhibitions held alternately between the *Biennale* years.

July. *Festival della danza*. A dance festival with open-air performances given in the city.

Third Sun of July. *Festa del Redentore*. A bridge of boats is constructed across the Giudecca Canal to the church of the Redentore which was built in thanksgiving for the lifting of the plague of 1576. On the previous evening there is a stunning display of fireworks, best seen from the Zattere, the Giudecca or a boat. It is traditional for Venetians to picnic in their boats, stay up all night and then row to the Lido for a dawn swim.

Late Aug–early Sept. International Film Festival at the Palazzo del Cinema on the Lido. Movies are shown night and day for about two weeks to an international jury. The last few days are hectic, with tickets scarce and expensive.

Fall: September, October, November

Fall is the most important season for music. There are concerts and recitals in the churches and theaters; there is also, usually, a Festival of Contemporary Music.

Major art exhibitions are also frequently held in autumn.

First Sun in Sept. *Regata Storica*. Venice's historic regatta. The races are preceded by a magnificent procession on the Grand Canal of historic boats rowed by Venetians in costume.

Nov. Opening of the opera season at the Fenice and Malibran, which usually lasts until May.

Nov. 21. *Festa della Madonna della Salute*. A votive procession to the Salute, commemorating the end of the plague of 1630, takes place on two floating bridges built across the Grand Canal from the Giglio and at the Dogana (the old Customs House).

When and where to go

May and October are the ideal months to visit Venice. The weather
is usually mild and sunny and the city is full of activity without
being overcrowded. Easter can be beautiful, but there is always a
risk of cold, rainy weather. June to September remains the peak
tourist season despite often intense heat, crowds and high prices.
Winter has become increasingly popular lately, especially since the
revival of **Carnival** (see *Calendar of events*), and many hotels now
stay open through the winter months. Prices are lower and a
tempting variety of package tours is available.

No matter when you go to Venice, the way to spend your time
will very much depend on the length of your stay. Outlined below
are suggestions for how to plan your time; all the sights mentioned
in Venice are described in *Sights and places of interest*, and the
places on the mainland or in the lagoon can be found in the
sections titled *The Mainland* and *The Venetian lagoon*.

Three days If you are a conscientious sightseer and this is your
first trip to Venice you will want to visit San Marco, the Doges'
Palace, the Accademia Galleries and the Rialto. *Walk 1* (see *Walks
in Venice*, which follows this section) will take you to these major
monuments, but try to leave some time for wandering off the
beaten track and to fit in a ride, by gondola or vaporetto, along the
Grand Canal. Allow yourself one trip into the lagoon, perhaps to
Murano. Ascend the *campanile* of San Marco, or, for an even better
view, of San Giorgio Maggiore.

One week A week should give time for seeing the main sights
mentioned above, as well as the Correr, Ca' Rezzonico and Santi
Giovanni e Paolo. Visit at least one of the *scuole*, perhaps San
Giorgio degli Schiavoni for the paintings by Carpaccio or San
Rocco for the works by Tintoretto. Follow *Walk 2* and find the
time to eat a pizza on the Zattere. Spend a day in the lagoon,
carrying on from Murano to Burano and Torcello. Visit Padua, at
least for the Giottos in the Arena chapel and the Donatellos in the
Santo; or Vicenza for Palladio's palaces. Or explore some of the hill
towns N of Venice; the most charming are Asolo, Bassano del
Grappa and Maróstica.

Two weeks There are still a great many major churches to visit,
including the Frari, the Salute, San Salvatore, the Madonna
dell'Orto, San Zaccaria, San Sebastiano and the Miracoli.
Nevertheless, two weeks should leave enough time to explore
Venice in a leisurely way according to your mood, personal taste
and interests. The Ca' d'Oro houses a good collection of
Renaissance art. If you are interested in the 18thC, you will know
Ca' Rezzonico, but have you visited the Querini Stampalia or the
Palazzo Mocenigo at San Stae? If you enjoy modern art, you will
already be familiar with the Guggenheim Collection, but have you
been to Ca' Pesaro? Specialty museums include the Naval
Museum, the Fortuny Museum and the Murano Glass Museum.

To get to know Venice more intimately follow *Walk 3*, or
explore another out-of-the-way neighborhood: N of the Ghetto,
perhaps, or around San Giacomo dell'Orio. Take the public
motoscafo no.5 all around the periphery of Venice, a most enjoyable
ride in itself.

Two weeks will also allow you time to discover some of the
pleasures of the Venetian mainland. You could make an overnight
trip to Verona, or rent a car and visit some or all of Palladio's villas
(see the two suggested tours on page 184).

Another pleasant way to spend a day is to take the Burchiello
water bus along the Brenta.

Walks in Venice

These itineraries are merely intended to introduce you to the pleasure of walking in Venice. They cover most of the city's major monuments and churches (cross-referenced to *Sights and places of interest*), but they do not begin to exhaust the wealth of visual splendors and oddities that the city has to offer at almost every twist and turn.

One of the most rewarding ways of spending time in Venice is simply to strike out on foot in any direction and allow yourself to get thoroughly lost. Although the main routes — to and from San Marco, the Rialto, the Station (*Ferrovia*) and Piazzale Roma — are clearly signed, it is much more fun to explore the less frequented byways. When, as inevitably happens in Venice, you lose your direction, you will find that Venetians are almost without exception delighted to set you straight.

When asking directions you can safely ignore the official address system, which is determined by the six Venetian *sestieri* or districts (and is explained in the introduction to *Sights and places of interest*). For purposes of getting around on foot, it is more useful to aim for the parish church nearest your destination. Street names are given here as they appear on street signs. These spellings are generally in dialect and do not always conform to the standard Italian given in printed matter and on maps. Just to confuse matters further, Venetians have a tendency to identify streets by the landmarks in them rather than by their proper or dialect names: so that, for example, the Calle Vallaresso becomes the "Harry's Bar Calle."

You will need confortable shoes: walking in Venice means climbing over bridges and in and out of *traghetti*. And do adopt the Venetian habit of stopping frequently for refreshment. Some of the most sympathetic bars and restaurants are in remote areas. Restaurants and bars named here in bold are individually described in the *Restaurants* and *Bars and cafés* sections of the book.

Detailed itineraries are given in Giulio Lorenzetti's classic, *Venice and its Lagoon*. The most delightful modern guidebook to walking in Venice is J.G. Links' *Venice for Pleasure*.

If you enjoy these walks remember that there are other areas waiting to be explored. Try western Cannaregio and eastern Castello. And if you fear you are losing the art of getting lost in Venice, spend a morning in labyrinthine Santa Croce.

Walk 1/The center (San Marco, the Rialto and the Accademia)

The most direct route from San Marco to the Rialto is along the Mercerie, the main shopping street; and from San Marco to the Accademia the shortest path is by way of San Moisè and the Calle Larga XXII Marzo, the wide street enlarged in the late 19thC and named after the revolution of 1848 against the Austrians. But these are well-trodden itineraries, clearly signposted and usually very crowded. This walk will take you, in a more leisurely, wandering way, to the three principal centers of Venice.

From San Marco to the Rialto via San Zaccaria and Santa Maria Formosa

Leave Piazza *San Marco* by way of the Piazzetta dei Leoni(**1**) and along the Calle de la Canonica(**2**) next to the Bishop's Palace at the far end. Ahead, across the bridge, is the early 16thC **Palazzo Trevisan**, where Bianca Cappello lived after her marriage to

Francesco de' Medici. Turn right into Fondamenta de la Canonica. At the top of the steps leading to the Ponte de la Canonica is a small courtyard where early fragments from the Basilica of San Marco are set into the walls (and where there is a back entrance to the Basilica itself). From the Ponte de la Canonica there is a fine **view** to the right of the Bridge of Sighs, the Ponte de la Paglia and the E wing of the *Doges' Palace*. *Sant' Apollonia* is on the far side of the bridge at the end of the short fondamenta, beyond the former church which now houses the showrooms of the famous Jesurum lace. From the foot of the Ponte de la Canonica take the Rughetta S. Apollonia(**3**), which widens into Campo SS Filippo e Giacomo, and continue straight into Salizada S. Provolo, over the bridge into Campo San Provolo and under the **Gothic archway**, surmounted by a *Madonna with Sts John the Baptist and Mark* by Bartolomeo Bon, into Campo *San Zaccaria*.

Returning under the archway, turn sharp right into Campo San Provolo, then under the sottoportico into Calle San Provolo which bends right into Fondamenta de l'Osmarin(**4**). At the far corner of the wide rio ahead on the left is the Gothic brick **Palazzo Pruili**, one of the noblest of 15thC Venetian palaces. Cross the Ponte del Diavolo into Calle dei Diavolo, turn left into Calle dei Preti and right into Campo S. Severo. Cross the Ponte S. Severo on your left into Salizada Zorzi(**5**), where no.4930 on the right, **Palazzo Zorzi e S. Severo**, is an elegant but dilapidated early-Renaissance palace attributed to Mauro Codussi. Turn right into Ruga Giuffa(**6**). Toward the end on the right, the short Ruga Grimani is closed by the entrance to **Palazzo Grimani**, no.4858, attributed to Michele Sanmicheli. The collection of antique sculptures assembled here in the 16thC may be returned and the palace opened as the Archeological Museum. Continue on straight into Campo *Santa Maria Formosa* which you enter at the apse end of the church.

Walk diagonally across the campo, leaving it through the narrow Ramo va in Campo. Turn right onto Fondamenta dei Preti, left across the canal, under the **archway** decorated with a *Madonna della Misericordia* (dated 1407), and into Calle del Paradiso(**7**). The restaurant **Ai Barbicani** is immediately on the left. The **Calle del Paradiso** is flanked by 13th-16thC artisans' and shopkeepers' houses with their upper stories projected over the street to provide maximum living space.

Under another Gothic arch, turn right into Salizada S. Lio, a long shopping street where the row of houses on the left preserves 13thC facades, with shop-fronts at ground level and biforate windows opening from the original main living rooms. The church of **San Lio** at the W end is of little interest inside apart from Pietro Lombardo's Gussoni Chapel. Carry on straight into Calle al Ponte S. Antonio (signs now point to the Rialto) and over the bridge into Calle de la Bissa. There are a number of good sandwich shops and *rosticcerie* on this side of Campo *San Bartolomio* which opens out from the Sotoportego de la Bissa. The *Rialto* Bridge is at the far end of Salizada Pio X.

From the Rialto to the Accademia via the Bovolo staircase and Santo Stefano

From Campo San Bartolomio take the Marzarieta (Merceria) 2 Aprile(**8**) passing the church of *San Salvatore* on the left. Carry on straight into Calle del Lovo, where there are a number of attractive bar/pastry shops. Turn left into Calle dei Fabbri (**9**), which leads to San Marco. But to reach the Accademia, turn right around the corner of Standa, the department store, into Calle del Magazen, left at the end into Calle dei Fuseri(**10**), where the first right, Calle de la Vida o della Locanda, is signed for the Scala del Bovolo (*Bovolo Staircase*), farther along and left in a courtyard.

The Calle de la Vida bends sharp right and then opens into **Campo Manin(11)**, where the Casa di Risparmio, built in 1968 by Pier Luigi Nervi and Angelo Scattolin, is one of the few ugly buildings in Venice. The square is otherwise dominated by the monument (1875) to the revolutionary leader Daniele Manin. Follow the sign for the Accademia over the bridge into Calle de la Cortesia, which becomes Calle de la Mandola, a crowded shopping street where there are several good patisseries. Toward the end a sign points right to the *Fortuny Museum*.

As you enter **Campo San Angelo** you will see the alarmingly tilted campanile of the church of Santo Stefano. The composer Cimarosa lived and died in no.3584, the large symmetrical Gothic palace on the left. The **cloister of Santo Stefano**, now belonging to the Intendenza di Finanza, is usually open. Cross the bridge to

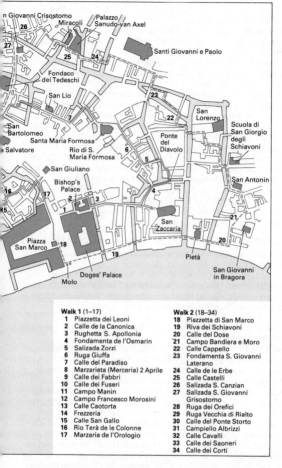

Walk 1 (1–17)
1 Piazzetta dei Leoni
2 Calle de la Canonica
3 Rughetta S. Apollonia
4 Fondamenta de l'Osmarin
5 Salizada Zorzi
6 Ruga Giuffa
7 Calle del Paradiso
8 Marzarieta (Mercería) 2 Aprile
9 Calle dei Fabbri
10 Calle dei Fuseri
11 Campo Manin
12 Campo Francesco Morosini
13 Calle Caotorta
14 Frezzeria
15 Calle San Gallo
16 Rio Terà de le Colonne
17 Marzaria de l'Orologio

Walk 2 (18–34)
18 Piazzetta di San Marco
19 Riva dei Schiavoni
20 Calle del Dose
21 Campo Bandiera e Moro
22 Calle Cappello
23 Fondamenta S. Giovanni Laterano
24 Calle de le Erbe
25 Calle Castelli
26 Salizada S. Canzian
27 Salizada S. Giovanni Grisostomo
28 Ruga dei Orefici
29 Ruga Vecchia di Rialto
30 Calle del Ponte Storto
31 Campiello Albrizzi
32 Calle Cavalli
33 Calle dei Saoneri
34 Calle dei Corti

the right of the cloister into Calle dei Frati which leads to **Campo Francesco Morosini(12)**, where the church of *Santo Stefano* is immediately on the left. The bar **Paolin** on the corner next to the church sells good ice cream and there is a convenient snack-bar and pizzeria on the other side of the square. The *Accademia Bridge* is at the end, across Campo San Vidal. The galleries are on the other side of the bridge.

From the Accademia to San Marco via the Fenice
Signs point the direct way from Campo Morosini to San Marco, but for a prettier route return to Campo San Angelo and take the narrow Calle Caotorta(**13**) from the SE corner. Cross the Ponte Storto and turn immediately left along Rio Menuo o de la Verona, over the next bridge and left under the colonnaded Sotoportego S. Cristoforo (by now you may hear the strains of music in rehearsal or performance at the Fenice theater). Turn right into Calle de la

39

Fenice which leads past Campiello Marinoni to **Campo San Fantin**, where the entrance to the *Fenice* is on the right. The Pizzeria Bar Ristorante **Al Theatro** is on the left, **Da Arturo** and **Ai Assassini**; are a minute's walk to the N; the **Antico Martini** and **Vino Vino** are just to the s.

Take the Calle del Frutariol to the left of the church of **San Fantin**, cross the bridge (on the right is the house where Mozart stayed during the Carnival of 1771) and carry on straight into the **Frezzeria(14)**, an important shopping street named after the arrows which were once sold here. In the Calle dei Fuseri (first left and across the bridge) is the restaurant **Da Ivo** and in a courtyard at the far end of the bridge **Al Campiello**. Nearby too is **La Colomba**.

Turn sharp right with the Frezzeria and take the first left into Calle Tron; cross the Ponte Tron into Campo Rusolo San Gallo. Turn left and then right into Calle San Gallo(**15**), left into Calle dei Fabbri and first right into the curving, colonnaded **Rio Terà de la Colonne(16)**. Turn second right under the Sotoportego dei Armeni, left into Calle Fiubera, over the bridge into Marzaria San Zulian — the church of *San Giuliano* is at the far end — then right into **Marzaria de l'Orologio(17)** and straight into Piazza *San Marco* under the Clock Tower.

Walk 2/San Marco, Castello, Cannaregio, San Polo

This walk makes a wider arc around the center than *Walk 1*. It takes you from San Marco into the *sestieri* of Castello, Cannaregio and San Polo, past the two most important Venetian Gothic churches, Santi Giovanni e Paolo and the Frari, as well as two of the city's most beloved small artistic treasures, San Giorgio degli Schiavoni and the church of the Miracoli.

From San Marco to the Rialto via San Giorgio degli Schiavoni and the Miracoli

From the Piazzetta di *San Marco* (**18**) turn left around the corner of the *Doges' Palace* on to the Molo, pausing to enjoy the sparkling view across the Bacino di San Marco of *San Giorgio Maggiore*, the *Giudecca* and the *Salute*. Cross the Ponte de la Paglio — the **Bridge of Sighs** is on your left — onto the **Riva dei Schiavoni(19)**, the broad, sunny street lined with open-air cafés and hotels which curves along the edge of the Bacino. The first building on the left houses the **prisons** (1560-1614), from which Casanova effected his famous escape. It is followed by the far grimmer modern extension of the Danieli Hotel, the main part of which occupies the 15thC Gothic Palazzo Dandolo next door. Over another bridge, the Ponte del Vin, you see the effusive monument to Victor Emmanuel. The next bridge crosses the Rio dei Greci, flanked by pretty palaces and dominated by the campanile of *San Giorgio dei Greci*.

Past the *Pietà* and across the next bridge is the house where tradition has it that Petrarch stayed during his visit to Venice in 1363. Turn left into the next street, the narrow Calle del Dose(**20**), which leads straight into the peaceful Campo Bandiera e Moro(**21**). The church of *San Giovanni in Bragora* is on the right side. Should you find yourself here around lunchtime interesting restaurants in the neighborhood are **Corte Sconta**, **Da Remigio**, **Ai Schiavoni**, and the Chinese **La Grande Muraglia** (*Castello 3958, closed Mon*). Cross the campo diagonally and turn left into Salizada S. Antonin, a domestic shopping street. Turn right around the church of San Antonin into Fondamenta dei Furlani, at the end of which is the tiny Scuola di *San Giorgio degli Schiavoni*.

Turn left over Ponte de la Comenda, right into Fondamenta S.

Giorgio dei Schiavoni, and left into Calle San Lorenzo which bends right and opens into Campo San Lorenzo. The church, which has an unfinished facade, is on the right. Turn left to cross the pretty **Rio di San Lorenzo**, which is the setting of Gentile Bellini's *Miracle of the Holy Cross* in the *Accademia*, then turn right onto Fondamenta S. Lorenzo. Take the second left, which is Calle Larga San Lorenzo and turn right under the archway into Calle Cappello(**22**).

Cross the Ponte Cappello and turn left into Fondamenta Seconda S. Giovanni Laterano, right at the end into Calle S. Giovanni Laterano, left into Fondamenta S. Giovanni Laterano(**23**) and right over Ponte de l'Ospealeto into Calle de l'Ospealeto. Turn left at the end and on the right you will pass the menacing Baroque facade of the *Ospedaletto*. Continue straight into Campo S. Zanipolo, with the swelling chapels of the church of *Santi Giovanni e Paolo* on your right.

At the far end of the campo turn left along the canal and right over the bridge into Calle de le Erbe(**24**) (where you leave the *sestiere* of Castello and enter Cannaregio). At the end, over the bridge, turn right into Fondamenta van Axel; no.6099 at the end is **Palazzo Sanudo-van Axel** (1473-79), a splendid palace now occupied by the Ministry of Public Education. If the door is open (it is the only original wooden door left on a Venetian palace of the period) be sure to look into the beautiful courtyard. Now turn right into the narrow Calle Castelli(**25**). At the end, to the right, is the facade of the church of *Miracoli*.

Now cross the Ponte dei Miracoli into Calle dei Miracoli, carry straight on into Calle Boldù and turn left into Salizada S. Canzian(**26**). **Boldrin** (*closed Sun*), on the right, is a good wine-bar serving hot and cold snacks. From Campiello Flaminio Corner turn left over Ponte S. Giovanni Crisostomo (the way to the Rialto is signed now) into Salizada S. Giovanni Crisostomo(**27**). The **Toscano Buffet** does good sandwiches. The red-stuccoed church of *San Giovanni Crisostomo* is on the left, and behind it in Corte Prima del Milion on the way to 'Marco Polo's house' is the Ostaria **Al Milion**. Continue along Salizada San Giovanni Crisostomo, which becomes more crowded as you approach the Rialto. Cross the bridge over Rio dei Fondego dei Tedeschi which is the boundary between the *sestieri* of Cannaregio and San Marco, into Salizada dei Fondego dei Tedeschi and Campo San *Bartolomeo*, from which Salizada Pio X on the right leads to the *Rialto* Bridge. If you want to eat before crossing the bridge, try **Al Volto** for a glass of wine and a snack or the restaurant **Stagnier**.

From the Rialto to San Polo and the Frari

At the other side of the *Rialto* Bridge the Ruga dei Orefici(**28**) stretches straight ahead, flanked by market stalls piled with fruit and vegetables. On the right it opens on to the arcaded Campo di Rialto watched over by the charming porticoed facade of the church of *San Giacomo di Rialto*. Good restaurants near this side of the bridge include the **Poste Vecie** and **La Regina**. Or have a drink in the delightful Cantina **Do Mori**.

Turn left into the broad Ruga Vecchia di Rialto(**29**). Immediately on the left is the handsome early 15thC campanile of the church of **San Giovanni Elemosinario**, which is worth looking into for Titian's paintings of *St John the Almsgiver* (*c*.1535) over the high altar. Continue straight along the Ruga, which leads into Rughetta del Ravano, and at the end you will see the church of San Silvestro which is at the bottom of Rio Terà S. Silvestro on your left. Take the next right into Campo Sant' Aponal, cross the campo

and leave it by Calle del Ponte Storto(**30**) and cross the Ponte
Storto. The early 16thC **Palazzo Cappello**, no.1280 on the right,
was the birthplace of Bianca Cappello.

Turn left and then first right into Calle del Tamossi which leads
straight into Campiello Albrizzi(**31**). The little square is dominated
by the tall, stately 17thC **Palazzo Albrizzi**, no.1940, which is still
occupied by the Albrizzi family. Leave the campiello from the far
corner by the well-named Calle Stretta (narrow street). Turn right
under the colonnaded Sottoportego de la Furatola and left over the
bridge into Calle Cavalli(**32**), which bends right and then left. As
you cross the canal notice on the left the impressive water facade of
the 18thC **Palazzo Tiepolo-Maffetti**. Passing under the
Sotoportego Cavalli you emerge from the labyrinth into Campo
San Polo, the largest open space in Venice after San Marco. You
are near two excellent restaurants: **Le Carampane** and **Da Fiore**,
the latter specializing in fish and shellfish.

Aiming now for the Frari, go to the left of the church of San
Polo and cross the Rio di S. Polo — the water facade of
Sanmicheli's **Palazzo Corner Mocenigo** faces the canal to your
right — into Calle dei Saoneri(**33**). Trattoria **Ignazio** on the left is a
popular fish restaurant. Turn left into Rio Terà dei Nomboli and
right into Calle dei Nomboli, where no.2793, Palazzo Centani,
houses the *Goldoni Museum*.

Now cross the Ponte San Tomà, turn right into Fondamenta S.
Tomà and left into Campiello S. Tomà. Notice the charming
15thC reliefs of the *Madonna della Misericordia* on the side of the
church of San Tomà, and the facade of the Scuola dei Calegheri
across the square. The trattoria **San Tomà** is a useful restaurant
and pizzeria. Take the Ramo Calegher to the right of the Scuola,
turn right into Calle dei Corti(**34**) and left into Calle della Passion
which leads to the *Frari*. On the fondamenta opposite the facade of
the Frari you will find the elegant little bar Topo. The Scuola di
San Rocco is behind the apse end of the church. There is a
vaporetto stop at San Tomà. If you prefer to go on walking, carry

on to *San Pantaleone* in the *sestiere* of Dorsoduro, which is
described in *Walk 3*.

Walk 3/Dorsoduro

Dorsoduro is the Greenwich Village, or Chelsea, of Venice. The
least densely populated of the *sestieri*, it is a privileged domestic
neighborhood, rarely explored by tourists, although some of the
city's major churches and its prettiest, most peaceful streets are to
be found here. The name Dorsoduro, meaning 'hard back,' refers
to the unusually hard subsoil of this southernmost section of the
historic center.

Western Dorsoduro

Start at the *Accademia*. Facing the galleries, walk around the
right side into Rio Terà della Carità(**1**) and turn right out of
Campiello Calbo into the narrow Calle del Pistor(**2**) which brings
you on to Fondamenta Nani, named after the handsome ogival
Palazzo Nani, no.960, now the Liceo Artistico. If you are already
in need of refreshment, stop for a glass of wine at the Cantine del
Vino già Schiavi. Cross the Ponte San Trovaso, noticing the
miscellany of relief carvings embedded in the walls of the house
opposite and on the campanile. Turn left past the side entrance of
the church of *San Trovaso* and walk diagonally across its campo
turning right into Fondamenta Bonlini(**3**), where trees and vines
spill over low garden walls.

Turn right before the bridge into Fondamenta di Borgo(**4**)
where, toward the end, you will find the Locanda **Montin**, one of
the best known of the artists' trattorias. Cross the bridge ahead
into Calle delle Turchette which leads to the Calle Lunga(**5**), a
busy shopping street where the fish restaurant **La Furatola** is on
the left. Turn left, crossing the bridge ahead into Calle
L'Avogaria(**6**). No.1590-91, a typical and handsome late 15thC
palace, is near the Ponte L'Avogaria. The next bridge leads
straight across the Rio di San Sebastiano to Paolo Veronese's glory

Walk 3		
1	Rio Terà della Carità	**13** Rio Terà Canal
2	Calle del Pistor	**14** Fondamenta della Toletta
3	Fondamenta Bonlini	**15** Calle Contarini Corfù
4	Fondamenta di Borgo	**16** Calle nuova S. Agnese
5	Calle Lunga	**17** Piscina Venier
6	Calle L'Avogaria	**18** Calle A. da Ponte
7	Fondamenta de la Pescaria	**19** Zattere
8	Fondamenta di Riello	**20** Fondamenta della Dogana
9	Fondamenta delle Terese	**21** Calle Bastion
10	Corte Maggiore	**22** Fondamenta Venier dai Leoni
11	Fondamenta Briati	**23** Calle della Chiesa
12	Campo Santa Margherita	**24** Piscina del Forner

and burial place, the church of *San Sebastiano*.

Behind San Sebastiano you enter the old working-class district once inhabited by fishermen and artists and nowadays by employees of the maritime station and the cotton factory of Santa Marta, both of which you will pass a little later.

Walk around the right side of San Sebastiano, bearing right across the raised Campo San Angelo Raffaele toward the twin towers of the church of *Angelo Raffaele*. Turning left into the Fondamenta de la Pescaria(**7**), you can see ahead the squat Romanesque campanile of the church of San Nicolò dei Mendicoli. The brick building on the left is the customs house of the maritime station. Turn right over the next bridge and left into Fondamenta di Riello(**8**). The large brick building ahead is the cotton factory. Turn right at the end into the campiello which is dominated by the campanile of the ancient fishermen's church of *San Nicolò dei Mendicoli*.

Walk around the church and across the Rio delle Terese by the bridge opposite the facade of San Nicolò, then turn right into Fondamenta delle Terese(**9**). To your right, across the rio, there is a picturesque row of typical 18thC working-class tenements with external chimney breasts. Walk past the 18thC former church of Santa Teresa and cross the bridge at the end of the fondamenta. Turn right into Corte Maggiore(**10**) and left at the end — the facade of Angelo Raffaele is over to your right across the rio — and straight ahead into Fondamenta Briati(**11**). Looking ahead and straight to the right you can see the campanile of the next church on the itinerary, the *Carmini*.

The most important of the fine palaces on Fondamenta Briati is **Palazzo Arian**, no.2376, much restored but preserving delicate tracery above its six-light central block of windows. Across the canal, no.2597 is the 17thC **Pallazo Zenobio**, by Antonio Gaspari. Its ballroom is decorated with frescoes by Louis Dorigni. The next bridge that you come to crosses the Rio Briati into Fondamenta Foscarini. Turn right over the Ponte Foscarini into Campo dei Carmini. No.2615 is known, for no reliable reason, as Othello's house. Walk around the left side of the church of the Carmini.

Now turn left around the corner of the Scuola Grande dei Carmini into **Campo Santa Margherita**(**12**), the liveliest and largest square in Dorsoduro. In the courtyard immediately to the right is a Chinese restaurant **Shuang Hsi**. The freestanding building in the center of this end of the campo is the 18thC Scuola dei Varotari (tanners). On the left side of the square, occupying nos. 2920-35, is a row of 14th-to-early 15thC houses incorporating a 12th or early 13thC doorway with an attractive terra-cotta lunette. Two more 14thC Gothic houses are nos. 2945-2962. Looking ahead you can see the campanili of San Pantaleone and the Frari. On the right corner of the Calle della Chiesa at the far end of the campo is the ruined campanile of the former church of Santa Margherita and across the bridge ahead is the church of *San Pantaleone*.

Returning to Campo Santa Margherita turn left into Rio Terà della Scoazzera and right into Rio Terà Canal(**13**). As you cross the Ponte dei Pugni ahead notice the marble footprints on its summit which mark the starting point for the traditional fist-fights which once took place here between the residents of the parish of San Nicolò (the Nicolotti) and those of Castello (the Castellani). The game was banned in the 18thC after it led to bloodshed and several deaths.

Turn left at the foot of the bridge and right into Campo San Barnaba, dominated by the frigid 18thC facade of the church of

San Barnaba. Leave the campo by way of the Sotoportego del Casin dei Nobili, crossing the bridge ahead into Fondamenta della Toletta(14). M. Zanon on the right is the best pastry and coffee shop in Dorsoduro; another good one farther along on the left is Callegari. The Toletta brings you out onto the rio above San Trovaso. Cross the Ponte delle Maravegia. A right turn will bring you straight to the Zattere (see below). Or turn left passing the pizzeria **San Trovaso**. Turn right into Calle Contarini Corfù(15), left into Campiello Gambara and right into Calle Gambara, which brings you back to the Accademia.

Eastern Dorsoduro

Start at the left of the *Accademia* complex, walking past the apse at the end of the former church of the Carità along the Palladian flank of its cloister. Turn left into Calle nuova S. Agnese(16), then right into Piscina Venier(17) which becomes Piscina S. Agnese. Of architectural interest here are no.834, a typical small 15thC Gothic house, and nos. 830-33, united in the 17th-18thC by a pedimented central block with a *Madonna* in its niche. Turn right into Calle A. da Ponte(18), cross Campo S. Agnese, then turn left into Rio Terà Gesuati, along the flank of the church of the *Gesuati*, emerging on to the Zattere.

The **Zattere**(19) — the word means rafts — which runs along the broad *Giudecca* Canal is one of the sunniest parts of Venice and one of the best places to stretch your legs. Looking across the canal to the Giudecca the two most prominent monuments are the church of the *Redentore* to the left and the Mulino Stucky to the right. You could catch a vaporetto over to the Giudecca and eat at **Altanella**, **Do Mori** or **Harry's Dolci**. But there are plenty of pizzerias on the Zattere, with tables on the rafts; the best ice cream is sold by Aldo. Turning left at the Gesuati, walk along the Zattere — after a few minutes the church of *San Giorgio Maggiore* comes into view across the water. Continue along the Zattere as it sweeps round to the left and eventually you will come to the Customs House Point at the farthest and easternmost tip of Dorsoduro.

After admiring the spectacular view, turn left into Fondamenta della Dogana(20), walk past the facade of the *Salute* and cross the neareest wooden bridge, the Ponte dell' Abazia. The door on the right after the sottoportico, no.172 (ring for admission), leads to the colonnaded Gothic cloister of the **abbey of San Gregorio**, one of the oldest monastic foundations in Venice. On the left is the 15thC Gothic former church of San Gregorio, now used for the restoration of pictures. Take the Calle S. Gregorio and continue westward along Calle Bastion(21), the Ramo and Calle Barbaro into Campiello Barbaro. Cross the Ponte Cristoforo into Calle Cristoforo, at the corner of which you will be confronted by the wrought-iron land gates of the Palazzo Venier dei Leoni, which houses the *Guggenheim Collection*. The nearby bar, the **Corner Pub**, is a favorite with employees of the Guggenheim; and the nearest restaurant is **Cugnai** (*San Vio 857, closed Mon*).

Take the Fondamenta Venier dei Leoni(22). No.707 preserves a 13thC Veneto-Byzantine archway; across the canal, no.375 is an interesting architectural composite, probably rebuilt in the 17thC, with a Gothic doorway and huge Renaissance chimneys. Calle della Chiesa(23) leads to Campo San Vio where the English church, still very much a center of expatriate life, is to be found on the left. In Fondamenta Bragadin, which runs s from San Vio, is the restaurant **Cantinone Storico**. Cross the Rio di S. Vio into the Piscina del Forner(24), which will bring you back to the Accademia.

Sights and places of interest

No one building or work of art is as remarkable as Venice itself. While it is not the business of a guidebook to discourage sightseeing, it must be said that ticking off stars in a day or two is no way to enjoy this particular city. The average tourist now stays less than 24 hours; a lifetime is not long enough, but try to give it at least a long weekend. Venice is a city for loitering, dreaming, wandering, making private discoveries, going home and planning to return.

You can walk across the historic center in less than an hour, and nothing is much more than half an hour by foot from the Rialto. Or you can explore it by water on the *vaporetti* (the water buses), the *traghetti* (the inexpensive ferry gondolas), or, if you are feeling flush, in a private gondola. Either way, by foot or by water, you will see almost nothing that is ugly, and much that is dazzlingly beautiful, charming or odd.

The central fish-shaped group of islands is divided into six districts, or *sestieri*: Cannaregio, San Marco, Castello, Santa Croce, San Polo and Dorsoduro. The inner suburbs, only a few minutes away by boat, are the Giudecca, the Lido, and Murano. Each *sestiere* has its own special character and social mix. (There are older Venetians who like to claim that they have never crossed the meandering boundaries that contain their native *sestieri*.) The walks on pages 36-45 will take you through most of them.

The *sestieri* are also the basis of the Venetian address system, which is by no means as illogical as it may at first seem. Each one is numbered from 1 to many thousands; a postal address consists simply of the name of the *sestieri* and its number, for example Castello 2341 or Dorsoduro 3. A useful aid to finding your way around the *sestieri* by numbers is a little book, readily obtainable from bookstores, called *Il nuovo indicatore anagrafico di Venezia*. The various Venetian designations for the words street and square are given on pages 196-97.

Opening hours

As in the rest of Italy, opening hours of individual sights vary from one to another and change frequently. There is talk about rationalizing and extending them, possibly to the more familiar 9-5 pattern. Meanwhile, those given below are correct for 1987. A list of up-to-date opening hours is available from the Tourist Information Office in the Piazza and is published in the tourist magazine *Un Ospite di Venezia*.

Museums and galleries are open at least in the morning; some close all day once a week. Ticket offices shut one hour before the published closing time. Many museums are occasionally forced to close off sections for restoration or due to staff shortages. Children under 12 accompanied by adults are admitted free. There is a maddening shortage of printed guidance to some of the museums, although the expensive Electa guides are sold at some, and at many good bookstores.

Churches, many of which still contain important works of art, are theoretically open from early morning to noon and again from late afternoon to early evening. They face the same problems as museums and some maintain irregular opening hours, although most are open at least for services. Carry a supply of 200 lira coins for the light boxes and tip the sacristan for any help.

The **scuole**, a number of which are open to the public as museums, played a vital role in the life and art of medieval and Renaissance Venice. They were not schools or guilds, but lay confraternities whose members, drawn from the middle classes, looked after one another's spiritual and material welfare and performed charitable works in the name of a patron saint. The richest of the *scuole* built impressive headquarters and commissioned leading artists to commemorate the lives of their patron saints, often in a Venetian setting. These large narrative canvases, known as *teleri*, have left us with vivid and often accurate pictures of the city as it was; some are major works of art. Two of the most important cycles remaining in their original *scuole* are by Tintoretto (in San Rocco) and by Carpaccio (in San Giorgio degli Schiavoni).

Major sights classified by type

Churches
Angelo Raffaele
Carmini
Frari
Gesuati
Gesuiti
Giglio
Madonna dell'Orto
Miracoli
Ospedaletto
Pietà
Redentore
Salute
Sant' Alvise
Santi Apostoli
San Bartolomio
San Cassiano
Sant' Elena
San Francesco della Vigna
San Giacomo dell' Orio
San Giacomo di Rialto
San Giobbe
San Giorgio dei Greci
San Giorgio Maggiore
San Giovanni in Bragora
San Giovanni Crisostomo
Santi Giovanni e Paolo
San Giuliano
San Marco (Basilica)
San Marcuola
Santa Maria della Fava
Santa Maria Formosa
Santa Maria Mater Domini
San Marziale
San Moisè
San Nicolò dei Mendicoli
San Nicolò da Tolentino
San Pantaleone
San Pietro di Castello
San Polo
San Rocco
San Salvatore
San Sebastiano
San Stae
Santo Stefano
San Trovaso
San Zaccaria
Scalzi

Museums and galleries
Accademia
Archeological Museum
Cini Collection
Correr Museum

Doges' Palace
Fortuny Museum
Franchetti Gallery (Ca' d'Oro)
Gallery of Modern Art (Ca' Pesaro)
Goldoni Museum
Guggenheim Collection
Museum of Icons (San Giorgio dei Greci)
Museum of Sacred Art (Sant' Apollonia)
Museum of the Venetian 18thC (Ca' Rezzonico)
Natural History Museum
Naval Museum
Querini-Stampalia

Palaces
Arian (San Sebastiano)
Ca' d'Oro
Ca' Pesaro
Ca' Rezzonico
Centani (Goldoni Museum)
Contarini (Bovolo Staircase)
Corner Mocenigo (San Polo)
Doges' Palace
Fondaco dei Turchi
Grassi
Gritti Badoer (San Giovanni in Bragora)
Labia (San Giobbe)
Mocenigo
Nani (San Trovaso)
Pesaro degli Orfei (Fortuny)
Querini-Stampalia
Soranzo-Van Axel e Barozzi (Miracoli)
Trevisan-Cappello (Sant' Apollonia)
Venier dei Leoni (Guggenheim)
Zen (Gesuiti)
See also *Grand Canal* and *Planning and walks.*

Scuole
Carmini, Scuola Grande dei
San Giorgio degli Schiavoni, Scuola di
San Giovanni Evangelista, Scuola di
San Marco, Scuola Grande di (Santi Giovanni e Paolo)
San Rocco, Scuola Grande di

Accademia ★
Map 14E2. Campo della Carità, Dorsoduro ☎ 5222247 ■
Open Mon-Sat 9am-7pm; Sun, hols 9am-1pm. Water bus 1
or 2 to Accademia.

The Accademia houses the most complete collection of Venetian paintings in existence. Even the most shamelessly rushed tourists will wish to visit it for the sake of Giorgione's *Tempest*, Carpaccio's *St Ursula Cycle*, Titian's *Presentation of the Virgin*, and the outstanding works by Bellini, Veronese and Tintoretto. Be warned though. The gallery suffers from acute staffing problems and often the most popular sections are closed without warning.

If you are approaching the galleries across the **Accademia Bridge** you may be detained at its summit by an irresistible view of the *Grand Canal*, as far as the *Salute* and Bacino di San Marco on your left and the bend of the canal at Palazzo Balbi on your right. The wooden bridge was built as a temporary structure in 1932 by Eugenio Miozzi, but has become as much a permanent landmark as if it were made of stone.

The galleries and the Accademia di Belle Arti (Academy of Fine Arts) occupy the former church, monastery and *scuola* of the Carità. The original appearance of the buildings from the San Marco side, now much altered, was lovingly recorded by Canaletto in his *Stonemason's Yard* in the National Gallery, London. The Neoclassical facade was applied when the complex was adapted to receive the Academy in the early 19thC. The facade of the former church retains in the lunette over its main door a carving of *The Coronation of the Virgin* (1445) by Bartolomeo Bon.

The Gothic portico to the left of the gallery gives access to the still flourishing art school. Special permission is required to visit the section of the monastery partially built by Palladio in 1561, of which only the E wing of the cloister, the sacristy or *tablinum* and the famous oval staircase survive.

The Accademia was founded in the mid-18thC under the direction of its first president, Giambattista Piazzetta, who was succeeded by Giambattista (G.B.) Tiepolo. The collection, which originally comprised works by the 18thC academicians, was later enriched with pictures from the churches and monasteries suppressed under Napoleon, with numerous bequests from Venetian private collections and, since the late 19thC, by state-funded purchases.

Five centuries of Venetian painting are represented, from the first named masters of the 14thC to the last burst of artistic genius in the 18thC. The pictures are arranged in approximately chronological order, but first-time visitors on a tight schedule might find it convenient to tour the galleries backward, picking out the highlights as follows: **Room XXIV**, Titian's *Presentation of the Virgin*; **Room XXI**, Carpaccio's *St Ursula Cycle*; **Room XX**, Bellini's *Corpus Domini Procession*; **Room X**, Veronese's *Feast at the House of Levi*; **Room VII**, Lotto's *Portrait of a Young Man*; **Room V**, Giorgione's *Tempest* and works by Giovanni Bellini.

Room I   This was the assembly hall of the Scuola Grande della Carità, one of the oldest and richest of the Venetian confraternities. The splendid wooden ceiling (1461-84) is attributed to Marco Cozzi. The pictures by the so-called Venetian Primitives date from the 14th and early 15thC, during which the traditional Venetian allegiance to Byzantium gradually gave way to Gothic influences. The Byzantine splendor of Paolo Veneziano's polyptych of the *Coronation of the Virgin with Scenes from the Lives of Christ and St Francis* (c.1340) owes much to the lavish use of gold and lapislazuli.

A more intimate and naturalistic work is the *Annunciation with Saints and Prophets* (1357) by Lorenzo Veneziano, the leading Gothic painter of his period. Although the Gothic persisted in Venice well into the 15thC, Jacobello del Fiore's *Coronation of the Virgin in Paradise* (1438), modeled on a fresco painted in the previous century by Guariento for the *Doges' Palace*, is unusually conservative for its date.

Room II The room was built in 1875 to exhibit Titian's *Assumption*, which was not returned to the *Frari* until 1919. Giovanni Bellini's *Madonna Enthroned with Sts Francis, John the Baptist, Job, Dominic, Sebastian and Ludwig* ★ (*c.*1487) is the earliest of the three altarpieces in this room painted for the Renaissance church of *San Giobbe*. Carpaccio's San Giobbe altarpiece, *The Presentation of Jesus* ✩ (1510), has a similar composition and one of the most charming of all musical angels. The latest of the San Giobbe altarpieces, Marco Basaiti's *Agony in the Garden* (1516), is one of the artist's most successful works; another is *The Calling of the Sons of Zebedee* (1510).

Room IV Andrea Mantegna, whose *St George* ✩ (*c.*1460) was probably painted before he left his native Padua for the Gonzaga court at Mantua, was married to Nicolosia Bellini and exercised a strong influence on his brother-in-law Giovanni Bellini's early

Accademia Galleries

work. Piero della Francesca's *St Jerome* (*c*.1450), an early work by one of the greatest Tuscan masters, may have been painted in Venice.

Another mainland artist represented here is the first of the great Ferrarese painters, Cosmè Tura, with his characteristically brittle *Madonna of the Zodiac* (*c*.1453) in its original frame. Giovanni Bellini's *Madonna and Child with St Catherine and the Magdalen* ★ (*c*.1490) is a masterpiece of modeling with light.

Room V The fame of Giorgione's *Tempest* ★ (*c*.1507), the best known painting in the Accademia, does not in any way vitiate its fascination. It is one of the few pictures that can be confidently attributed to Giorgione, but the story behind its subject, a soldier and a woman nursing a baby under a lowering sky, remains a mystery. Giorgione's *Old Woman* ☆ (*c*.1508) is an unusually compressed and forceful treatment of a familiar warning about the ravages of time.

The *Madonna of the Trees* ☆ (1487) is one of the most serenely tender and justly celebrated of Giovanni Bellini's many madonnas. Bellini was an old man when he painted the *Pietà* ★ and *Madonna and Child with the Baptist and a Female Saint* ★ (both *c*.1505); but he was not too old to explore the limits of his undiminished versatility or to respond to the revolutionary new art of his pupil Giorgione. Whereas the *Pietà* is set against a landscape studded with real buildings, the background of the *Madonna and Child* emphasizes the abstract surface pattern of the buildings in a way that makes one think back to Byzantine mosaics and ahead almost four centuries to Cézanne.

Room VI Titian's *St John the Baptist* (*c*.1535) is posed like a self-conscious athlete in a wonderfully evocative landscape. In Paris Bordone's *Presentation of the Ring to Doge Bartolomeo Gradenigo* (1534) the fisherman offers the ring as proof of his encounter with St Mark on the occasion when the saint saved the city from a flood in 1340.

Five of the early 16thC artists represented in this and the next two rooms were from the part of Lombardy ruled by Venice since the middle of the previous century. Lorenzo Lotto and Palma il Vecchio were born in Bergamo, Girolamo Savoldo, Girolamo Romanino and Moretto in Brescia.

Room VII The quizzically brooding *Portrait of a Young Man in his Study* ★ (*c*.1525) is one of the few pictures by Lotto in Venice, where the artist's extraordinary gifts were never fully recognized. The character and thoughts of the subject are established by the objects around him: the mandolin, the hunting horn, the fallen rose petals (the transience of life), the salamander (immortality).

Room VIII Palma il Vecchio's *Sacra Conversazione* ☆ (*c*.1525) shows the influence of Titian, who may have finished the picture after Palma's death. Romanino's *Pietà with Saints* (1510) is the artist's earliest dated work.

Room IX The *Madonna of the Taylors* (1533) and *The Eternal Father Protecting Venice*, which gives a view of the Piazza San Marco as it was in the 1530s, are by Bonifacio de' Pitati, a pupil of Palma il Vecchio.

Room X Veronese's *Feast at the House of Levi* ★ (1573) was painted as a Last Supper for the monks of *Santi Giovanni e Paolo*. Not surprisingly, perhaps, given the moral climate of the Counter-Reformation, the artist was summoned before the Inquisition and ordered to erase the dogs, dwarfs, drunkards and especially the Germans, all of which were judged offensive elements in the treatment of a sacred subject. Another oddity is the presence of 15 people rather than the 13 normally required for a

Last Supper. By an inspired piece of lateral thinking, Veronese managed to meet the objections of the Inquisition without changing anything — except the title. A recent cleaning has relieved the picture of 18thC overpainting.

Tintoretto's *St Mark Freeing the Slave* ★ (1548), painted for the Scuola di San Marco at Santi Giovanni e Paolo, established his reputation with its brilliant theatricality. He resumed the San Marco cycle in 1562 with the phantasmagoric *Translation of the Body of St Mark* and the *St Mark Rescuing a Saracen* (both ★). Pordenone, whose *St Lorenzo Giustiniani with Sts Francis, Augustine, Bernardino and John the Baptist* (1532) was painted for the *Madonna dell'Orto*, was a northern Italian artist who influenced the young Tintoretto. Admirers of Tintoretto's work should also be sure to visit the Scuola di *San Rocco*, and lovers of Veronese, the church of *San Sebastiano*.

Titian's *Pietà* ✫ (1576) is the artist's last work and the one he wished to be placed above his tomb in the Frari. The canvas is made up of several pieces, which suggests that he began with the central figures of Christ and the Madonna and enlarged the composition later. The picture was finished by Palma il Giovane.

As it was the inevitable destiny of Venice to be painted, and painted with passion, so the wide world of the picture becomes, as we live there, and however much we go about our affairs, the constant habitation of our thoughts.
Henry James, *Italian Hours*, 'The Grand Canal,' 1892

Room XI In the **first section** are several paintings by Tintoretto, including *Sts Jerome and Andrew* (*c*.1552) and its pendant *St George and the Princess with St Louis* (*c*.1553), and the Old Testament scenes: the scurrying *Creation of the Animals, Adam and Eve* and *Cain and Abel* (*c*.1550). The spiritual intensity of Tintoretto's art is in total contrast to the sensual worldliness of his younger contemporary, Paolo Veronese, who was the supreme colorist of the 16thC. Three of Veronese's most radiant pictures are the *Madonna Enthroned with the Baptist and Sts Joseph, Francis and Jerome* ★ (1562) painted for the sacristy altar of *San Zaccaria; The Mystic Marriage of St Catherine* ★ (1575), of which a 17thC admirer wrote that it might have been painted in gold, pearls, rubies, emeralds, sapphires and diamonds; and *Ceres Paying Homage to Venice* ★ (1575), painted for a ceiling in the *Doges' Palace*.

The most exciting paintings produced in 17thC Venice were by non-Venetians. The Neapolitan Luca Giordano, the Genoese Bernardo Strozzi, the Florentine Sebastiano Mazzoni and the Vicentine Francesco Maffei are represented in the **second section** of **Room XI** (and also in **Room XIV**). Notice here especially Strozzi's *Feast in the House of Simon* (*c*.1629) and Giordano's *Crucifixion of St Peter* (*c*.1660).

In the 18thC, the native Venetian genius reasserted itself. The greatest painter of this last golden age, G.B. Tiepolo, developed his art through close study of Veronese and of his older contemporaries Sebastiano Ricci and G.B. Piazzetta. The Tiepolos in this room were originally designed for churches. *The Bronze Serpent* (1732-35) was the frieze of a choir; *St Helena Discovers the True Cross* (*c*.1745) was the central tondo of a ceiling; *The Faithful Worshipers* survives from the decorations of the *Scalzi* which were largely destroyed during World War I.

Room XII The first part of the long corridor is devoted to 18thC landscapes by Marco Ricci, the leading Venetian practitioner of the genre, by Giuseppe Zais and by the Tuscan Francesco Zuccarelli.

Room XIII This room is devoted to late 16thC Venetian and mainland artists, including Jacopo Bassano, Jacopo and Domenico Tintoretto, Andrea Schiavone and Palma il Giovane.

Room XIV Outstanding paintings by 17thC non-Venetians include Jan Liss' *Sacrifice of Isaac*, Domenico Fetti's *David* (*c*.1620), *Meditation* (1623) and *Parable of the Good Samaritan* (1623), and Sebastiano Mazzoni's startlingly original *Annunciation* ☆ (*c*.1650).

Room XV The elegant *Abraham and the Angels* (1773) is by G.B. Tiepolo's son and disciple Giandomenico.

Room XVI *The Rape of Europa* (*c*.1725) is the loveliest of three youthful works by G.B. Tiepolo.

Room XVIA Compare G.B. Piazzetta's *Fortune-teller* ☆ (1740), a light-hearted genre subject dashingly treated by a great painter, with Pietro Longhi's appealing but wooden little genre scenes in **Room XVII**.

Room XVII 18thC view painters are represented here. Canaletto's *Capriccio of a Colonnade opening on to a Courtyard* ☆ (1765), the only Canaletto exhibited in the gallery, was presented to the Accademia on his election. The *Scuola di San Marco* (1738-40) is by Canaletto's nephew and close disciple Bernardo Bellotto. Like Canaletto and Bellotto, Francesco Guardi painted his views of Venice primarily as souvenirs for tourists. His more poetic and impressionistic vision of the city is exemplified here by the *Island of San Giorgio Maggiore* (*c*.1780) and the *Fire at San Marcuola* (1789).

Pietro Longhi's six *Scenes from Venetian Life* (1741-*c*.1752) convey a sociability, charm and intimacy rare in Venetian art. G.B. Tiepolo's *Transfer of the Holy House from Nazareth to Loreto* (*c*.1742) is a sketch for the ceiling of the *Scalzi*, which was destroyed in World War I. Rosalba Carriera, the sister-in-law of Gian Antonio Pellegrini, was one of the most popular and prolific 18thC portraitists. The seven pastels, which include a self-portrait, were painted in the 1730s.

Room XIX The terra cotta *Apollo* (1779) was Antonio Canova's presentation piece to the Accademia, which originally represented sculptors as well as painters.

Room XX The pictures in this room, **Room XXI** and **Room XXIV** are outstanding examples of the large narrative canvases commissioned in the 15th and early 16thC by the Venetian *scuole* or benevolent confraternities. These *teleri* filled the double function of depicting the lives and legends of the confraternities' patron saints and of portraying prominent members. They were often set in a real or pastiche Venetian background. The eight *Stories of the Holy Cross* were painted for the Scuola di San Giovanni Evangelista, which housed a miracle-working relic of the True Cross. Gentile Bellini's *Corpus Domini Procession* ★ (1496) records the appearance of the Piazza San Marco as it was before the gilding faded on the Porta della Carta, then newly built. The two 12thC Byzantine procuracies were replaced by the present wings of the Piazza in the 16thC and the brick paving was changed to stone and marble in the 18thC.

In Gentile Bellini's *Miracle of the Cross on the Canal of San Lorenzo* ☆ (1550), Caterina Cornaro, Queen of Cyprus, kneels in the left foreground opposite a group of men among whom are Gentile and his brother Giovanni. In Carpaccio's *Recovery of a Man Possessed by Demons* ☆ (1496) the miracle itself takes place on an imaginary loggia on the left while the center of attention is the wooden *Rialto* Bridge, which was not replaced by the present stone bridge until late in the 16thC. Beyond, on the right, you can see the old Fondaco dei Tedeschi that was destroyed by fire in 1505, the Ca' da Mosto, now much altered, and the former campanile of *Santi Apostoli*, rebuilt in the 17thC.

Room XXI Carpaccio's *St Ursula Cycle* ★ (1475-95) was painted for the Scuola di Sant' Ursula whose headquarters at Santi Giovanni e Paolo were destroyed by fire in the early 19thC. Along with the cycle Carpaccio finished 16yrs later, which remains in its original Scuola di *San Giorgio degli Schiavoni*, these scenes are among the most universally loved pictures in Venice. Ruskin, who fell in love with them 20yrs after he had written *The Stones of Venice*, was almost driven mad by his obsession with them. According to the legend told by Jacobus de Voragine, Ursula, daughter of the Christian king of Brittany, accepted a proposal of marriage from the pagan king of England on condition that their union remained unconsummated for 2yrs, while she and 11,000 virgins made a pilgrimage to all the holy sanctuaries of the world.

Carpaccio's narrative begins with the *Arrival of the English Ambassador at the Court of Ursula's Father* and ends with the *Martyrdom and Funeral* and *Apotheosis* of St Ursula. Although the architecture is mostly imaginary, the costumes, textiles, furnishings and ships of late 15thC Venice are all accurate.

Room XXIII This is part of the former church of Santa Maria della Carità, built between 1441-52 by the studio of Bartolomeo Bon. The four large triptychs displayed in the apse were painted for the church by the young Giovanni Bellini when he was still strongly under the influence of Donatello and Mantegna.

Room XXIV This was the *albergo*, or committee room, of the Scuola della Carità. The blue and gold wooden ceiling was installed when the room was redecorated in 1444. Titian's *Presentation of the Virgin* ★ (1534-38), in its original position on the entrance wall, is the only picture painted by the artist for a Venetian confraternity. Against a landscape that evokes Titian's native Friuli, members of the confraternity watch the tiny figure of Mary climb the steps of Solomon's temple. Three of the spectators at the foot of the staircase are borrowed from a tapestry design by Raphael, while the old egg-seller is taken from a painting by Cima da Conegliano. These references demonstrate the artist's commitment both to the most advanced developments in 16thC Italian painting and to the specifically Venetian conventions of this particular kind of narrative work. In the same way, the pink and white patterned brickwork of one of the houses recalls the *Doges' Palace*, while other architectural elements, such as the classical loggia and rusticated steps, belong to the Roman High Renaissance.

In their jointly executed transitional work, the *Madonna Enthroned with Sts Gregory, Jerome, Ambrogio and Augustine* ☆ (1446), Antonio Vivarini and Giovanni d'Alemagna set their monumental Gothic figures in a marble enclosure that is sumptuously decorated in the International Gothic style and skillfully simulates real space according to the principles of the Florentine Renaissance.

Angelo Raffaele †

Map 8F3. Campo Angelo Raffaele, Dorsoduro. Water bus 1, 2 or 4 to Accademia, 1 to Ca' Rezzonico or 5 to San Basilio.
A church dedicated to the Archangel Raphael has occupied this site in the sw corner of Venice since the 7thC. The present building dates from 1618-39. The facade facing the canal was added in 1735 and could hardly be duller; however, partly because

of the ineptitude of its builders, the interior is graced with five of the most attractive 18thC pictures in Venice.

The facade collapsed while under construction, destroying the organ on the interior facade. The new organ is decorated with five enchanting *Scenes from the Story of Tobias* ★ by Gianantonio Guardi, possibly with the collaboration of his brother Francesco.

In the same area, other notable churches include *San Sebastiano*, *San Nicolò dei Mendicoli* and the *Carmini*.

Archeological Museum *(Museo Archeologico)*
Map 15D4. Piazza San Marco 17 ☎5225978 ▥ Open Mon-Sat 9am-2pm; Sun, hols 9am-1pm.

The Archeological Museum is temporarily installed in a sequence of rooms in the Procuratie Nuove originally built by Scamozzi. It will eventually be transferred to the Palazzo Grimani at S. Maria Formosa, which is where the most important parts of the collection were originally assembled in the 16thC by two members of the Grimani family.

The collection is particularly interesting because of the unusually large number of original Greek and Roman sculptures. These works affected the style of Venetian painters and sculptors from Giovanni Bellini to Canova.

Arsenale *(Arsenal)* ▥
Map 12E9. Castello. Water bus 1 to Arsenale.

This vast, walled dockyard in eastern Venice was once the largest and most efficient industrial complex in Europe. Run as a strictly controlled government monopoly, it pioneered methods of prefabricated construction to produce the galleys on which Venetian trade and naval power depended.

It was called *arsenale* after the Arabic *Dar Sina'a*, meaning house of construction, and its fame was such that all subsequent arsenals were named after it. The arsenal was established in the 12thC when Doge Ordelafo Falier nationalized Venetian shipbuilding. At its peak in the Renaissance it employed over 4,000 specialized workers and the galleys were assembled at a rate of one every few hours.

The arsenal remained active until World War I and was then used as a naval base for stores and repairs.

The **ceremonial land gate** which faces the canal from the Campo Arsenale was the first example of Renaissance classical architecture in Venice (although the capitals of the freestanding columns were taken from an 11thC Veneto-Byzantine building). It was erected in 1460 by Antonio Gambello, who adopted the form of a Roman triumphal archway. The winged lion of St Mark over the gate holds a closed book. Possibly the book's traditional inscription, *Pax tibi Marce* (Peace be with you, Mark), was considered inappropriate to the place where Venice prepared itself for war.

An endearing pride of four Greek lions stands in front of the gate. Those on either side of the terrace were sent from Athens by Francesco Morosini after the recapture of the Morea in 1687. The one on the left bears an inscription in ancient Scandinavian referring to the exploits of Norse mercenary soldiers employed by the Byzantine Emperor in the 11thC. The lion that has a new head (center right) originally came from Delos and was placed here to commemorate the recapture of Corfu in 1716.

Parts of the Arsenal are open to the public by the *Naval Museum*. Other sections may be opened in the near future and are well worth visiting for their historical associations as well as for some works of art, notably Jacopo Sansovino's *Madonna and Child* (1533) in the atrium.

Bovolo Staircase *(Scala del Bovolo)* 🏛 ★
Map 15D4. Palazzo Contarini, Calle della Vida (s of Campo Manin), San Marco. Water bus 1, 2 or 4 to Rialto or 1 to Sant' Angelo.

This external staircase (*bovolo* in Venetian dialect means snail shell or spiral staircase) in the open courtyard of the Palazzo Contarini is one of the curiosities of Venetian Renaissance architecture and one of its more remarkable feats of engineering. It was built *c*.1499, probably by Giovanni Candi, a follower of Mauro Codussi. The staircase is contained within a loggiaed tower inspired by the cylindrical *campanili* once common in the Veneto and elsewhere, notably at Pisa. You will see that the turns of the spiral had to be adjusted to the differing heights of the five arcaded stories of the earlier garden facade to which it was attached.

In front is a miscellaneous collection of wellheads including one 11thC Byzantine example.

Ca' d'Oro *(Franchetti Gallery)* 🏛 ★
Map 15A4. Grand Canal, Cannaregio 3922 ☎5238790 🖼 Open Mon 1.30-7pm, Tues-Sat 9am-7pm; Sun, hols 9am-1pm. Water bus 1 to Ca' d'Oro.

No domestic building in Venice so perfectly expresses both the Venetian love of surface decoration for its own sake and the Venetian resistance to the organizing principles of mainland Gothic and Renaissance architecture as does the Ca' d'Oro. Admiring its facade from the *Grand Canal*, which is the only way to see it properly, you may find it incredible that the Ca' d'Oro was built within a few years of, and only a few hundred kilometers away from, Brunelleschi's rigorous Innocenti Loggia, the building that launched the Florentine classical Renaissance. The comparison becomes all the more remarkable if one imagines the original appearance of the Ca' d'Oro, when its carvings were picked out in real gold leaf (hence the name House of Gold), set off by ultramarine and red.

The Ca' d'Oro was begun in 1424 for the wealthy patrician Marino Contarini; he closely supervised its construction, which was carried out jointly by the workshops of the Milanese sculptor Matteo Raverti and the Venetian stonemason Giovanni Bon. Raverti probably executed the six-light window on the *piano nobile* — a direct borrowing from the *Doges' Palace* — while Bon is thought to have been responsible for the single-balconied windows on the right, the cornice and the pinnacles on the roofline. The water gate and inlaid carvings on the facade were preserved, according to Contarini's instructions, from a previous Veneto-Byzantine palace.

In 1840 the Russian Prince Alexander Trubetskoy romantically, but as it turned out disastrously, made a present of the Ca' d'Oro to the ballerina Marina Taglioni. Taglioni's barbarous alterations to the house included the demolition of Raverti's external staircase in the courtyard and of the portal of the street entrance. Fortunately the Ca' d'Oro was bought in 1894 by Baron Giorgio Franchetti, who undertook a painstaking restoration and, in 1915, bequeathed it, together with his large collection of paintings, sculpture and furniture, to the State.

The **Franchetti Gallery ★**, which was reopened to the public in 1984 after years of closure, has been brilliantly designed to take the greatly enlarged collection. On the first floor, important exhibits include Andrea Mantegna's late, famous *St Sebastian* ★ (*c.*1506); Pier Jacopo Alari's *Apollo* (1498); the bronzes in rm 3; and Tullio Lombardo's superb carving of *Two boys*.

A 15thC wooden staircase, a reconstruction from another palace, leads to the second floor. In rm 9, the finest of the portrait busts by Alessandro Vittoria are those of Benedetto Manrini and Giovanni Donà. In the portego, atrium and rm 16 are the remains of detached **frescoes** that originally adorned the exteriors of buildings in the city. The most interesting are those by Titian and Giorgione from the Fondaco dei Tedeschi. Executed in 1508, they were public manifestos of the revolutionary new art of the Venetian 16thC. In the last rooms, do not miss the two modellos by Bernini for his *Fountain of the Rivers in Rome*; or the two *Views of Venice* by Francesco Guardi, which are among the few left in Venice.

The magnificent Verona-marble **wellhead** ☆ (1427) in the courtyard is carved with the figures of *Fortitude, Justice and Charity* by Bartolomeo Bon. Baron Franchetti retrieved this wellhead from the Paris dealer to whom it had been sold; he also rebuilt the external staircase from its original fragments.

Ca' Pesaro *(Gallery of Modern Art and Oriental Museum)* 🏛 ☆
Map 14A3. Grand Canal, Santa Croce. Water bus 1 to San Stae. Entrance in Calle Pesaro.

The greatest Baroque palaces on the *Grand Canal*, both designed by Baldassare Longhena, are *Ca' Rezzonico* and Ca' Pesaro. Ca' Pesaro, the earlier and more flamboyant of the two, was begun in 1652 for Giovanni Pesaro, who was elected Doge six years later. (His funerary monument in the *Frari* is also by Longhena.) The palace remained incomplete at Longhena's death and it was not until 1710 that the second *piano nobile* and the simpler facade facing the Rio Due Torre were eventually added by Antonio Gaspari.

The design of the facade is closely based on Sansovino's Palazzo Corner near San Maurizio, with its surface texture elaborated and enriched — most notably by the diamond-cut rustication on the water story; this feature had been used in Venice only once before, on the mid-15thC Ca' del Duca.

The first two floors of the palace are occupied by the Gallery of Modern Art and the third by the Oriental Museum. The entrance is through the impressive courtyard designed by Longhena but completed after his death.

Gallery of Modern Art *(Galleria Internazionale d'Arte Moderna)*
☎ 721127 ▨

The gallery was founded in 1897 as a permanent exhibition of works of art acquired from the Biennale. Closed since 1983, it will eventually house a representative collection of works by Italian and international contemporary artists. The 19thC art formerly displayed here may be moved to a separate museum.

Oriental Museum *(Museo Orientale)*
☎ 5227681 ▨ *Open Tues-Sat 9am-2pm, Sun 9am-1pm. Closed Mon.*

The top floor contains a notable collection, beautifully displayed, of Japanese art of the Edo period (1614-1868) as well as other Oriental works of art, decorative objects, armor and costumes collected in the 19thC by the Conte di Bardi during an extensive voyage in the Far East.

The Japanese displays include parade and combat armor; 18th and 19thC swords; 17th and 18thC Toso screens; and paintings.

Ca' Rezzonico *(Museum of the Venetian Eighteenth Century)* ☆

Map 14D2. Grand Canal, Dorsoduro ☎5224543 Open Mon-Thurs, Sat 10am-4pm; Sun 9am-12.30pm. Closed Fri. Water bus 1 to Ca' Rezzonico. Entrance from Fondamenta Rezzonico, near Campo San Barnaba.

If you approach Ca' Rezzonico by water you will see that it is one of the most imposing palaces on the *Grand Canal*. It was begun in 1667 by Baldassare Longhena for the procurator Filippo Bon. The design, like that of Longhena's other great palace, *Ca' Pesaro*, derives from Sansovino's Palazzo Corner near San Maurizio.

The Bon family ran out of money when the palace was completed only as far as the first *piano nobile* and, in 1712, they sold the unfinished building to the vastly wealthy Rezzonico family, who had recently bought themselves into the Venetian aristocracy. The palace was completed for them in 1752 by Giorgio Massari.

The poet Robert Browning died at Ca' Rezzonico in Dec 1889 while visiting his son Pen.

Here you come with your old music, and here's all the good it
  brings.
What, they lived once thus at Venice where the merchants were
  the kings,
Where Saint Mark's is, where the Doges used to wed the sea
  with rings?

Did young people take their pleasure when the sea was warm in
  May?
Balls and masks begun at midnight, burning ever to mid-day,
When they made up fresh adventures for the morrow, do you
  say?

Robert Browning, *A Toccata of Galuppi's*, 1855

The palace has housed the Museum of the Venetian Eighteenth Century since 1936. Furniture, decorative objects, pictures and ceiling paintings were brought from elsewhere and arranged to recreate the atmosphere of one of the more splendid of the 18thC Venetian palaces. Some of the rooms will remain closed until the · restoration of the palace is completed.

Massari's grand ceremonial staircase leads to the **first piano nobile**, the floor which in all Venetian palaces was used for entertaining and where the most impressive ceiling paintings and furniture were found. The **ballroom**, which Massari built on to the back of the palace, has a splendid ceiling fresco by G.B. Crosato. The **ebonized vase-stands upheld by moors** ☆ around the walls, are by the early 18thC sculptor Andrea Brustolon and are part of a remarkable suite of furnishings, the rest of which is in the **Sala del Brustolon** (see below), entered through the left-hand door.

The right-hand door leads to the **Sala della Allegoria Nuziale**, named after G.B. Tiepolo's ceiling painting, an allegorical celebration of *The Marriage of Ludovico Rezzonico to Faustina Savorgnan* ☆ (1758). The Savorgnan were one of the most powerful families of the Veneto, and the marriage, as you can see, represented an ecstatic climax to the Rezzonico family's rapid social climb. The other great family event of 1758 was the election of Carlo Rezzonico to the papacy as Clement XIII. A staircase leads to the mezzanine apartments he occupied, and where Robert Browning died.

The Sala della Allegoria Nuziale leads on to the **Sala dei**

Pastelli, where pastels and miniatures by Rosalba Carriera decorate the walls. In the **Sala del Trono**, the next room but one, the carved and gilded throne and other pieces are by Antonio Corradini who, like Brustolon, worked primarily as a sculptor. G.B. Tiepolo's ceiling fresco shows *Merit between Nobility and Virtue* (1758). The long reception hall or *portego* commands fine views across the Grand Canal of Massari's *Palazzo Grassi*. The two statues of *Atlantes* are by Alessandro Vittoria.

Across the *portego* from the Sala del Trono is the **Sala del Tiepolo**, with a ceiling painting by G.B. Tiepolo representing *Fortitude and Wisdom* (1745). Beyond a corridor is the **library**, containing 18thC books published in Venice. The five *Mythological Scenes* on the ceiling are by the early 17thC artist Francesco Maffei. The chandelier was made in Murano. Moving through a room with paintings by Giorgio Lazzarini, you come to the **Sala del Brustolon**, which is decorated with elaborately fantastic **furnishings** ☆ by Andrea Brustolon. The ceiling paintings of allegorical and mythological figures are by Maffei.

A staircase from the *portego* leads to the **second piano nobile**. Here the *portego* is hung with 18thC paintings including G.B. Piazzetta's *Death of Darius*, G.A. Pellegrini's *Mucius Scaeuola*, and Jan Liss' *Judith and Holofernes*. The left door opposite the stairs leads to the **Sala dei Longhi**, hung with the largest collection in Venice of Pietro Longhi's spirited, affectionate *Scenes from Venetian Life* ☆ In the 18thC nearly everybody, it seems, went about their business with a smile. The ceiling by G.B. Tiepolo represents the *Triumph of Zephyr and Flora* (1730). Next door, in the **Sala delle Lacche Verdi**, the suite of green and gold lacquer furniture is an unusually fine example of Venetian chinoiserie. The ceiling painting of the *Triumph of Diana* is by Gian Antonio Guardi. In the **Sala del Guardi**, the three damaged frescoes of *Minerva, Apollo* and *Venice* are by G.A. Guardi. The next room, the **Camera dell'Alcova**, is an exact reconstruction of an 18thC bedroom, with a pretty stuccoed boudoir behind.

Across the *portego*, the door to the left of the stairs leads to a delightful group of rooms devoted to the **frescoes** ☆ by Giandomenico (G.D.) Tiepolo — son of Giambattista (G.B.) — originally painted for the Tiepolo family house near Mestre. They include the *New World* (1791), his famous satirical depiction of Venetians watching a peep-show at a Sunday fair, and the cavorting *Clowns* which were among his favorite subjects. The earliest works in the series are the frescoes in the adjacent chapel.

The **Camera della Spinetta** off the *portego* contains an 18thC spinet and in the passageway is a rosarymaker's signboard by Francesco Guardi. In the last room on this floor, the **Sala del Ridotto**, overlooking the Grand Canal, are two marvelously painted and evocative representations of 18thC Venetian life by Francesco Guardi: *The Nuns' Parlor at San Zaccaria* ☆ recording one of the city's most fashionable rendezvous, and *The Long Room of the Ridotto* ☆ showing a favorite gambling house near San Moisè.

On the **third floor** are ceramics, costumes, a marionette theater and a reconstruction of an 18thC pharmacy.

Carmini *(Santa Maria del Carmelo)* †
Map 8F3. Campo Carmini, Dorsoduro. Water bus 1 to Ca' Rezzonico or 5 to San Basilio.

The church and *scuola grande* of the Carmelite order stand at the sw corner of the extensive market square of Santa Margherita. The **church** (Santa Maria del Carmelo) was built in the 14thC but was subsequently much altered. Its brick facade facing the little Campo dei Carmini was added in the 16thC. The tall Baroque campanile (1688) by Giuseppe Sardi is surmounted by a statue of *The Virgin Holding the Scapular*. The scapular, two patches of cloth, is the distinguishing badge of the Carmelites. Entrance to the church is through the 16thC portico, decorated with Byzantine carvings, on the left flank.

Nothing requires more care, as a long knowledge of Venice works in, than not to lose the useful faculty of getting lost.
Henry James, *Italian Hours*, 'Two Old Houses,' 1899

The arcades of the nave were decorated in the 17thC with gilded wooden statues and a series of Baroque canvases illustrating the history of the Carmelite order. The best — and most peculiar — is the *Dream of Honorius III* (1669) by the Florentine Sebastiano Mazzoni, which is fifth on the left. Over the second altar on the right is a serene *Adoration of the Shepherds* ✪ (before 1510) by Cima da Conegliano. Opposite, over the second altar on the left, is Lorenzo Lotto's *St Nicholas Bari with Sts John the Baptist and Lucy* ✪ (1529) with a spacious harbour landscape. The choir lofts at either side of the entrance to the chancel are decorated with paintings of the *Annunciation, Adoration of the Shepherds, Adoration of the Magi* and *Flight into Egypt* by Andrea Schiavone. In the chapel to the right of the high altar there is a bronze low relief of the *Lamentation over the Dead Christ* by the Sienese sculptor and architect Francesco di Giorgio.

Scuola Grande dei Carmini ✪
☎5226553 🚼 *Open Mon-Sat 9am-noon, 3-6pm. Closed Sun.*
The Scuola Grande dei Carmini, the headquarters of the Carmelite confraternity, was built in 1663. Two facades (1668-80) were designed with advice from Baldassare Longhena. The interior is decorated throughout with 18thC frescoes, of which the great glory is the ceiling of the first-floor **salone superiore**, painted in the early 1740s by G.B. Tiepolo. In the center of the ceiling is a sensuous, visionary representation of *St. Simon Stock Receiving the Scapular from the Virgin* (1744). It is one of Tiepolo's religious masterpieces. In the four corners of the ceiling are voluptuous figures of *Virtues*, which were received with such enthusiasm when unveiled in 1743 — before the central panel was completed — that the artist was unanimously elected a memeber of the confraternity. 'In their quiet way these paintings are a quintessence of Tiepolo's mature style . . . even the most severe Virtue appears relaxed.' (Michael Levey)

Tiepolo's master, G.B. Piazzetta, is represented in a passageway between the next two rooms by a fine *Judith and Holofernes* (after 1748).

Cini Collection *(Raccolta d'Arte Vittorio Cini)* 🏛
Map 14F3. Dorsoduro 864, Campo San Vio ☎710755. *Open Tues-Sun 2-7pm summer only. Closed Mon. Water bus 1 or 2 to Accademia.*
Count Vittorio Cini, who made his fortune as an industrialist between the wars, was the 20thC Venetian Maecenas, his greatest gift to the city, and indeed to Europe, being the Cini Foundation at *San Giorgio Maggiore*. He lived here, in the 15thC Palazzo Valmarana, which was opened to the public after his death. His private collection, arranged on the two *piano nobili* very much as it was in his lifetime, consists of some 30 Tuscan school paintings as well as distinguished furniture and *objets d'art*.

Correr Museum *(Museo Correr)* 🏛 ★
*Map **15D5**. Piazza San Marco, San Marco ☎5225625,
5222185, 5229006 🔲 ✈ Open Mon, Wed, Thurs 10am-4pm;
Fri, Sat 10am-9pm; Sun 9am-9pm. Closed Tues. Water bus
1, 2, 4 or 5 to San Marco or San Zaccaria. Entrance under
arcades of Ala Napoleonica at w end of Piazza.*

The civic museum of Venice occupies most of the Procuratie
Nuove, the range of buildings that line the s side of the Piazza *San
Marco*. It consists of three separate sections: a large and
instructive historical collection, a museum devoted to souvenirs of
the Risorgimento, and a gallery of Venetian-school paintings
which contains a number of masterpieces and one famous
curiosity, Carpaccio's *Courtesans*.

The nucleus of the collection was left to the city in 1830 by the
nobleman Teodoro Correr. Enlarged by further bequests and
acquisitions, it was transferred from Correr's private palace first to
the Fondaco dei Turchi (now the *Natural History Museum*) and
finally in 1922 to its present premises. Other works belonging to
the museum are now displayed in *Ca' Rezzonico*, the *Goldoni
Museum* and the Murano Glass Museum.

At the top of G.M. Soli's monumental staircase is the large oval
ballroom (1822) completed by Lorenzo Santi under the Austrian
occupation. It is now used for important temporary exhibitions,
which unfortunately obscure the elegant Neoclassical decorations.

The first floor houses the **historical collection** *(raccolte storiche)*,
the objects in this section occasionally being exchanged with others
from deposit or on loan. The first rooms retain their Neoclassical
decorations and contain works by Antonio Canova, the last great
Venetian sculptor. The *Orpheus* ★ and *Eurydice* ★ (1773-76) are
among his earliest sculptures and the *Daedalus and Icarus* ★ (1779)
is the piece that made him famous. Gesso models by Canova
include the one he intended for the monument to Titian in the
Frari but which was used instead for his own tomb in the same
church.

Exhibited in the next rooms are many items of historical
interest. Early carvings of the Lion of St Mark include a *bocca di
leone* (lion's mouth), in which secret denunciations were placed for
the attention of the Council of Ten. There is material relating to
the doges and the procedure by which they were elected, as well as
costumes worn by officials of the Republic.

A library lined with 17thC bookcases contains 15th-17thC
commissioni, illuminated bound manuscripts made to
commemorate the appointment of Venetian patricians to
important offices of state. You can see an uninterrupted series of
coins minted under every doge from Sebastiano Ziani (1172-78) to
Lodovico Manin (1789-97) and a collection of the silver medals
known as *oselle* (birds) which 16thC doges gave to noble families
every New Year.

Arms and armor from the 16thC are displayed, and souvenirs of
the naval victory over the Turks at Lepanto in 1571 include
Alessandro Vittoria's bust of *Francesco Duodo*, Captain of the
Venetian fleet. A 17thC model of the *bucintoro*, the ceremonial
ducal barge, is displayed near the remains of the gilded carvings by
Antonio Corradini that decorated the last *bucintoro*, built in 1724
and destroyed at the fall of the Republic. There are documents
relating to Venetian shipping and commerce as well as a copy of a
gilded idol from Canton, said to be an effigy of Marco Polo. The
last rooms contain objects connected with the career of Francesco
Morosini, Captain General of the Venetian army in the wars
against the Turks, and Doge from 1688-94.

On the second floor, to the left of the stairs, the **Museo del Risorgimento** traces the history of Venice from the fall of the Republic in 1797, through its annexation to the United Kingdom of Italy in 1866 and up to the present day, by means of paintings, drawings, prints and other memorabilia. A special display is devoted to the hero Daniele Manin who led the doomed rebellion against the Austrians in 1848.

The **Quadreria** (Picture Gallery) is to the right of the stairs on the second floor. The paintings are clearly labeled and arranged in chronological order. **Rooms 1 and 2** are devoted to Veneto-Byzantine and early Gothic art, including a 13thC wooden chest decorated with an early example of Venetian painting on wood. **Room 3** has works by Lorenzo Veneziano. The fresco fragments of *Virtues* in **Room 4** are rare, possibly unique, examples of painting executed in this medium in 13thC Venice; the artist was probably from the N Italian mainland.

Room 5 has Gothic paintings from the end of the 14thC.

Room 6 has paintings in the International Gothic style, of which the two leading Venetian interpreters were Jacobello del Fiore and Michele Giambono; each of them is represented here with a *Madonna and Child*. **Rooms 7 and 8** are devoted to the Ferrarese school, including Cosmè Tura's nervously expressive little *Pietà* ✭ (1468) and the *Portrait of a Young Man in Profile*, with a shipyard in the background, by the court painter Baldassare Estense. **Room 9** has 15thC wooden sculptures.

Rooms 10 and 11 contain Flemish paintings. The Flemish technique of oil painting was introduced to Venice by the Sicilian artist Antonello da Messina, who visited the city in 1475-76; the damaged *Dead Christ with Angels* ✭ in rm 11 is the only one of his works remaining in Venice. Two other fine Flemish paintings in this room are the *Crucifixion with the Virgin and St John* ✭ by Hugo van der Goes and the *Madonna and Child* ✭ by Dirk Bouts.

Room 13 is devoted to works by the Bellini family. The *Crucifixion* on the wall is by the father, Jacopo, possibly with assistance from the young Giovanni. Giovanni Bellini's *Transfiguration* ✭ (c.1465-70), set against a landscape at sunset, has in the past been attributed to his brother-in-law Mantegna, who was an early formative influence on his style. The *Dead Christ Supported by Angels* ✭ (c.1465) demonstrates the impact on Giovanni's work of the Florentine sculptor Donatello. The angels are in fact direct copies of bronzes by Donatello in the Santo at Padua. The profile *Portrait of Giovanni Mocenigo*, Doge from 1478-85, is by Giovanni's brother Gentile. **Room 14** has works by Alvise Vivarini, most notably his precisely imagined *St Anthony of Padua* in its original frame; also followers of Bellini.

Carpaccio's well-known *Courtesans* ✭ can be seen in **Room 15**. The fame of this genre scene is scarcely justified either by its artistic qualities or by its two charmless subjects, who are probably not courtesans at all since they are dressed in the curious fashion adopted by respectable Venetian women in the late 15thC.

When the diarist John Evelyn visited the city in the 17thC he was fascinated by the unusual personal appearance of Venetian women which, in some respects, had not changed since Carpaccio's day. He was told that their high shoes were invented to keep them at home, 'it being very difficult to walk with them . . . their other habits are also totally different from all nations. They weare very long crisped haire, of several strakes and colours, which they make so by a wash, dishevelling it on the brims of a broade hat that has no head, with an hole to put out their heads by; they drie them in the sunn, as one may see them at their windows.'

A more distinguished Carpaccio is the striking *Portrait of a Young Man in a Red Beret*, to be found in **Room 16**.

The 16thC paintings and sculptures in **Room 17** include a small *Madonna and Child* (c.1525) painted in Bergamo by Lorenzo Lotto. **Room 18** is devoted to works by the Greek artists known as the *madonneri*, who kept the Byzantine style of painting alive into the 17thC. There is a good collection of Italian maiolica in **Room 21**, including the supremely graceful, 17-piece Ridolfi service (c.1520), probably painted by Nicola da Urbino, who has been called the Raphael of maiolica painting.

Other rooms contain a library, more ceramics, bronzes, medals and topographical prints and paintings. The most accurate and detailed early map of Venice was made in 1500 by Jacopo de' Barbari; an impression of it hangs near the original wooden printing blocks.

Doges' Palace *(Palazzo Ducale)* 🏛 ★

Map 15D5. Piazzetta San Marco, San Marco ☎ 5224951 ▦ Open Mon-Sun 8.30am-7pm. Water bus 1, 2, 4 or 5 to San Marco or San Zaccaria. 'Secret' itineraries (Itinerari segreti) of parts of the palace hitherto closed to the public may be booked in advance (☎5204287 ▦). Tours of the backstairs quarters include the Inquisitor's room; the prison under the roof — the famous piombi — from which Casanova escaped; and a view from above of the ceiling of the Great Council room.

The Doges' Palace was the official residence of the dukes of Venice and the seat of the Venetian government from the 9thC until the fall of the Republic in 1797. No visible traces of the first Byzantine palace remain. The external appearance of the building dates mainly from a program of enlargement carried out in the 14th and early 15thC.

By the 14thC, Venice was governed as an aristocratic republic according to a complex system of checks and balances which restricted the power of individuals and prevented the factional rivalries that plagued the cities of the Italian mainland. The lagoon, furthermore, acted as a natural defense against foreign invasion. The airy, graceful structure of the Doges' Palace celebrates the unique political stability and sovereign independence of the Most Serene Republic. Its style is in striking contrast to the grim fortified civic palaces of the mainland, for example the Florentine Palazzo della Signoria, which was completed only 26yrs before this waterfront facade was begun.

Exterior

The waterfront facade was begun in 1340 to accommodate an enlarged Great Council Hall (Sala del Maggior Consiglio). The **ceremonial balcony** surmounted by the figure of *Justice* (1404) is by Pier Paolo and Jacobello dalle Masegne. The two lower windows on the right belong to the earlier council hall and have the only remaining Gothic traceries; those of the new council hall were destroyed by fire in 1577. The sculptures on the outer corners of the portico represent, at the Piazzetta end, *Adam and Eve* ★ (late 14thC) and at the rio end, *The Drunkenness of Noah* (early 15thC). The **capitals of the portico columns** were carved in the early 15thC; although all have been frequently restored and some replaced by 19thC copies, they are well worth examining. The proportions of the portico have been altered over the centuries by repeated raisings of the pavement in front of the palace. The **waterfront facade** originally extended N into the Piazzetta only as far as the seventh column, which is thicker than the others and

marked by a relief tondo of *Justice*. The palace assumed its
shoe-box shape after 1424 when the Piazzetta facade was extended
toward the Basilica by Bartolomeo and Giovanni Bon, who
faithfully copied the earlier Gothic architecture.

The decorations for the new wing were mostly executed by
Tuscan stonecutters. The beautiful sculpture of the *Judgment of
Solomon* ★ on the corner nearest the Basilica echoes the design of
Adam and Eve and *The Drunkenness of Noah* on the waterfront
corners but is a work of far higher quality and energy. Scholars are
divided about its attribution, some giving it to Bartolomeo Bon,
others to a Tuscan sculptor, possibly Jacopo della Quercia. Below
is the finest of the capitals, carved by Pietro di Niccolò Lamberti
with a figure of *Justice* and scenes illustrating the qualities of good
government. The balconied window in the center is a 16thC
imitation of the one facing the water.

The area of the Piazzetta outside the w facade of the palace was
known as the *broglio*. Although patricians were strictly forbidden
to solicit for votes, it was here that they did so, hence the word
imbroglio for political intriguing.

Porta della Carta ★
Entrance to the palace is through the ceremonial gateway built in
1438-43 (restored 1976-79). This magnificent example of Venetian
High Gothic architecture was designed by Bartolomeo and
Giovanni Bon to form a physical and stylistic link between the
Basilica and the Doges' Palace. Its name, which means gate of
paper, may refer to the proximity of the state archives.

Once She did hold the gorgeous east in fee;
And was the safeguard of the west: the worth
Of Venice did not fall below her birth,
Venice, the eldest Child of Liberty.

William Wordsworth,
On the Extinction of the Venetian Republic, 1802

The gate was commissioned by the ambitious and forceful Doge
Francesco Foscari (1423-57), who is shown above the doorway
kneeling before the winged lion of St Mark. The carving is a 19thC
copy of the original, most of which was destroyed in 1797; the
original head survived and is preserved inside the palace. Above
the window is a medallion containing the bust of St Mark
supported by angels and surrounded by putti climbing through a
wonderfully carved foliated frieze. On top of the gate the serene
personification of *Venice as Justice* sits, like the *Justice* over the
seventh column of the Piazzetta facade, on two lions. In the
flanking niches of the gate are statues of the four guiding virtues of
Venetian government: *Temperance, Fortitude, Prudence* and *Charity*.

Courtyard ★
The E side of the courtyard opposite the entrance was erected in
1483-98 by Antonio Rizzo, who was appointed architect in charge
of rebuilding the palace after important sections were destroyed by
fire in 1479 and 1483. The carved decorations are by the
Lombardo family. The lower parts of the other two sides were
completed in the 17thC in a similar style. The magnificent twin
bronze **wellheads** (1554-59) were made by master metal-casters
from the *Arsenale* foundries.

The triumphal arch on the Basilica side of the courtyard is the
Arco Foscari, begun by the Bon family and completed in 1462,
five years after Doge Foscari's death, by Antonio Bregno and
Antonio Rizzo. The statues of *Francesco Maria I della Rovere*
(1587) by Giovanni Bandini and of *Adam and Eve* (after 1483) by

63

Antonio Rizzo are copies of the originals, now kept in the palace.

Rizzo's major architectural contribution to the palace was the grand ceremonial staircase (1484-1501) at the head of which the doges were crowned and important ambassadors welcomed. It is called the **Scala dei Giganti** (Staircase of the Giants) after Jacopo Sansovino's colossal statues of *Mars* and *Neptune* (1567), symbols of Venetian power on land and sea.

Interior ★

Entrance to the rooms of the Doges' Palace is from the left-hand corner of the courtyard behind the Scala dei Giganti.

Even Ruskin, that obsessive student of Venetian art, confessed that the unselective visitor to the Doges' Palace would be 'merely wearied and confused' by its multitude of paintings. Some, notably the Veroneses and Tintorettos, are among the greatest works of art in Venice, but others are of purely historical interest.

Many of the rooms inside the palace were rebuilt in the 16thC after a series of fires destroyed the original Gothic decorations. The paintings, executed by 16thC Venetian artists, were without exception designed to serve the State: to inflate the ego of the aristocratic governing class who spent much of their time here, to impress visiting dignitaries with the incorruptible impersonality of the Venetian government, and to exemplify the virtues and victories that made Venice the only rich and independent state in northern Italy after the 16thC.

From the first-floor loggia, the **Scala d'Oro** or Golden Staircase (1538-59), designed by Sansovino and gorgeously decorated with stuccoes on a gilded background by Alessandro Vittoria, leads to the **first piano nobile** on the second floor. To the right are the doges' private apartments, rebuilt after a fire in 1483 and now frequently used for large temporary exhibitions. The most important of these rooms is the first, the **Sala degli Scarlatti** or

---

There never happened unto any other Common-wealth, so undisturbed and constant a tranquility and peace in her self, as is that of Venice.

James Harrington, *The Common-wealth of Oceana*, 1656

Robing Room, which has a good chimneypiece by Tullio and Antonio Lombardo and a superb relief by Pietro Lombardo of *Doge Leonardo Loredan at the Feet of the Virgin* (c.1501).

The Scala d'Oro continues to the **second piano nobile** on the third floor. At the top of the stairs is the **Atrio Quadrato**, its 16thC gilded wooden ceiling containing Tintoretto's painting of *Justice Presenting the Sword and the Scales to Doge Girolamo Priuli* (1559-67). The route through the palace is usually as follows:

Sala delle Quattro Porte This room was built in 1575, after a fire in the previous year, by Antonio da Ponte to designs by Palladio and Giovanni Rusconi. Palladio's ceiling is decorated with splendid stuccowork by Giovanni Cambi. To the right of the entrance the central canvas is Titian's *Doge Antonio Grimani Kneeling before Faith*, largely a studio work and probably completed after the artist's death. On an easel between the windows is G.B. Tiepolo's *Venice Receiving the Homage of Neptune*.

Anticollegio This is where ambassadors, Venetian mercenary captains and deputations from Venice's subject territories waited before being admitted to the Sala del Collegio. The room was rebuilt to plans by Palladio and Alessandro Vittoria after the 1574 fire. The rich stuccoed ceiling is by Marco del Moro and the fireplace by Scamozzi. Opposite the window wall is Veronese's radiantly beautiful *Rape of Europe* ★ (1580), which Henry James

The Doges' Palace

Second piano nobile

First piano nobile

1 Sala degli Scarlatti
2 Sala della Quarantia Civil Vecchia
3 Sala dell'Armamento
4 Andito del Maggior Consiglio
5 Sala del Maggior Consiglio
6 Sala dello Scrutinio
7 Chiesetta
8 Antichiesetta
9 Sala del Senato
10 Sala del Collegio
11 Anticollegio
12 Sala delle Quattro Porte
13 Atrio Quadrato
14 Sala del Consiglio dei Dieci
15 Sala della Bussola
16 Saletta dei Tre Inquisitori
17 Sale d'Armi del Consiglio dei Dieci

called 'the happiest picture in the world.' On the door walls are Tintoretto's *Vulcan's Forge, Mercury and the Graces* ★ *Bacchus and Ariadne* ★ and *Minerva Dismissing Mars* (c.1577).

Sala del Collegio The *collegio* was the cabinet of the Venetian government. It comprised the doge and his personal councillors, the heads of the Council of Ten and selected senators representing the Senate's three spheres of interest: foreign affairs, mainland interests and maritime concerns. The sumptuously carved and gilded **ceiling** contains some of Veronese's loveliest paintings (1575–c.1577). The masterpiece is in the center at the far end, representing *Venice Enthroned Receiving the Sword and Scales from Peace and Justice* ★. In the center of the near end is a panel depicting *Mars and Neptune with the Campanile and Lion of St Mark*. Other sections contain allegorical figures. On the wall above the tribune is Veronese's *Doge Sebastiano Venier Offering Thanks to Christ for the Victory of Lepanto*. The best of the three works by Tintoretto on the wall opposite the fireplace is the *Marriage of St Catherine*.

Sala del Senato This was the center of Venetian government, where foreign, economic, military and domestic policies were debated and decided. The Senate was chaired by the doge and was about 200 strong. The room was rebuilt by da Ponte after the 1574 fire. The ornate ceiling contains pictures by Tintoretto and his assistants. Over the tribune is Tintoretto's *Descent from the Cross with Doges Pietro Lando and Marcantonio Trevisan*.

The door to the right of the tribune leads to the **antichiesetta,** which contains Sebastiano Ricci's cartoons for the 18thC mosaics on the facade of San Marco. This room commands a fine view over tiled roofs to the facade of *San Zaccaria*. The adjoining **chiesetta** was designed as the doges' private chapel in 1593 by Scamozzi. Over the altar is a marble *Madonna and Child* by Jacopo Sansovino. After returning through the Sala delle Quattro Porte, you enter the section of the palace which was devoted to the administration of justice.

Sala del Consiglio dei Dieci In spite of its name, the Council of Ten was usually at least 30 strong. It was responsible for state security: the quashing of treason, the vetting of foreigners employed by the State, and the conduct of diplomacy considered too secret for the multiple ears and mouths of the Senate. It employed a corps of spies, informers and assassins, and had its own armory and prison for state offenders. The ceiling paintings by Veronese were his first works in Venice, painted in 1553-54 according to an allegorical scheme dictated by his patron, the humanist Daniele Barbaro. The central oval showing the *Vices Struck Down by Job's Thunderbolts* is a copy of the original, which was taken to Paris in 1797 and is now in the Louvre. Others by Veronese include *The Old Man in Oriental Costume with a Young Woman* in the far right-hand corner, and *Juno Offering Gifts to Venice* in the center of the left side.

Sala della Bussola This was the antechamber of the Sala del Consiglio dei Dieci. The marble chimneypiece is by Sansovino. To the right of the exit door is a lion's mouth (*bocca di leone*) in which denunciations were placed anonymously for the attention of the Council of Ten.

Saletta dei Tre Inquisitori The need for close secrecy in certain investigations involving treason led in 1539 to the creation of a special committee of three Inquisitors of State. This is the room in which cases were discussed. A staircase leads to the **Sale d'Armi del Consiglio dei Dieci** (the State armory). One of the outstanding armories in Europe, and the only state armory to be preserved intact, it contains weapons for the defense of the palace, prestige armor loaned to patricians appointed to military commands, presents from foreign governments — which often took the form of fine armor or weapons — and one-off examples of experimental weapons, the trials of which were authorized by the Council of Ten. The armory has been housed in these rooms since 1532.

Items of particular interest in **Room I** include the 16thC suit of armor known as Gattamelata's — although its date is too late for it to have been worn by Gattamelata (subject of Donatello's celebrated statue in Padua) — and an unusual 14thC helmet shaped like a sparrow's beak. The magnificent **suit of white armor** in **Room II** was presented to the Republic in 1603 by King Henry IV of France. In **Room III** the 868 pieces of armor are arranged as they were in the 17thC. **Room IV** commands a marvelous view across the Bacino di San Marco to *San Giorgio Maggiore* and contains 620 pieces, including a 17thC cannon, 15th and 16thC swords, side arms and instruments of torture.

The **Scala dei Censori** leads to the **first piano nobile** on the second floor. On the left is the L-shaped **Andito del Maggior Consiglio**. The shorter *liagò* or veranda, at the far end facing the water, is where nobles relaxed during sittings of the Great Council. On display here are Antonio Rizzo's softly modeled marble statues of *Adam* ☆ and *Eve* ☆ (after 1483) and Giovanni Bandini's statue of the mercenary soldier *Francesco Maria I della Rovere* (1587), all from the Foscari Arch in the palace courtyard. To the left of the long section of the Andito is the **Sala della Quarantia Civil Vecchia**, one of the oldest rooms in the palace. It was originally occupied by the Magistry of Forty, the central body of government before the creation of the Senate in the 13thC. A fragment of Gothic mural decoration has been revealed beneath the paneling on the right wall.

In the adjoining **Sala dell' Armamento**, formerly the armory, are displayed the remains of the vast fresco of the *Coronation of the Virgin* (1365-68) painted by Guariento for the Sala del Maggior Consiglio. The work was spoiled by the fire of 1577 and replaced by Tintoretto's *Paradise*. These fragments were discovered when the *Paradise* was removed temporarily.

To the right of the Andito is the huge **Sala del Maggior Consiglio**, the Great Council Hall built in 1340 and gutted by fire in 1577. It was redecorated from 1578-85 by leading Venetian artists, with paintings commemorating significant events in the history of the Republic. Any adult male patrician (the rank of patrician was limited to those whose family names were recorded in the so-called Libro d'Oro or Golden Book) was qualified to sit on the Great Council. There were nearly 2,000 members, too many for efficient decision-making, so the Council's business was restricted to electing men to the smaller government councils. Elections were made by nominations on name slips which were drawn by lot to prevent favoritism.

The E wall above the benches where the doge and Senate presided over Council meetings is entirely covered by Tintoretto's 'monster picture,' as Mark Twain called it, the *Paradise* (1588-90), which has been restored so often that its quality has deteriorated and it is now chiefly remarkable only as the largest oil painting in the world. The pictures on the N wall, overlooking the courtyard, celebrate the reconciliation in 1172 of Pope Alexander III and Emperor Frederick Barbarossa, which was brought about by the diplomatic tactics of Doge Sebastiano Ziani. Those on the S wall, facing the water, commemorate the Fourth Crusade led in 1202 by the blind Doge Enrico Dandolo.

More enticing than the historical paintings is the view on a fine day from the balcony, embracing, from the left, the island of *San Giorgio Maggiore*, the churches of the Zitelle and *Redentore* on the *Giudecca*, the gilded ball of the Customs House Point, and the *Salute*. On the short W wall facing the Piazzetta is the *Triumph of Doge Andrea Contarini after the Victory at the Battle of Chioggia in 1379* by Veronese and assistants.

Running above the paintings around three of the walls is a frieze of portraits of the first 76 doges. It begins chronologically in the middle of the N wall and runs clockwise. On the E wall, a black-painted veil conceals the portrait of Doge Marin Falier who was executed for treason in 1355.

The **ceiling** of the hall is divided into 35 panels. The oval nearest the E end contains one of Veronese's most glorious masterpieces, the *Apotheosis of Venice* ★ (*c*.1583). In the central rectangle is *Venice Surrounded by Gods Giving an Olive Branch to Doge Nicolò da Ponte* by Tintoretto and assistants. In the oval at the W end, *Venice Welcoming the Conquered Nations Around her Throne* is by Palma il Giovane.

Sala dello Scrutinio Elections to the most important offices took place here, including those of successive doges, which were the most elaborate of all. A complex procedure was designed, at least in theory, to prevent anyone from pushing himself, or a favored candidate, into office. All state offices, apart from that of doge, were for only one or two years, so there were plenty of elections.

On the end wall opposite the tribune is the **triumphal arch** (1694), designed by Antonio Gaspari, honors Francesco Morosini, Captain General of the Venetian army in the wars against the Turks, and doge from 1688-94. The paintings on the side walls record naval victories in the Orient. Those on the ceiling depict victories over rival naval powers. Above the tribune, the *Last Judgment* (1587-94) is by Palma il Giovane.

A narrow doorway to the left of the tribune in the Sala del Maggior Consiglio leads to a loggia, off which there are several rooms (closed during exhibitions) where miscellaneous treasures are displayed. They include Carpaccio's *Winged Lion of St Mark* and a *Pietà* by Giovanni Bellini.

I stood in Venice, on the 'Bridge of Sighs';
A Palace and a prison on each hand:
I saw from out the wave her structures rise
As from the stroke of the Enchanter's wand!
A thousand Years their cloudy wings expand
Around me, and a dying Glory smiles
O'er the far times, when many a subject land
Looked to the winged Lion's marble piles,
Where Venice sate in state, throned on her hundred Isles!
　　　　　　Byron, *Childe Harold's Pilgrimage*, Canto IV, 1816

Stairs lead down to the **Bridge of Sighs** ☆ or Ponte dei Sospiri, which crosses the rio to the **new prisons** built in 1560-1614. (The old prisons, from which Casanova made his brilliant escape, were known as I Piombi because they were under the lead roof of the palace.) The bridge itself is built of Istrian stone to a design by Antonio Contino. The delicate ornamentation includes marble trellising over the windows, presumably to preserve the anonymity of prisoners. Although they may well have sighed as they crossed over the bridge, by the time it was built in the early 17thC the conditions of their incarceration were probably more salubrious than in other European prisons. Only one political prisoner is known to have been led across the bridge; those who served sentences in these dungeons were mostly petty criminals. You can still make out the graffiti they left on the cell walls.

After returning across the Bridge of Sighs, the exit is through rooms used by the Avogaria, a branch of the judiciary instituted in 1517. From the **Bridge of Straw**, or Ponte della Paglia, linking the Molo to the Riva degli Schiavoni, there is a good view of both the Bridge of Sighs and the Renaissance E facade of the Doges' Palace, begun by Antonio Rizzo after the fire of 1483 and completed in the 17thC.

Fenice *(Teatro La Fenice)*
Map 15D4. Campo San Fantin, San Marco ☎23954. Water bus 1, 2 or 4 to San Marco or Accademia.

The Fenice is the largest, oldest and most important theater in Venice and one of the most delightful opera houses in the world. It was built between 1790-92 by Antonio Selva. The forbiddingly sober Neoclassical facade has always been controversial and certainly gives no hint of the deliciously frivolous atmosphere of the theater within.

In 1836 the Fenice was partially destroyed by a fire. True to its name, which means phenix, it rose from the ashes. The rebuilding was completed within a year and the auditorium was redecorated in the opulently pretty late-Empire style which makes it such a suitable setting for 19thC Italian operas. Rossini, Bellini and Verdi are among the composers who wrote operatic masterpieces for the Fenice, including Rossini's *Tancredi* and Verdi's *Rigoletto* and *La Traviata*.

Opposite the theater is the Renaissance church of **San Fantin**, begun in 1507 by Antonio Scarpagnino and completed in 1564 by Jacopo Sansovino. The interior is remarkable for the handsome, domed chancel designed by Sansovino.

The late 16thC building to the left of the church was originally the headquarters of the Scuola di San Girolamo, the confraternity responsible for comforting condemned criminals in their last hours. It is now occupied by the Ateneo Veneto, a learned society founded by Napoleon.

Fondaco dei Turchi This palace on the *Grand Canal*, once the warehouse of Turkish merchants, now houses the *Natural History Museum*.

Fortuny Museum *(Museo Fortuny)* 🏛
Map 14D3. Palazzo Pesaro degli Orfei, Campo San Benedetto, San Marco ☎5200995. Water bus 1 to San Angelo.
Mariano Fortuny (1871-1949) is best known internationally for the featherweight pleated silk Fortuny dresses which were once worn by cosmopolitan beauties and are now museum pieces. In Venice, he is remembered as a little Leonardo: as well as making dresses and textiles he was an engraver, sculptor, architect, photographer, stage designer and the inventor of the Fortuny Dome, a version of the cyclorama that revolutionized modern stage lighting.

Born in Spain, he spent the last 42yrs of his life in Venice, living and working in the splendid 15thC Gothic Palazzo Pesaro degli Orfei. The palace and its contents were left to the city as a museum by his wife Henriette on her death in 1956.

The museum conveys the personality of the man, but it does not do full justice to his genius. There are too many paintings of coy nudes — painting was the one art at which he did not excel — and too few of the pleated dresses; but Fortuny textiles, which reproduce the pattern and sheen of materials otherwise seen only in Venetian painting, are well represented.

Temporary **photographic exhibitions** held in the museum are usually of considerable interest.

The church of **San Benedetto** opposite the Palazzo Pesaro is sometimes open in the mornings. It contains three outstanding 17thC pictures — *St Sebastian* by Bernardo Strozzi and two representations of *St Benedict* by Sebastiano Mazzoni — as well as *St Francis of Paola* by G.B. Tiepolo.

Frari *(Santa Maria Gloriosa dei Frari)* 🏛 † ★
Map 14C2. Campo dei Frari, San Polo 🚋 Open Mon-Sat 9.30am-noon, 2.30-6pm, Sun 2.30-6pm. Water bus 1 or 4 to San Tomà.
The two most important Gothic churches in Venice are the Franciscan Frari and the Dominican *Santi Giovanni e Paolo*. The resemblance between these two red-brick, factorylike monastic churches is very close; and yet people who know Venice well often express a strong preference for one or the other.

The Franciscans were granted their plot of land in 1236 — ten years after the death of St Francis and two years after the Dominicans received their site across the city. By the 14thC the Franciscan order was attracting large congregations and was wealthy enough to replace an earlier, smaller church. Building began in the 1330s — as always with Gothic churches, at the apse end — and was substantially completed by the mid-15thC. The church was consecrated in 1492.

The bridge that crosses the canal opposite the church facade is an 18thC reconstruction of one built by the Franciscan friars in 1428. To the right of the church is the former monastery which now houses the State Archives, one of the richest collections of historic documents relating to any city in the world. The handsome Gothic **campanile** that rises from the left flank of the church is the tallest in Venice after that of San Marco. It was built between 1361-96 by Jacopo Celega and his son Pier Paolo. In the flank of the left transept, over the door, is a beautiful and moving relief of the *Madonna and Child with Two Angels* ☆ by the Master of the Mascoli Chapel in San Marco. The apse end of the church — the central apse was rebuilt in the 15thC — abuts onto one side of the Campo *San Rocco*.

The plain brick church facade, sparsely decorated with Istrian stone, is broader and softer in outline than that of Santi Giovanni e Paolo. Over the main portal the statue of *The Risen Christ* (1581) is by Alessandro Vittoria and those of *The Virgin* and *St Francis* are attributed to Bartolomeo Bon and his studio. Entrance is normally through the left flank of the church.

The **interior** ★ like that of Santi Giovanni e Paolo, is organized according to the Cistercian model. Its superstructure is given lateral support by wooden tie-beams, and the colors of the building materials — red brick and white Istrian stone — are used with maximum decorative effect and are repeated in the red and white marble floor.

But the Frari makes a different, less coherent impression than its Dominican counterpart. This is partly because the apsidal chapels are not, as they are at Santi Giovanni e Paolo, aligned with the aisles of the nave; this means that the only prospect of the length of the church is from the beginning of the nave itself. The nave is separated from the chancel by the only **monks' choir** ★ in Venice still *in situ*. The **screen** was begun in the Gothic style by Bartolomeo Bon and completed in Renaissance fashion by the Lombard studio (1475). The 124 **intarsiaed stalls** were carved by Marco Cozzi (1468) and show the influence of the Lendinara brothers' work at the Shrine of St Anthony in Padua.

A tour of the church should begin from the bottom of the **nave**. From here the vista is dominated, as the artist intended, by Titian's enormous painting of *The Assumption of the Virgin* (see below). On the holy-water stoups next to the first two columns of the nave are fine **bronze statuettes** (1593) by Girolamo Campagna. In the right aisle, notice first the grandiose **monument to Titian**, erected in 1836 — 276 years after the artist was buried here. The low reliefs illustrate some of the Titians that especially appealed to 19thC academic taste, including a *Visitation* which is now known not to be by Titian. On the third altar is Alessandro Vittoria's marble statue of *St Jerome* (before 1568) based on Michelangelo's *Dying Slave* (in the Louvre in Paris).

In the right transept, to the right of the sacristy door and against a frescoed background of imitation drapery, is the **Beato Pacifico monument** (1423-27), decorated with attractive terra-cotta sculptures and reliefs. To the left of the sacristy door is the **monument to Paolo Savelli** (*died* 1405), who was a Roman-born commander of the Venetian army. His monument is the first equestrian statue of a mercenary soldier in Venice.

The **sacristy** was commissioned by the Pesaro family in the mid-15thC. Over the altar is one of Giovanni Bellini's greatest paintings, the *Madonna and Child with Sts Nicholas, Peter, Benedict and Mark* ★ (1488) in its original frame. 'Nothing in Venice is more perfect than this,' wrote Henry James. 'It is one of those things that sum up the genius of a painter, the experience of life, the teaching of a school. It seems painted with molten gems, which have only been clarified by time, and it is as solemn as it is gorgeous and as simple as it is deep.' On the entrance wall is the refined 15thC Renaissance **Tabernacle of the Reliquary of Christ's Blood**. Opposite is the exuberant, melodramatic, 18thC Rococo **Altar of the Reliquaries**, decorated with gilded angels by Andrea Brustolon and marble high reliefs by Cabianca. Off the sacristy is the chapter room of the monastery, leading into a Palladian cloister, lately restored; the wellhead and sculptures in the cloister are 18thC.

In the **apse chapels** to the right of the chancel, the altarpiece of the *Madonna and Child with Sts Peter, Paul, Andrew and Nicola* (1482) is by Bartolomeo Vivarini. In the Florentine Chapel, immediately next to the chancel, is Donatello's starkly realistic wooden statue of *St John the Baptist* ✩. It used to be considered one of his latest works, but a recent restoration has revealed it to be as early as 1438.

The **chancel** is dominated by Titian's astounding *Assumption of the Virgin* ★ (1516-18), commissioned especially for the high altar. It was the largest and, stylistically, the most innovatory and sophisticated altarpiece ever painted in Venice. The triangular composition, emphasized by the pattern of the colors, gives momentum to the upward sweep of the Virgin, who soars above the gesticulating apostles toward God the Father. The attendant angels 'seem to be there only to sing the victory of a human being over his environment,' wrote Bernard Berenson. 'They are embodied joys, acting on our nerves like the rapturous outbursts of the orchestra at the end of *Parsifal*.'

On the right wall is the **monument to Doge Francesco Foscari** (1423-57) by Antonio Bregno in the Gothic-Renaissance style — 'the refuse of one style encumbering the embryo of another,' was how Ruskin described it. On the left wall, the enormous **monument to Doge Niccolò Tron** (1471-73), executed in 1476 by Antonio Rizzo, carries forward the Renaissance tendencies of the Foscari monument.

1 Monks' choir
2 Campagna's bronze statuettes
3 Monument to Titian
4 Vittoria's St Jerome
5 Beato Pacifico monument
6 Monument to Paolo Savelli
7 G. Bellini's Madonna and Child
8 Tabernacle of the Reliquary of Christ's Blood
9 Altar of the Reliquaries
10 B. Vivarini's Madonna and Child
11 Donatello's St John the Baptist
12 Titian's Assumption of the Virgin
13 Monument to Doge Francesco Foscari
14 Monument to Doge Niccolò Tron
15 A. Vivarini and M. Basaiti's St Ambrogio
16 J. Sansovino's St John the Baptist
17 B. Vivarini's St Mark Enthroned
18 Titian's Pesaro Madonna
19 Monument to Bishop Jacopo Pesaro
20 Monument to Antonio Canova

Entrance

Frari

In the **apse chapels** to the left of the chancel, the altarpiece of *St Ambrogio* (1503), crowded with rather bland figures of saints, is by Alvise Vivarini and Marco Basaiti. In the Corner Chapel, the next chapel to the left, the delicate marble statue of *St John the Baptist* (1554) on the font is by Jacopo Sansovino and the altarpiece of *St Mark Enthroned with Sts John the Baptist, Jerome, Nicholas and Paul* (1474) is by Bartolomeo Vivarini.

> The only way to care for Venice as she deserves it is to give her a
> chance to touch you often — to linger and remain and return.
> Henry James, *Italian Hours*, 'Venice,' 1882

In the left aisle, Titian's *Pesaro Madonna* ★ (1519-26) is next to the **monument to Bishop Jacopo Pesaro**, who commissioned the picture in commemoration of a naval victory he led against the Turks in 1502. Bishop Pesaro and members of his family are shown giving thanks to the Madonna who is surrounded by Sts Peter, Francis and Anthony of Padua. On the left, a warrior saint leads two Turkish captives toward the Madonna. Another early 16thC Venetian artist would have painted this altarpiece as a symmetrical *Sacra Conversazione* with the donor kneeling to one side of the Madonna's throne. Titian's diagonal composition, which gives equal emphasis to the Madonna and the Pesaro family, was the first asymmetrical altarpiece painted in Venice and was regarded as a solecism by some contemporaries.

In the penultimate section of this aisle is the **monument to Antonio Canova** (*died* 1822), executed in 1827 by a group of the sculptor's disciples; the design had been prepared by Canova in 1794 for a monument to Titian that was never realized. (The model can be seen in the *Correr Museum*.) Canova's body was buried in his native village of Possagno, but his heart is enshrined in a porphyry urn inside this pyramid.

On your way to the nearest vaporetto stop, in **Campo San Tomà**, you can see two appealing relief carvings on the facade of the former Scuola dei Calegheri (Confraternity of Shoemakers). *St Mark Healing the Shoemaker Anius* (1478) in the lunette of the doorway is attributed to Pietro Lombardo; above is a 15thC *Madonna of Mercy*.

Gesuati *(Santa Maria del Rosario)* †
Map 9G4. Fondamente delle Zattere, Dorsoduro. Water bus 1, 2 or 4 to Accademia or 5 to Zattere.

The Gesuati (1726-36) was the first Venetian church built by the greatest of the native Rococo architects, Giorgio Massari. It was commissioned by the Dominicans who had bought the site previously occupied by the minor Gesuati order. The Gesuati were suppressed in the 17thC, apparently for disreputable behavior, but their name has always been attached to this distinguished church.

Massari's design deliberately reflects that of the *Redentore* across the *Giudecca* Canal. The giant Corinthian order of the facade, the domed chancel and twin campanili derive from Palladio's great church, as does the arrangement of the **interior** (restored in 1975). Here Massari transposed the solid Roman grandeur of his Palladian theme into the more delicately graceful key of his own period. The painted and sculptured decorations, which were completed only a few years after the building itself, are in perfect stylistic harmony with Massari's supremely lucid architecture.

The paintings refer to the Dominican order. G. B. Tiepolo's sparkling **ceiling frescoes** ☆ (1737-39) celebrate *The Institution of* *the Rosary* (which, according to Dominican orthodoxy, was offered to St Dominic by the Madonna, to whom the church is dedicated), *The Apotheosis of St Dominic,* and *St Dominic Blessing a Dominican Monk.*

Over the first altar on the right is another of Tiepolo's most joyous religious paintings, the *Virgin and Child with St Catherine of Siena, St Rose and St Agnes* ✪ (before 1740). The third altarpiece on the right, depicting three Dominican martyrs, *Sts Vincent Ferraris, Hyacinth and Lawrence Bertrando* ✪ (*c*.1739), is one of the most handsome of G.B. Piazzetta's masterpieces. The statues and relief carvings are all by G.M. Morlaiter, one of the most accomplished Rococo sculptors working in Venice.

Immediately to the left of the Gesuati is the cloister and Renaissance church of **Santa Maria della Visitazione** (1493-1522) which was originally owned by the Gesuati order and has a fine coffered wooden ceiling.

Gesuiti *(Santa Maria Assunta)* †
Map 6C7. Campo dei Gesuiti, Cannaregio. Water bus 5 to Fondamenta Nuove.

Because of their close association with the Papacy, the Jesuits were held in extreme suspicion by the Venetian Republic, and it was not until 1715 that their position in the city was secure enough to allow the building of a Jesuit church. The project was entrusted to Domenico Rossi, whose flair for dramatic effects had been demonstrated by the facade of *San Stae.* Rossi was given explicit instructions: to follow the ground plan of the Gesù, the Jesuit mother church in Rome, and to create an interior so magnificent that it would dazzle the Venetians. Whether or not you regard the result as a monstrous piece of bad taste you will never, even in Rome, see a church interior quite like it.

The portentous Baroque architecture of G.B. Fattoretto's facade and its swarm of gesticulating statues does not quite prepare you for the **interior** ✪. The entire wall surface appears swathed in green and white damask and, as a finishing touch, more green and white damask appears to be draped over the pulpit. The illusion persists even after you realize that the material is in fact green and white marble.

The ceiling frescoes, framed in elaborate stuccowork, are by Francesco Fontebasso. The high altar, designed by Giuseppe Pozzo, enshrines a lapis-lazuli tabernacle and marble group of *God the Father and Christ Seated on the World* by Giuseppe Torretto who also made the impressive figures of the *Archangels* at either side. At the foot of the altar is the family tomb of the Manin, who financed this astonishing church.

One great painting survives from the previous church on this site. Titian's *Martyrdom of St Lawrence* ★ (1548-57), over the first altar on the left, was one of the first successful night scenes in the history of painting; a recent cleaning has revealed that it is still one of the most dramatic.

The **Oratorio dei Crociferi** (*open Fri, Sat, Sun 5am-noon* ☎ 716088) opposite the church contains some of Palma il Giovane's finest works. At the far end of the campo, on the corner of the Fondamenta Zen, at nos.4922-25, are three 16thC **Zen Palaces.** Designed by a member of the great seafaring family in an odd, nostalgic Gothic-Renaissance style, they were originally frescoed on the outside by Andrea Schiavone and Tintoretto.

In the Campo Tiziano, behind the Fondamenta Nuove, at nos.5179-83, is the house, now much altered, where Titian lived from 1531 until his death in 1576.

Ghetto ☆

Map 5C4. Cannaregio X (including five synagogues) three times every morning, except Sat, from Museo Israelitico in the Ghetto Nuovo. Water bus 1 to San Marcuola.

The idea of locking a Jewish community into a ghetto is of Venetian origin, as is the word 'ghetto' itself. But Venice cannot be blamed entirely for the shameful connotations the word has subsequently acquired.

All aliens under the strict and suspicious rule of the Venetian Republic were segregated and curfewed. Jews represented the largest, most successful and most problematic of many foreign mercantile communities. The size of the Jewish population, which reached a peak of around 5,000 in the 17thC, testifies that Venice was regarded as a refuge, certainly not a trap, as well as a city where Jewish commercial and professional talents could be employed profitably.

I will buy with you, sell with you, talk with you, walk with you, and so following; but I will not eat with you, drink with you, nor pray with you. What news on the Rialto?

Shakespeare, *The Merchant of Venice* (Shylock to Bassanio,
Act I, Scene iii), 1600

Jews were denied the right to own property; but business, banking and shipping were permitted. Some of the most illustrious doctors, philosophers and printers were Jews; other Jews grew rich in the antique trade, especially after they were granted the exclusive privilege of furnishing all ambassadorial apartments.

The Jewish presence in Venice dates at least from the 11thC, and by 1290 Levantine Jews were permitted to warehouse their goods on the *Giudecca*. From 1496 Jews were required to wear a distinctive badge.

On Mar 20 1516 the government decreed that all Venetian Jews should be confined on an island N of the Cannaregio Canal. The island was the site of an old iron foundry, from which the word *ghetto*, a corruption of the Venetian *getar* meaning to cast, derives. The maximum permitted height of buildings in the Ghetto was one-third higher than in the rest of the city, hence the characteristic 'skyscrapers' of the Ghetto Nuovo, which were leased to Jews at exorbitant rents. The Ghetto gates were torn down (traces of the hinges can be seen at the entrances) under the Napoleonic regime.

Today there are about 1,000 Jews in Venice, of which some 20 families still reside in the Ghetto. It is an increasingly fashionable and prosperous domestic neighborhood served by well-stocked shops and good restaurants. The three sections of the Ghetto are misleadingly named. The **Ghetto Vecchio** (Old Ghetto), dating from 1541, is actually 25yrs newer than the original Ghetto, which is confusingly known as the **Ghetto Nuovo** (New Ghetto). The Ghetto was further enlarged in 1633 with the **Ghetto Novissimo** (Newest Ghetto).

There is a dramatic view of the Ghetto Nuovo's high tenements from the Calle del Ghetto Novissimo; no.2911 in the campo was occupied by one of the three banks managed by Jews in the Ghetto from 1591. The **Ghetto Nuovo Bridge** (1866), with its exquisite wrought-iron railings, was one of the last of the iron bridges built by the Austrians who occupied Venice at different periods between 1797-1866.

While you are in this remote area visit also *San Giobbe*, the *Madonna del Orto*, and the Franchetti Gallery in *Ca' d'Oro*.

Museo Israelitico
Campo del Ghetto Nuovo, Cannaregio ☎ 715359 📷 Open Mon-Fri 10.30am-5pm; Sun 10.30am-1pm; or by appointment. Closed Sat and Jewish hols.

A permanent exhibition of ritual Hebrew art is housed in the building occupied by the Schole (synagogues) Tedesca and Canton. Among many important objects on display are 17th and 18thC parocheths (arcs where sacred scrolls are traditionally kept), a collection of elaborate silver rimmonin (ornaments) and ataroth (badges of sovereignty), a large silver pignaton (chandelier) in the main hall, and fine 17th and 18thC furniture and textiles.

The Synagogues *(Tempii Israelitici)*
Guided tours only.

The five surviving Venetian synagogues are the most numerous and the oldest continuously functioning synagogues in any uropean city. Originally they were both temples of worship and benevolent confraternities, which is why they are known as *schole*. They are distinguished one from another not by nationality but by rite. The **Schola Tedesca**, built by the Ashkenazi community in *c.*1528, is the oldest. The **Schola Spagnola** in the Ghetto Vecchio, rebuilt by Longhena *c.*1654, is the largest and most famous. Opposite is the **Schola Levantina** (1538-61), with an elegant pulpit attributed to Andrea Brustolon. The last two have entrancing interiors, like miniature opera houses.

Many illustrious Venetian Jews lie buried in the 14thC Jewish Cemetery on the *Lido*.

Giardini Pubblici *(Public Gardens)*
Map 12G10. Castello. Water bus 1 to Giardini.

The formal gardens in SE Castello were laid out in 1810 by Antonio Selva as part of a scheme fostered by the Napoleonic regime; the object was to improve the urban fabric of Venice according to Neoclassical ideals. The E end of the gardens is occupied by the national pavilions of the Biennale (see *Calendar of events* in *Planning and walks*).

Giglio *(Santa Maria del Giglio or Santa Maria Zobenigo)* ✝ 🏛
Map 14E3. Campo Santa Maria Zobenigo, San Marco. Open mornings only. Water bus 1 to Santa Maria del Giglio.

The Baroque facade of the Giglio (1680-83) is the funerary monument of Antonio Barbaro, a high-ranking patrician who died in 1679 leaving money and instructions for a scheme that glorified his family and career. The architect was Giuseppe Sardi, and this was his last facade.

Barbaro's portrait statue by Giusto Le Court stands above the entrance and is flanked by statues of the virtues with which he wished to be identified. The niches of the lower order are occupied by representations of members of his family. But the most unusual and attractive feature of the facade is the **relief carvings**: on the bases of the lower columns, these represent fortified cities where Barbaro had held administrative or ambassadorial posts — Zara (Zadar), Candia (Heraklion), Padua, Rome, Corfu, Spalato (Split) — and, on the bases of the upper order, the vessels with which Barbaro was associated as a naval commander.

The rectangular **interior** has a ceiling decorated by Antonio Zanchi with three episodes from the *Life of the Virgin* (1690-95). The Molin Chapel to the right side of the nave was restored and rearranged in 1975 and is now a little museum of reliquaries, furniture and pictures; it contains Rubens' *Sacred Family*. The

best pictures are hung in the sacristy and include Tintoretto's paired *Evangelists* (1552), formerly the organ doors, as well as Zanchi's *Abraham Instructing the Egyptians in Astrology* and his four small canvases from the choir gallery.

Giudecca
Maps 8, 9, 10. Water bus 5 or 8 to Le Zitelle.

The slim stretch of eight connected islands facing the Zattere across the Giudecca Canal is the most accessible of the lagoon suburbs. The name Giudecca is thought to derive either from the Jews (*Giudei*) or politically undesirable nobles (*giudicati* or 'judged') who were segregated here in the Middle Ages.

From the early Renaissance, rich Venetians built pleasure villas here on the s bank facing the lagoon. Michelangelo sought peace of mind living on the Giudecca during his exile from Florence in 1529, as did Alfred de Musset three centuries later. Its special atmosphere, enlivened by the intense activity of fishing craft, still attracts working artists, a number of whom maintain studios on the Giudecca.

Leave the vaporetto at Le Zitelle and walk w along the Fondamenta. The pleasant Palladian facade of the church of **Le Zitelle** (*open Sun mornings only*) was built between 1572-76. In the 18thC its convent was a home for poor girls famous for their lacemaking. Nearby, no.43 is the delightful Neo-Gothic **Casa de' Maria** (1910-13) designed and lived in by the Bolognese painter Mario de' Maria. Farther w is the outstanding monument of the Giudecca, Palladio's masterpiece of ecclesiastic architecture, the church of the **Redentore**. The Rio di Ponte Lungo bisects the Giudecca and offers a tantalizing glimpse of the lagoon beyond.

If you are lucky enough to find the church of **Sant'Eufemia** open, be sure to go in. The portico dates from 1596. The interior is an intriguing mixture of styles: 11thC nave and aisles with some Veneto-Byzantine colums and capitals, boudoirlike stuccowork and paintings from an 18thC restoration.

The massive, Teutonic fortress at the w end of the Giudecca is the **Mulino Stucky**, built as a flour mill from 1895 by the Hanoverian architect Ernst Wullekopf. This confident piece of 19thC industrial architecture was abandoned in the 1920s, and plans are occasionally put forward to convert it into much-needed housing. The vaporetto from Sant'Eufemia will ferry you across the canal to the Zattere.

Goldoni Museum *(Casa Goldoni)* 🏛
Map 14C2. Palazzo Centani, San Polo ☎5236353. Open Mon-Sat 8.30am-1.30pm. Closed Sun. Water bus 1 to San Tomà. Entrance in Calle dei Nomboli.

The pretty 15thC Palazzo Centani was the birthplace of Carlo Goldoni (1707-93), the most prolific and, at his best, one of the greatest of Italian playwrights. His house (unfortunately often closed) now contains a center for theatrical studies and a small theater museum. Notice the delightful courtyard with external stone staircase leading to the *piano nobile*.

Grand Canal *(Canal Grande)* ★
Choose a fine evening, an hour or two before sunset, preferably in late spring or early fall. Equip yourself for the journey with sandwiches or pastries and a bottle or two of chilled Prosecco. If you are in love, all the better; if not, be sure your companion is someone with whom you can relax and be silent or talkative as the mood takes you.

76

Now you are ready to accept the invitation of the nearest gondolier, who will not be very far away if you are in the San Marco area. It takes a little more than an hour to travel the full course of the Grand Canal, but since you will certainly want to linger you had better hire him for two hours. If you are shocked by the high price he asks, you can always check it against the official tariff. And it will be more than worth it, because to glide along the Grand Canal on a golden evening is one of the supreme pleasures life can offer, an experience that will enrich the memory long after the dust has settled on your Murano glass.

If you make friends with your gondolier and do not ask him to sing Santa Lucia, which is a Neapolitan song, he will probably tell you about the buildings you are passing, the people who live in them and a great deal more of the kind of local information that cannot be discovered from guidebooks and tourist offices.

In my opinion, if the Earthly Paradise where Adam dwelt with Eve were like Venice, Eve would have had a hard time to tempt him out of it with any fig. For it would have been another matter to lose Venice, where there are so many lovely things, than to lose that place where there are nothing but figs, melons and grapes.

Pietro Aretino, 1492-1556

A trip by gondola is the ideal way to see the Grand Canal for the first time. It can also be seen, economically and more rapidly, from a water bus. Take the slow vaporetto, no.1, which is perversely called the *accelerato*, from San Zaccaria or San Marco to Ferrovia (railroad station) and allow about half an hour.

Either way — gondola or vaporetto — it would be a shame to spoil a first experience of the Grand Canal with too many facts. Most of the 100 or more buildings along its course are beautiful or interesting in one way or another, but nobody can be expected to remember all of their names. What follows, therefore, is for reference or for a second or third journey.

The Grand Canal, known to Venetians as the Canalazzo, follows the course of an ancient river bed which cuts through the city in the shape of an inverted S from SE to NW. It is about 3.5km (2¼ miles) long, 30-70m (130-230ft) wide and 5m (18ft) at its deepest. It is crossed by only three bridges, at the Accademia, Rialto and Scalzi, which leads to the railroad station, bordered by only a few stretches of pavement (*fondamente*), and punctuated by the landing stages of the vaporetti and ferries. The Grand Canal is therefore mostly hidden from the pedestrian, and one of the reasons it is so difficult to find your way around the backstreets of Venice is that you can rarely see where you are in relation to this tortuous main street.

STREETS FULL OF WATER PLEASE ADVISE
Cable sent home by Robert Benchley on his first visit to Venice

Although the palaces of the Grand Canal date from the 12th-18thC, most of them share a common basic plan, which survived six centuries of stylistic changes. The main entrance, which always faces the water, opens on to an *androne*, or entrance hall, flanked on either side by warehouses. Above are one or two *piani nobili*, the main floor (s), with a *portego*, or reception hall, running from front to back and lit by a row of closely grouped windows. There is a subsidiary land entrance, often through a courtyard where, in palaces built before *c.*1500, there is usually an external staircase. The word Ca', short for Casa, was generally used even for the grandest Venetian houses until the 19thC and the usage still survives for some important palaces.

If you are setting off from *San Zaccaria*, before entering the Grand Canal proper, the boat will pass: the prisons, built in the 17thC and connected to the *Doges' Palace* by the Bridge of Sighs; the Piazzetta of *San Marco* with its twin columns topped by St Theodore and St Mark, successive patron saints of Venice; the Marciana Library and Zecca or Mint, both by Sansovino; the Giardinetti Reali with an elegant Neoclassical Coffee House (1838) by Lorenzo Santi; the Capitaneria di Porto (Port Authority) on the far side of the rio; behind the San Marco landing stage, the Calle Vallaresso (where Harry's Bar can be found); and the Hotel Monaco.

The Grand Canal is entered where the Customs House Point, or Punta della Dogana, projects into the Bacino di San Marco opposite Ca' Giustinian.

From the Customs House Point to the Accademia: left bank

Beyond the Customs House Point and the **Customs House** tower, surmounted by its gilded ball of fortune, stretch the customs warehouses, the 17thC **Patriarchal Seminary** and Longhena's immense domed church of the *Salute* ★ the outstanding Baroque monument in Venice. Across the rio is the 14thC Abbey of San Gregorio. After a row of less interesting buildings comes the endearingly lovely **Palazzo Dario** ★ (*c*.1488), attributed to Pietro Lombardo, its crooked, asymmetrical facade inlaid with marble roundels and topped by outsized chimney pots. Henry James thought it looked 'like a house of cards that hold together by a tenure it would be fatal to touch.'

The next palace but one, the long, low **Palazzo Venier dei Leoni** (1749), houses the *Guggenheim Collection*. It is more commonly known as Palazzo Nonfinito because it was completed only as far as the first story. In the nearby **Casa Biondetti**, the painter Rosa Carriera died in 1757.

After the Rio di San Vio there are two palaces followed by a garden, next to which is the harmonious Renaissance **Palazzo Contarini dal Zaffo**, built by a collaborator of Pietro Lombardo and now owned by the Polignac family. Passing under the **Accademia Bridge** (1932) you can see the flank of the former church of the **Carità**, followed by the prim Neoclassical facade of the *Accademia* galleries.

The large 15thC Gothic palace opposite the Customs House is **Ca' Giustinian**. Now headquarters of the municipal tourist offices and of the Biennale, it was once a hotel which numbered Verdi, Gautier and Proust among its patrons. Next is the modern Hotel Bauer Grünwald. After the Rio di San Moisè comes the 17thC **Palazzo Treves de' Bonfili**.

Next is the Hotel Europa, built in the 17thC for the Tiepolo family, followed by the Hotel Regina. Beyond the spacious 15thC **Palazzo Contarini** is the delightful little **Palazzetto Contarini-Fasan**, known as the House of Desdemona, with charming late 15thC Gothic decorations. The Hotel Gritti occupies the severely restored early 15thC **Palazzo Pisani**.

After several smaller buildings there rises the majestically classical **Palazzo Corner** ✪ called Ca' Grande, commissioned in 1537 and built after 1545 by Sansovino for the immensely rich and powerful Corner family. It was they who later blocked the completion of the Guggenheim palace opposite, which would have obscured their view of the lagoon. The architecture of this important palace was influenced by Codussi's Vendramin-Calergi palace at the station end of the Grand Canal; in its turn, it had a strong effect on Longhena's designs for Ca' Rezzonico and Ca' Pesaro. The palace is now the police headquarters. In the garden next to it is a little red house, the **Casina delle Rose**, where Canova had his studio in the 1770s and d'Annunzio lived during World War I.

I was conducted through the principal street, which they call the Grand Canal . . . . It is the fairest and best-built street, I think, in the world, and goes quite through the city; the houses are very large and lofty, and built of stone; the old ones are all painted . . . . In short, it is the most triumphant city that I have ever seen.
Philip de Commines, French Ambassador to Venice, 1495

Before the Accademia are the two **Palazzi Barbaro**. The Gothic palace was built in 1425. Next to it is the wing added in 1694-98 by Antonio Gaspari to house a ballroom. The upper floors of the palace were bought in 1882 by the Curtis family, whose distinguished guests included John Singer Sargent, Robert Browning, Claude Monet and Henry James (who wrote *The Aspern Papers* while staying here). Across the rio is the 15thC **Palazzo Franchetti**, spoiled by a 19thC restoration and pompous addition. Beyond its garden at the foot of the Accademia Bridge is Campo San Vitale.

Beyond the Accademia galleries is the British Consulate at the 18thC **Palazzo Querini**. Next but one is **Palazzo Contarini degli Scrigni** (1609) designed by Scamozzi as an extension of the adjacent 15thC Gothic **Palazzo Corfù**. Second after the Rio di San Trovaso is the large, symmetrical 15thC Gothic **Palazzo Loredan**, which bears two good Lombard statues of pages on its first floor; it is known as 'dell' Ambasciatore' because it was the Austrian Embassy in the 18thC. Across the Rio di San Barnaba rises Longhena's monumental *Ca' Rezzonico*, now the Museum of the Venetian 18thC.

After some lower buildings comes an impressive row of three mid-15thC Gothic edifices. The first two are the **Palazzi Giustinian**. Wagner spent the winter of 1858-59 in the second, composing *Tristan and Isolde*. The third is **Ca' Foscari** ✪ now a department of the University, which Ruskin called 'the noblest

example in Venice of the 15thC Gothic.' Doge Francesco Foscari
died of a broken heart here in 1457 after his dismissal from office.

The Grand Canal takes a sharp bend (known as the Volta del
Canal), around the mouth of the Rio Foscari. This is part of the
Rio Nuovo, one of the widest of the internal canals, and used by
fast water buses as a short-cut to the railroad station. On the far
corner of the rio the palace with obelisks on its roof is **Palazzo
Balbi** (1582-90), which was probably designed by Alessandro
Vittoria. Frank Lloyd Wright's unrealized center for Foreign
Architectural Students (1953) would have been situated to the left
of Palazzo Balbi, had the latter's owners not blocked the plans.
The most splendid of the palaces between the San Tomà landing
stage and the Rio di San Polo is the large, symmetrical mid-15thC
Gothic **Palazzo Pisani-Moretta**. Its great reception hall, once
decorated by Veronese, Tiepolo and Piazzetta, is still used for
grand balls. From here you can catch a first glimpse of the *Rialto*
Bridge ahead.

We returned up the Grand Canal in our gondola. We watched the
double line of palaces between which we passed reflect the light
and angle of the sun upon their rosy surfaces, and alter with them,
seeming not so much private habitations and historic buildings as a
chain of marble cliffs at the foot of which people go out in the
evening in a boat to watch the sunset . . . . And thus any
excursion, even when it was only to pay calls or to go shopping,
was threefold and unique in this Venice where the simplest social
coming and going assumed at the same time the form and the
charm of a visit to a museum and a trip to the sea.
                                    Marcel Proust, *Remembrance of Things Past*, 1925

The red 16thC **Palazzo Cappello-Layard** on the far side of the
wide Rio di San Polo was the home of Sir Austen Layard, the
English ambassador whose collection of paintings is now in the
National Gallery, London. Next is the graceful 16thC **Palazzo**

Left Bank
1 Accademia Galleries
2 Pal. Querini
3 Pal. Contarini d. Scrigni
4 Pal. Corfù
5 Pal. Loredan
6 Ca' Rezzonico
7 Palazzi Giustinian
8 Ca' Foscari
9 Pal. Balbi
10 Pal. Pisani-Moretta
11 Pal. Cappello-Layard
12 Pal. Grimani
13 Pal. Bernardo
14 Palazzi Donà
15 Pal. Coccina-Papadopoli
16 Pal. Businello
17 Pal. Barzizza
18 Pal. Ravà
19 Pal. d. Dieci Savi

Right Bank
20 Pal. Giustinian-Lolin
21 Ca' del Duca
22 Pal. Grassi
23 Pal. Moro-Lin
24 Pal. Contarini
25 Case Mocenigo
26 Pal. Corner Spinelli
27 Pal. Benzon
28 Pal. Corner Contarini
29 Pal. Grimani
30 Casa Corner Martenigo-Ravà
31 Pal. Farsetti
32 Pal. Loredan
33 Pal. Dandolo
34 Pal. Bembo
35 Pal. Dolfin-Manin

Grimani, and next but one the **Palazzo Bernardo** (1442), one of
the best preserved Gothic palaces on the Grand Canal. The two
Palazzi Donà, on either side of the *traghetto* landing stage, date
originally from the 12th-13thC and preserve Veneto-Byzantine
windows and decorations.

The fine classical palace with obelisks is the **Palazzo Coccina-
Papadopoli**, built by Giangiacomo dei Grigi around 1560. On the
far side of the Rio dei Meloni are two palaces, the **Businello** and
Barzizza, which preserve Veneto-Byzantine features. After the San
Silvestro landing is the picturesque but modern (1906) **Palazzo
Ravà** and the Fondamenta del Vin which stretches all the way to
the Rialto Bridge. At the foot of the near side of the bridge is the
16thC **Palazzo dei Dieci Savi** by Scarpagnino.
From the Accademia to the Rialto: right bank
The second building upstream from the Accademia Bridge is
Palazzo Giustinian-Lolin (1623), Longhena's first palace. Next
but one is the **Ca' del Duca**, which incorporates part of the
rusticated base and columns of an ambitious palace begun by
Bartolomeo Bon in the 15thC for the Cornaro family, bought from
them by Francesco Sforza, Duke of Milan, and never completed;
Titian had a studio here in 1514. Past the San Samuele landing
stage is the large and handsome 18thC **Palazzo *Grassi***, built by
Giorgio Massari, who also completed Longhena's Ca' Rezzonico
on the opposite side of the Grand Canal. Palazzo Grassi is now the
International Center of Arts and Costume and is used for
temporary exhibitions of all kinds.

The broad **Palazzo Moro-Lin**, known as the House of Thirteen
Windows, was built in the 17thC for the painter Pietro Liberi to
the design of the Florentine painter and poet Sebastiano Mazzoni.

At the bend of the canal is the **Palazzo Contarini**, called 'delle
Figure' after the carved figures over the doorway. It was built in
the early 16thC for Palladio's patron Jacopo Contarini. Next are
the four **Case Mocenigo**, built for the great Mocenigo family
which produced four doges. The two central houses are united by a
long facade bearing Neoclassical decorations. Giordano Bruno
stayed in the first in 1592. Byron lived in the second from 1818-20,
began *Don Juan* there, and later moved into the one nearest the
Rialto. The *Rialto* Bridge comes into sight after the San Angelo
landing stage. It is followed by the exceptionally fine Renaissance
Palazzo Corner Spinelli ☆ (1485-90) with rusticated base and
round-headed windows characteristic of the style of Mauro
Codussi who almost certainly designed it.

After two more palaces comes the pink **Palazzo Benzon**, once
the home of Contessa Marina Querini-Benzon, who inspired the
still-popular love song *La Biondina in Gondoletta* and who
entertained great artistic and literary figures, including Byron and
Canova.

Farther along, on the near side of the Rio di San Luca, is the
pretty mid-15thC Gothic **Palazzo Corner Contarini** with a
graceful row of central windows. The palace is known as 'dei
Cavalli' after the reliefs of horses on its facade. On the other corner
of the rio is the towering facade of the early 16thC **Palazzo
Grimani**, a masterpiece of High Renaissance architecture by
Sanmicheli, now the Court of Appeals. Next but one is the 17thC
Casa Corner Martenigo-Ravà, a hotel favored in the 19thC by
artists and writers including Sir Thomas Lawrence, J.M.W.
Turner and James Fenimore Cooper.

The Fondamenta del Carbon and the Riva del Ferro, which run
alongside the canal, are named after the coal and iron boats that
once unloaded here. Next to the **Palazzo Martenigo-Ravà** are two

heavily restored 13thC Veneto-Byzantine palaces, the **Palazzo Farsetti** and **Palazzo Loredan**, now the town hall. The little 14thC **Palazzetto Dandolo** was the birthplace of the blind Doge Enrico Dandolo, who led the Fourth Crusade and the Sack of Constantinople in 1202-4. Then follows a small house where Pietro Aretino, the 16thC scholar, wit and friend of Titian, spent the last years of his life. The large Gothic building on the near side of the Rio di San Salvatore is **Palazzo Bembo**, and on the far side is the 16thC **Palazzo Dolfin-Manin**, Sansovino's first domestic palace in Venice, begun in 1538, now the Banca d'Italia. The boat now passes under the *Rialto* Bridge (1588-92) built by Antonio da Ponte.

From the Rialto to the railway station: left bank

Angled around the bend of the canal at the upstream foot of the Rialto Bridge are the graceful facades of **Palazzo dei Camerlenghi** ☆ (1523-25), designed by Guglielmo dei Grigi as the seat of the Exchequer; its ground floor was used as a state prison, after which the adjacent Fondamenta delle Prigioni is still named. The long arcaded building beyond the Camerlenghi Palace is the fruit and vegetable market, the **Fabbriche Vecchie di Rialto**, built by Scarpagnino after a fire devastated the area in the early 16thC.

Then you pass the **Fabbriche Nuove di Rialto** (1552-55) by Sansovino, now the Court of Assizes, which follows the curve of the canal to the **Campo della Pescheria**, the fish market since the 14thC. The new fish market building or *pescheria* (1907) beyond the campo is in imitation Gothic style.

Past the **Fondamenta della Riva dell' Olio** and the Gothic **Palazzo Brandolin** is the small red **Casa Bragadin Favretto**, now the Hotel San Cassiano, a 14thC house where in the 19thC the painter Giacomo Favretto had a studio. Next to it rises the handsome 18thC **Palazzo Corner della Regina** built by Domenico Rossi for the branch of the Corner family descended from Caterina Cornaro, Queen of Cyprus, who was born in the house which occupied this site in 1454. The palace now houses the Biennale archives of contemporary art. After two smaller houses comes Longhena's splendid *Ca' Pesaro*, begun in the late 17thC and now occupied by the Gallery of Modern Art and the Oriental Museum.

Left Bank
1 Pal. d. Camerlenghi
2 Fabbriche Vecchie di Rialto
3 Fabbriche Nuove di Rialto
4 Pescheria
5 Pal. Brandolin
6 Casa Bragadin Favretto
7 Pal. Corner d. Regina
8 Ca' Pesaro
9 S. Stae
10 Pal. Belloni-Battagia
11 Depositi d. Megio
12 Fondaco d. Turchi
13 S. Simeone Piccolo

16 Ca' da Mosto
17 Pal. Mangilli-Valmarana
18 Pal. Michiel
19 Pal. Sagredo
20 Ca' d'Oro
21 Pal. Fontana
22 Pal. Gussoni-Grimani d. Vida
23 Pal. Soranzo
24 Pal. Erizzo alla Maddalena
25 Pal. Marcello
26 Pal. Vendramin Calergi
27 S. Marcuola
28 Pal. Correr Contarini
29 Pal. Labia

Right Bank
14 Fondaco d. Tedeschi
15 Pal. Lion-Morosini

30 S. Geremia
31 Pal. Flangini
32 Scalzi

The Baroque facade of the church of *San Stae* (1709) is by Rossi.
On the far corner of the next rio is the Baroque **Palazzo
Belloni-Battagia**, with obelisks on its roof, by Longhena.

The fortress-like brick building that follows was erected in the
15thC as the **Depositi del Megio** (Granaries of the Republic) ; the
relief of the *Lion of St Mark* is a modern replacement of the
original, which was destroyed at the fall of the Republic. Next is
the **Fondaco dei Turchi**, named after the Turkish merchants to
whom it was leased as warehouse and residence in the 17thC. It
dates from the 13thC, but a drastic restoration in the 19thC left no
more than the outlines and a few fragments of the original
Veneto-Byzantine building. It now houses the *Natural History
Museum*.

After a stretch of unremarkable buildings the boat passes under
the steep railroad bridge, or **Ponte degli Scalzi** (1934), by Eugenio
Miozzi. The copper-domed church opposite the railroad station is
San Simeone Piccolo, an eclectic building of the 18thC.

From the Rialto to the railroad station: right bank

The first building upstream from the Rialto is the **Fondaco dei
Tedeschi**, named after the German merchants to whom it was
leased by the Republic. It is now the central post office. It was
built in 1505 by Spavento and Scarpagnino after a fire destroyed an
earlier building. The exterior walls were decorated by Giorgione
and Titian, whose frescoes have now disappeared, apart from
fragments preserved in the *Ca' d'Oro*. Before the Rio di San
Giovanni Crisostomo is the charming little **Campiello del Remer**
(taking its name from the local oarmakers), where the 13thC
Palazzo Lion-Morosini has an unusual external staircase.

A Venetian palace that has not too grossly suffered and that is not
overwhelming by its mass makes almost any life graceful that may
be led in it. With cultivated and generous contemporary ways it
reveals a pre-established harmony.

Henry James, *Italian Hours*, 'The Grand Canal,' 1892

The fourth palace in the next group is **Ca' da Mosto**, a good
example of the Veneto-Byzantine style. In the 16th-18thC it was
the grand hotel of Venice, the Albergo del Leon Bianco. The house
on the far side of the Rio dei Santi Apostoli, **Palazzo Mangilli-
Valmarana**, was built in the 18thC for Joseph Smith, the English
consul and Canaletto's patron. **Palazzo Michiel**, next to it, is
called 'dal Brusà' after the great fire that destroyed the original
Gothic building in 1774.

On the far side of the *traghetto* landing is **Palazzo Sagredo**, with
pretty 14thC Gothic central windows and some Veneto Byzantine
features. The *Ca' d'Oro* (1425-*c*.1440) is probably the most
famous and certainly the most flamboyantly beautiful of all the
Gothic palaces on the Grand Canal. It is called the Golden House
because the rich decorations of its facade were once gilded. It
houses the important Franchetti Collection of art. The next large
palace, the 17thC **Palazzo Fontana,** was the birthplace in 1693 of
Count Carlo Rezzonico, later to become Pope Clement XIII.

On the far side of the Rio di Noale is the harmoniously
proportioned 16thC **Palazzo Gussoni-Grimani della Vida,**
attributed to Sanmicheli, where Sir Henry Wotton, the English
ambassador, lived in 1614-18. In the center of the group of houses
after the Rio della Maddalena are the graceful 16thC **Palazzo
Soranzo**, probably by Sante Lombardo, the 15thC Gothic **Palazzo
Erizzo alla Maddalena**, and **Palazzo Marcello**, rebuilt in the
18thC, where the composer Benedetto Marcello was born in 1686.

Now your eyes will probably be drawn to the crowning architectural masterpiece of the Grand Canal, and indeed one of the greatest Renaissance buildings in Italy, the **Palazzo Vendramin Calergi ★** the first facade in Venice on which the classical orders were correctly expressed according to the principles of Alberti. It was designed and begun in the first decade of the 16thC by Codussi and completed by one of the Lombardo family. Wagner died here in 1883. It is now the winter home of the Casino.

Behind the next landing stage is the unfinished facade of the church of *San Marcuola*, followed by a row of mostly 17thC palaces including the **Palazzo Correr Contarini**, the home of Teodoro Correr (1750-1830), whose collection formed the nucleus of that in the *Correr Museum*, to which it was transferred in 1922 from the Fondaco dei Turchi.

At the far corner of the Cannaregio Canal, which is the widest of the internal canals and leads to the lagoon, is the **Palazzo Labia**, headquarters of the Italian Broadcasting Network, RAI. The most famous and elaborate parties in 18thC Venice were held in its ballroom which is still decorated with some of G.B. Tiepolo's most glorious paintings. (*Visits on Wed, Thurs and Fri afternoons by appointment* ☎716666).

Next to it is the 18thC church of **San Geremia**, followed by Giuseppe Sardi's unfinished **Palazzo Flangini**. Between the railroad bridge and the station (1955) is the Baroque facade of Sardi's church of the *Scalzi*.

Grassi Palace *(Palazzo Grassi)* 🏛

Map 14D2. San Marco 3231, Campo San Samuele ☎5235133/5231680. Open 10am-7pm. Water bus 2 to San Samuele.

Giorgio Massari's imposing Neoclassical palace (begun 1749) facing the Grand Canal is now a center for large and important temporary exhibitions. Financed mainly by Fiat and adapted in the mid-1980s by the architects Gae Aulenti and Antonio Foscari, it contains a small theater, library, projection rooms, conference rooms, a branch of **Harry's Dolci** (see *Restaurants*), an overpriced shop, countless prominently signposted rest rooms and innumerable public telephones. In short, it contains all the amenities and the atmosphere of a smart, anonymous international airport hotel.

Massari built the palace around a large interior courtyard (an unusual plan in Venice) which was glassed over in 1951. The frescoes are by Michelangelo Morlaiter.

The church of San Samuele next to the palace retains its 12thC romanesque *campanile*.

Guggenheim Collection *(Raccolta Peggy Guggenheim)* 🏛 ■■ ☆

Map 14F3. Palazzo Venier dei Leoni, Dorsoduro 701, Calle Cristoforo ☎ 5206288 ☒ Open Apr-Oct Wed-Mon noon-6pm; Sat 6-9pm. Closed Tues. Groups are advised to telephone. Water bus 1 to Salute or 1, 2 or 4 to Accademia.

Peggy Guggenheim began buying Cubist, Abstract and Surrealist art in Europe in the years immediately before World War II. She took the collection to New York in 1942 and displayed it in her 'Art of this Century' gallery. It was a key inspiration for the as yet unknown Abstract Expressionists — Robert Motherwell, Mark Rothko, David Hare, Clifford Still and (Peggy Guggenheim's star discovery) Jackson Pollock — whose works she now began to acquire.

In 1949 she bought the Palazzo Venier dei Leoni on the Grand Canal, transferred her entire collection there and opened it to the public. She lived in Venice and continued buying contemporary art (although with diminishing enthusiasm from the 1960s) until her death in December 1979. The collection is now managed under the aegis of the Solomon R. Guggenheim Foundation.

The **Palazzo Venier dei Leoni** was begun in 1749 by the Neoclassical architect Lorenzo Boshchetti. It is known as Palazzo Nonfinito because it was never finished; probably the Corner family, whose palace faces it across the Grand Canal, blocked the plans for a building which would have obscured their view. The result is that what would certainly have been a pompously oversized intrusion is one of the most attractive oddities on the Grand Canal.

Since Peggy Guggenheim's death, her collection has been cleaned, rehung, well lit and properly labeled, and the gallery is staffed with efficient young guides bilingual in English and Italian. It is one of the most important privately assembled collections of 20thC art outside America, a monument but not a shrine to the personality of Miss Guggenheim.

The elegant **land gates** (1961) are to a design by Claire Falkenstein. Marino Marini's sculpture *Angel of the Citadel* (1949) faces the Grand Canal from the water gate. In the **galleries** don't miss the Cubists in the former dining room, the Mondrians in the living room, the Joseph Cornell boxes, and the Pollocks and the Surrealists in the garden gallery. Among the best-known modern classics are Picasso's *La Baignade* (1937), Duchamp's *Sad Young Man on a Train* (1911), De Chirico's *Red Tower* (1913), Max Ernst's *The Attirement of the Bride* (1940) and Magritte's *Domain of Lights* (1954).

The **garden** has been replanted as a setting for sculptures by, among others, Arp, Moore, Giacometti, Paolozzi and Ernst. Peggy Guggenheim is buried here with her beloved dogs.

Madonna dell' Orto �𝕞 † ☆

Map 5B6. Campo Madonna dell' Orto, Cannaregio. Water bus 5 to Madonna dell' Orto.

The Madonna dell' Orto, which is situated in the remote northern region of Cannaregio, is one of the loveliest Gothic churches in Venice. It was originally built in the mid-14thC to enshrine a miraculous statue of the Virgin found in a nearby orchard; it was subsequently reconstructed at the end of the 14thC and again, definitively, in 1473.

In 1968-69 the British Italian Art and Archives Fund undertook a comprehensive restoration of the building and its contents. This was the first of the large-scale restoration programs carried out in Venice after the 1966 flood and has been the model for all others.

The graceful facade — a less forbidding variation on the style of the *Frari* and *Santi Giovanni e Paolo* facades is essentially that of the original church, but the windows and sculptural decorations are later additions. The *St Christopher and Child* over the main door is thought to be by Bartolomeo Bon. *The Virgin* and *Angel Gabriel* on the gate posts are attributed to Antonio Rizzo, and *The Twelve Apostles* in the niches to the dalle Masegne brothers. The campanile (1503) is the first to be seen distinctly when approaching Venice by water from the airport.

The Madonna dell' Orto was the parish church of Tintoretto and contains a number of his masterpieces. The two most spectacular are in the chancel. These giant paintings were executed *in situ*, possibly from 1562-64, just before Tintoretto started work at *San Rocco*. On the left wall is *The Adoration of the Golden Calf* ☆ and on the right wall is *The Last Judgment* ☆ which Ruskin considered the only true painted interpretation of 'this unimaginable event.' The two paintings by Tintoretto behind the high altar, *The Beheading of St Paul* and *The Vision of the Cross to St Peter*, originally decorated the inside of the organ doors.

Perhaps the most appealing of all the Tintorettos is *The Presentation of the Virgin* ☆ (*c.*1552-53), at the altar end of the right aisle, which deliberately rivaled Titian's treatment of the same subject in the *Accademia*. It was originally painted in two halves to form the outside of the organ doors. In the Contarini Chapel, off the left aisle, *St Agnes Reviving Licinio* was commissioned in the 1560s by Tomasso Contarini, whose portrait bust by Alessandro Vittoria is on the right wall. Tintoretto is buried in the family chapel to the right of the chancel.

Two other outstanding paintings in the church are Cima da Conegliano's *St John the Baptist with Sts Peter, Mark, Jerome and Paul* over the first altar in the right aisle, and Giovanni Bellini's tiny *Madonna and Child* in the early-Renaissance Valier Chapel off the entrance end of the left aisle. In the Chapel of San Mauro, entered under *The Presentation of the Virgin*, is the miraculous statue of *The Madonna* for which the church was built, now largely a plaster reconstruction of the original.

Across the canal is the N facade of the **Palazzo Mastelli**, known as 'del Cammello' after the sculpture of a man leading a camel. If you cross the Madonna dell' Orto Bridge into the Campo dei Mori and turn left you will see, set into the walls of the palace, the famous worn statues of the Mastelli brothers, Levantine merchants who built the palace in the 12thC.

The house where Tintoretto lived, and died in 1594, is farther along the fondamenta at no.3399.

Miracoli *(Santa Maria dei Miracoli)* 🏛 ✝ ★
Map 15B5. Campo dei Miracoli, Cannaregio. Irregular opening hours. Water bus 1, 2 or 4 to Rialto.

The Miracoli is a small, exquisitely-crafted church built from 1481-89 by Pietro Lombardo, with the assistance of his sons Antonio and Tullio, to contain a miracle-working image of the Virgin. Clad in sheets of softly-colored, smoothly-joined marble, rising sheer from the water of the canal on one side, it seems both quintessentially Venetian and not quite real — a building from the background of a painting by Bellini or Carpaccio.

Although the architecture of the Miracoli is superficially that of the Tuscan Renaissance — the style introduced to Venice by Pietro Lombardo — the emphasis is on the beauty of its materials is in the Veneto-Byzantine tradition. The two orders of the exterior, derived perhaps from the Florence Baptistry, are applied to enliven the surface appearance of the building rather than to reveal its structure. The marble facings have been tragically damaged by time; a major restoration has been in progress since 1988.

The **facade**, topped by a large, semi-circular lunette, is inlaid like that of the Palazzo Dario on the *Grand Canal* with roundels and small panels of porphyry and *verde antica* marble.

The **interior** is lined with panels of gray and rose marble which are reflected in Giovanni Bellini's *Annunciation*, originally painted for the organ doors but now, alas, in the *Accademia*. The deep curve of the unusual, early 16thC barrel-vaulted ceiling is decorated with 50 busts of saints and prophets. On the elegant balustrade of the raised chancel are half figures of *St Francis, The*

Archangel Gabriel, The Virgin and *St Clare* by Tullio Lombardo, who also carved the lacy marble screen that surrounds the high altar and the tondo bust of *The Evangelists* in the spandrels of the cupola.

The Calle Castelli leads from the Campo dei Miracoli to the Fondamenta Sanudo. No.7009, the fine late-Gothic **Palazzo Soranzo-Van Axel e Barozzi** (1473-79), retains its original curved wooden doors, the only ones in Venice to survive from the 15thC, and has an attractive courtyard with an outdoor staircase and Renaissance loggia.

Misericordia 🏛
Map 6B6. Cannaregio. Waterbus 5 to Madonna dell'Orto.

The Sacco della Misericordia, the large square inlet that interrupts the Fondamenta Nuove, was originally used as a floating storage space for timber brought by water from the mainland.

This part of Cannaregio is dominated by the immense brick Scuola Nuova della Misericordia, begun *c.*1534 by Jacopo Sansovino. Although left unfinished it is one of the city's most impressive architectural monuments. It is occupied, rather inappropriately, by basketball courts; but there is talk of turning it one day into a much-needed museum of Venetian sculpture.

The Church of the Misericordia is used as a center of stone restoration. The Ponte Chiodo, which crosses the Rio di San Felice, is the last surviving example in Venice of a bridge built at a low enough gradient to take horses.

Mocenigo Palace *(Palazzo Mocenigo)* 🏛
Map 14A3. Salizzada San Stae 1992 ⬛ ☎ Open Sat 8.30am-1.30pm. Water bus 1 to San Stae.

The Palazzo Mocenigo at S. Stae, inhabited until recently by a branch of one of the great Venetian families, offers a rare opportunity to view the interior of a domestic aristocratic palace which has hardly changed since 1778 when the last of the seven Mocenigo doges died.

The exterior is 17thC. The interior was redone in the 18thC, and the controlled magnificence of the furnishings and decorations of the first *piano nobile* typify patrician taste on the eve of the fall of the Republic: frescoed ceilings, Murano chandeliers, 18thC furniture, mirrors and monumental paintings richly framed (notice for example the frame of the portrait of Giulio Contarini from the workshop of Antonio Corradini).

The palace also houses a library and study collection of costumes and textiles.

Modern Art, Gallery of
The gallery and the Oriental Museum are housed on different floors of the splendid late 17thC palace *Ca' Pesaro* on the Grand Canal.

Natural History Museum *(Museo di Storia Naturale)* 🏛
Map 14A2. Fondaco dei Turchi, Grand Canal, Santa Croce ☎5240885 ⬛ ✱ Open Tues-Sat 9am-1.30pm; Sun 9am-1pm. Closed Mon. Water bus 1 to San Stae.

The Natural History Museum occupies the second floor of the **Fondaco dei Turchi** which faces the *Grand Canal* opposite San Marcuola. The building takes its name from the Turkish merchants to whom it was leased by the government as a residence and warehouse from 1621-1838. The original 13thC Byzantine palace was almost entirely rebuilt in 1869.

Objects on display in the museum include dioramas of

underwater fauna; a gondolalike pre-Roman canoe found in the lagoon in 1893; one of the largest dinosaur skeletons in the world, brought from the Sahara in 1973; and a 19thC collection of model fishing boats and nets.

Naval Museum *(Museo Storico Navale)*
Map 12F9. Campo San Biagio, Castello ☎5200276 ▨ ☀
Open Mon-Fri 9am-1pm, Sat 9am-noon. Closed Sun. Water bus 1 to Arsenale.

The Naval Museum is housed in one of the old granaries of the Republic near the *Arsenale*. It commemorates the water life of Venice from the great age of galley warfare to the present and is one of the richest and most attractively displayed collections of its kind in Europe. The models of Venetian watercraft for which the museum is famous are irresistible even to nonspecialists.

One **ground floor** room is devoted to Admiral Angelo Emo, the last naval commander of the Republic, who is commemorated here by a monument (1795) by Canova. Elsewhere on this floor you can see a World War II 'human torpedo,' and Renaissance and 17thC bronze artillery. The **first floor** contains a model of a 16thC 224-oar fighting galley, an early 19thC model of the *bucintoro*, the barge in which the doge conducted the annual ceremonial marriage to the sea, and a large model of the 80-cannon ship *Caesar*, launched under the Napoleonic regime. On the **second floor** are models of modern war and passenger ships. The **third floor** has an exhibition devoted to the construction of gondolas and a model of the *squero*, the boatyard at *San Trovaso* where gondolas are still made and repaired. In addition, there are models of fishing boats and nets and a collection of votive paintings recording miraculous deliverance from accidents at sea. The naval museum has recently expanded into parts of the *Arsenale*, where real Venetian craft, mostly from the 19th and 20th centuries, are displayed.

Next to the museum is the 18thC naval chapel of **San Biagio,** in which there is a startlingly naturalistic reclining statue of *Admiral Emo* (1792) by Giovanni Ferrari.

Ospedaletto *(Santa Maria dei Derelitti)* ☒ †
Map 11D8. Salizzada Santi Giovanni e Paolo, Castello. Water bus 1, 2 or 4 to Rialto, or 5 to Fondamenta Nuove. Open for concerts only.

The bizarre Baroque facade of the Ospedaletto dominates the narrow street running back past the s apse of *Santi Giovanni e Paolo.* The church was built between 1662-74 by Guiseppe Sardi and Baldassare Longhena who designed the deliberately shocking facade, which was later singled out by Ruskin as 'the most monstrous example of the Grotesque Renaissance which is to be found in Venice; the sculptures on its facade representing masses of diseased figures and swollen fruit.'

The interior is decorated with good 17th and early 18thC Venetian pictures including *The Annunciation* by Palma il Giovane and *The Sacrifice of Isaac* (1715-16), by G.B. Tiepolo.

The 18thC music room in the adjacent *Ospizio* may be visited on request.

Pietà †
Map 11F8. Riva degli Schiavoni, Castello. Rarely open. Water bus 1, 2 or 4 to San Zaccaria, or 1 to Arsenale.

Some of Antonio Vivaldi's finest music was composed for the choir of orphan girls under the protection of the state hospital of the Pietà. The church of the Pietà, which was begun four years after

Vivaldi's death, was destined to become one of the leading concert halls of 18thC Venice. Giorgio Massari won a competition to design it in 1736, the year his more ambitious *Gesuati* was completed. It was built between 1745-60 but the facade was not applied until 1906.

The chief attraction of the **interior**, if you should be lucky enough to catch it open, is G. B. Tiepolo's dazzling ceiling painting of *The Coronation of the Virgin* (1755).

Querini-Stampalia *(Palazzo Querini-Stampalia)*
Map 11E7, 15C6. Campiello Querini, Castello ☎5225235. Water bus 1, 2 or 4 to Rialto, or 1, 2, 4 or 5 to San Zaccaria.

The early 16thC Palazzo Querini-Stampalia stands across the canal from the SE corner of Campo *Santa Maria Formosa*. The palace and its contents were left to the city of Venice in 1869 by Count Giovanni Querini. The access bridge, ground floor and garden were designed in the early 1960s by the Venetian architect Carlo Scarpa. The first floor houses a public lending library *(open Mon-Sat 2.30-11.30pm, Sun 3-7 pm)*, which has an excellent range of Italian books and periodicals on open stacks.

Gallery
🖼 *Sun. Open Tues-Sun 10am-7pm. Closed Mon. Ring bell for admission.*

The gallery, on the second *piano nobile*, was decorated by the patrician Querini-Stampalia family in the years before and after the fall of the Venetian Republic. It retains its late 18thC lacquer furniture, mirrors, Rococo stuccowork, painted ceilings and an undemanding collection of 14th-18thC pictures. Visitors may borrow a detailed list of the contents of the 20 rooms, from which the following is only a brief selection.

Room I, to the left of the *portego* or reception hall, is hung with 69 *Scenes from Venetian Public Life* executed in the late 18thC by Gabriele Bella — naïve, clumsily executed works which nevertheless do bring the period alive. The rest of the gallery leads off from the far side of the *portego*. **Room III** has portraits of public figures by Sebastiano Bombelli, the leading 17thC Venetian portrait painter who established the tradition of the full-length patrician portrait, typically represented here by *Girolamo Querini in a Red Toga*. **Room VII** is notable for its Neoclassical decor, 17thC genre pictures and, in the center of the room, the clay model for Canova's *Portrait of Napoleon's Mother*.

The most important Renaissance pictures in the collection are in **Room VIII**. *The Presentation of the Virgin* by the young Giovanni Bellini is closely based on a Mantegna *Presentation*, a photograph of which hangs nearby. The tondo of *The Virgin and Child* is by the Florentine Lorenzo di Credi. Also of interest are Palma il Vecchio's late, unfinished portraits of *Francesco Querini* and his bride *Paola Priuli* (1528), for whom this palace was built. Another late work by Palma il Vecchio is the *Sacra Conversazione* in **Room IX**. The most striking work in this room is the *Judith* by Vincenzo Catena, a 16thC follower of Giorgione. The ceiling panels representing *Midday, Dawn* and *Evening* may be youthful works by Sebastiano Ricci.

A corridor leads to the second wing of the gallery. In **Room XI** are works by the engaging 18thC genre painter Pietro Longhi, including doll-like group portraits of *The Sagredo Family* and *The Michiel Family*. Of the delightful paintings of *Venetian Monks, Canons and Friars*, Longhi wrote that he intended to distinguish among the religious orders 'who amuse themselves, who study and who pray.' His *Temptation of St Anthony* is an unusual and unsuccessful attempt to depict a serious religious subject. **Room XII** has more paintings by Pietro Longhi, including *Venetians Receiving the Sacraments* and *The Geography Lesson*. The finest of Longhi's hunting scenes is the *Party of Venetians Shooting Duck on the Lagoon* in **Room XIII**.

The next rooms contain characteristic 18thC furnishings. **Room XV** is furnished as a bedroom, with attractive lacquer furniture, Flemish tapestries and an engraved Venetian mirror; **Room XVI** is a boudoir with *boule* pieces, a gilded 18thC pendulum clock and a Querini barometer. **Room XVIII** is dominated by two large 18thC portraits of awesomely self-important public officials: *Procurator Daniele Dolfin* by Alessandro Longhi (son of Pietro) and *Procurator Giovanni Querini* by G.B. Tiepolo. There are two good 17thC pictures in **Room XIX**: a *Madonna and Child* by the Genoese Bernardo Strozzi and *The Death of Milo of Crotona* by Francesco Maffei of Vicenza.

Redentore 🏛 † ★

Map 9H5. Campo Redentore, Giudecca. Water bus 5 to Redentore.

In 1577 the Venetian Senate vowed to express its gratitude for the lifting of a plague that had carried off one third of the population, by building a temple of worship dedicated to Christ the Redeemer (*Redentore*). Andrea Palladio, by now the most eminent architect in Venice, was commissioned to design the church. The site on the *Giudecca* was chosen both for its conspicuous position and because it was sufficiently remote to allow for a spectacular annual procession to the votive church from the center of the city. The Feast of the Redentore, celebrated on the third Sunday in July by a procession that crosses the Giudecca Canal on a bridge of boats, remains one of the highlights of the Venetian calendar (see *Calendar of events* in *Planning*).

The Redentore was completed in the unusually short space of 15yrs. After Palladio's death in 1580 the work was supervised by Antonio da Ponte. Nevertheless, its design reflects Palladio's original intentions more completely than any other Venetian building with which he was associated.

The **facade** is a subtler and more complex development on that of the nearby *San Giorgio Maggiore*. The pediments of the overlapping temple fronts and the flight of steps on which the entrance is raised, in accordance with the principles of Vitruvius, lead the eye, when approaching across the water, to the great dome with its lantern surmounted by the figure of Christ the Redeemer. The statues of *St Mark* and *St Francis of Assisi* in the niches flanking the entrance are attributed to Girolamo Campagna.

The facade prepares you for the proportions of the **interior** but not for its forceful, incandescent beauty. Ideas from the classical and contemporary buildings Palladio had studied in Rome 20yrs earlier are unified here with a confident originality never matched by his numerous disciples. The rectangular nave is illuminated by huge thermal windows cut into the thickness of the vaulting (as in classical Roman baths). Architectural features are picked out in white Istrian stone, against a background of white stucco.

In the colonnaded curve of the apse, the high altar, like the exterior entrance, is flanked by statues of *St Mark* and *St Francis of Assisi* by Girolamo Campagna. The monks' choir behind the high altar and the exterior of the apse facing the monastic buildings are deliberately plain in contrast to the grandeur of the rest of the church — which, apparently, offended the Capuchin monks to whom the care of the church was entrusted.

Rialto ★
Map 15C4. Water bus 1, 2 or 4 to Rialto.

Rialto, from the Latin *rivo alto* — high bank — was the name given to the central part of the Venetian archipelago by its first permanent inhabitants, and it still refers to the area where they settled, around the middle bend of the *Grand Canal*. The bridge is always called Ponte di Rialto; the San Marco bank around Campo *San Bartolomio* is the *Rialto di quà* (this side) and the market bank is the *Rialto di là* (that side).

Rialto Bridge
The Istrian-stone bridge was built from 1588-92 by Antonio da Ponte who, although aptly named for the job, was a far less distinguished architect than his competitors, Michelangelo, Palladio, Vignola, Sansovino and Scamozzi, all of whom produced plans that were rejected in favor of his. It replaced the wooden bridge that you can see in Carpaccio's painting of *The Miracle of the True Cross* in the *Accademia*, and it remained the only pedestrian crossing point on the Grand Canal until 1854.

The chief interest of the bridge is not its rather clumsy design or even its shops but the views from it, which extend upstream (toward the railroad station) from the Fondaco dei Tedeschi to Ca' da Mosto and downstream (toward the Bacino di San Marco) as far as Palazzo Pisani-Moretta on the right.

Rialto markets
Venice was the greatest commercial power in Renaissance Europe and the Rialto was its business center. Precious cargoes of spices, silks and dyes from the Far East were unloaded in the markets where vegetables are now sold, and there was a cluster of banks around the Campo di Rialto, where merchants came to raise small loans, to speculate, and to hear the latest shipping news.

In 1514 the markets were devastated by a fire which spared only the ancient church of *San Giacomo di Rialto*. The Fabbriche Vecchie di Rialto, the arcaded buildings at the foot of the bridge, were rebuilt in the following year to the functional design of Antonio da Scarpagnino. The *erberia* (wholesale vegetable market) was erected later to an uninspired plan by Jacopo Sansovino. Farther upstream can be found the modern *pescheria* (wholesale fish market).

Salute *(Santa Maria della Salute)* 🏛 † ★
Map 15F4. Campo della Salute, Dorsoduro. Water bus 1 to Salute.

The massive round votive church of the Salute dominates the inner harbor of San Marco where the *Grand Canal* and Giudecca Canal run into it. It is the greatest Baroque church in Venice, the masterpiece of its architect Baldassare Longhena and, as Bernard Berenson wrote, 'the building which occupies the center of the picture Venice leaves in the mind.'

It was built as a thanksgiving offering to the Virgin, bringer of health (*salute*), for lifting the devastating plague of 1630. More than 1 million piles were sunk to support the immense structure, the building of which occupied Longhena for the last 50yrs of his life. It was consecrated in 1687, five years after his death.

The architect wrote that he adopted the circular form to signify 'a crown to be dedicated to the Virgin.' A statue of *The Virgin* surmounts the lantern above the dome. Like the vision described in Revelations, she is 'clothed in the sun, the moon under her feet and upon her head a crown of twelve stars.' The figures of *The Twelve Apostles* — the stars in her crown — stand on the gigantic scrolled buttresses of the dome.

Longhena's design was carefully attuned to the most prominent of the surrounding buildings. His two soaring domes echo those of the Byzantine Basilica of *San Marco*. The dome at the rear is flanked, like that of Palladio's *Redentore*, by twin bell towers, and the thermal windows of the side facades reflect the facade of the other Palladian church on the *Giudecca*, Le Zitelle. The interior arrangement of Composite and Corinthian orders is taken from the interior of *San Giorgio Maggiore*.

The Salute was conceived, not as a monastic foundation or place of regular worship, but as a prominent commemorative landmark and the destination point of an annual votive procession from *San Marco*. The procession still takes place on the Feast of the Presentation of the Virgin, Nov 21, when a bridge of boats is built across the *Grand Canal* from the Giglio and the central doors of the church are thrown open.

And the red tower looked gray, and all between
The churches, ships and palaces were seen
Huddled in gloom; — into the purple sea
The orange hues of heaven sunk silently.
We hardly spoke, and soon the gondola
Conveyed me to my lodging by the way.
                              Shelley, *Julian and Maddalo*, 1818

Entering the church by a side door, as you must on most days, you miss the full theatrical impact of Longhena's processional approach. This focuses your eye on the main altar from the top of the 35 steps until, as you reach the center of the octagonal nave, you see the six subsidiary altars for the first time dramatically revealed.

Most of the sculptural decorations of the church are by Giusto Le Court, including the group on the high altar of *The Virgin* flanked on one side by a personification of *Venice* and on the other by the figure of an ugly old woman representing the vanquished plague.

The three altarpieces on the right side of the church representing *The Presentation*, *The Assumption* and *The Birth of the Virgin* are by Luca Giordano. Over the third altar on the left is a disappointing painting by Titian of *The Descent of the Holy Spirit*, which he repainted, apparently without enthusiasm, in the 1540s after an earlier version had been destroyed by damp.

The best pictures are in the **sacristy** 🖼 to the left of the high altar. Those by Titian were painted for the Monastery of Santo Spirito in Isola and transferred here in 1656. The altarpiece *St Mark Enthroned with Sts Cosmos, Damian, Roch and Sebastian* ☆ (saints all associated with healing) was painted during the plague of 1509-14. Thirty years later Titian painted the brutal, audaciously foreshortened **Old Testament scenes** ☆ on the ceiling representing *Cain and Abel*, *The Sacrifice of Isaac* and *David and Goliath*. On the wall to the right of the altar is a dramatic Tintoretto, The *Marriage at Cana* ☆ (1561).

The building to the left of the Salute is the **Seminario Patriarcale** (Patriarchal Seminary) designed by Longhena in 1670 and now housing the **Manfrediana Collection** (*visits by appointment only* ☎5225558). The collection includes sculptures, architectural fragments and pictures.

Beyond the Seminario is the **Customs House** (Dogana), also built in the 17thC; the outside walls of the warehouses were rebuilt in the 19thC. The golden ball surmounted by *Justice* on the Customs House tower was designed by Bernardo Falcone. The

Customs House Point (Punta della Dogana) commands a
wonderful view, as from the prow of a ship, of the harbor of San
Marco.

On the other side of the Salute, across the Rio della Salute, are
the red-brick Gothic church and monastery of **San Gregorio**. The
church is now used as a restoration center for paintings.

Sant' Alvise †

*Map 5B5. Campo Sant'Alvise, Cannaregio. Water bus 5 to
Sant'Alvise.*

Sant' Alvise is one of the most remotely situated and rarely visited
of Venetian churches, although it is within easy reach of the
Ghetto and the *Madonna dell'Orto*. It is a simple, late 14thC
Gothic building standing next to a shady square. The interior was
rebuilt and redecorated in the 17thC when the flat ceiling was
frescoed with engagingly inept architectural perspectives and
sacred subjects. The eight Biblical scenes hung beneath the
monks' choir are by an unknown naive painter of the 15thC. The
outstanding picture from the church, G.B. Tiepolo's *Road to
Calvary*, has been removed to the *Accademia*.

Sant' Apollonia *(Museum of Sacred Art)* 🏛

*Map 15D6. Fondamenta Sant'Apollonia, San Marco
☎5229166. Open Mon-Sat 10.30am-12.30pm. Closed Sun.
Water bus 1, 2, 4 or 5 to San Zaccara.*

The former convent of Sant' Apollonia is situated behind the
Basilica of *San Marco* on the other side of the Rio di Palazzo. The
charming little cloister, built in the late 13thC and restored in
1969, is the only surviving example in Venice of Northern
European Romanesque architecture. Embedded in its walls are
decorative fragments and tombs from the first Basilica of San
Marco.

The rooms upstairs have been organized as a museum where
religious objects and paintings, temporarily removed from
churches under restoration, are displayed.

From the **Ponte Canonica** there is a good view of the Bridge of
Sighs and the E facade of the *Doges' Palace*. The fine 16thC
Renaissance palace at the E foot of the Ponte Cappello is the
Palazzo Trevisan-Cappello, now used as showrooms for Murano
glass, where Bianca Cappello lived after her marriage to Francesco
de' Medici.

Santi Apostoli †

*Map 15B5. Campo Santi Apostoli, Cannaregio. Water bus 1
to Ca' d'Oro.*

The church of Santi Apostoli stands on the site of one of the
earliest settlements founded by refugees fleeing the barbarian
invasions on the mainland. It owes its present appearance to
radical restorations in the late 16th and mid-18thC. Apart from the
campanile (1672), one of the prominent landmarks of the Venetian
skyline, the exterior is of no architectural interest. The domed
belfry was added to the campanile in the 1720s to designs by
Andrea Tirali.

The interior dates mainly from the 16thC with the notable
exception of the elegant late 15thC **Corner Chapel**, attributed to
Mauro Codussi. Over its altar hangs G.B. Tiepolo's small, radiant
Communion of St Lucy ☆ (1748), and on the right wall is the **tomb
of Marco Corner** (father of Caterina Cornaro, Queen of Cyprus),
attributed to Tullio Lombardo. In the chapel to the right of the
chancel are fragments of one of the two surviving 13thC

Romanesque fresco cycles in Venice; their subject is *The Deposition and Burial of Christ*. In the chapel to the left of the chancel, the altarpiece of *The Guardian Angel* is by 17thC Vicentine painter Francesco Maffei.

San Bartolomio †
Map 15C4. Campo San Bartolomio, San Marco. Water bus 1, 2 or 4 to Rialto. Entrance in Salizzada Pio X.
The last section of the Merceria, the principal route from *San Marco* to the *Rialto*, opens into Campo San Bartolomio, the city's busiest intersection and gossip trap. In the center of the campo, Antonio del Zotto's bronze statue of *Carlo Goldoni* (1883), the great Venetian playwright, surveys the scene with an expression of sardonic amusement. The church of San Bartolomio, which has been in restoration for years and rarely open, was used by the German community, whose trading center was in the nearby Fondaco dei Tedeschi (now the central post office). Its most important works of art, the four figures of saints (1507-9) by the young Sebastiano del Piombo were painted for the organ doors and are now displayed in the *Accademia*.

The 18thC campanile of the church is protected from evil spirits by a splendidly leering grotesque above its door.

San Cassiano †
Map 14B3. Campo San Cassiano, San Polo. Water bus 1 to San Stae.
This 17thC church between *Ca' Pesaro* and the *Rialto* has an uninviting, harshly restored exterior, but should be visited for Tintoretto's stunning painting of *The Crucifixion* ☆ (1568) in the chancel.

Sant' Elena
Map 13H12. Water bus 1, 2 or 4 to Sant' Elena.
The island of Sant' Elena at the extreme SE of the city is the garden suburb of Venice. It was largely manmade in the 19thC around a much smaller island. The pretty Gothic church of **Sant' Elena** at the far end of the Viale Sant' Elena was founded in the 13thC and rebuilt by Olivetan monks from 1435. Its fine **portal** (*c*.1475) by Antonio Rizzo is one of the earliest specimens of Renaissance architecture in Venice. In the lunette above is Rizzo's moving **monument to Vittore Cappello**, showing the soldier kneeling before the figure of St Helen.

San Francesco della Vigna 🏛 †
Map 11E9. Campo della Confraternita, Castello. Water bus 1 to Arsenale.
An earlier church of San Francesco della Vigna was built in the 13thC by Observant Franciscan monks on the site of the vineyard (*vigna*) where legend has it that St Mark rested on his journey from Aquilea. In 1534 Doge Andrea Gritti laid the foundation stone of an ambitious new Franciscan church, the building costs of which were underwritten by some of the wealthiest Venetian nobles. It was the architect Jacopo Sansovino's most important religious commission.

The **facade** was not begun until 1568. Although Sansovino was still living, it was entrusted instead to Andrea Palladio, who modified the older architect's plan. This was the first example in Venice of the superimposed temple fronts Palladio was to design later and with greater success for the facades of the *Redentore* and *San Giorgio Maggiore*. The campanile, one of the tallest in

Venice, is easily mistaken for the campanile of San Marco when seen from the water to the N. Built in 1581, it was remodeled in 1758.

Sansovino's largest church **interior** is not his most inspired, but it contains some notable works of art. On the holy water stoups are fine bronze statuettes of *St John the Baptist* and *St Francis* by Alessandro Vittoria. In the right transept, the elaborately decorative and appealing *Madonna and Child* ✿ (*c*.1450) is the only signed work by the Greek artist Antonio da Negroponte. The **Giustiniani Chapel** to the left of the chancel is decorated with charming marble carvings (1478-*c*.1480) by Pietro Lombardo and his studio. Giovanni Bellini's *Madonna and Child with Sts John the Baptist, Francis, Jerome, Sebastian and a Donor* (1507) has now been cleaned and returned to the Cappella Santa, off the left transept. A door nearby gives access to the beautiful 15thC cloister which you should try to see.

Off the left nave, in the fifth chapel, the *Madonna Enthroned with Sts John, Joseph, Catherine and Anthony Abbot* (1551) is a very early work by Veronese, painted before he moved permanently to Venice. The altar of the second chapel off the left nave is decorated with magnificent marble statues of *St Roch, St Anthony Abbot* and *St Sebastian* (1561-64) by Alessandro Vittoria; the figure of St Sebastian was modeled on a *Dying Slave* by Michelangelo.

Returning to the center of the city via Campo San Lorenzo you cross the **Rio di San Lorenzo**, which is flanked by the beautiful palaces depicted by Gentile Bellini in his *Miracle of the True Cross* in the *Accademia*.

San Giacomo dell 'Orio †

*Map **14**B2. Campo San Giacomo dell' Orio, Santa Croce. Water bus 1 to San Stae or Riva di Biasio.*

The Campo San Giacomo dell' Orio is one of those secret places in the heart of Venice, to which access seems to be deliberately concealed in a labyrinth of narrow *calli* and covered passageways. It is a leafy, homey square dominated by the swelling apses of its church, the facade of which, partly obscured by the modest priest's house, faces the canal across Campiello del Piovan.

The church is a 9thC foundation greatly altered over the centuries. The peculiar magic of its **interior** ✿ owes something to the genial mixture of styles and something also to the archaic method of construction. As can be seen at the crossing, the building is held together and supported by a network of wooden beams without benefit of stone arches. The 14thC ship's-keel ceiling is one of only two of its kind in Venice, the other being in *Santo Stefano*.

Two of the columns were plundered from Byzantium during the Fourth Crusade. The one in the right transept was described by d'Annunzio as 'the fossilized condensation of an immense verdant forest'; the other is at the corner of the nave and left transept behind the pulpit. Nearby hangs the *Martyrdom of St Sebastian with Sts Lawrence and Roch* (1498-1500), one of the best works by the Vicentine painter Marescalco. In the apse, the *Madonna and Child with the Parish Priest Giovanni Maria da Ponte*. The **new sacristy** has a ceiling and altarpiece by Veronese.

The custodian also has the keys to the nearby 11thC church of **San Giovanni Decollato** (San Zan Degola), a remarkably intact example of a Veneto-Byzantine church, containing fragments of Byzantine frescoes. Close by, in the Fondamenta del Megio, no.1757 was the house of Marin Sanudo (1466-1536), whose diaries are the most detailed source of information about his period.

San Giacomo di Rialto 🏛 † ☆

Map 15B4. Campo San Giacomo, San Polo. Water bus 1, 2 or 4 to Rialto.

San Giacomo di Rialto, affectionately known to Venetians as San Giacometto, is the oldest church in Venice. Its traditional foundation date is 421, the year of the first settlement at the *Rialto*. The present structure, built in the 11th-12thC as a place of worship for merchants using the Rialto market, is one of the few surviving small Veneto-Byzantine churches in the city. The Gothic portico and the round blue clock are 15thC additions.

The **interior** preserves its original Greek-cross plan and freestanding Greek marble columns which support the only brick dome erected in Venice during the Byzantine period (apart from those of *San Marco*). The Baroque altarpieces, which are disastrously out of proportion in the tiny space, were added during a restoration in the early 17thC.

The church faces the **Campo di Rialto** which was opened as a market in 1097 and became the principal emporium of the Republic. Bankers and insurance brokers conducted their business from booths under the arcades, which were rebuilt in 1515 after a fire devastated the whole Rialto area, sparing only this church.

San Giobbe 🏛 †

Map 4C3. Campo San Giobbe, Cannaregio. Water bus 1, 2, 4 or 5 to the railroad station, or 5 to Ponte Tre Archi.

The Franciscan church of San Giobbe in western Cannaregio is the building which introduced modified Tuscan Renaissance architecture to Venice. It was begun in the mid-15thC by the Gothic architect Antonio Gambello to commemorate a recent visit by the Sienese preacher St Bernardino. In the 1470s a program of enlargement and decoration was entrusted to Pietro Lombardo, who had only recently arrived in Venice. He completed the church in the new classical style he had assimilated on the mainland.

The doorway is surmounted by the figures of *St Bernardino*, *St Anthony of Padua* and *St Louis of Toulouse* with *St Job* and *St Francis of Assisi* in low relief in the lunette — all carved by Pietro Lombardo in 1471. Lombardo also designed the domed **chancel** (*c*.1472) and the magnificent triumphal arch that separates it from the nave. With the help of his son Tullio, he executed the decorative carvings on the arch and below the cupola as well as the *Evangelists* in the spandrels.

The best of the altarpieces painted for this church — Giovanni Bellini's *Sacra Conversazione*, Carpaccio's *Presentation of Jesus* and Marco Basaiti's *Agony in the Garden* — are now in the *Accademia*, having been removed when the monastery of San Giobbe was suppressed under Napoleon. Two notable pictures that remain are the *Nativity* (1540), a late work by the Brescian artist Gerolamo Savoldo in Gambello's ogival **Contarini Chapel**, to the right of the chancel end of the nave; and Antonio Vivarini's triptych of the *Annunciation with Sts Michael and Anthony* (*c*.1450) over the altar of the **Da Mula Chapel** which leads off from the far end of the Renaissance sacristy.

The **Martini Chapel**, second left from the entrance, was built in Tuscan Renaissance style for a wealthy family of silk weavers originally from Lucca. Its design, recalling the Cardinal of Portugal's Chapel in the Florentine church of San Miniato, is attributed to Bernardo Rossellino and the sculptures over the altar to his brother Antonio. The glazed terra-cotta medallions of *Christ* and the *Evangelists* are unique examples in Venice of the art of the Florentine Della Robbia studio.

The fabric of this important church is threatened by rapidly accelerating rising damp which has noticeably affected much of the interior stonework. If the condition is allowed to continue unchecked it could lead to the tragic loss of Pietro Lombardo's carvings on the chancel arch.

Returning to the *Grand Canal* along the Fondamenta San Giobbe, you pass the large 18thC **Palazzo Labia**, the Venetian headquarters of the Italian broadcasting network RAI. The ballroom (*visits by appointment only, Wed, Thurs, Fri 3-4pm* ☎716666) is one of the most stunningly beautiful rooms in the world, let alone in Venice, and is frescoed with scenes from *The Story of Anthony and Cleopatra* ★ by G.B. Tiepolo in a style which unforgettably blends intimacy with grandeur.

San Giorgio dei Greci †
Map 11E8. Calle dei Greci, Castello. Water bus 1, 2, 4 or 5 to San Zaccaria.

Like all ethnic minorities in Republican Venice, the Greeks enjoyed the freedom to worship according to their own faith and to maintain their language and cultural traditions. The colony was substantially enlarged by refugees from Constantinople after it fell to the Turks in 1453, and in 1498 a Greek confraternity was founded under the protection of St Nicholas of Myra.

The church of San Giorgio dei Greci, where the Orthodox community still worships, was built from 1536-61. The interior is richly decorated and hung with paintings in the Byzantine style. The precariously tilted campanile dates from 1587-92. Next to the church are the Greek College and the former Scuola di San Niccolò dei Greci, both 17thC buildings designed by Baldassare Longhena.
Museum of Icons of the Hellenic Institute *(Museo di Icone dell' Instituto Ellenico)*
☎5226581 🖼 🖾 *Open 9am-12.30pm, 2.30-5pm, Sun 9am-noon. Closed Tues.*

The museum is housed in Longhena's Scuola di San Niccolò dei Greci. Exhibits include some 80 paintings by the Greek artists known as the *Maddoneri*, who remained faithful to the manner of Byzantine icon painters into the 17thC.

San Giorgio Maggiore 🏛 † ★
Map 11G8. Isola San Giorgio Maggiore. Open Mon-Sun 9am-12.30pm, 2.30-6.30pm. Water bus 5 or 8 to San Giorgio.

The church of San Giorgio Maggiore floats on its own island in strict, icy majesty, surrounded by the low brick buildings of its monastery and guarded by a tall soldierly campanile and a pair of tiny Neoclassical lighthouses. It is one of that astounding trio of buildings — the others are the *Doges' Palace* and the *Salute* — which play the overture to Venice across the water of its inner harbor.

The island of San Giorgio was occupied from the 10thC by a Benedictine monastery founded and specially favored by the doges. When in 1110 St Stephen's body was brought to Venice from Constantinople this valuable status symbol was personally delivered to San Giorgio by Doge Ordelafo, and the monastery was rededicated to St Stephen as well as St George. The complex was destroyed by an earthquake in 1223 and the buildings you see today date from the 15th-17thC.

In 1565 Andrea Palladio, who had begun a refectory for the monastery five years earlier, was commissioned to build a new church. It was completed in 1576, apart from the facade, which was erected to Palladio's plan in 1611 by Simone Sorella. With the

Redentore, San Giorgio is one of only two Venetian churches designed in their entirety by Palladio. The Istrian stone **facade** is composed of two overlapping temple fronts, supported respectively by four giant Composite columns and eight Corinthian piers. In the niche on the far left is a 16thC portrait bust of *Doge Tribuno Memmo* (held office 979-91), the first permanent memorial to a medieval doge. The otherwise ineffectual Doge Memmo was one of the early benefactors of the monastery, as was Doge Sebastiano Ziani (held office 1172-78) whose **memorial** is in the niche on the far right. The **campanile** modeled on that of San Marco, was erected in 1791 by the Bolognese Benedetto Buratti. It gives one of the most beautiful and extensive views of the lagoon. (☎5289900 ✆ *Open Mon-Fri 9am-12.30pm, 2.30-4.30pm, Sun 11am-12.30pm, 2-4.30pm. Closed Sat*). The facade of the dormitory wing, with its three semi-circular tympana, which faces the lagoon was begun in 1508 by Giovanni Buora.

Of all the colors, none is more proper for churches than white, since the purity of the color, as of life itself, is particularly satisfying to God.
Andrea Palladio, *Quattro Libri dell'Architettura*, 1570

The vast, white, luminous **interior** is in the form of a Latin cross. Its austerity and the disposition of its parts reflect the spirit of the Counter-Reformation — the Council of Trent had come to an end only three years before the church was begun — but the confidently exaggerated use of classical Roman forms was Palladio's own personal invention. The great thermal windows, derived from Roman baths, are of a type which was later to become one of the hallmarks of Palladianism. The giant Composite order of half columns emphasizes the grandeur of the space while the lower Corinthian order of the pilasters gives the interior a human scale.

Over the first altar in the right aisle is a fine *Nativity* (1582) by Jacopo Bassano. Over the altar to the right of the high altar is one of the inaugural Venetian Rococo paintings, *The Madonna and Child with Nine Saints* (1708) by Sebastiano Ricci, influenced by Veronese's *Marriage of St Catherine* in the *Accademia*.

The entrance to the **chancel** is flanked by two elegant bronze **candelabra** (1598) by Niccolò Roccatagliata. The high altar is dominated by Girolamo Campagna's splendid bronze *Globe Surmounted by God the Father and Supported by the Four Evangelists* (1591-95). Tintoretto's *Last Supper as the Institution of the Mass* ☆ on the right wall and *Gathering of the Manna* on the left wall (both 1594) are vigorous masterpieces painted when the artist was nearly 80.

On the rail of the monks' choir behind the altar are fine bronze statues of *St Stephen* and *St George* (1593) by Niccolò Roccatagliata. The choir stalls (1594-98) are decorated with low-relief carvings representing scenes from *The Life of St Benedict* by the Flemish sculptor Albert van der Brulle.

A corridor to the right of the chancel leads to the **Deposition Chapel,** named after Tintoretto's *Deposition* ☆ (1592-94), probably the artist's last work, and one of his most moving masterpieces. The **Coro Invernale** (winter choir) is reached by a spiral staircase. The altarpiece of *St George and the Dragon* (1516) is a studio version of Carpaccio's painting in *San Giorgio degli Schiavoni*.

A covered passage to the left of the chancel leads to the elevator by which you can ascend the **campanile**.

Monastery/Cini Foundation *(Fondazione Giorgio Cini)*
☎89900. *Open for special exhibitions, otherwise visits by
appointment only.*

The monastery has been occupied since 1951 by the Cini
Foundation, one of Italy's most important cultural institutions,
which was given to the city by Count Vittorio Cini in memory of
his son. The architectural highlights of the complex include the
Palladian **Cloister of the Cypresses** (1579-1614), the simpler
Cloister of the Bay Trees (1516-1640), probably designed by
Giovanni and Andrea Buora, and the **Refectory** ☆ (1560),
Palladio's first work in Venice and one of the great rooms of the
world. The **Dormitory** (1493-1533) is by Giovanni Buora. The
monumental **double staircase** ☆ (1641-47), which is among
Longhena's most impressive designs, leads to the **Library** (1641-
53), also by Longhena, which replaced a library built in 1433 by
the Florentine architect Michelozzo.

Plays and operas are performed in the **Teatro Verde** in the
gardens behind.

San Giorgio degli Schiavoni *(Scuola di San Giorgio degli Schiavoni)*★

Map 11E8. Calle Furlani, Castello ☎5228828 📷 *Open
Tues-Sat 9.30am-12.30pm, 3.30-6.30pm; Sun 9.30am-
12.30pm. Closed Mon. Water bus 1, 2 or 4 to San Zaccaria.*

The Schiavoni (Slavs) were Dalmatian merchants who formed an
active trading colony in Venice and in 1451 built their own
confraternity a little way to the N of the Riva degli Schiavoni where
they moored their boats. Their tiny *scuola* contains one of the most
irresistibly appealing sequences of pictures in Venice. Executed by
Vittore Carpaccio between 1502-8, the series depicts scenes from
the lives of the Dalmatian patron saints, Sts George, Tryphon and
Jerome. It is the only one of the five narrative cycles Carpaccio
painted for Venetian confraternities to remain in its original
building.

Inspired, perhaps, by the exotic origins of his clients and the
intimate scale of their *scuola*, Carpaccio gave these stories all the
vivid, immediate charm of fables. One, *St George and the Dragon*,
is a horror story with a happy ending; another, *St Jerome Leading
his Lion into a Monastery*, is a joke about the timidity of friars.
Settings are in some cases Oriental fantasies, in others precisely
described late 15thC Venetian scenes, sometimes a mixture of the
two.

The series represents, on the left wall, *St George Killing the
Dragon* and *The Triumph of St George;* on the altar wall, *St George
Baptizing the Heathen King and Queen* and *St Tryphon Exorcizing
the Daughter of the Emperor Gordianus* (the altarpiece of *The Virgin
and Child* is by Benedetto Carpaccio, Vittore's less talented son) ;
on the right wall, from the altar end, *The Agony in the Garden, The
Calling of St Matthew, St Jerome Leading his Lion into a Monastery,
The Funeral of St Jerome*, and *St Augustine in his Study* ☆.

The last, and by far the greatest, of these pictures is set in a
faithful reconstruction of a late 15thC Venetian study. St
Augustine, who is portrayed as the Greek humanist scholar
Cardinal Bessarion, has been reading a letter from St Jerome
requesting his opinion on a theological matter. Carpaccio has
frozen the story at the precise instant when the saint's study is
filled with light and a miraculous voice reveals to him that St
Jerome is now dead. St Augustine has just taken up his pen to
reply to the letter, the books he has been consulting lie open
around him and his little dog, who will doubtless begin to bark

when the action resumes, is momentarily transfixed by the light.

In the nearby church, San Giovanni dei Cavalieri di Malta, is a charming *Baptism of Christ* by the school of Giovanni Bellini, with some touches perhaps by the master himself.

San Giovanni in Bragora 🏛 †
Map 11F8. Campo Bandiera e Moro, Castello. Water bus 1 to Arsenale.

The pretty Gothic church of San Giovanni in Bragora stands in one corner of this large, peaceful campo just behind the Riva degli Schiavoni. No one knows what *bragora* means, but the name may derive from the Venetian *bragola* (market place) or *bragolare* (fishing trade). The building dates from 1475-90 and the interior retains its pleasant Gothic character despite modifications in the 18thC. Antonio Vivaldi was baptised in this church in 1678.

The church contains three important late 15thC pictures which illustrate the transition from the late Gothic to Renaissance styles. In the chapel to the left of the chancel is a triptych of *The Virgin with Sts John the Baptist and Andrew* (1478) by Bartolomeo Vivarini. The gold background and artificially posed figures remind one how long Venetian painters clung to Gothic traditions. To the right of the chancel is a *Resurrection* (1498) by Bartolomeo's nephew Alvise Vivarini. This picture was as innovatory for its date as Bartolomeo's triptych was conservative. It was admired by Giorgione and Titian and in some respects looks forward even further, to the late 16thC. The vigorous figure of Christ, dramatically thrust into the foreground, is based on a statue of *Apollo* in the *Archeological Museum*. Behind the high altar, the *Baptism of Christ* ✰ (1492-95) is one of Cima da Conegliano's masterpieces, set in an inviting mountain landscape.

On the other side of the campo, no.3608 is the handsome 15thC Gothic **Palazzo Gritti Badoer**, now the hotel La Residenza. Above its central windows there is a 10thC Byzantine relief of a peacock.

San Giovanni Crisostomo 🏛 † ✰
Map 15B5. Campo San Giovanni Crisostomo, Cannaregio. Water bus 1, 2 or 4 to Rialto.

Mauro Codussi's last church, begun in 1497 and completed by the year of his death in 1504, is modestly dressed in terra-cotta colored stucco and squeezed into a tiny campo just N of the *Rialto*. San Giovanni Crisostomo was built for a poor and densely populated Venetian parish.

The interior is one of Codussi's most satisfying spaces, spoiled only by the flat ceiling of the choir, which replaced the original barrel vault in the 17thC. The central dome is supported, like that of *San Giacomo di Rialto*, by freestanding pillars. As in his *Santa Maria Formosa*, Codussi followed the Greek-cross plan of a Veneto-Byzantine church. Nevertheless, the effect of this interior is very different from that of the earlier church. Here the upward sweep of the vaulting gives a vertical emphasis; and the classical orders are more fully expressed, with Corinthian capitals on the pilasters carrying a full entablature.

The church contains two masterpieces of early 16thC painting, both influenced by Giorgione. Over the first altar in the right aisle is Giovanni Bellini's *St Jerome with Sts Christopher and Augustine* ★ (1513), one of the few Bellinis in which there is no Madonna. The pillar in the center of the church is carved in the style of Tullio Lombardo, who is represented over the second altar in the left aisle by one of his most confidently classical carvings, *The Coronation of the Virgin* (1500-2).

Over the high altar is Sebastiano del Piombo's painting of the church's patron saint, *St John Chrysostomus with Six Saints* ★ (1508-10). The composition is a deliberate improvement on Carpaccio's similarly organized but rather stilted *Presentation of Jesus* in the *Accademia*. The novelist Henry James described the central female figure, the Magdalen, as if she were the inspiration for one of his own heroines, 'leaving the susceptible observer with the impression of having made, or rather having missed, a dangerous, but most valuable acquaintance.'

An archway behind the church leads to two courtyards called 'del Milione' after the nickname given to Marco Polo by those who thought he exaggerated his account of his voyages to the Far East. In the second, the **Corte Seconda del Milione**, a round-headed Veneto-Byzantine arch survives from what may have been the Polo family palace.

San Giovanni Evangelista *(Scuola di San Giovanni Evangelista)* 🏛

*Map **14**B2. Campiello di San Giovanni, San Polo.*
☎ 5224134 ⊡ *Visits by previous appointment Mon-Fri 9.30am-12.30pm. Closed Sat and Sun. Water bus 1 to San Tomà.*

The Scuola di San Giovanni Evangelista, which stands just to the N of the *Frari*, is approached through a **marble screen and courtyard** ★ (1481) designed by Pietro Lombardo. The lunette over the screen contains the eagle, symbol of St John the Evangelist, patron saint of the confraternity, and is surmounted by a cross signifying the relic of the True Cross that was presented to the *scuola* in 1369. The possession of this precious relic greatly enhanced the prestige of the confraternity, which had been founded in the previous century, and occasioned the building of a new headquarters, completed in 1454. The more elaborate of the two doorways to the *scuola* was added in 1512.

She looks a sea Cybele, fresh from Ocean,
Rising with her tiara of proud towers
At airy distance, with majestic motion,
A Ruler of the waters and their powers:
Byron, Childe Harold's Pilgrimage, Canto IV, 1816

The principal attraction of the interior is Codussi's domed and barrel-vaulted double-ramp **staircase** ★ (1498), a masterpiece of Renaissance architecture and one of Codussi's most brilliant designs. It leads to the *albergo*, or committee room, which was redecorated in 1727 by Giorgio Massari. In the adjoining oratory, the relic of the True Cross is preserved in a silver and crystal Gothic **reliquary** (1379) on the altar. The cycle of canvases painted for this oratory by Gentile Bellini, Carpaccio and others, depicting miracles performed by the True Cross, is now in the *Accademia*.

Opposite the *scuola* is the church of **San Giovanni Evangelista**, a 15thC building much restored from the 16th-18thC.

Santi Giovanni e Paolo 🏛 ✝ ★

*Map **10**D7. Campo Santi Giovanni e Paolo, Castello. Water bus 1, 2 or 4 to Rialto, or 5 to Fondamenta Nuove.*

After the Piazza *San Marco*, the most spectacular square in Venice, architecturally, sculpturally and historically, is the Campo Santi Giovanni e Paolo. The great, gaunt Dominican church dedicated to Sts John and Paul (their names are conflated by Venetian dialect to San Zanipòlo) is the largest Gothic religious building in the city and, as the pantheon of Venetian political and military leaders, gives through its monuments a clear impression of the development of Venetian sculpture. Its importance is rivaled only by the Franciscan *Frari* across the city. The church is flanked by two of the most outstanding achievements of the Italian Renaissance: the **Scuola Grande di San Marco** and the **equestrian monument to Bartolomeo Colleoni**.

These three monuments to the Venetian preoccupation with religious reform, organized charity and military leadership were erected over a period of some two and a half centuries on a marshy island granted to the Dominicans by Doge Giacomo Tiepolo in 1234. The site was originally on the edge of the lagoon, which was later filled in to the N of the Scuola di San Marco. The most dramatic approach to the church is from the Calle Larga Gallina to the W.

The church of Santi Giovanni e Paolo was begun in the mid-13thC, two decades after the site was granted, but was not completed and consecrated until 1430. The lower section of the facade remains from the original building. The magnificent Gothic-Renaissance **portal**, attributed to Antonio Gambello, was erected after 1458. To the left is the tomb of *Doge Giacomo Tiepolo* (1229-49), the first of 25 doges to be buried in this church between 1248 and 1778. Before entering the church, walk around the s flank, noticing the handsome 16thC **wellhead**, and admire the polygonal **apse**, a rare example in Venice of 14thC Gothic architecture uncompromised by later accretions.

The **interior** ★ makes a stronger and more coherent first impression than that of the Frari and all the more so since the recent cleaning of its stone monuments. Both monastic churches are in the form of a Latin cross terminating in apsidal chapels; they are approximately the same length and width, but the nave of Santi Giovanni e Paolo is taller. Entering the church by the W door, you have a clear view down the length of the nave, which is divided into three aisles by monumental, widely-spaced columns, to the slender ogival windows of the central apse.

This vista was originally interrupted by a monks' choir — as it still is in the Frari — but this was removed in the 17thC. The beautiful color combination of dusky red brick and pale gray stone is characteristic of Venetian Gothic churches, as are the wooden tie-beams that give the light, flexible structure its lateral support.

On the interior facade are tombs of the Mocenigo family. The **monument to Doge Giovanni Mocenigo** (1478-85) near the N corner is by Tullio Lombardo. Near the s corner, Pietro Lombardo's **monument to Doge Pietro Mocenigo** ☆ (1474-76), erected in 1485, celebrates the Doge's military career. In the right aisle, over the second altar, is Giovanni Bellini's early masterpiece, the polyptych of *St Vincent Ferrer* ★ (after 1465). The towering figures of Sts Vincent Ferrer, Sebastian and Christopher originally gazed upward toward a panel of *God the Father*, now lost. The original gilded frame was one of the first in Venice carved in the style of the classical Renaissance.

Farther along is the **Chapel of the Addolorata**, built in the 15thC, with its Gothic appearance now disguised by 17thC Baroque decorations. Off the top end of the aisle before the crossing is the **San Domenico Chapel** (1690-1716), built by Andrea Tirli to designs by Antonio Gaspari. G.B. Piazzetta's soaring *Glory of St Dominic* ★ (1727) is the artist's only ceiling painting and one of the most exhilarating examples of its period. The chiaroscuro tondos of *The Cardinal Virtues* at the corners are also by Piazzetta. The powerful bronze high reliefs on the walls

Santi Giovanni e Paolo

portraying *Scenes from the Life of St Dominic* (1715-20) are by Giuseppe Mazza.

The **right transept** is lit by the magnificent **stained-glass window** (*c*.1470-73) made in Murano by the master glazier Antonio Lincinio da Lodi to designs by Bartolomeo Vivarini and Cima da Conegliano. The window has recently been restored. Two notable pictures in the transept are Alvise Vivarini's *Christ Carrying the Cross* (1474) and Lorenzo Lotto's *St Antonino Pieruzzi, Archbishop of Florence, Giving Alms* (1542). In the first **apse chapel**, the altar and the bronze statues of *The Virgin* and *St John the Evangelist* are by Alessandro Vittoria. The **monument to Sir Edward Windsor** (*died* 1574), an English ambassador to Venice, is also attributed to Vittoria.

The Baroque high altar in the **chancel** is thought to be by Longhena. On the right wall are the 15thC **monument to Doge Michele Morosini** (1382), which Ruskin called 'the richest monument of the Gothic period in Venice' and the clumsily portentous **monument to Doge Leonardo Loredan** (1501-21), built in 1572 to a design by G.G. Grapiglia, with allegorical statues and reliefs by Danese Cattaneo.

On the left wall, nearest the altar, the **monument to Doge Andrea Vendramin ★** (1476-78), designed after 1493 by Pietro Lombardo and carved by Tullio Lombardo, is generally considered to be the masterpiece of Venetian Renaissance funerary art. This 'manifesto of Venetian classicism' (John Pope-Hennessy) inspired one of Ruskin's bitterest tirades against the 'dishonesty,' 'coldness of feeling' and 'moral degradation' of the 'pestilential art of the Renaissance.'

The two **warrior saints** in niches by Lorenzo Bregno replace Tullio Lombardo's *Adam* and *Eve*. The *Adam* is now in the Metropolitan Museum of Art, New York; the *Eve* is in the Vendramin Calergi Palace in Venice. To the left of the Vendramin monument, above the incomplete Gothic **monument to Doge Marco Corner**, are statues of the *Madonna and Child with Saints* by Nino Pisano.

The far wall of the **left transept** is occupied by monuments to the Venier family including, over the door, the **monument to Doge Antonio Venier** (1382-1400), one of the earliest doges' tombs in the church, by the International Gothic sculptor Pier Paolo Dalle Masegne. To the right of the door is the **monument to Doge Sebastiano Venier** (1577-78), who had commanded the Venetian fleet at the Battle of Lepanto in 1571.

The door leads to the **Chapel of the Rosary** built by the Confraternity of the Rosary in thanksgiving for the victory of Lepanto on the Madonna's feast day in 1571. Originally decorated with important works by leading late 16thC Venetian artists, it lost its precious contents in a fire in the 19thC. The most tragic loss was Titian's masterpiece, *St Peter Martyr*, a copy of which hangs in the left aisle of the church. The chapel was restored in 1913. The ceiling paintings by Veronese are from another church and the chancel is a reconstruction. The engaging *Archangel St Michael Defeating Lucifer* on the right wall is attributed to the Brescian painter Moretto or to the Veronese Bonifacio de' Pitati.

Returning to the **left aisle** of the church, under the funerary monument the painter Palma il Giovane designed for himself, is the entrance to the 16thC **sacristy**, which contains two paintings by Palma: *The Crucifixion* over the altar and *The Resurrection* to its right. Next to the sacristy door is the **monument to Doge Pasquale Malipiero** (1457-62), the first work Pietro Lombardo executed in Venice and the first Venetian tomb to show the influence of the Florentine Renaissance — although the canopy over the effigy is still in the Gothic style.

Farther along is the eclectic **monument to Doge Tommaso Mocenigo** (1414-23) by the Tuscans Pietro Lamberti and Giovanni di Martino da Fiesole, which Ruskin overpraised as a 'noble image of a king's mortality' in order to contrast it with the loathed Vendramin monument. Next to it is the fine Renaissance **monument to Doge Nicolò Marcello** ☆ (1473-74) by Pietro Lombardo. On the altar nearest the entrance, the statue of *St Jerome* ☆ (1576) is a late, powerful work by Vittoria modeled on Michelangelo's *Rebellious Slave*, and can now be seen in the Louvre in Paris.

We have seen thirteen thousand St Jeromes, and twenty-two thousand St Marks, and sixteen thousand St Matthews, and sixty thousand St Sebastians, and four millions of assorted monks, undesignated, and we feel encouraged to believe that when we have seen some more of these various pictures, and had a larger experience, we shall begin to take an absorbing interest in them like our cultivated countrymen from *Amerique*.

Mark Twain, *The Innocents Abroad*, 1867

The **monument to Bartolomeo Colleoni** ★ to the s of the church facade is the most exciting and, along with Donatello's *Gattamelata* monument in Padua, the most famous Renaissance equestrian statue in northern Italy. It was modeled by the Florentine sculptor Andrea Verrocchio from 1481-88, cast in Venice after Verrocchio's death, and set up in the square in 1496.

The rider is an idealized portrait of one of these esteemed mercenary commanders, a native of Bergamo who died in 1475 leaving the government a large bequest on condition that a bronze statue of himself should be raised near the Basilica of San Marco. With Colleoni dead and his money invested in the Turkish war, the government, always unwilling to commemorate any individual, much less a foreigner, in the city's political center, played him the small-minded trick of placing his memorial in front of the Scuola rather than the Basilica of San Marco.

The **Scuola Grande di San Marco** ★ (now the civic hospital, to which visitors are welcome on application) is one of the oddest buildings in Venice. It was begun c.1488 on the foundations of an earlier Gothic building which had been destroyed by fire, and was erected in two stages.

The architects of the lower order were Pietro Lombardo and Giovanni Buora. The four illusionist arcades — filled with boldly foreshortened **lions of St Mark** on either side of the main door and with reliefs of *Scenes from the Legend of St Mark* on each side of the subsidiary entrance — were carved by Tullio Lombardo. Although the perspective — which recedes to a vanishing point behind each door, leaving the viewer cross-eyed — only works on a decorative level, it represents the first attempt by a Venetian sculptor to integrate his work into its architectural setting. The relief of *St Mark Venerated by Members of the Confraternity* and the figure of *Charity* over the main door are attributed to Bartolomeo Bon.

Mauro Codussi completed the upper order of the facade c.1495. The lunettes of the roofline, which emphasize the asymmetry of the facade and may be intended to echo the domes of the Basilica of San Marco, are characteristic of his style.

The **interior** is chiefly worth visiting for the **double-branched staircase**, a reconstruction of Codussi's original, which was pulled down in 1819, and for the **coffered ceiling** of the Sala dell' Albergo, now the Medical Library. The *Scenes from the Legend of St Mark* painted for the Confraternity by Gentile and Giovanni Bellini, Carpaccio and Tintoretto are now in the *Accademia* and the Brera in Milan.

On the Fondamenta dei Mendicanti, which follows the flank of the hospital to the Fondamente Nuove, is the hospital church of **San Lazzaro dei Mendicanti** with a restrained Palladian facade (1673) by Giuseppe Sardi. Inside is a splendidly youthful work by Tintoretto, *St Ursula with the Eleven Thousand Virgins*.

San Giuliano *(San Zulian)* 🏛 †
Map 15D5. Campo San Zulian, San Marco. Water bus 1, 2 or 4 to San Marco or Rialto.

The facade of San Giuliano (1553-55) was designed by Jacopo Sansovino and his pupil Alessandro Vittoria for Tommaso Rangone, a fashionable philosopher-physician whose **bronze effigy** is over the main door. Rangone is portrayed in his role as scholar, further emphasized by the Greek and Hebrew inscriptions and allegorical carvings decorating the facade.

While the facade was under construction the ceiling of the church collapsed. The interior was rebuilt and redecorated in the sumptuous taste of the late 16th and early 17thC. The central ceiling painting of *The Apotheosis of St Julian* (1585) is one of Palma il Giovane's better works. The first altarpiece on the right, the *Pietà above Sts Roch, Mark and Jerome* (1584), is a late work by Veronese. Over the second altar on the left is a serene, early 16thC *Madonna and Four Saints* by the Ferrarese Boccaccio Boccaccino. On the walls of the sanctuary hang two huge, violent Baroque fantasies, *A Miracle of St Julian* and *The Martyrdom of St Julian* (1674), by Antonio Zanchi.

The **Sacramental Chapel** to the left of the sanctuary was designed by Giovanni Antonio Rusconi. The splendid **altar** (1583) is carved with a marble relief of *The Dead Christ with Angels* and flanked by bronzed terra cottas of *The Virgin* and *The Magdalen*, all by Girolamo Campagna.

San Marco ★
*Map 15D5. Water bus 1, 2, 4 or 5 to San Marco or San
Zaccaria.*

For Venetians there is only one Piazza. The other squares of
Venice are called *campi* (literally, fields) ; and as for the piazzas of
other great Italian cities, which of them bears comparison with this
most exciting and improbable of all public spaces, the central
square of Venice which, as Goethe said, can only be compared to
itself? 'I don't know that there can be anything like it on this
earth,' exclaimed Petrarch, one of the earliest of the countless
writers and artists who have described this unique piazza in all its
many moods.

Sometimes it seems like an Oriental bazaar, a little tawdry you
might think if you are a fastidious Florence-lover; at other
moments, it is how Napoleon saw it — the most elegant
drawing-room in Europe. But it always remains a theater, where
each tourist plays a dramatic role under the ever-shifting Venetian
light, whether in the festive crowd scenes of midsummer or in the
melancholy romance of a misty winter's evening.

The Piazza San Marco has always been animated by various
kinds of popular entertainment, some more suitable than others.
In the past it had executions and gambling. Today it has 'the
insupportable café orchestras that never give one a moment's
respite,' as Lorenzetti complained in an uncharacteristically
irritable moment; and, of course, the pigeons, which delight
visitors, but worry the conservationists who have tried to find a
merciful way of controlling their population since discovering that
they are a major cause of stone erosion.

But it has also been the stage for the solemn official celebrations
recorded by Venetian painters from Gentile Bellini — whose
Corpus Domini Procession in the *Accademia* gives us the most
vivid and detailed picture of the Piazza at the end of the 15thC —
to Canaletto.

The buildings around the Piazza span the thousand-year history
of the Venetian Republic from the 9thC, when the Basilica and
Campanile were begun, to the early 19thC, when Napoleon tore
down a church at the far end to make way for a ballroom.

In the early 16thC the Byzantine N wing of the Piazza, which
appears in Bellini's painting, was replaced by Mauro Codussi's
Procuratie Vecchie, the residences of the Procurators of San
Marco, the highest government officials after the doge who were
responsible for the fabric of the Basilica and the Piazza.

In 1529, the Procurators hired the architect and sculptor Jacopo
Sansovino, who had fled to Venice after the Sack of Rome, to
continue the process of dignifying and modernizing the Piazza.
Sansovino's **Marciana Library**, which forms the corner into the
Piazzetta facing the *Doges' Palace*, was one of the earliest
classical Roman buildings in the city; its design was later repeated
along the s side of the Piazza when a new procurators' residence,
the **Procuratie Nuove**, was built.

The pavement of the Piazza, in Euganean trachyte and white
Istrian stone, was laid in 1723 to a design by Andrea Tirali.
Basilica 🏛 ✝ ★
Open Mon-Sun 9.30am-5.30pm.
In 828, the body of St Mark, stolen from his tomb in Alexandria,
was brought to Venice. The event, known in Venetian mythology
as the *traslatio*, was one of the most significant in the history of the
Most Serene Republic. St Mark quickly displaced the Greek
soldier St Theodore as patron saint of Venice, and his role grew
into something far greater than that played by the protector saints

of other cities. He became the law-giver, the chief alibi for political and military ambition. It was in his name that Venice conquered, and his winged lion, the symbol of Venetian power and justice, was installed throughout the city and its expanding empire.

The church of San Marco was built to enshrine the body of the saint, who was not only a political figurehead but also the rival of St Peter, patron saint of the church of Rome. St Peter's church (*San Pietro di Castello* — formerly the cathedral of Venice) was located on the remote island of Castello until the patriarchal seat was finally transferred to San Marco in 1807.

A treasure-heap, it seems, partly of gold, and partly of opal and mother-of-pearl . . . . a confusion of delight, amidst which the breasts of the Greek horses are seen blazing in their breadth of golden strength, and the St Mark's lion, lifted on a blue field covered with stars, until at last, as if in ecstasy, the crests of the arches break into a marble foam, and toss themselves far into the blue sky in flashes and wreaths of sculptured spray, as if the breakers on the Lido shore had been frost-bound before they fell.
Ruskin, *The Stones of Venice*, 1851-53

Under the Republic, the Basilica of San Marco was the doges' private chapel, the church of the Venetian government. It was a government that sought to enhance its social prestige while holding its sword to the East and its shield to the West. Under its administration, Venetian merchants grew fabulously rich through dealing in precious goods and this wealth is reflected in the splendid decorations of the Doges' Chapel.

Only traces of the first 9thC church remain visible. The present building, modeled on the Church of the Holy Apostles in Constantinople, dates essentially from the end of the 11thC, although the exterior appearance has been radically altered. In the 13thC, the domes were raised to their present soaring height and surmounted by their onion-shaped lanterns, and in the 14th and 15thC, the plain round arches of the roofline were surmounted by their exhilarating Gothic carvings.

Over the centuries, the walls of the Doges' Chapel were encrusted with a magnificent miscellany of mosaics, sheets of rare marble and carvings. Some of these embellishments were plunder, some were executed by visiting Byzantine craftsmen, but after the 13thC they were made by Italians whose workmanship increasingly reflected the prevailing styles of Western Europe. The spirit in which they were applied, like jewels to a giant reliquary, remained essentially Oriental. The result, as Bernard Berenson wrote, is 'the most typical, the most complete and the most satisfactory Byzantine edifice now in existence.'

Exterior ☆

A picture of the Basilica as it appeared in the 13thC is seen in the lunette mosaic of *The Translation of the Body of St Mark* ☆ above the northernmost of the five doors. This is the only original mosaic left on the facade. Over the next door, the 18thC mosaic of the *Magistrates Adoring the Body of St Mark* is from a cartoon by Sebastiano Ricci. The other mosaics are 17th-19thC.

The **relief carvings ☆** (1225-60) on the three receding arches of the main entrance are the earliest Romanesque sculptures in Venice and among the most important in Italy. Notice especially those of Venetian trades and crafts on the inner curve of the outer arch. The centerpiece of the upper order comprised until recently **four gilded bronze horses**, now thought to be Hellenistic Roman sculptures of the early 4thC, stolen from Constantinople during the Fourth Crusade. When placed on the facade in 1222, they were potent emblems of Venetian imperial pride. Napoleon delivered a painfully significant blow when he carried them off to Paris in 1797, where they remained until the sculptor Canova helped negotiate their return in 1815. They are now threatened by another enemy, atmospheric pollution, and have been removed inside to the Basilica's museum; those now on the facade are copies.

A grand and dreamy structure, of immense proportions; golden with old mosaics; redolent of perfumes; dim with the smoke of incense; costly in treasure of precious stones and metals, glittering through iron bars; holy with the bodies of deceased saints; rainbow-hued with windows of stained glass; dark with carved woods and coloured marbles; obscure in its vast heights and lengthened distances, shining with silver lamps and winking lights; unreal, fantastic, solemn, inconceivable throughout.

Dickens, *Pictures from Italy*, 1844

The **Gothic carvings** ☆ that bristle from the roofline were begun in 1385, probably by the dalle Masegne brothers, and continued in the early 15thC by Lombard and Tuscan sculptors. They are best studied from the **Loggia dei Cavalli**, where the bronze horses once stood. The carvings on the central arch and the statue of *St Mark* above are by Pietro di Niccolò Lamberti. The statues in the outer aedicules of the *Virgin Annunciate* and *Angel* are attributed to Jacopo della Quercia.

The s facade, facing the waterfront next to the entrance to the *Doges' Palace*, was originally the ceremonial entrance to the Basilica; it was also the first facade to be seen from the water by visiting dignitaries, who were forcefully reminded of Venice's military power by the display of trophies looted during 13thC conquests. The apprehensive-looking porphyry figures on the corner, known as *The Tetrarchs* and traditionally said to represent Diocletian and three other rulers, are 4thC Egyptian sculptures taken from Byzantium during the Fourth Crusade.

The two freestanding pillars bearing rare 6thC Syrian carvings were brought from Acre after the victory over Genoa in 1256, as was the porphyry stump known as the *Pietra del Bando* (proclamation stone), from which Venetian laws were announced to the public.

There is more plunder set into the n facade facing the Piazzetta dei Leoncini. In the fourth bay, the **Porta dei Fiori** has finely carved 13thC Moorish arches enclosing a pleasing Romanesque relief of the *Nativity*.

Interior ★

San Marco will never reveal itself fully to the sightseer who, however diligently, visits it only once. It should be seen in as many different lights as possible: when the gold ground of the mosaics blazes in the reflected sunlight of a fine midday, in the smoky glow of evening, and, best of all, in the flickering candlelight of a high service.

The **portico** (or narthex) of the Basilica originally ran around three sides but was later closed on the s by the Zen Chapel and Baptistry. The 13thC **mosaics** in the arches and cupolas depict scenes from the Old Testament, beginning in the s cupola where the liveliest of the Genesis stories is the *Creation of Adam and Eve* ★ The mosaics of *Apostles* on either side of the central doorway survive from the early 12thC Basilica.

Before entering the main body of the church, take your bearings by climbing the steep staircase from the portico to the **galleries** above (■ ☎ *5225205. Museum, Pala d'Oro and Treasury open Mon-Sat 9.30am-5.30pm, Sun 1.30-5.30pm. Keep the ticket for the museum which can be visited later*). From the catwalk which runs all the way around the nave and transepts you can see that, although San Marco is always called a basilica, its plan is actually that of a Greek cross slightly elongated to bring it closer to a Western Latin cross. It is surmounted by five domes, erected in the 11thC, each of which takes its lateral support from four thick barrel vaults. The galleries are enclosed by a balustrade bearing 6th-11thC Byzantine **relief panels** and supported by Greek marble columns with exquisite Byzantine and classical **capitals** ✩ The lower walls are coated in sheets of Oriental marble.

Mosaics ★

Above the level of the galleries the entire wall surface, an area of 4,046sq.m (about one acre) is covered with 11th-19thC mosaics executed in a variety of styles and heavily restored (only a third of the surface is original). Many of the mosaics are most easily examined from the galleries, but the full impact of their glittering opulence can only be appreciated from the church below.

Whereas the mosaics in the portico represent the world of the Old Testament, anticipating the coming of Christ, those inside the church depict scenes from the New Testament after the triumph of Christ's teaching. Thus, passing from the portico into the church, you enter the era of grace. The most important of the Byzantine mosaics are in the first two cupolas, on the walls of the aisles and in the right transept.

The oldest mosaics in the church, dating from the 11thC are the figures of *The Evangelists* in the portico and *Sts Peter and Nicholas* in the main apse.

Some of the most impressive are the early 13thC *Passion Scenes* in the w vault and the *Ascension of Christ* in the central cupola over the crossing. On the walls of the aisles are the figures of the *Madonna* and *Four Prophets* (right wall) and *Christ Blessing* and *Four Prophets* (left wall). These vibrant, magnificently hierarchical mosaics dating from *c.*1230 are superb examples of the fusion of Byzantine and Romanesque styles.

The cupola over the chancel shows the *Religion of Christ as Foretold by the Prophets*. Over the left transept, the cupola mosaics illustrate *Scenes from the Life of St John*. In the right transept, notice particularly among the 12th-13thC *Scenes from the Life of Christ* in the arch nearest the nave, the *Temptation of Christ in the Desert*.

Other monuments and works of art

The **marble mosaics** of the pavement, dating from the 12thC but often restored, are laid in a wide variety of designs.

The **iconostasis**, the marble rood screen that divides the raised chancel from the nave, bears **marble statues** ★ of *The Virgin*, *The Twelve Apostles*, and *St Mark* (1394), mature, naturalistic works by the Gothic sculptors Jacobello and Pier Paolo dalle Masegne.

In the **left transept**, set in a jewelled frame on the altar, is the miraculous icon of the *Madonna of Nicopeia, Bringer of Victory* (10thC), which Byzantine emperors carried into battle before it was stolen by the Venetians in 1204. There are two chapels built out from the head of the transept. The **St Isidore Chapel** (1355) enshrines the remains of St Isidore, whose body was stolen from Chios in 1125. Mosaics and carvings on the tomb tell his story.

The 15thC **Mascoli Chapel** ✩ is named after the male (*mascoli*) members of a confraternity who worshiped here in the 17thC. The altar statues of the *Madonna*, *St Mark* and *St John the Evangelist* are by an unknown master whose style suggests the

San Marco

Mosaics
A   Stories from Genesis, including the *Creation of Adam and Eve* (13thC)
B   The *Apostles* (12thC)
C   *Pentecost* and *Apostles Preaching to the Nations* (mid-12thC)
D   *Ascension of Christ* (early 13thC)
E   *Madonna and Four Prophets* (early 13thC)
F   *Christ Blessing and Four Prophets* (13thC)
G   *Religion of Christ as Foretold by the Prophets* (12thC)
H   *Sts Nicholas, Peter, Mark and Hermagorus* (early 13thC)
I   *Scenes from the Life of St John* (end 12thC)
J   *Scenes from the Life of Christ,* including *Temptation in the Desert* (12th-13thC)
K   *Scenes from the Life of the Virgin,* including (left) *Birth* and *Presentation* and (right) *Visitation* and *Death* (15thC)
L   *Scenes from the Lives of the Baptist and Christ,* including *Banquet of Herod* (14thC)

influence of the Venetian dalle Masegne brothers and the Florentine Donatello.

The pictorial styles of 15thC Venice and Florence meet in the **vault mosaics** depicting *The Life of the Virgin.* On the left side, *The Birth* and *The Presentation* are signed by the Gothic Venetian artist Michele Giambono. On the right are *The Visitation,* attributed to Jacopo Bellini, and *The Death of the Virgin,* which makes confident use of the Florentine technique of focused perspective and has been attributed to Andrea Castagno.

The **chancel** (🎟 *ticket also admits you to the treasury*) houses the Pala d'Oro and is entered from the right through the **St Clement Chapel,** which contains sculptures by the dalle Masegne brothers. The baldachino above the altar is supported by four alabaster columns carved with beautiful but baffling *Scenes from the New Testament,* which could be either 6thC Byzantine or mid-13thC

Venetian. The **sarcophagus of St Mark** lies beneath the altar.

The bronze statues of *The Evangelists* (1550-52) on the balustrade and the reliefs of the *Martyrdom and Miracles of St Mark* (1537-44) on the walls on either side of the altar are by Jacopo Sansovino. The concave **sacristy door** (1546-69) behind the altar on the left is Sansovino's last masterpiece. The reliefs, based on Ghiberti's *Gates of Paradise* in Florence, represent *The Entombment* and *The Resurrection*. Among the busts in the small surrounding panels are a self-portrait and portraits of Sansovino's contemporaries, Aretino, Titian, Veronese and Palladio.

The **Pala d'Oro** ★ — the most renowned of San Marco's treasures and the most important ecclesiastical object in Venice — stands behind the high altar. This extraordinary gold altarpiece, enriched with precious stones and cloisonné enamelwork, was originally made in Constantinople in 976 for Doge Pietro Orseolo, enlarged with more panels in the 12thC and again in the 13thC, and finally rearranged in 1342 and placed in the Gothic frame that we see today.

In the upper section, the Archangel Michael is surrounded by roundels of saints flanked by scenes from the New Testament. In the lower part, the Pantocrator is surrounded by 14thC Venetian-made panels and enamels made in Constantinople; in the border are scenes from the lives of the Evangelists, perhaps from the 12thC altarpiece.

The **treasury** ★ (■ *ticket also admits you to the chancel and Pala d'Oro*) is entered from the top of the right transept under a sinuously curved Moorish arch. It contains the richest hoard of Byzantine gold and silver work in the world, much of it plundered during the conquest of Constantinople. The prize piece is the 12th-13thC **gilded silver incense burner** in the form of a Byzantine church.

The **baptistry**, entered from the bottom of the right aisle, was built into the s wing of the portico on the instructions of Doge Andrea Dandolo (1343-54), the scholar-prince who was Petrarch's friend. Dandolo's Gothic tomb was described by Ruskin as 'the best existing example of Venetian monumental sculpture.' In front of it is the font designed by Sansovino, who lies buried at the E end of the chapel.

The **mosaics** (1342-54) illustrating *Scenes from the Lives of the Baptist and Christ*, are an interesting demonstration of the Byzantine style giving way to the more naturalistic tendencies of Gothic painting, especially evident in the *Banquet of Herod* over the entrance door. The altar is made from a granite slab on which Christ is supposed to have stood when he preached in Tyre.

The **Zen Chapel** ★ (1504-21), entered from the s end of the portico, has recently been restored and reopened. It was designed by Paolo Savin and Antonio Lombardo as the funerary chapel of Cardinal Giovanni Battista Zen, who left his fortune to the Republic on condition that he be buried in the Basilica of San Marco. His bronze tomb, in the antique style, and the bronze altar were begun by Alessandro Leopardi and Antonio Lombardo and finished by Paolo Savin. The beautiful bronze statue on the altar, the *Madonna and Child* ★ known as the *Madonna of the Shoe* (1515), is by Antonio Lombardo.

The **museum** (■) located in the galleries above the church, is reached by a steep, narrow staircase from the portico. As well as the four gilded bronze horses brought inside from the loggia, the collection includes fragments of early mosaics from the Basilica, panel paintings, Oriental carpets, and tapestries. Of special interest is the painted wooden **cover made for the Pala d'Oro**

(1345), signed by Paolo Veneziano and his two sons, which depicts in the lower section seven *Scenes from the Life of St Mark* and in the upper part, *Christ, the Virgin and Saints*.

Among the tapestries displayed in the second part of the museum, notice especially the ten *Scenes of the Passion* (*c.*1420) woven from cartoons by Niccolò di Pietro. The splendid 15thC silk Persian carpets, interwoven with gold and silver threads, were gifts from Persian ambassadors in the 17thC.

There is a fine view of the Piazza from the Loggia dei Cavalli (see above).

Piazza ★

The **flagstaffs** in front of the Basilica rise from ornate bronze pedestals (1505) cast by Alessandro Leopardi.

The **Piazzetta dei Leoncini** to the left of the Basilica is named after the two red marble lions, favorite mounts of Venetian and visiting children since they were carved in 1722. On the E side of the Piazzetta is the Neoclassical **Bishop's Palace**, built after San Marco became the cathedral of Venice. To the N, the former church of **San Basso** (1675), with a facade by Longhena, is used for temporary exhibitions.

The **Torre dell'Orologio** ★ or Clock Tower (1496-1500) (☎5231879 ▥ *open Tues-Sat 9am-noon, 3-5pm; Sun, hols 9am-noon; closed Mon*) forms the archway to the **Mercerie**, one of the principal shopping streets and a short cut to the *Rialto*. The central tower was designed by Mauro Codussi and the two wings were added in 1506, possibly by Pietro Lombardo. During Ascension Week and at Epiphany the figures of the Magi emerge hourly from the side doors above the clock and bow to the Madonna. The two so-called Moors that strike the hours from the top of the tower are made of gun-metal cast in the *Arsenale* in 1497. The mechanism of the clock may be examined inside the tower.

Wonderful San Marco, the Saint Sophia of the West, the colossal reliquary of Venetian civilization, a gilded cavern, diapered with mosaics, a vast heaping up of jasper, porphyry, alabaster, and fragments of antiquity, a pirate cathedral enriched with the spoils of the universe.

Théophile Gautier, Voyage en Italie

To the left of the Clock Tower, the long building that forms the N wing of the Piazza is the **Procuratie Vecchie** (1500-12), designed by Mauro Codussi as residences for the Procurators of San Marco, and partially rebuilt by Bartolomeo Bon and Guglielmo dei Grigi after a fire. The rapid rhythm of the arcading reflects the design of the Byzantine building it replaced and of the Orseolo hospice which stood opposite until 1582, when it was torn down to make room for a new procurators' residence. The stately **Procuratie Nuove** (1584-1640) was begun by Vincenzo Scamozzi in the style of Sansovino's Marciana Library (see below), which it joins at the E corner, and later extended to the W by Longhena.

During the Napoleonic regime, the Procuratie Nuove became the Royal Palace (its official address today is ex-Palazzo Reale) and the two Procuratie were joined at the W end of the Piazza by the Neoclassical **Ala Napoleonica** (1808-14), designed by Giovanni Maria Soli to house a grand ballroom. The Ala Napoleonica and parts of the Procuratie Nuove are occupied by the *Correr Museum*.

The massive brick **Campanile** ★ of San Marco (☎5224064 ▥ *open for ascent 9.30-10pm*) is the tallest in Venice at nearly 100m (325ft). It was begun in the 9thC shortly after the first Basilica and assumed its present appearance in 1514 when the stone spire and gilded angel were added during a restoration directed by Bartolomeo Bon. The Campanile has served as lighthouse, watchtower and astronomical observatory. It survived a thousand years of earthquakes and lightning strikes, until in July 1902 it became in imminent danger of collapse. On the morning of July 14 it fell in upon itself, smashing the *loggetta* at its base and all but the largest of the bells, but inflicting no further damage. It was decided that evening that the Campanile would be rebuilt '*com'era, dov'era*' (as it was, where it was) ; and a new tower, an exact replica, was inaugurated in 1912.

The belfry may be reached by elevator or by a spiral of ramps originally designed to take visitors up on horseback. Few have disagreed with Thomas Coryat, the 17thC traveler, that the view from the top must be 'the fairest and goodliest prospect that is in all the world.' The most beautiful, densely built and topographically baffling of cities is laid out below like a model of itself in a setting which, on a clear day, extends E over the domes of the Basilica to the Istrian Peninsula, N over the Procuratie Vecchie to Monte Grappa and the Alps, w over the Ala Napoleonica to the Euganean Hills and s over the Procuratie Nuove to the open waters of the Adriatic.

At the base of the Campanile is the **loggetta** ☆ built by Jacopo Sansovino between 1538-40 as a meeting place for patricians. A painstaking restoration completed in the late 1970s has revealed the rich colors of its materials, red Verona marble and Istrian stone, with carved details in Carrara marble and *verde antica*.

The **loggetta** is in the form of a Roman triumphal arch and its sculptural decoration is an allegorical glorification of the Venetian government. Sansovino's supremely elegant bronze statues ★ in the niches represent the qualities and aims of good government: *Pallas* (wisdom), *Mercury* (eloquence), *Apollo* (harmonious administration) and *Peace*. The oblong marble reliefs above show *Venice as Justice* flanked by allegories of *Crete* and *Cyprus*, Venice's two largest overseas colonies. Inside is Sansovino's moving terra-cotta group of the *Madonna and Child with St John*.

Piazzetta

The Piazzetta di San Marco extends from the Basilica to the waterfront, with the *Doges' Palace* to the E and the Marciana Library to the w. The two great granite **columns** were brought from the Levant in the 12thC. One is surmounted by the figure of *St Theodore*, the first patron saint of Venice, the other by the *Lion of St Mark*. The engineer who accomplished the difficult feat of raising these columns was rewarded with the right to set up gambling tables between them. Executions also took place here; and in the early 16thC before Sansovino was given the task of dignifying the Piazza, the space between the columns was occupied by food stalls and latrines.

The **Marciana Library** ★ or Library of St Mark (1537-88) was designed by Sansovino to house the collection of manuscripts bequeathed to the Republic in the previous century by Cardinal Bessarion, the Greek emigré and humanist. Palladio judged it 'the richest, most ornate building since Antiquity,' and ever since it has been considered Sansovino's architectural masterpiece. The state rooms of the interior, frescoed by Titian, Veronese and Tintoretto and containing among their printed treasures the **Grimani Breviary**, the famous 15thC world map drawn by Fra Mauro, and Marco Polo's will, are unfortunately closed to the public. The reading rooms (*open Mon-Fri 9am-7pm, Sat 9am-1.30pm, closed Sun: telephone application only* ☎*5208788*) are entered from no.7.

San Marcuola

Facing the water next to the library is the **Zecca** ☆ the state treasury and mint. Begun in 1536, this fortress-like building was Sansovino's first important architectural commission in Venice. It replaced the earlier mint where the first golden ducat was issued in 1284.

San Marcuola *(Santi Ermarcora e Fortunato)* †
Map 5C5. Campo San Marcuola, Cannaregio. Water bus 1 to San Marcuola.

The church of San Marcuola stands across the *Grand Canal* from the Fondaco dei Turchi (which houses the *Natural History Museum*). It has one of the few unfinished facades in Venice but the **interior** (1728-36) is an elegant and unusual design by Giorgio Massari, lavishly decorated with statues by Giovanni Morlaiter. The outstanding work of art in the church, on the left wall of the chancel, is Tintoretto's *Last Supper* (1547), his first treatment of this subject and a fine example of his early style.

Santa Maria della Fava †
Map 15C5. Campo Santa Maria della Fava, San Marco. Water bus 1, 2 or 4 to Rialto.

This early 18thC church not far from the *Rialto* is named after the bean-shaped sweets that were once made in a nearby *pasticceria*. It contains two fine 18thC paintings, G.B. Tiepolo's *Education of the Virgin* (1732), an early work which hangs over the first altar on the right, and G.B. Piazzetta's *Virgin and Child with St Philip Neri* (1725-27), which is over the second altar on the left.

Santa Maria Formosa �III † ☆
Map 15C6. Campo Santa Maria Formosa, Castello. Water bus 1, 2 or 4 to Rialto or 1, 2, 4 or 5 to San Zaccaria.

The lively market square of Santa Maria Formosa is one of the largest and most attractive open spaces in Venice. Although only a short walk from *San Marco*, it preserves a special domestic character of its own and, perhaps because it lies off the main route to the *Rialto*, has the atmosphere of a place which is miles rather than minutes from the tourists' Venice. The eccentrically rambling perimeter of the campo, studded with handsome palaces, takes in at its SE end Mauro Codussi's parish church, one of the few freestanding churches in the city.

The church of Santa Maria Formosa is dedicated to the Virgin who is said to have appeared in the guise of a buxom *(formosa)* matron to the Bishop of Oderzo in the 7thC and caused him to found the church. The present building was begun in 1492 by Codussi, who died before the exterior was completed. The two principal facades, one facing the campo (1604), the other facing the canal (1542), were financed by members of the Cappello family who are commemorated on both. At the base of the Baroque **campanile** (1688) is a grotesque mask, 'leering in brutal degradation,' wrote the appalled Ruskin, 'too foul to be either pictured or described, or to be beheld for more than an instant.'

Codussi's **interior** plan follows the foundations of the original Greek-cross church but with the nave slightly elongated to form a Latin cross. The church possesses two pictures of special interest.

In the first chapel to the right of the canal entrance is a triptych of *The Madonna of Mercy* (1473) by Bartolomeo Vivarini, painted for the high altar of the original church and paid for by the congregation. In the right transept is Palma il Vecchio's masterpiece, *The Martyrdom of St Barbara* ☆ (*c.*1509). St Barbara was the patron saint of gunners and this work was painted for the first Venetian artillerymen's training school, headquartered at Santa Maria Formosa. George Eliot was impressed by the robust femininity of this St Barbara, whom she described as 'an almost unique presentation of a hero-woman.'

Of the palaces in the campo the finest is no.5250 (across the canal from the apse end of the church), the early 16thC **Palazzo Malipiero-Trevisan**, attributed to Sante Lombardo, Tullio's son. No.5246, with Veneto-Byzantine decorations above its central windows, is **Palazzo Vitturi**. No.5866, the soberly classical **Palazzo Ruzzini-Priuli** (c.1580), closes the end of the campo opposite the church. Nos.6125-26 are the ogival **Palazzi Donà**.

Off the Rialto end of the campo, across the Ponte del Paradiso, there is an early 15thC Gothic **archway** bearing a charming relief of the *Madonna of Mercy* and the coats of arms of the Foscari and Mocenigo families.

Santa Maria Mater Domini ⌂ †
Map 14B3. Calle della Chiesa, Santa Croce. Water bus 1 to San Stae.
The recently restored church of Santa Maria Mater Domini was built between 1504-40. The architect is unknown, but the crisp early Renaissance style of the interior suggests Mauro Codussi, Pietro Lombardo or Giovanni Buora. The second altarpiece on the right, depicting *The Vision of St Christina* ★ (1521), is the masterpiece of Vincenzo Catena, a follower of Bellini and Giorgione.

In the picturesque campo next to the church there is a fine 14thC **wellhead** and some good palaces. The earliest of these, no.2174, is the **Casa Zane**, with a 13thC four-light window and Byzantine carvings embedded in the wall above. No.2120, **Palazzo Viaro-Zane**, has a row of 14thC Gothic windows on the first story and a Renaissance second story.

Santa Maria dei Miracoli   See *Miracoli*.

Santa Maria della Salute   See *Salute*.

San Marziale †
Map 6C6. Campo San Marziale, Cannaregio. Water bus 1 to San Marcuola.
The Baroque church of San Marziale is chiefly visited for the soaring, luminous **ceiling paintings** (1705) which established the reputation of Sebastiano Ricci as the leading Venetian painter of his day. They represent *God the Father Surrounded by Angels*, *The Glory of St Martial*, *The Miraculous Arrival of the Image of the Virgin*, and *The Image of the Virgin Carved on a Tree Trunk*.

San Michele in Isola   The cemetery island of Venice, graced by Mauro Codussi's beautiful white church, is only a 5min boat ride away from the city. (See *San Michele* in *The Venetian lagoon*).

San Moisè †
Map 15E4. Campo San Moisè, San Marco. Water bus 1, 2 or 4 to San Marco.
The church of San Moisè faces the San Marco end of the Calle Larga XXII Marzo — one of the most conspicuous positions in Venice. Ruskin called it 'one of the basest examples of the basest school of the Renaissance,' but many people today find the riotous confusion of its Baroque facade more appealing than the slick

modernity of the Bauer Grünwald hotel next door, which was built in the 1960s.

The **facade** was erected in 1668 to a design by Alessandro Tremignon and its overbearingly crowded carvings were executed by Heinrich Meyring. Tremignon and Meyring also collaborated on the high altar, a supercharged monument of bad taste which represents *Moses on Mount Sinai Receiving the Tablets*. The **interior** is otherwise lavishly decorated with 17th and 18thC paintings and sculptures, but the only major work of art is in the sacristy. Here, the altar frontal contains a bronze relief, *The Allegory of Redemption with the Dead Christ Surrounded by Angels* (1633) by Niccolò and Sebastiano Roccatagliata, one of the first Venetian relief sculptures to look forward to the Baroque style.

San Nicolò dei Mendicoli 🏛 †

Map 8F2. Campo San Nicolò, Dorsoduro. Water bus 5 to San Basilio.

The parish church of the working-class district of Santa Marta in the extreme sw corner of Venice is one of the oldest and most endearingly individual buildings in the city. Founded in the 7thC, it was rebuilt in the 12thC and subsequently modified in the variety of styles which contribute to its special charm.

The squat campanile survives from the 12thC. The 15thC portico on the w facade is the only remaining example in Venice, apart from that at *San Giacomo di Rialto*, of a once common architectural feature. The entrance portal facing the campo was applied in the 18thC.

The intimate atmosphere of the **interior** is created by an appealing mixture of simple and splendid elements. The oldest parts are the apse and the 12thC columns of the nave, which have 14thC capitals. The nave is decorated in a similar way to that of the *Carmini*, with gilded wooden statues and panel paintings on the upper walls. These date from the 16thC, as does the organ above the w door.

In the apse is a large wooden statue of *St Nicholas* by the Bon studio. A comprehensive restoration of the fabric of the church and its contents was completed in 1977.

While you are in this slightly remote corner of Venice, you might also visit the churches of *Angelo Raffaele* and *San Sebastiano*.

San Nicolò da Tolentino 🏛 †

Map 4E3. Campo dei Tolentini, Santa Croce. Water bus 1, 2, 4 or 5 to Piazzale Roma.

This handsome church near Piazzale Roma is a striking example of the enduring influence exercised by Andrea Palladio on Venetian architecture. It was begun in 1590 for the recently established Theatine order by Vinceno Scamozzi, who based the plan of the chancel and crossing on a design by Palladio. Scamozzi was dismissed from the job in 1599 before the facade was completed. From 1706-14 Andrea Tirali, inspired by some of Palladio's mainland villas, added the severely correct Corinthian **portico**, the first projecting temple front erected in Venice.

The church contains two remarkable 17thC pictures by mainland artists, both anticipating the Rococo style developed in the next century by Piazzetta and Tiepolo. Outside the first chapel on the left is the Genoese Bernardo Strozzi's vigorous, tightly painted *St Lawrence Giving Alms*. On the left wall outside the chancel is an exuberant, freely-executed *St Jerome Surrounded by Angels* by the German-born artist Jan Liss.

On the left wall of the chancel is the **monument to Francesco Morosini** (died 1678) by Filippo Parodi, one of the most splendid Baroque monuments in Venice.

San Pantalon †

Map 9E4. Campo San Pantalon, Dorsoduro. Water bus 1 or 4 to San Tomà.

The church of San Pantalon, located between the *Frari* and Campo Santa Margherita, was built between 1668-86. Despite the stark appearance of its exterior — it has one of the few unfinished facades in Venice — it contains one of the city's major surprises. The vaulted **ceiling** ✰ of the Palladian interior is surrounded by a loggia, open to the sky at its center, and populated by a crowd of boldly foreshortened figures re-enacting the events leading to *The Martyrdom and Apotheosis of St Pantalon*.

The scale and style of this vast illusionist canvas, a synthesis of the perspective techniques perfected by Veronese and Tintoretto and the fantasy of Roman Baroque painting, are unique in Venice. It is the masterpiece of Gian Antonio Fumiani, who worked on it from 1680-1704.

There are two other important paintings in the church. In the second chapel on the right, *San Pantalon Healing a Boy*, recently cleaned, is Paolo Veronese's last work, completed by his son Carletto Caliari. In the Chapel of the Holy Nail to the left of the chancel is a *Coronation of the Virgin* (1444) by Antonio Vivarini and Giovanni d'Alemagna.

The elaborate Baroque **high altar** (1668-71) is by Giuseppe Sardi.

San Pietro di Castello †

Map 13F11. Isola di San Pietro. Water bus 1 to Giardini.

The island of Castello, at the E edge of the central Venetian archipelago, was the first to be inhabited by settlers from the original lagoon communities. In 775 a bishopric was founded and a church built in the previous century was dedicated to St Peter and designated as the cathedral of Venice.

San Pietro di Castello remained the cathedral church of Venice throughout the thousand-year life of the Venetian Republic. Since relations between the Church and the Venetian state were generally characterized by mutual distrust and occasionally even outright hostility, it suited the Republican government that the patriarchal seat (as it became in 1451) should be physically remote from the administrative and commercial centers at *San Marco* and the *Rialto*. It was only in 1807, 10yrs after the fall of the Republic, that the title of cathedral was transferred from St Peter's church to St Mark's — to the Basilica of San Marco, formerly the private chapel of the doges.

The name Castello, now given to the easternmost *sestiere* of Venice, is thought to have derived from a Roman-built fortress of which no trace remains.

The church stands in a grassy, tree-fringed square facing the broad San Pietro canal. The building is unremarkable apart from its charming situation and its lofty, leaning **campanile** ✰ rebuilt from 1482-88 by Mauro Codussi. Although Codussi retained the Gothic lines of the earlier bell tower, he clad the new structure with Istrian stone. This was the first, and is still among the most impressive, of the gleaming white Venetian bell towers.

The **facade** was originally designed by Palladio in 1557 but, as realized by Franco Smeraldi in 1596, it was reduced to a mere pastiche of the Palladian style. The **interior**, also loosely based on a plan by Palladio, was completed in 1621. It contains a number of 17thC paintings by Pietro Liberi, Pietro Ricchi and Luca Giordano. In the Lando Chapel, off the right aisle, is a bust of *San Lorenzo Giustiniani*, the first Patriarch of Venice, by a follower of Antonio Rizzo.

San Polo †

Map 14C3. Campo San Polo, San Polo. Water bus 1 to San Silvestro or 1 or 4 to San Tomà.

Campo San Polo is the largest square in Venice after San Marco. It was once the scene of bull baiting, military parades and masked carnival balls. Nowadays it is usually filled with children, careening around the perimeter on bicycles and playing soccer in the center.

The church, which faces away from the SE corner, is a medieval foundation largely rebuilt in 15thC Gothic style and drastically restored and oversimplified in the early 19thC. It retains its Gothic lancet windows and doorway. At the base of the **campanile** (1362) across the *salizzada* from the entrance are two 12thC lions, rare examples in Venice of Romanesque carving.

The **interior** contains some fine works by the Tiepolos, father and son. In the chapel entered under the organ there are 14 *Stations of the Cross* (1747), vivid and moving youthful works by Giandomenico. His father, Giambattista, is represented over the second altar on the left by *The Virgin Appearing to St Julian Nepomuk* (1754). On the high altar are impressive bronze statues of *St Paul* and *St Anthony Abbot* by Alessandro Vittoria.

The **campo** is surrounded by some notable palaces. No.2128 is the **Palazzo Corner Mocenigo.** Its principal facade (*c.*1543), designed by the great Veronese architect Michele Sanmicheli, faces the Rio di San Polo and can be seen from the San Polo Bridge. Frederick Rolfe, alias Baron Corvo, wrote his novel, *The Desire and Pursuit of the Whole*, here; the manuscript so shocked his hosts that they turned him out onto the streets. On the opposite side of the square, nos.2169-71 are the 15thC Gothic **Palazzi Soranzo** and no.1957 is the 18thC **Palazzo Tiepolo** (no connection whatever with the artists), with its main facade facing the Rio della Madonnetta.

After a few minutes' walk toward the *Rialto* you come to **Campo Sant' Aponal**. Over the door of the church there are late 13thC carvings of *The Crucifixion* and scenes from *The Life of Christ*. A right turn out of Campo Sant' Aponal toward the *Grand Canal* brings you into **Campo San Silvestro**, where the 19thC church contains a dramatic painting by Tintoretto of *The Baptism of Christ* (*c.*1580).

San Rocco ★

Map 14C1. Campo San Rocco, San Polo. Water bus 1 or 4 to San Tomà.

The *scuola* and church of San Rocco stand at right angles to each other in a little campo at the apse end of the *Frari*.

Scuola Grande di San Rocco
☎ 5234864 ▥ ▨ *Open summer Mon-Sun 9am-1pm, 3.30-6.30pm.*

The Scuola Grande di San Rocco, one of the great charitable institutions of Renaissance Venice, was founded in 1478 under the protection of St Roch, patron saint of plague victims. The building was begun in 1516 by Bartolomeo Bon and completed in 1549 by Antonio Scarpagnino. The elaborately carved and inlaid decorations of the asymmetrical facade were made possible by donations from citizens seeking protection against the plague of

1527; unfortunately they do nothing to reconcile its stylistic incoherence.

The **interior** is hung with one of the most important Italian painting cycles, executed between 1564-87 by Jacopo Tintoretto, the greatest Venetian painter to succeed Titian. The San Rocco pictures were Tintoretto's major achievement and only here can you experience the full impact of his fervent, visionary, unresolved artistic personality. ' . . . .We shall scarcely find four walls elsewhere that enclose within a like area an equal quantity of genius,' wrote Henry James. 'The air is thick with it and dense and difficult to breathe; for it was genius that was not happy, inasmuch as it lacked the art to fix itself for ever. It is not immortality that we breathe at the Scuola di San Rocco, but conscious, reluctant mortality.'

It was a great mastery of light and shadow which enabled Tintoretto to put into his pictures all the poetry there was in his soul without once tempting us to think that he might have found better expression in words. The poetry which quickens most of his works in the Scuola di San Rocco is almost entirely a matter of light and color.
Bernard Berenson, *The Venetian Painters of the Renaissance*, 1894

To follow the series in chronological order, climb Scarpagnino's grand staircase to the first floor and begin in the **albergo**, or committee room, where Tintoretto worked from 1564-66. The ceiling panel of *St Roch in Glory* is the work which won him the commission to decorate the rest of the *scuola*. His competitors — Veronese, Salviati and Zuccari — submitted sketches, but Tintoretto outdid them by producing a completed painting. It is said that he was accused of cheating.

On the wall opposite the entrance is *The Crucifixion* ★ (1565), the largest, most spectacular and moving work in the cycle. Tilting outwards from the crowded stage, the figure of Christ compels our own participation in the central drama of Christianity. The other pictures on the walls represent *Christ before Pilate* ✪ *Christ Carrying the Cross* and an *Ecce Homo*. On one of the easels is another *Christ Carrying the Cross* ✪ traditionally attributed to Giorgione although recent evidence suggests that it was painted by Titian around 1508-9.

The large **upper hall** was decorated between 1576-81. On the wall opposite the altar are paintings of *St Roch* and *St Sebastian*. On the long wall opposite the staircases *The Nativity* ✪ is an almost journalistic account, transfigured by Tintoretto's sense of the power of its meaning; also on this wall are paintings of *The Baptism*, *The Resurrection*, *The Agony in the Garden* and *The Last Supper*. On the staircase wall are: *The Miracle of the Loaves and Fishes*, *The Resurrection of Lazarus*, *The Ascension*, *The Pool of Bethesda* and *The Temptation of Christ*. These New Testament scenes are prefigured by Old Testament stories on the **ceiling**, also selected to emphasize the three charitable obligations of the confraternity, which followed St Roch's example in alleviating thirst, hunger and illness.

On easels in front of the altar are an *Annunciation* by Titian, a *Visitation* by Tintoretto and two early paintings by G.B. Tiepolo of *Abraham and the Angels* and *Hagar and the Angels*. Near the door to the *albergo* is a portrait, possibly a self-portrait, by Tintoretto. The *trompe-l'oeil* **bookcase** that runs around the lower walls of the room is decorated with curious Baroque carvings by the 17thC sculptor Francesco Pianta.

On the staircase leading to the ground floor is a painting by Antonio Zanchi depicting *The Plague of 1630*.

The eight pictures in the **ground floor hall** were begun in 1583 and completed in 1587 when Tintoretto was nearly 70. On the wall opposite the staircase is his *Annunciation* ✰. No earlier treatment of this theme had shown such a brutal invasion of private life and no work in San Rocco so clearly displays Tintoretto's bitter belief that God could only prise mankind free by force. Other paintings on the same wall include *The Adoration of the Magi*, *The Flight into Egypt* ✰ set in one of the most hauntingly beautiful landscapes ever painted, *The Slaughter of the Innocents* and *St Mary Magdalen* ✰. On the staircase wall are *St Mary of Egypt* ✰, *The Circumcision* and *The Assumption of the Virgin*.

Church of San Rocco
The 18thC facade repeats the classical motifs of the *scuola*. Just inside the door are two splendid Rococo sculptures of *David* and *St Cecilia* (1743) by Giovanni Marchiori. In the left nave, the paintings of *St Martin* and *St Christopher* are by the early 16thC N Italian artist Giovanni Antonio Pordenone. The walls of the chancel are hung with four large canvases by Tintoretto, depicting miracles performed by St Roch. The most powerful is *St Roch Healing the Plague Victims* (1549) on the right wall.

San Salvatore ⅏ † ★
Map 15C4. Campo San Salvador, San Marco. Water bus 1, 2 or 4 to Rialto.
San Salvatore was built for the wealthy monastic order of the Augustinian Regular Canons. It has a rather routine Baroque facade (1663) by Giuseppe Sardi, but the **interior** (1505-34) is one of the most powerful and original of all Italian Renaissance churches. The plan, devised by Giorgio Spavento, was carried forward after his death in 1509 by Tullio Lombardo and brought to completion by Jacopo Sansovino. The lanterns were cut into the cupolas in 1574 by Vincenzo Scamozzi.

The immaculately controlled geometric divisions of the space and the combination of gray stone and white plaster are reminiscent of 15thC Tuscan architecture. But the design is actually based on a traditional type of Veneto-Byzantine church, of which the most notable example is of course *San Marco*. Mauro Codussi had already revived the Greek-cross plan for his nearby church of *San Giovanni Crisostomo*. Here, three domed Greek crosses are joined together to form a long nave and side aisles which, with the addition of short transepts at the E end, make the overall plan that of a Latin cross. The architectural unity of the interior is emphasized by the use of capitals. This was the first Venetian church in which capitals fully expressed support: Corinthian capitals bear the entablature; Ionic capitals, rising from the same pedestals, carry the arches around the aisle domes.

The church is well endowed with good 16thC Mannerist sculpture. In the right aisle, between the second and third altars, Jacopo Sansovino's **monument to Doge Francesco Venier** (1556-61) is, like his loggia at San Marco, in the form of a triumphal arch displaying allegorical figures — in this case *Charity* and *Faith*. The *Faith* was Sansovino's last work.

Titian's *The Annunciation* (1559-66) over the third altar is also the work of an artist in old age. Some admire it as an example of his late, so-called impressionistic manner; others cite the murky colors and areas of inept drawing as evidence that it must be largely a studio work. Vasari, at any rate, wrote that Titian himself did not much care for it. At the bottom of the right transept is the huge

monument to **Caterina Cornaro, Queen of Cyprus** (1580-84) by
Bernardino Contino, which seems to anticipate, even if rather
awkwardly, the cold simplicity of Neoclassicism. The relief shows
The Queen Handing over her Kingdom to the Doge.

Over the high altar is a *Transfiguration* (*c.*1560) by Titian,
painted as the cover for the silver-gilt reredos; and in the chapel
which opens to the left of the sanctuary there is a copy of a lost
Supper at Emmaus by Giovanni Bellini. The third altar of the right
aisle is **the altar of the Luganegheri**, or Sausagemakers' Guild. It
was designed by Alessandro Vittoria, who also carved the emotive
figures of *St Roch* and *St Sebastian* (*c.*1600). The *St Sebastian*, one
of Vittoria's masterpieces, was modeled on Michelangelo's *Dying
Slave*, now in the Louvre in Paris.

In the campo to the left of San Salvatore is the former **Scuola di
San Teodoro**, now used for temporary exhibitions. Its facade
(1655), like that of the church, was designed by Sardi.

San Sebastiano 🏛 † ★

*Map 8F3. Campo San Sebastiano, Dorsoduro. Water bus 1,
2 or 4 to Accademia. Irregular opening hours.*

San Sebastiano is Paolo Veronese's church. It was here that he
made his reputation 2yrs after he had moved to Venice from his
native Verona, and here that he was buried in 1588, having
transformed the unprepossessing little 16thC church at the sw
corner of the city into one of the most joyously beautiful interiors
in Venice. San Sebastiano is virtually a museum of Veronese, just
as *San Rocco* is of his very different contemporary, Tintoretto.

To follow Veronese's magnificent pictorial cycle in chronological
order, begin your visit in the **sacristy**, reached by the door under
the organ. The virtuoso ceiling panels of *The Coronation of the
Virgin* and *The Four Evangelists* are the earliest works by Veronese
in the church, painted in 1555. They made him famous but they
show his style not yet fully matured. Only a year later, when he
was still in his 20s, he demonstrated the lyrical range of his palette,
and his mastery of perspective, with the radiant, brilliantly
composed ceiling paintings of *The Story of Esther* ★ in the nave.
They represent *Esther Taken to Ahasuerus, Esther Crowned Queen
by Ahasuerus* and the *Triumph of Mordecai.*

Now climb the stairs to the monks' choir. Veronese painted the
chiaroscuro frieze of sybils, prophets and *trompe-l'oeil* columns
after the nave ceiling with the help of his studio, and in 1558 he
frescoed the E end of the choir with *St Sebastian before Diocletian*
and *The Martyrdom of St Sebastian.* In the following year, 1559, he
began the painting for the high altar, *The Virgin in Glory with Sts
Sebastian, Peter, Catherine and Francis* ★ and in 1560 he
completed the paintings on the **organ doors** ★ in the left nave
which show, on the outside, *The Presentation of Jesus at the Temple*
and, on the inside, *The Pool of Bethesda.*

Finally, in 1565, Veronese began the two enormous scenes from
the life of St Sebastian in the chancel: *St Mark and St Marcellino
Encouraged by St Sebastian* ★ on the left, and on the right the
Martyrdom of St Sebastian. The radiant sensuality of these pictures
makes it hard to remember that they are tragic subjects. Veronese
is buried near the organ.

Looking across the rio from the N end of the Fondamenta di San
Sebastiano you can see the 14thC **Palazzo Arian** (no.2376), one of
the earliest Venetian Gothic palaces, with delicate window tracery
on the second floor that gives it an almost Moorish quality.

Two other notable churches in the area are *Angelo Raffaele*
and *San Nicolò dei Mendicoli.*

San Stae 🏛 ✝

Map **14**A3. Campo San Stae, Santa Croce. Water bus 1 to San Stae.

The striking Neo-Palladian facade of San Stae, facing the *Grand Canal* near *Ca' Pesaro*, was the masterpiece of the Swiss-born architect Domenico Rossi. It was applied to the church in 1709 and adorned with animated Baroque statues by contemporary sculptors, including Antonio Corradini who carved the figures of *The Redeemer, Faith* and *Hope*.

The 17thC **interior** is chiefly interesting for the pictures in the chancel where many of the leading 18thC Venetian artists are represented with youthful works. The best are, on the right side, *The Martyrdom of St Bartholomew* by G.B. Tiepolo and *The Crucifixion of St Andrew* by Antonio Pellegrini; on the left side, *The Martyrdom of St James the Great* by G.B. Piazzetta and *The Liberation of St Peter* by Sebastiano Ricci, who also painted the ceiling fresco above the altar, representing *The Adoration of the Sacrament*.

Santo Stefano 🏛 ✝ ☆

Map **14**D3. Campo Francesco Morosini, San Marco. Water bus 1, 2 or 4 to Accademia or 1 to Sant'Angelo.

The handsome Gothic church of Santo Stefano stands at the N end of one of the city's most elegant large squares and most natural of children's playgrounds. You will rarely see the central statue of *Niccolò Tommaseo* without a swarm of children at his feet and a roosting pigeon on his head. The long building on the W side of the square (no.2945) is **Palazzo Loredan**, built in 1536 by Antonio Scarpagnino and now the headquarters of the Venetian Institute of Sciences, Letters and Arts.

The church presents its S flank to the square. It was built in the 14th and 15thC for the Augustinian friars. The flamboyant spray of Gothic foliage over the doorway was carved in the 1430s by the studio of Bartolomeo Bon.

The **interior** is graced with unusually rich architectural decorations. The magificent **ship's-keel ceiling** is one of only two of its kind in Venice, the other being in *San Giacomo dell'Orio*. The carved wooden tie-beams are characteristic of Venetian Gothic churches, as is the red and white color scheme carried out by the slender columns of polished Greek and Verona marble. The ogival arches are frescoed with rampant foliage and the brickwork of the walls above is diaper-patterned as in the *Doges' Palace*. The most notable sculptures on the interior facade are the **monument to Giacomo Surian** (1488-93), by Pietro Lombardo and his sons, and Antonio Canova's **monument to Giovanni Falier** (1808), the sculptor's first patron. A slab tomb in front of the first altar on the left marks the burial place of the composer Giovanni Gabrielli.

In the **sacristy** there are two late works by Tintoretto, *The Agony in the Garden* and *Christ Washing the Disciples' Feet*, also *The Last Supper* by the school of Tintoretto — all very badly lit. The **monks' choir** behind the high altar is furnished with elaborately carved Gothic stalls (1488) by Marco and Francesco Cozzi.

The 16thC **cloister**, entered from the left aisle, retains fragments of a frescoed frieze by Pordenone. The monastery is now occupied by the Ministry of Finance.

From the far end of the cloister a door leads into **Campo Sant' Angelo**. From here you can look back at the alarmingly tilted 16thC **campanile** of Santo Stefano. The composer Domenico Cimarosa died in the Gothic **Palazzo Duodo**, no.3584, in 1801.

At the *Accademia* end of Campo Morosini is the deconsecrated

church of **San Vitale**, now an art gallery. It has an early 18thC
Neo-Palladian facade by Andrea Tirali and inside, over the high
altar, a painting by Carpaccio of *St Vitalis on Horseback* (1514).

San Trovaso †

*Map 14E1. Campo San Trovaso, Dorsoduro. Water bus 1, 2
or 4 to Accademia or 5 to Zattere.*

The present building was begun around 1585 after the partial
collapse of an earlier church on the site. One of its two blandly
Palladian facades faces the canal (notice the 12th-13thC relief
carvings of *St Peter* on the house next to the campanile) ; the other
faces the peaceful campo. The original purpose of the raised block
in the middle of the campo was to provide storage space for the
clay cases that purified water collected from the well.

In the chapel to the right of the altar you can see the outstanding
artistic treasure of the church, the painting of *St Chrisogonus on
Horseback* ✰ (*c*.1450) by Michele Giambono, the leading Venetian
interpreter of the International Gothic style. In the chapel in the
right transept, the altar carving of *Angels Carrying the Instruments of
the Passion* (1470) is one of the earliest low reliefs of the Venetian
Renaissance.

The picturesque **Squero di San Trovaso** (*squero* is Venetian for
boatyard), where gondolas have been built and repaired for
centuries, is best seen from the Fondamenta Nani across the canal.
No.960-61 on the Fondamenta Nani is the splendid Gothic
Palazzo Nani.

San Zaccaria ▥ † ★

*Map 11E8. Campo San Zaccaria, Castello. Water bus 1, 2, 4
or 5 to San Zaccaria.*

The first church of San Zaccaria was built in the 9thC to enshrine
the remains of John the Baptist's father, which had been presented
to the Doge as a gesture of friendship by the Byzantine Emperor
Leo V. The Benedictine monastery that grew up around the
foundation continued to enjoy the favor of emperors and doges and
soon acquired extensive properties, including what is now the
Piazza *San Marco*. The wealth and prestige of San Zaccaria
explain the successive programs of rebuilding which eventually
eclipsed all but a few traces of the first 9th and 12thC churches,
culminating in the remarkable Gothic-Renaissance building we see
today.

To the right of the tall, tiered Istrian-stone facade are the
remains of the previous church, finally rebuilt in the mid-15thC
except for its 13thC **campanile**, one of the oldest bell towers in
Venice. To the left of the new church the campo is enclosed by the
arcaded portico of the late 15thC cloister.

The **new church** of San Zaccaria was financed by the Senate and
begun in 1458 by the Gothic architect Antonio Gambello, who
worked on his ambitious but traditional plan until his death in
1481. In 1483 the project was entrusted to the innovatory
Renaissance architect Mauro Codussi, who had established his
reputation in Venice with the church of *San Michele in Isola*.
San Zaccaria was finally completed in 1515, nine years after
Codussi's death.

On the high, elegant Gothic base of the **facade**, Codussi lightly
piled three airy, arcaded tiers, terminating in the semi-circular
lunette that was one of his favorite devices. He respected the
Gothic plan and the proportions of Gambello's unfinished **interior**
but continued building the upper parts — arches, vaulted ceiling,
cupola — in the radically different style of the Renaissance.

Architecturally, the most interesting sections of the church are the **ambulatory** which runs around the back of the high altar (it is the only post-Byzantine ambulatory in Venice), where Codussi replaced the original rib vaults with a ring of elliptical cupolas and the **choir**, where Gothic and Renaissance styles are marvelously well-integrated.

In front of the first two pillars at the entrance end of the nave are two holy water stoups surmounted by finely carved statues of *The Baptist* and *St Zaccharias* by Alessandro Vittoria (who lies buried in the tomb he designed for himself, next to the sacristy door at the top of the left aisle). Over the second altar in the left aisle is Giovanni Bellini's *Madonna and Child with Sts Peter, Catherine, Lucy and Jerome* ★ (1505), the last of Bellini's *Sacre Conversazioni* and, some would say, the greatest, especially since the successful restoration carried out in 1976.

The walls of the nave are crowded with Baroque canvases hung during a misguided redecoration in the late 17thC. Most of these may be safely ignored, apart from Bernardo Strozzi's *Tobias Healing his Father* over the entrance to the St Athanasius Chapel at the top of the right aisle.

The two chapels off the right side of the church were incorporated from the old church when door. (*If closed, apply to the custodian for admission.*) The **St Athanasius Chapel** was created in 1595 out of the central section of the old church, from which the carved wooden **choir stalls** (1455-64) by Francesco and Marco Cozzi survive. The 15thC **St Tarasius Chapel** was the apse of the former church. The **mosaic floor** around the altar remains from the 12thC building and the **crypt** of the original 9thC church may be inspected below.

In the fan vaults of the St Tarasius Chapel are damaged frescoes of *God the Father, the Evangelists and Saints* ★ (1442). These rounded, human figures are the earliest works attributed to the Tuscan Renaissance artist Andrea del Castagno. Like the mosaics in the Mascoli Chapel in *San Marco*, which have also been attributed to Castagno, they were executed in a style which was totally alien to the artistic mood of mid-15thC Venice. One can appreciate this by comparing them with the three magnificent but mannered **polyptychs** on the altar and side walls, painted only 1yr later by Giovanni d'Alemagna and Antonio Vivarini.

Scalzi *(Santa Maria di Nazareth)* 🏛 ✝

Map 4C3. Fondamenta Scalzi, Cannaregio. Water bus 1, 2, 4 or 5 to the railroad station.

The church of the Scalzi, which faces the *Grand Canal* next to the station, was built in 1670-72 by Baldassare Longhena for the barefoot (*scalzi*) order of the Carmelites. The elaborate Baroque facade (1672-80), erected by Giuseppe Sardi, reflects the huge sum spent on it by Sardi's socially ambitious patron Gerolamo Cavazza.

The **interior** is clad in marble of different colors and lavishly decorated with Baroque sculptures. Its greatest treasure was lost in 1915 when G.B. Tiepolo's ceiling painting of *The Transfer of the Holy House to Loreto* was destroyed by an Austrian shell. The surviving fragments and one of Tiepolo's sketches for the central panel may be seen in the *Accademia*. Three works by Tiepolo remaining in the church are *St Theresa in Glory* (1720-25) in the vault of the second chapel on the right, and the chiaroscuro *Angels of the Passion* and *Agony in the Garden* (c.1731) in the vault of the first chapel on the left.

Lodovico Manin, the last of the doges (1789-97), is buried in the second chapel on the left.

Where to stay

Venetian hotels are among the most expensive in the world. If this fact does not bother you, stay at the **Gritti Palace**, which remains the most fashionable of the luxury hotels, or at the **Cipriani** for its swimming pool and tennis courts. Of the very expensive hotels, just below the super deluxe class, two of the most congenial are the **Europa e Regina** and **Monaco**.

If, by contrast, you are young and broke in Venice, be warned that it is technically against the law to sleep rough; if you try, free accommodations may be provided in a disused factory on the mainland. The Youth Hostel is at Giudecca 86 (☎*5238211*). A list of other hostels, mostly run by religious orders, is obtainable from the tourist information office. Of the inexpensive *locande* the most fashionable is above the restaurant **Montin**.

In the medium range hotel prices remain dismayingly high (a modest room will cost you about twice what it would on the provincial mainland), and standards are surprisingly variable. The main hazards are cramped rooms (space in the historic city is at a premium), dark rooms (about half of habitable Venice, 'City of Light,' receives little or no sunlight), and noise. It is always worth asking for a room on an upper floor or facing the hotel garden if there is one. If you suffer from claustrophobia, look for a room in an old palace where planning laws prohibit the partitioning of rooms. And if you are on your own, remember that single rooms are usually the least comfortable; a double room in a third or fourth-class hotel may prove better value than a single in a first or second.

Italian hotels are classified in four categories, *pensioni* in three, and in the cheapest category of all are the *locande*. A complete list of all hotels, *pensioni* and *locande*, with current prices is published annually by the Provincial Tourist Board and issued free by the **Italian Government Travel Office** (*630 5th Ave., Suite 1565, New York, NY 10011* ☎ *(212) 245-4825*).

Seasoned travelers in Italy soon learn that hotel breakfasts are expensive and meagre. A coffee and sweet roll at the nearest bar (see *Bars and cafés*) is usually a more pleasant way to start the day. Remember too that hotels can charge what they like for long-distance telephone calls, which can be made conveniently and at the official rate from the post office at the Rialto (see *Post and telephone services* in *Basic information*).

During peak seasons — the February Carnival, Easter and June to Sept — it can be difficult to find any hotel accommodations at all at the last minute, so be sure to reserve well in advance (see sample reservation letter in *Words and phrases* in *Special information*). There are on-the-spot hotel reservation offices at the airport, at the mainland end of the bridge across the lagoon, at the railroad station and at Piazzale Roma.

Even when Venice is most crowded it is sometimes possible to find accommodations in the Lista di Spagna, a wide street near the railroad station, and around Piazzale Roma. These are not the city's most salubrious neighborhoods, but many of the hotels face the Grand Canal and are less expensive than those in the tourists' center. Four adequate hotels in these areas are the **Etap-Park**, the **Carlton Executive**, the **Principe** and the very inexpensive **Hotel S. Geremia** in Campo S. Geremia.

Finding pleasant accommodations in Venice is much less of a problem in winter (apart from the Carnival period). Some hotels close in Jan, but many now stay open throughout the rest of the year. Prices are generally 10-15 percent lower and even the luxury

Hotels

hotels offer remarkably inexpensive package deals, available through such tour operators as Pegasus and CIT. As a further incentive, some of the larger hotels stage programs of concerts, lectures and other entertainments.

In the descriptions that follow, the first part of the address (e.g. *Dorsoduro 1058*) is all you will need when writing — the *sestieri* are shown on the *Orientation map* in *Planning*. Hotels on the Lido are described separately on page 148; and for some suggestions for staying on the mainland near Venice see page 153.

Hotels classified by area

Cannaregio
Madonna dell'Orto *I□*
Giorgione *III□* to *IIII□*
Castello
Atlantico *II□*
Bisanzio *III□* to *IIII□*
Bucintoro *II□*
Danieli *IIIII*
Gabrielli Sandwirth *IIII*
Londra Palace *IIII*
Metropole *IIII*
Paganelli *II□*
La Residenza *II□*
Savoia e Jolanda *III□* to *IIII□*
Scandinavia *II□*
Trovatore *II□*
Dorsoduro
Accademia *II□* to *III□*
American *III□*
Calcina *II□* to *III□*
Casa de' Stefani *□*
Pausania *III□*
Alla Salute Da Cici *II□*
Seguso *III□*
Giudecca
Casa Frollo *II□*
Cipriani *IIIII*

Santa Croce
San Cassiano *III□* to *IIII□*
San Marco
Ala *III□* to *IIII□*
Bauer Grünwald *IIIII*
Bel Sito *III□* to *IIII□*
Bonvecchiati *III□* to *IIII□*
Casanova *II□* to *III□*
Cavalletto e Doge Orseolo *III□* to *IIII□*
Concordia *III□* to *IIII□*
Do Pozzi *III□*
Europa e Regina *IIII*
La Fenice e des Artistes *III□* to *IIII□*
Flora *III□*
Gritti Palace *IIIII*
Luna *IIII*
Monaco e Grand Canal *IIII*
Montecarlo *III□* to *IIII□*
San Marco *III□* to *IIII□*
Saturnia e International *IIII*
Torino *III□*
San Polo
Carpaccio *III□* to *IIII□*

Accademia ✿ 🏛
Map 14E2. Dorsoduro 1058, Fondamenta Maravegie ☎5237846 *II□* to *III□* 26 rms 🛏 18 AE ⊙ ⊙ VISA *Landing stage: Accademia.*
A well-known *pensione* in a 17thC villa with two pleasant gardens — an unusual luxury in Venice. But the rooms on the canal side are noisy and some guests complain that the simple charm has been spoiled by surly management.
🖼 🏊 ⚓ ◁≡ ☯

Ala
Map 14E3. San Marco 2494, Campo Santa Maria del Giglio ☎5208333 ⊚ 410275 *III□* to *IIII□* 81 rms 🛏 81 ▦ AE ⊙ ⊙ VISA *Closed one month in winter. Landing stage: Santa Maria del Giglio.*
A centrally placed, adequately comfortable but charmless package tourists' hotel.
✥ □ 🖼 🏊

American *(ex-Dinesen)*
Map 14F3. Dorsoduro 628 (near Campo San Vio) ☎5204733 ⊚ 410508 *III□* 30 rms 🛏 30 AE ⊙ ⊙ VISA *Landing stage: Accademia.*
A friendly, practical hotel on a pretty side canal in one of the city's most peaceful domestic neighborhoods, but very near the Accademia Gallery and Guggenheim Collection. Packages can be arranged in the off season.
⌂ □ 🖼 🏊 ⚓ ◁≡

Atlantico 🏨 ✿
Map 15C5. Castello 4416, Calle Rimedio ☎5209244 *II□* 36 rms 🛏 26 VISA *Closed sometimes in winter. Landing stage: San Zaccaria.*
Tucked away behind San Marco, with some rooms overlooking the Bridge of Sighs, this cheerful, recently modernized *pensione* is a very good choice for student groups.
🖼 🏊 ☯

Bauer Grünwald 🏨
*Map 15E4. San Marco 1459,
Campo San Moisè ☎5207022/
5231520 📠 410075 ▥▥▥ 210 rms ▭
▭ 210 ▤▤ ⇄ AE ⓪ ⓒ VISA
Landing stage: San Marco.*

The building at San Moisè, erected
in the 1960s, is an esthetic scandal;
but what the Bauer Grünwald lacks
in charm it makes up for in
spaciousness, luxury and efficiency.
The hall porter at this hotel is
famously well-connected with
theaters and restaurants.
‡ ⟨ ▢ ⟩ ⟨ ▥ ⟩ Y

Bel Sito
*Map 14E3. San Marco 2517,
Campo Santa Maria del Giglio
☎5223365 📠 433077 ▥▥▯ to ▥▥▥ 36
rms ▭ 36 ▤▤ AE ⓪ Landing
stage: Santa Maria del Giglio.*

A central, handsomely furnished
hotel. Bedrooms are small but fifteen
of them overlook the church of Santa
Maria del Giglio.
▱ ▥ Y

Bisanzio
*Map 11F8. Castello 3651, Calle
della Pieta ☎5203100/5204114
▥▯ to ▥▥▥ 45 rms ▭ 40 ▤▤ AE CB
⓪ ⓒ VISA Closed Jan. Landing
stage: San Zaccaria.*

A smart, efficient hotel in a peaceful
area not far from San Marco.
‡ ▱ Y

Bonvecchiati
*Map 15D4. San Marco 4488, Calle
Goldoni ☎5285017 📠 410560 ▥▯
to ▥▥▥ 86 rms ▭ 75 ⇄ ▤▤ AE
ⓒ VISA Landing stage: Rialto.*

A centrally-located hotel under the
same management as the **Colomba**
(see *Restaurants*) — its hallways are
hung with part of the proprietor's
well-known collection of 20thC art,
and the food in its restaurant is
unusually good. Best rooms, some
with views over surrounding
rooftops, are on the upper floors.
‡ ▱ ⟨ ⟩ Y

Bucintoro ✿
*Map 12F9. Castello 2135, Riva
degli Schiavoni ☎5223240 ▥▯ 17
rms ▭ 6 ⇄ pensione obligatory
in summer ⓒ Open 1 Mar-15
Nov. Landing stage:
Arsenale.*

All bedrooms in this modest, clean,
hospitable old *pensione* command
stunning views of the harbor.
Whistler stayed here when it was a
lodging house favored by American
art students and etched the Riva
from a window.
▱ ▰ ⟨

Calcina
*Map 9G5. Dorsoduro 780,
Fondamenta Zattere dei Gesuati
☎5206466 ▥▯ to ▥▥▥ 35 rms ▭ 20
AE CB ⓪ ⓒ VISA Closed Dec to
Jan. Landing stage: Zattere.*

This *pensione* is one of the places
Ruskin stayed while writing *The
Stones of Venice*, and it retains a
faintly gloomy, high-minded
atmosphere which appeals especially
to British scholars and intellectuals.
There are marvelous views across the
Giudecca Canal.
⟨

Carpaccio 🏛
*Map 14C2. San Polo 2765, corner
of Rio di San Polo ☎5235946 ▥▥▯
to ▥▥▥ 20 rms ▭ 17 VISA Closed
mid-Nov to mid-Mar. Landing
stage: San Tomà.*

A small, second-class hotel on the
Grand Canal in the unfinished 16thC
Palazzo Barbarigo della Terrazza.
Bedrooms are unusually spacious; six
of them and the *salone* look onto the
Grand Canal.
⟨ ▢ ▱ ⟨ ⟩ Y

Casa Frollo ▰ ✿ 🏛
*Map 10H7. Giudecca 50,
Fondamenta delle Zitelle
☎5222723 ▥▯ 26 rms ▭ 9.
Closed Dec-Feb. Landing stage:
Zitelle.*

This old-fashioned *pensione*, in an
unspoiled, spacious and light-filled
17thC pleasure villa facing Venice
across the Giudecca Canal, appeals,
as ever, to writers and artists.
⟨ ▱ ▰ ⟨ ⟩ Y

Casa de' Stefani ✿
*Map 9F4. Dorsoduro 2786, off
Campo San Barnaba ☎5223337
▢ 11 rms AE. Closed for two
weeks in Nov or Jan. Landing
stage: Ca' Rezzonico.*

Perhaps the most sympathetic of the
low-budget students' *pensioni*. It may
be a bit run-down, but the frescoes
and stained glass are wonderful.
Accommodations range from
windowless garrets suitable for
starving young artists to spacious
four-bedded *salons*.
⟨ ▰ ▰

Casanova
*Map 15D4. San Marco 1284,
Frezzeria ☎5223217 📠 22553 ▥▥▯
to ▥▥▥ 45 rms ▭ 40 ▤▤ AE VISA
Landing stage: San Marco.*

An extremely central and carefully
managed hotel decorated in restful
good taste and popular with visiting
Italian business people.
⟨ ‡ ▱ Y

127

Hotels

Cavalletto e Doge Orseolo
Map 15D4. San Marco 1107, Bacino Orseolo ☎ 5200955
☎ 410684 ▥ to ▥ 81 rms ▭ 81
▤ ⇌ AE VISA *Landing stage: San Marco.*

Superbly positioned immediately behind the Piazza on a canal packed with parked gondolas. The more elegantly furnished rooms face the water. Elsewhere, the functional decor might lead you to wonder if you really are in Venice, and there are occasional complaints of unfriendly management.
‡ □ ▱ ⌘ ᐅ Ⴤ

Cipriani ▥
Map 11H7. Giudecca 10
☎ 5207744 ☎ 410162 ▥ 94 rms
▭ 94 ▤ ⌂ ⇌ AE ⓞ VISA
Landing stage: Zitelle.

The Cipriani, which is under the same management as the much publicized Venice Simplon Orient-Express, occupies three tranquil acres at the E end of the Giudecca. It has the only swimming pool and tennis courts in central Venice, not to mention a private harbor for yachts and one of the best of the hotel-restaurants (described under *Restaurants*). Bedrooms are exquisitely furnished in every detail, with Fortuny fabrics and tiled or marble bathrooms. Sixty rooms overlook the lagoon and there are lavish new suites around the pool. Although it is only 5mins by the hotel's private motor launch to San Marco, many guests find it difficult to leave this hedonists' paradise for the real Venice.
▱ ‡ & □ ▱ ᐅ ᐅ≈ ⌀ ᐅ
Ⴤ

Concordia
Map 15D5. San Marco 367, Calle Larga San Marco ☎ 5206866 ▥
to ▥ 60 rms ▭ 60 ▤ AE ⓞ VISA
Landing stage: San Marco.

The only hotel in Venice overlooking San Marco has 20 bedrooms with a full view of the Piazzetta dei Leoni.
▱ ‡ ▱ ᐅ

Danieli ▥ ▥
Map 15D6. Castello 4196, Riva degli Schiavoni ☎ 5226480
☎ 410077 ▥ 250 rms ▭ 250 ▤
⇌ AE CB ⓞ ⓞ VISA *Landing stage: San Zaccaria.*

The largest of the Venetian luxury hotels occupies the 15thC Palazzo Dandolo and its stark modern extension, both overlooking the lagoon. The lobby, built around the Gothic courtyard of the palace, is spectacular; but some guests

complain of impersonal management and slipshod service. In the 19thC, distinguished residents included Ruskin, Wagner and Georges Sand.
▱ ‡ □ ▱ ▱ ᐅ ᐅ Ⴤ

Do Pozzi
Map 15E4. San Marco 2373, Calle Larga XXII Marzo ☎ 5207855 ▥
35 rms ▭ 35 ⇌ AE ⓞ ⓞ VISA
Landing stage: San Marco.

A decent, friendly, central little hotel with some rooms overlooking a pretty garden. But beware of the single rooms, which are cramped and dark. *Pensione* available at the restaurant **Da Raffaele**.
▱ ‡ ▱ ᐅ

Europa e Regina ▥
Map 15E4. San Marco 2159, Calle del Traghetto ☎ 5200477
☎ 410123 ▥ 205 rms ▭ 160 ▤
⇌ AE VISA *Landing stage: San Marco.*

An elegant and particularly well-managed Ciga hotel on the Grand Canal. 29 rooms, some with terraces, command full views of the Salute.
▱ ‡ & □ ▱ ᐅ ᐅ Ⴤ

La Fenice et des Artistes
Map 15D4. San Marco 1936, Campiello de la Fenice
☎ 5232333 ☎ 411150 ▥ to ▥ 68
rms ▭ 68 ▤ *Landing stage: San Marco.*

An exceptionally pleasant hotel near the opera house. The bedrooms are attractively furnished as in a private house.
▱ ‡ ▱ ᐅ ᐅ

Flora
Map 15E4. San Marco 2283a, Calle Larga XXII Marzo
☎ 5225324 ☎ 410401 ▥ to ▥ 44
rms ▭ 43 ▤ AE ⓞ ⓞ VISA
Closed Nov-Jan. Landing stage: San Marco.

The abundantly planted, secluded garden of the Flora seems just the setting for a romantic idyll. Some of the best double bedrooms live up to this promise, but other rooms, especially singles, are claustrophobic and spartan.
‡ ▱ ᐅ ᐅ

Gabrielli Sandwirth ▥
Map 11F8. Castello 4110, Riva degli Schiavoni ☎ 5231580
☎ 410228 ▥ 120 rms ▭ 82 ▤
⌂ ⇌ AE ⓞ ⓞ VISA *Closed mid-Nov to mid-Mar except for Carnival. Landing stage: San Zaccaria.*

This hotel in a Gothic palace is especially alluring in summer when

you can cool off in its lush English rose garden, take a drink in the interior courtyard, or sunbathe on the roof terrace overlooking the lagoon. Other features include stately marble-tiled bathrooms.
🏨 ‡ 🖾 🗼 ⟨ 👗 Ⴤ

Giorgione
Map 6D6. Cannaregio 4587, off Campo Santi Apostoli
☎ 5225810 ▥ to ▥ 56 rms
▭ 56 🖾 ⇌ AE ⓄⒹ ⅦⅣ *Landing stage: Ca' d'Oro.*

A roomy and peaceful hotel in a domestic neighborhood behind the Ca' d'Oro.
🏨 ‡ 🖾 🗼 🚿 🗼 Ⴤ

Gritti Palace 🏩 🏛
Map 14E3. San Marco 2467, Campo Santa Maria del Giglio
☎ 794611 ⓄⒹ 410125 ▥ 92 rms
▭ 92 🖾 🖾 ⇌ AE ⓄⒹ ⅦⅣ *Landing stage: S.M. del Gigli.*

The Gritti is one of the most distinguished luxury hotels in Europe, with a deserved reputation for comfort and cordial management. The terrace bar on the Grand Canal is a fashionable rendezvous and the restaurant **Terrazza del Doge** serves above-average hotel food. Service apartments in a separate section of the hotel may be rented for a minimum of one week.
🏨 ‡ 🖾 🗼 🖾 🚿 🗼 ⟨ 👗 Ⴤ

Londra Palace
Map 11F8. Castello 4171, Riva degli Schiavoni ☎ 5200533
ⓄⒹ 431315 ⓄⒹ 70 rms ▭ 70 🖾 🖾
⇌ AE CB ⓄⒹ ⅦⅣ *Landing stage: Arsenale.*

A first-class hotel with '100 windows looking onto the lagoon,' comfortably appointed reception rooms and an aggressively multilingual style of management.
🏨 ‡ 🖾 🗼 🖾 🚿 🗼 ⟨ 👗 Ⴤ

Luna
Map 15E4. San Marco 1243, Calle Vallaresso ☎ 5289840 ⓄⒹ 410236
▥ 125 rms ▭ 125 🖾 ⇌ AE ⓄⒹ ⅦⅣ *Landing stage: San Marco.*

Although the Luna boasts that it is 'the oldest hotel in Venice,' it has long since been modernized in an anonymous style suitable for superior package tourists.
‡ 🖾 🗼 🖾 🗼 👗 Ⴤ

Madonna dell'Orto 🏛
Map 5B6. Cannaregio 3499, Fondamenta Madonna dell'Orto
☎ 5200555 ▥ 39 rms ▭ 14 🖾
🖾 ⇌ ⅦⅣ *Landing stage: Madonna dell'Orto.*

The remote location of this charming hotel, in an old palace near the church of Madonna dell'Orto, is not convenient for short-term sightseers. But it might well suit those on a more leisurely family vacation. Some of the spacious rooms retain original stuccoes and Murano mirrors, and a huge garden planted with mature trees stretches back to the lagoon.
🏨 🖾 🗼 👗 Ⴤ

Metropole
Map 11F8. Castello 4149, Riva degli Schiavoni ☎ 5205044
ⓄⒹ 410340 ▥ 64 rms ▭ 64 🖾 AE
Ⓒ ⓄⒹ ⅦⅣ *Landing stage: San Zaccaria.*

Once a traditional, family-run hotel, the Metropole has now jumped upscale into the first category. Its most attractive features are still the pretty, painted Venetian furniture and views of the lagoon.
🏨 ‡ 🖾 🗼 🖾 🖾 ⟨ 👗 Ⴤ

Monaco e Grand Canal
Map 15E4. San Marco 1325, Calle Vallaresso ☎ 5200211 ⓄⒹ 410450
▥ 80 rms ▭ 75 🖾 🖾 ⇌ AE ⅦⅣ *Landing stage: San Marco.*

One of the most congenial of the first-class hotels on the Grand Canal, decorated in classic good taste and with an excellent restaurant, the Grand Canal, and pleasant bar with an open fire in winter.
‡ 🗼 🖾 🖾 🖾 ⟨ 👗 Ⴤ

Montecarlo
Map 15D5. San Marco 463, Calle Specchieri ☎ 5207144 ⓄⒹ 411098
▥ to ▥ 48 rms ▭ 48 🖾 🖾 AE
Ⓒ ⓄⒹ ⅦⅣ *Landing stage: San Marco.*

Two attractions of the Montecarlo are its central position and the charm of its proprietor, who edits the excellent tourists' magazine *Un Ospite di Venezia* and is eager to share his knowledge of the city with his guests.
‡ 🗼 🖾 Ⴤ

Paganelli
Map 11F8. Castello 4182 and 4687, Riva degli Schiavoni
☎ 5224324 ▥ 23 rms ▭ 14 ⇌
pensione obligatory. Restaurant closed mid-Nov to mid-Mar. Landing stage: San Zaccaria.
A modest hotel with fine views. Some rooms look onto the lagoon — Henry James stayed in one and described the view in the preface to *Portrait of a Lady* — others onto Campo San Zaccaria. Those facing the water are also the prettiest and most characteristically Venetian.
🏨 🖾 🚿 ⟨ Ⴤ

Hotels

Pausania 🏨 ♿ 🏛
*Map 9F4. Dorsoduro 2824, off
Campo San Barnaba ☎ 5222490/
5200067 ☻ 41176 ▥ 26 rms
▭ 26 ▦ Landing stage: Ca'
Rezzonico.*
A recently modernized hotel in a
pretty palace on one of the city's
liveliest internal canals.
🛏 ☐ ⌨ ⌣ ⊻

La Residenza ♿ 🏛
*Map 7F8. Castello 3608, Campo
Bandiera e Moro ☎ 5285315 ▥
17 rms ▭ 14 AE CB VISA Landing
stage: Arsenale.*
A sympathetic and attractive private
hotel in a splendid Gothic palace, on
a busy domestic square.
🛏 ⌨ ﹪

Alla Salute Da Cici
*Map 15F4. Dorsoduro 222, near
Salute ☎ 5235404/5222271 ▥ 50
rms ▭ 12. Closed 15 Nov-20 Dec,
10 Jan, Carnival. Landing stage:
Salute.*
A third-class *pensione*, conveniently
located, with two pleasant gardens.
🛏 ⌨ ﹪ ⌣ ⊰ ⊻

San Cassiano 🏛
*Map 14B3. Sante Croce 2232,
Calle della Rosa ☎ 721033
☻ 223479 ▥ to ▥▥ 35 rms ▭ 35
▦ AE ☻ Landing stage: S. Stae.*
This hotel, located in the little Gothic
Ca' Favretto on the Grand Canal with
some rooms overlooking the Ca'
d'Oro, was the studio of the 19thC
painter Giacomo Favretto. Although
it was completely restored in the
1960s it retains some original
architectural features but is
predictably decorated with
reproduction furniture, Persian rugs
and Murano chandeliers.
🛏 ☐ ⌨ ﹪ ⌣ ⊰ ⊻

San Marco
*Map 15D5. San Marco 877, Calle
Fabbri ☎ 5204277 ☻ 215660 ▥
to ▥▥ 60 rms ▭ 60 🛏 ⊟ AE CB
☻ ☻ VISA Landing stage: S. Marco.*
The clean-lined modern furniture
and recessed lighting — if not
characteristically 'Venetian' — are
restful and there is a view of the
campanile of San Marco from the
penthouse terrace.
⇕ ⌨ ﹪

Saturnia e International 🏛
*Map 15E4. San Marco 2399, Calle
Larga XXII Marzo ☎ 5208377
☻ 410355 ▥▥▥ 97 rms ▭ 97 ▦ ⊟
AE ☻ ☻ VISA Landing stage: San
Marco.*
An ambitiously luxurious hotel in a

14thC palace with overly dramatic
Neo-Byzantine decor. Package
guests don't always get the best rooms.
⇕ ☐ ⌨ ⌣ 🛟 ⊻

Savoia e Jolanda
*Map 11F7. Castello 4187, Riva
degli Schiavoni ☎ 5206644
☻ 410620 ▥ to ▥▥ 72 rms ▭ 46
🛏 ⊟ AE VISA Landing stage:
San Zaccaria.*
A clean, unpretentious family hotel
overlooking the lagoon.
🛏 ⇕ ⌨ ﹪ ⊰

Scandinavia
*Map 15C6. Castello 5240, Campo
Santa Maria Formosa ☎ 5223507
☻ 311879 ▥ 27 rms ▭ 17 ⊟ ⊟
AE VISA Landing stage: Rialto or
San Zaccaria.*
The Scandinavia aims to be the best
third-category family hotel in
Venice. Bedrooms (doubles only,
each with an extra single bed) are
clean, but the imitation Venetian
palace decor is unconvincing.
🛏 ⌨ ⌣

Seguso
*Map 9G5. Dorsoduro 779,
Fondamenta Zattere dei Gesuati
☎ 5222340 ▥ 36 rms ▭ 13 🛏
🛏 ⊟ ☻ Closed Dec-Feb.
Landing stage: Zattere.*
This solidly old-fashioned *pensione*
overlooking the Giudecca Canal is a
traditional favorite with Anglo-Saxon
visitors. Children are made very
welcome and they enjoy the open
position.
🛏 ⇕ ⌡ ⊰

Torino
*Map 4E3. San Marco 2356, Calle
Larga XXII Marzo ☎ 5205222
☻ 223534 ▥ 20 rms ▭ 20 ▦ AE
CB ☻ ☻ VISA Landing stage:
Santa Maria del Giglio.*
A small, sensible hotel in the center
which is less cramped than it looks.
Bedrooms (doubles only) have high
ceilings and leaded windows; some
overlook a neighboring garden.
☐ ⌨ ⊻

Trovatore
*Map 10F7. Castello 4534, Calle
delle Rasse ☎ 5224611 ▥ 35 rms
▭ 18 AE CB ☻ ☻ Closed
mid-Nov to mid-Mar, but open
for Christmas and Carnival.
Landing stage: San Zaccaria.*
A small, serviceable hotel not far
from the center. Decor is minimal
and charmless, but some of the upper
rooms have terraces with views of the
surrounding rooftops.
⇕

Eating in Venice

The visual splendors of the Venetian food markets, where exotic species of fish are laid out as in a Byzantine mosaic, hold out a promise all too rarely fulfilled by the city's restaurants. There are now more than 300 restaurants in Venice: most cater deliberately to tourists, and most offer food that is both dull and over-priced by the standards of the mainland Veneto. For the freshest fish, the most plentiful variety of local vegetables, game and cheeses, the more time-consuming of the traditional regional recipes and the fairest prices you must leave your fellow tourists behind and go on to the *terra firma*. For advice about where to eat on the mainland see pages 152-53.

In Venice itself the more limited culinary repertory includes *pasta e fagioli, bigoli in salsa, seppie in nero, fegato alla Veneziana* and *polenta*. Fish and shellfish, offered as an antipasto, with pasta or grilled, boiled or baked as a main course can be the greatest treat of all, but only if the fish in question is chosen from the pick of the day's catch and quickly cooked to order. Remember that fish, even in Venice, is often imported frozen and is always expensive. Among the most reliable of the fish restaurants listed below are **Corte Sconta**, **Da Fiore** and the **Poste Vecie**.

Nevertheless, after a few days of fish with everything you may crave a change. **Da Arturo** specializes in meat of good quality; **Zorzi** (*San Marco 4352, Calle Fuseri* ☎5225350, *closed Sun*) is a vegetarian restaurant, café and store.

There are only a few Chinese restaurants in the city where Marco Polo is said to have introduced pasta from China. Two of the most agreeable are **China Town**, listed below, and **La Grande Muraglia** (*Castello 3958, Calle del Forno* ☎5232382, *closed Mon*).

Light, relatively inexpensive meals and snacks are widely available throughout the day. The most inviting of the pizzerias are on the Zattere, where you can sit in the sun on the quays overlooking the Giudecca canal. Many bars serve hot and cold snacks as well as delicious *tramezzini*. And there is a welcome revival of the *bacaro*, the traditional Venetian wine bar. *Bacari* worth seeking out for atmosphere as well as good value include **Antica Adelaide**, **Ai Assassini**, **Al Mascaron** and **Al Milion**.

It is useful to remember that most of the grand hotel restaurants stay open on Sunday and Monday evenings, when other restaurants tend to close. The expensive hotel restaurants have greatly improved in recent years. Especially recommended are those in the **Bonvecchiati**, **Cipriani**, **Gritti**, **Londra**, **Monaco** and **Saturnia** hotels. Smaller hotels sometimes reserve their restaurants for guests only.

Venice retires early, even in summer. Most restaurants take their last orders at 10.30pm; this is the case unless otherwise stated below. Restaurants that stay open much later are the **Antico Martini**'s Martini Scala, **Al Campiello**, **La Caravella**, **Al Paradiso Perduto** and **Al Theatro**.

Restaurants classified by area

Restaurants

San Trovaso ▯▭
Giudecca
Altanella ▯▭
Do Mori ▯▭ to ▥▭
Harry's Dolci ▥▭
Santa Croce
Antica Bessetta ▥▭
La Regina ▥▥
San Marco
Antico Martini ▥▥▥
Da Arturo ▥▭ to ▥▥▥
Ai Assassini ▥▭
Al Campiello ▥▭ to ▥▥
La Caravella ▥▥▥
La Colomba ▥▭ to ▥▥▥
Al Conte Pescaor ▥▥▥

Il Cortile ▥▥▥
Do Forni ▥▥▥
Al Graspo de Ua ▥▥▥
Harry's Bar ▥▥▥
Da Ivo ▥▥▥
Da Raffaele ▥▥▥
Stagneri ▯▭
Al Theatro ▯▭ to ▥▭
San Polo
Caffè Orientale ▥▥ to ▥▥▥
Le Carampane ▯▭ to ▥▭
Da Fiore ▯▭ to ▥▥▥
Da Ignazio ▥▭
Alla Madonna ▥▭
Poste Vecie ▥▥▥
Trattoria San Tomà ▯▭ to ▥▭

Altanella ♣
*Map 9H5. Giudecca 268, Calle dell'Erbe ☎5227780 ▯▭ ▭ ▭
Last orders 9pm. Closed Mon evening, Tues, 2 weeks in Aug. Landing stage: Redentore.*

This small, rough-and-ready, family-run fish restaurant is charming in fine weather when you can sit outside overlooking the Giudecca's pretty central canal.

Antica Adelaide ♣
Map 6C6. Cannaregio 3728, Calle Priuli, near Ca' d'Oro ☎5203451 ▭ ▱ Closed Mon. Landing stage: Ca' d'Oro or Fondamenta Nuove.

A particularly sympathetic wine bar and simple restaurant. Good cold vegetables and wholesome snacks.

Antica Bessetta ♣♣
Map 14A2. Santa Croce 1395, Salizzada Zusto (near San Giacomo dell'Orio) ☎721687 ▥▭ ▭▰▱ Last orders 9.30pm. Closed Tues, Wed. Landing stage: Riva Biasio.

One of the best, and best known, of the modest restaurants — despite its remote location. No menu, but if you take the proprietor's advice you will enjoy honest, traditional Venetian cooking, with an emphasis on fish, and good risottos and homemade pasta.

Antica Mola ♣
Map 5B5. Cannaregio 2800A, Fondamenta degli Ormesini (near the Ghetto) ☎717492 ▯▭ ▭ ▱ ▱ Closed Wed and Aug. Landing stage: San Marcuola.

Known affectionately to its regulars as La Mola, this no-nonsense, everyday trattoria is nicest in good weather when you can eat in its walled garden. The *risotto di pesce* preceded by *prosciutto* and melon makes an ideal summer lunch.

Antico Martini
*Map 15D4. San Marco 1983, Campo San Fantin ☎5224121 ▥▥▥ ▭▱▰▱ ▱ ▱ AE CB ◉ ◐ VISA
Closed Tues, Wed lunch, and Dec-Feb. Landing stage: San Marco.*

The opulent belle époque ambience, polished service and extensive international menu appeal especially to wealthy foreigners of a certain age. The food usually justifies the high prices; and those with more adventurous palates can request well-prepared Venetian specialties not necessarily on the menu. The piano bar, **Martini Scala**, serves a limited selection from the menu at lower prices from 10pm to 2.30am and stays open until 3.30am.

Da Arturo
*Map 14D3. San Marco 3656, Calle degli Assassini (near the Fenice) ☎5286974 ▥▭ to ▥▥▥ ▭ ▱▰
Closed Sun and two weeks in Aug. Landing stage: Santa Maria del Giglio.*

A tiny, popular wood-paneled restaurant, which serves more imaginative food than most, including unusual mixed salads, spaghetti with gorgonzola or *carciofi*, and tagliatelle with *radicchio*. There is no fish, for a change, but meat dishes are substantial. Reservations are essential.

Ai Assassini ♣
*Map 15D4. San Marco 3695, Rio Terà dei Assassini (near the Fenice) ☎ 5230862 ▯▭ ▱▰
Closed Mon. Landing stage: Giglio.*

Recently opened in the old wine stores of a palace, this *bacaro* (the Venetian word for wine bar) is a fashionable venue for young Venetians. Good for a light, informal lunch or supper; but go early or book because it does get very crowded.

Al Bacco ♣
Map 4B4. Cannaregio 3054, Fondamenta Capuzine (near the Ghetto) ☎717493 ⅢⅢ *Closed Tues. Landing stage: Ponte Tre Archi.*
A simple, reasonable neighborhood restaurant, which serves mainly fish in a comfortably authentic Venetian atmosphere.

Ai Barbicani
Map 6E7. Castello 5746, Calle del Paradiso (near San Lio) ☎5210234 ⅢⅢ ▭ ⬛ ▭ 🍽 AE ⊙ CD VISA *Closed Mon and Jan. Landing stage: Rialto or San Zaccaria.*
A snug, country-style restaurant where meat, fish and mushrooms in season are grilled over an open fire.

Caffè Orientale
Map 5D4. San Polo 2462, Rio Marin (near San Giovanni Evangelista) ☎719804 ⅢⅢ to ⅢⅢ 🍴 AE CB ⊙ CD VISA *Closed Mon. Landing stage: San Tomà.*
The minimalist-chic decor of this fish restaurant is unusual for Venice, and in fine weather there are tables outside on the canal.

Al Campiello
Map 15D4. San Marco 4346, Calle dei Fuseri ☎5206396 ⅢⅢ to ⅢⅢ ▭ 🍽 🍴 AE ⊙ CD VISA *Last orders midnight. Closed Mon and Aug. Landing stage: Rialto.*
A somewhat louche late-night restaurant, useful for a snack or full meal after the opera. The pastas and Venetian specialties can be good.

Cantinone Storico
Map 9G5. Dorsoduro 661, Fondamenta Bragadin (near Accademia) ☎5207528 ⅢⅢ ▭ ▭ 🍴 AE CB VISA *Closed Sun. Landing stage: Accademia.*
A snappily decorated high-bohemian restaurant with a nice native repertoire of both Venetian and non-Venetian dishes, including *ossobuchi al marsala* as well as game in season and fresh fish.

Le Carampane ♣
Map 14C3. San Polo 1911 (near Campo San Polo) ☎5240165 ⅢⅢ to ⅢⅢ *Closed Sun evening, Mon and Aug. Landing stage: San Silvestro or San Tomà.*
Tourists may receive a brusque greeting, but that is worth braving for the sake of uncorrupted traditional Venetian cooking at very reasonable prices. The emphasis is on fish. The restaurant's name

derives from Ca Rampani, which housed a brothel in the days of the Republic. Prostitutes bared their breasts from the balcony in order to discourage homosexual tendencies of passers by.

La Caravella
Map 15E4. San Marco 2398, Calle Larga XXII Marzo ☎5208901 ⅢⅢ ▭ ▬ 🍽 🍴 AE ⊙ CD VISA *Last orders 1am. Closed Wed in winter. Landing stage: San Marco.*
This is the grander of the two restaurants in the **Saturnia e International** hotel; the other is **Il Cortile**. Americans, who especially enjoy this restaurant, may be reminded by the mock ship-board decor that Columbus sailed to America with caravels. Venetians and would-be Venetians scorn the fancy parchment menu and unctuous service of this restaurant, but there is no doubt that the food is among the best to be had in Venice, especially if you choose the more expensive items such as shellfish and fillet of beef.

China Town ♣
Map 5C4. Cannaregio 408, Ponte Guglie (near the Ghetto) ☎716154 ⅢⅢ *Closed Tues. Landing stage: Ponte Guglie.*
The prettiest and most authentic of the Chinese restaurants in Venice run by a Formosan family. Some of the dishes, for example the *gamberi in nido di rondine*, are exquisite.

La Colomba
Map 15D4. San Marco 1665, Frezzeria (near the Fenice) ☎5221173 ⅢⅢ to ⅢⅢ ▭ 🍽 🍴 AE CB ⊙ CD VISA *Closed Wed (summer only). Landing stage: San Marco or Santa Maria del Giglio.*
The walls of this large, well-known restaurant are hung with the most impressive collection of 20thC paintings on public view in Venice outside the Guggenheim Collection. The menu offers a vast selection of traditional Venetian dishes, mostly fish.

Al Conte Pescaor
Map 15D5. San Marco 544, Piscina San Zulian ☎5221483 ⅢⅢ ▭ 🍽 🍴 AE *Closed Sun, Mon lunch, early Aug and one month in Jan-Feb. Landing stage: San Marco or Rialto.*
A busy, attractively old-fashioned fish restaurant staffed by a spirited team of waiters. Specialties include *spaghetti al conte, grigliata di pesce,*

Restaurants

and less familiar risottos and gnocchi.

Corte Sconta
Map 11F8. Castello 3886, Calle del Pestrin (near San Giovanni in Bragora) ☎5227024 ∎∎∎ to ∎∎∎∎ 🍷 AE *Closed Sun, Mon, Jan and July. Landing stage: Arsenale.*

This fish restaurant is named after the hidden courtyard where the characters created by its owner, the cartoonist Hugo Pratt, begin their adventures. Although well and truly hidden it is now nearly as famous, in its very different way, as **Harry's Bar**, and perhaps even more fashionable with discriminating tourists. The unique high-tech, low-profile ambience may be a bit studied given the prices, but the fish is nearly always delicious.

Il Cortile
Map 15E4. San Marco 2402, Calle Larga XXII Marzo ☎5208938 ∎∎∎∎ ⊡ ∎ ⚑ ⊞ 🍷 AE ⓪ ⓪ VISA *Closed Wed in winter. Landing stage: San Marco.*

The courtyard of the **Saturnia e International** hotel is one of the most pleasant outdoor settings in Venice. Food is similar to but less ambitious than that served at **La Caravella**.

Do Forni
Map 15 D5. San Marco 457, Calle dei Specchieri ☎5232148 ∎∎∎ ⚑ ⊞ 🍷 AE CB ⓪ ⓪ VISA *Last orders 11.30pm. Closed Thurs in winter. Landing stage: San Zaccaria.*

A big, brash so-called 'trattoria' much recommended by hall porters. You won't eat badly but may suffer from bossy service and a padded bill.

Do Mori ♣
Map 9H4. Giudecca 588, Fondamenta San Eufemia ☎5225452 ∎∎ to ∎∎∎ *Closed Sun.*

A noisy, deliberately unpretentious trattoria and pizzeria run by two former Harry's Bar waiters. Pizzas (served in the evening only) are among the best in town, and pastas, made in the kitchen, are unusual and very good. The more expensive main courses can be dull.

Da Fiore
Map 14B2. San Polo 2202, Calle del Scaleter (near Campo San Polo) ☎721308 ∎∎∎ to ∎∎∎∎ ⊡ ⊞ 🍷 AE ⓪ *Closed Sun, Mon, Aug and Christmas. Landing stage: San Tomà.*

In Venice 'did I eate the best Oysters

that ever I did in all my life,' wrote Thomas Coryat in 1611. If you wish to recapture his enthusiasm, take the trouble to seek out this restaurant of dignified domestic character, which serves only absolutely fresh fish and shellfish of the highest quality (as well as homemade bread and sweets). Reservations are usually advisable.

La Furatola
Map 9F4. Dorsoduro 2870A, Calle Lunga San Barnaba (near Campo San Barnaba) ☎5208594 ∎∎∎ ⊡ 🍷 *Last orders 9.30pm. Closed Wed dinner, Thurs, sometimes Mon and July, Aug. Landing stage: Ca' Rezzonico.*

A cheerful and unfussy little restaurant, serving only the best and freshest fish available that day.

Al Graspo de Ua
Map 15C4. San Marco 5094, Calle dei Bombaseri (near San Bartolomeo) ☎5200150/5223647 ∎∎∎ ⊡ ⊞ AE ⓪ ⓪ *Closed Mon, Tues and mid-Dec to mid-Jan. Landing stage: Rialto.*

This venerable restaurant, now 100yrs old, has the confident, expansive character nowadays found more often on the provincial mainland than in Venice. An international clientele is offered a large and complicated choice of regional as well as specifically Venetian dishes.

Harry's Bar
Map 15E4. San Marco 1323, Calle Vallaresso ☎5285777 ∎∎∎∎ ⊡ ∎ ⊞ ◁≪ 🍷 AE CB ⓪ ⓪ VISA *Closed Mon and Jan. Landing stage: San Marco.*

This of course, is *the* original Harry's Bar, founded more than half a century ago by Giuseppe Cipriani, known to his friend Ernest Hemingway as 'Harry.' Today Harry's Bar is an institution, one of the essential glamorous Venetian experiences for visiting celebrities and celebrity watchers who can afford the ridiculously high prices. The service is as reassuringly practiced as ever, and it scarcely seems to matter that the food, which is sometimes over-rich, is not quite what it once was.

Harry's Dolci
Map 8G3. Giudecca 773, Fondamenta San Biagio ☎5224844/5208337 ∎∎∎ AE VISA *Closed Sun evening, Mon and in winter. Landing stage: San Eufemia.*

This popular offshoot of **Harry's Bar** has the cheerful airy atmosphere of a country restaurant. Also nice for tea (ice creams and pastries are among the best in Venice) on a sunny day. Service can be slow, especially on Sun when it's jammed with Venetians. There is another branch in Palazzo Grassi.

Da Ignazio
Map 14C2. San Polo 2749, Calle Saoneri (near San Polo and the Frari) ☎5234852 ▥◫ ▱ AE CB ◉ ◐ VISA *Closed Sat, two weeks in March. Landing stage: San Tomà.*

A comfortable old-favorite among the fish restaurants, with a spacious garden.

Da Ivo
Map 15D4. San Marco 1809, Ramo dei Fuseri ☎5285004 ▥◫ ◻ ▦ AE CB ◉ ◐ VISA *Last orders 11.30pm Closed Sun and Jan. Landing stage: San Marco.*

Da Ivo retains a certain chic thanks perhaps to the Tuscan bias of the cooking — *bistecca Fiorentina* makes a welcome change in Venice — and to its position overlooking a pretty canal. But there have been increasing complaints, especially from non-habitués, of dull food and rude service.

Alla Madonna
Map 15C4. San Polo 594, Calle della Madonna (near Rialto) ☎ 5233824 ▥◫ ◻ ▦ *Closed Wed and Jan. Landing stage: Rialto.*

This large, bright, bustling fish restaurant used to be one of the best in Venice. It's still useful.

Malamocco
Map 11F7. Castello 4650, Campiello del Vin (near San Zaccaria) ☎5227438 ▥◫ to ▥▥ ◻ ▦ ▱ ▦ AE CB ◉ VISA *Closed Thurs and Jan. Landing stage: San Zaccaria.*

One of the best-known of the traditional fish restaurants. Now rather overpriced, over decorated and anxious to please the tourists, but with a romantic garden.

Al Mascaron ♣
Map 11E7. Castello 5225, Calle Lunga Santa Maria Formosa (near S. Maria Formosa and SS. Giovanni e Paolo) ☎5225995 ▥◫ to ▥◫

A rough, plain, justly popular bar and restaurant.

Al Milion ♣
Map 15B5. Cannaregio 5841, San Giovanni Crisostomo (near the Rialto) ☎5229302 ▥◫ *Open 10.30am-2.30pm, 5.30-10.30pm. Closed Wed. Landing stage: Rialto.*

This useful, homey old *bacaro* near the remains of Marco Polo's family house has been smartened up but not spoiled.

Montin
Map 9F4. Dorsoduro 1147, Fondamenta di Borgo (near San Trovaso) ☎5227151 ▥◻ ▱ ▦ AE CB ◉ ◐ VISA *Closed Tues evening, Wed, 2 weeks Jan and 2 weeks Aug. Landing stage: Accademia.*

Montin is the most consistently successful of the artists' trattorias, treated by its regulars as a club. They may complain about the haphazard quality of the cooking, the whistle-stop service and the ever-rising prices, but they remain regulars nevertheless. No one can fail to be charmed by the romantic location on a beautiful side canal or by the huge informal garden. If you catch the cook on a good day you will enjoy the *malfatti alla panna*, *fegato alla Veneziana*, *torta di noce* or *tirami su*. Also a *locanda*, with decent, inexpensive accommodations upstairs.

Al Paradiso Perduto ♣
Map 5C5. Cannaregio 2540, Fondamenta Misericordia ☎720581 ◻ ▱ *Last orders 11.30pm. Closed Mon. Landing stage: Madonna dell'Orto.*

A large, lively late-night restaurant popular with young people. Pasta and vegetables are excellent. Interesting jazz concerts on weekends.

Poste Vecie
Map 15B4. San Polo 1608, Pescheria ☎721822 ▥◫ ◻ ▦ ▱ ▦ ◉ *Closed Tues. Landing stage: Rialto.*

An exceptionally charming fish restaurant approached by its own bridge from the fish market. A new management, which also runs **La Regina** (see below) and Dall'Amelia in Mestre, has much refined the food.

Da Raffaele
Map 15E4. San Marco 2347, Fondamenta delle Ostreghe ☎5232317 ▥◫ ◻ ▱ ▦ AE ◉ ◐ VISA *Closed Thurs and Jan to mid-Feb. Landing stage: Santa Maria del Giglio.*

It would be a mistake to dismiss this restaurant, with its outside tables spread so invitingly along a conspicuous central canal, as a mere tourist trap. You'll find plenty of discriminating Venetians inside, in the mock baronial hall. Inside or out, service is pleasant and the special dishes — *risotto di pesce*, *risotto di seppie*, *branzino allo chef*, *granzeola*, *filetto al gorgonzola* — are consistently well prepared.

La Regina
Map 14B3. Santa Croce 2330, Calle della Regina (near the Rialto) ☎5241402 ▥▥ ▰ ▱ *Closed Mon and Aug. Landing stage: S. Stae.*

This classy new restaurant is one of the few in Venice influenced by the *nouvelle cuisine*. It offers a short, ambitious menu, which changes every month. Excessively fussy presentation of dishes does not always enhance their flavor — although some of the first courses in particular are outstanding. The lugubrious organ music is a mistake, but the international wine list is superbly judged and fairly priced.

Da Remigio
Map 11E8. Castello 3416, Salizzada dei Greci ☎5230089 ▯ *to* ▥▥ ▱ *Closed Mon dinner and Tues. Landing stage: Arsenale.*

A plain but reliable family-style trattoria more popular with Venetians than tourists.

Trattoria San Tomà
Map 14C2. San Polo 2864A, Campo San Tomà (near the Frari) ☎5238819 ▯ *to* ▥▥ ▰ ▱ ▱ *Closed Tues. Landing stage: San Tomà.*

Useful, everyday trat specializing in pizzas (also to take away) and fresh pastas. Or try the unusual *prosciutto salmonato* (smoked like salmon) from the Tyrol.

San Trovaso ♣
Map 14E2. Dorsoduro 1016, Fondamenta Priuli (near San Trovaso) ☎5203703 ▯ ▱ ▰ ▤ ▾ ▱ ▱ ▱ ▱ *Closed Mon evening and Tues. Landing stage: Accademia or Zattere.*

A useful and very popular pizzeria, which also serves basic Venetian dishes such as *zuppa di pesce* and *pasta e fagioli*.

Ai Schiavoni
Map 11F8. Castello 3734, Calle del Dose (behind Riva degli Schiavoni) ☎5226763 ▥▥ ▰ ▱ ▱ ▱ *Closed Wed and sometimes Jan. Landing stage: S. Zaccaria or Arsenale.*

This pretty and hospitable green-and-white striped osteria serves old-fashioned Venetian specialties prepared with loving care. The black *risotto* or *spaghetti con seppioline*, for example, is wonderful.

Stagneri ♣
Map 15C5. San Marco 5246, Calle Stagneri ☎5227341 ▥▥ ▱ *Closed Fri and mid-Jan to mid-Feb. Landing stage: Rialto.*

A tiny restaurant run with great care by two women who take justifiable pride in their pasta. Try the *spaghetti alla rugola* or *al pesto*, the salads and the *fegato di Veneziano*.

Al Theatro
Map 15D4. San Marco 1916, Campo San Fantin ☎5221052 ▯ *to* ▥▥ ▱ ▰ ▰ ▤ ▾ ▱ ▱ ▱ *Last orders midnight. Closed Mon and Nov. Landing stage: Santa Maria del Giglio.*

This is one of the most useful places in Venice: a bar, pizzeria and restaurant all in one, where you can have breakfast or a drink or eat a full meal after a performance at the Fenice or buy cigarettes and newspapers until midnight.

Bars and cafés

The bar is a vital center of Italian daily life. It is a place to stop in, at any time of day, for a coffee or something stronger, a snack (*spuntino*), a gossip, or the use of the telephone or rest room. You can start the day at a bar with a *cappuccino* and a sweet roll and end it there with a *grappa*; and if in the intervening hours you should suffer from that chronic sightseers' ailment, exhaustion, you will surely find a cure at the bar, be it a *caffè normale* (a short, potent *espresso*), *lungo* (weaker), *macchiato* (with a dash of milk), or *corretto* (laced with brandy); an '*ombra*' (small glass of wine); or a *spremuta* (freshly squeezed fruit juice).

In Venice any patch of sunlight is likely to be occupied by bar tables; and each bar, inside or out, has its own personality. Some, run by waiters trained at Harry's Bar or the grand hotels, specialize in fancy cocktails and delicate sandwiches. Others are *enoteche* where you can sample a wide variety of local wines by the glass. Many are *bacari*, or wine bars, where you can eat a plate of pasta or risotto as well as cold snacks (the distinction between restaurants and bars is not absolute). There are slick modern bars and pretty old-fashioned bars with circular open galleries on their first floors and charming rustic bars and cheap humble bars.

No one will be surprised if you while away the whole day in a bar or if you move on after five minutes. Either way, if you sit down, inside or out, the price doubles.

Al Cherubin
Map **14D3**. San Marco 4118, Calle San Antonio (near the Rialto) ☎5238239 Open 6pm-2am. Closed Mon.
This slick, late-night 'American' Bar is *the* meeting place for the young.

Corner Pub
Map **14F3**. Dorsoduro 684, Calle della Chiesa (near the Guggenheim) ☎5231606.
Sophisticated cocktails (e.g., the 'orgasmo') and a limitless variety of sandwiches in a big, lively bar with a more tranquil room behind.

Do Mori
Map **6D6**. San Polo 429, Ramo Primo Calle Galiazza (near the Rialto) ☎5225401. Open 9am-1pm, 5pm-10pm. Closed Sun.
A beautiful old bar of character where you can sample local wines by the glass. Irresistible sandwiches too.

Florian
Map **15B5**. Castello 5719, near San Giovanni Crisostomo ☎5285338 Open 9am-11.30pm. Closed Wed.
The most Venetian of all cafés has been here since 1720. The elegantly intimate decorations of the rooms were done in 1858 in a nostalgic 18thC style. Under the Austrian occupation Florian's was patronized exclusively by Venetians while the Austrians sat across the Piazza at **Quadri**.

Haig's Bar
Map **14E3**. San Marco 2477, Campo del Giglio ☎5289456 Open 3pm-1am. Closed Wed.
A useful late-night meeting place for sophisticated foreigners, gay and straight. But do check the bill.

Harry's Bar
Map **15E4**. San Marco 1323, Calle Vallaresso ☎5285331/5285777 Open 10.30am-11pm. Closed Mon.

Still, after more than 50yrs, the place to see and be seen in. The dry martinis, Bellinis (peach juice and Prosecco, also bottled to take out) are sublime, as are the sandwiches. But you may choke on the bill.

Alla Maddalena
Map **5C5**. Cannaregio 2348, Rio Terrà della Maddalena ☎5226638. Open 7.30am-8pm. Closed Sun.
A bar near the Casino which serves exceptionally good snacks.

Marchini
Map **14E3**. San Marco 2769, Calle del Spezier ☎5229109/5287507 Open 8am-8pm. Closed Tues.
The best *pâtisserie* in central Venice sells a luscious selection of cakes, pastries and savories.

Paolin
Map **14D3**. San Marco 2962A, Campo Santo Stefano ☎5225576. Open 7am-9pm (11pm in summer). Closed Fri.
A bar and *gelateria* that does some of the best ice cream in the center.

Quadri
Map **15D5**. Piazza San Marco 120-124 ☎5222105. Open 9.30am-11pm. Closed Mon (except July-Sept).
The advantages of drinking at Quadri's are morning sun and the privilege of asking its vigorous orchestra to change their tune to one of your *own* old favorites. Venetians, however, have remained faithful to **Florian**, across the Piazza, since the Austrian occupation officers patronized Quadri's.

E. Rosa Salva
Map **15D5**. San Marco 951, Calle Fiubera ☎710544. Open 8am-1pm, 3-8pm. Closed Sun.
A rather forbiddingly hygienic bar attached to the most fashionable party caterers in Venice.

137

Al Theatro
Map 15D4. San Marco 1916, Campo San Fantin ☎5221052. Open 8am-midnight. Closed Mon and Nov.

One of the few bars in Venice regularly open until midnight where you can also buy cigarettes and newspapers.

Vino Vino
Map 15D4. San Marco 2007A, Ponte delle Veste (near the Fenice) ☎5224121. Open 10am-2pm, 5pm-1am. Closed Tues.

The wine bar of the Antico Martini, convenient for a light meal at the bar or served at tables. There is also a take out service.

Toscano Buffet
Map 15B5. Cannaregio 5747 (near San Giovanni Crisostomo) ☎5235544. Open until 10.30pm. Closed Sat.

A convenient, animated bar and sandwich shop located on the main drag between San Marco and the Rialto.

Al Volto
Map 15C4. San Marco 4081, Calle Cavalli, off Fondamenta del Carbon ☎28945. Open 9am-1pm, 4.30-9pm. Closed Sun.

The most impressive *enoteca* in Venice (see *Wines of northeast Italy* in *Special information*). There is also a tempting array of snacks.

Nightlife and the arts

Venice goes to sleep early and most small bars and restaurants close their shutters well before midnight. Nevertheless, there is enough to do after that if you know where to look.

Casino Municipale
Apr-Sept on the Lido (map 16E3, Lungomare G. Marconi 4 ☎760626/760696); Oct-Mar in Palazzo Vendramin Calergi (map 5C5, 2040 Cannaregio, Strada Nuova ☎710211). Open 3pm-3am.

The Venice Casino is one of the most glamorous in Europe. You can play roulette, chemin de fer, trente et quarante, black jack or craps; and there are nightclubs, floorshows and restaurants at both venues.

The nightclub on the Lido is **La Perla** (*☎761354, open 10pm-3am* ♀ ❀ ♫ ♥) and, at the Palazzo Vendramin Calergi, **Casanova** (*☎710211, open 10pm-3am* ♀ ❀ ♫ ♥).

Music and theater

The main opera house is the **Fenice** (*San Marco 2549, Campo San Fantin ☎5223954/5225191*), one of the most entrancingly pretty theaters in the world. The opera season is irregular and there is no repertory, but usually at least six major productions are staged during the winter; and the concerts and recitals are performed at other seasons. Other theaters are the **L'Avogaria**, **Goldoni**, **Ridotto**, and those in **Palazzo Grassi** and behind the **Cini Foundation**. Concerts and recitals are also given in some of the churches, such as the **Pietà**, **Ospedaletto** and **San Stae**.

Nightclubs

There are piano bars at some hotels, notably the **Monaco e Grand Canal** and **Cipriani**, as well as some restaurants such as the **Do Leoni** (*4171 Castello, Riva degli Schiavoni*) and **Antico Martini**. Both casinos have their own nightclub (see above).

Independent late-night bars are **Al Cherubin** (where young people meet), **Haig's Bar** and **Al Theatro** (where you can buy cigarettes and newspapers).

El Souk
Map 14E2. Dorsoduro 1056A near Accademia ☎ 5200371 ▐▐▐ ♀ ◉ ♥ Open 9.30pm-2am. Closed Wed.

Shopping in Venice

The most glamorous Venetian shops are to be found in the central triangle determined by San Marco, the Rialto, and the Accademia. You will find plenty of temptation under the arcades of Piazza San Marco, in the Mercerie, Frezzeria, Calle Vallaresso, Salizzada San Moisè, Calle Larga XXII Marzo and in the narrow streets around the Fenice. But when shopping, as when sightseeing, it pays to wander off the beaten track. There are beguiling small shops and artisans' *botteghe* all over the city.

Prices are sometimes negotiable. Don't, however, expect many bargains. Venice is now one of the most expensive shopping cities in Europe.

Antiques
There are a number of amusing antique shops around Campo Santa Maria del Giglio and the Fenice, but if you are tempted to buy important antique furniture in Venice, remember that the Veneto is an active centre of fabrication. Furniture made of old wood qualifies under Italian law as 'antique'; but if you are importing into another country you may be charged full duty on objects which are not genuine antiques.

Auctions are held about six times a year at **Franco Semenzato** (*Palazzo Giovanelli, Cannaregio 2292, Strada Nuova* ☎*5200811*), and an antique market takes place from time to time in **Campo San Maurizio**.

See also *Artisans, Books, Glass, Jewelry and silver.*

Artisans
Craftsmanship is still very much alive in Venice, with glass and lacemaking (listed separately below) being only the most renowned of the native skills. Venetian artisans also excel in the making and restoration of fine furniture, carved picture frames, wrought iron, lacquerwork, stucco, mosaics, silver, brass and costume jewelry. You can often buy direct from their workshops scattered all over the city, two especially interesting areas being San Tomà and San Barnaba.

A representative selection of small handcrafted articles is sold by **Veneziartigiana** (*San Marco 412, Calle Larga San Marco* ☎*5235032* AE CB ⊙ ⊙ VISA); and an annual crafts exhibition, **Venice Mart**, is usually held in Sept (*information from the Associazione Artigiani Venezia, Dorsoduro 878* ☎*5220788*).

Antonio Gallina da Monte (*San Marco 1864, Calle del Fruttarol* ☎*5220468*) makes fine reproductions of antique stringed instruments, made to order for clients all over the world.

See also *Glass, Jewelry and silver, Lace, linen and textiles, Masks, Paper.*

Books
In the 16thC more books were printed in Venice than by all the rest of the Italian presses together; and it was here, at the Aldine Press, that the pocket classic was invented. While no longer a printing or publishing capital, Venice is still well-supplied with good bookstores.

Three of the best general bookstores in the center, all of which stock a wide selection of guidebooks and maps, are **Libreria Goldoni** (*San Marco 4742, Calle dei Fabbri* ☎*5222384*), **Libreria Internazionale Sangiorgio** (*San Marco 2087, Calle Larga XXII Marzo* ☎*5238451* AE VISA) and **Libreria Sansovino** (*Piazza San Marco 84* ☎*5222623* AE CB ⊙ ⊙ VISA).

For antiquarian books and prints try **Manilio Penso** (*San Polo 2916A, Calle del Mandoler, off Campo San Tomà* ☎5238215 AE) and the **Studio Bibliografico 'La Fenice'** (*San Marco 1850, Calle del Fruttarol* ☎5238006).

Alberto Bertoni
Map 14D3. San Marco 3636, Calle della Mandola ☎5229583.
A jumble of second-hand books on every subject, especially art and architecture.

Fantoni Libri
Map 15D4. San Marco 4119, corner of Salizzada San Luca and Calle Sant'Antonio ☎5220700 AE CB VISA
A first-class selection of recent art and architecture books in their original languages. Fantoni stocks all publications by Electa.

Il Libraio a San Barnaba
Map 14E1. Dorsoduro 2835A, off Campo San Barnaba ☎5228737.
English books, including children's fiction, are sold in a sympathetic environment where you may also sit and read.

Libreria Editrice Filippi
Map 15C5, San Marco 5762, Calle del Paradiso ☎5235635. *Also map 15C5, San Marco 5458, Calle della Bissa* ☎5236916.
Facsimile reprints of old Venetian books and maps, including Francesco Sansovino's early guide to Venice, Sanudo's diaries and Grewemboch's watercolors.

Clothes for men, women and children

Venetians have been noted since the Renaissance for the gorgeous materials and the eccentric manner of their dress; and even in the early years of this century the clothes made by the Venetian-based artist Mariano Fortuny were worn by unconventional women bold enough to defy the rules of Paris. The revival of interest in Fortuny has had a strong effect on the work of many young Venetian designers, whose dreamy, opulent clothes and textiles remain outside the mainstream of Italian fashion.

Nevertheless, you can also find all the up-to-date non-Venetian designer labels — including Armani, Fendi, Krizia, Missoni, Valentino, Versace — in the main shopping streets between San Marco, the Accademia and the Rialto.

Among the most stylish high-fashion boutiques are **Alma** (*San Marco 1811, Ramo Fuseri* ☎ 5237555 AE CB ⊙ VISA), **Laura Biagiotti** (*San Marco 4600A, Calle del Teatro* ☎5223709 AE CB ⊙ ⊙ VISA), **La Coupole** (*San Marco 2366, Calle Larga XXII Marzo* ☎ 5224243 AE CB ⊙ ⊙ VISA *and San Marco 1674, Frezzeria* ☎5206063), **Elisabetta alla Fenice** (*San Marco 1996, Campo San Fantin* ☎5229315 AE CB ⊙ ⊙ VISA), and **Betta Scarpa** (*San Marco 1797, Frezzeria* ☎5287051 AE CB ⊙ ⊙ VISA). And men who like the classic English look will find tailored wools and tweeds of beautiful quality at **Duca d'Aosta** (*San Marco 4922 and 4945* ☎5220733 AE ⊙ ⊙ VISA) and **Élite** (*San Marco 284, Calle Larga San Marco* ☎5230145 AE CB ⊙ ⊙ VISA).

At the other end of the price scale look out for the **Benetton** label, a local success story based in Treviso with several outlets in the center and a new upscale store at *San Marco 1485, Frezzeria* ☎5224762 AE CB ⊙ ⊙ VISA. It is also worth a visit to **Coin** (*Cannaregio 5788, near San Giovanni Crisostomo* ☎5227192 AE CB ⊙ VISA), the biggest department store in Venice, which stocks a full range of clothing and accessories for men, women and children.

But for something specifically Venetian, try the following.

Camiceria San Marco
Map 15E4. San Marco 1340, Calle Vallaresso ☎5221432 [AE] [◉] [◉]
[VISA]

Shirts, blouses and pajamas are made to order within the day from an
extensive choice of fine materials.

Emilio Ceccato
Map 15C4. San Polo 16-17, Sotoportego di Rialto ☎5222700.
This shop has been supplying gondoliers with their characteristic 'uniform'
since 1902. The striped T-shirts and heavy cotton jackets also look good
when worn by nongondoliers with jeans.

Fiorella
Map 14E3. San Marco 2806, Campo Santo Stefano ☎5209228/
5226036 [AE] [◉] [◉] [VISA]

Fiorella Mancini is the successful Venetian designer who was among the first
to revive and popularize the Fortuny style. The dresses are all hand-dyed and
printed. The shop also sells carnival masks, T-shirts, sculptures — some
serious, some bizarre.

Franz
Map 14E3. San Marco 2765a, Calle del Spezier, near San Maurizio
☎ *5227846/5285408* [AE] [◉] [VISA]
Fine, hand-finished lingerie, baby clothes, silk ties and custom-made men's
shirts.

Venetia Studium
*Map 6E7. Palazzo Vitturi Errera; Castello 5204, Calle dei Orbi, near
Santa Maria Formosa* ☎5236953
Faithful copies of Fortuny's pleated silk 'Delphos' dresses, hand-dyed in a
rainbow of colors and weighted with Murano glass beads are sold — for a
price — in the atelier of a private palace.

Glass
Venetians have been making glass for at least a thousand years.
The furnaces were transferred to the island of Murano in 1291, and
by the 16thC Murano glass was in demand all over the world, its
technical secrets closely guarded by order of the Council of Ten
and its beauty celebrated in paintings by Titian, Veronese and
Tintoretto.

  Glass of the highest quality is still made in Venice although you
might not guess it from the ubiquitous glass animals and free-form
paperweights. In fact, delightful objects can sometimes be found
among the rubbish, but if you intend to invest seriously in
Venetian glass you will want to choose from the work of the most
distinguished glass-makers, some of whom who are listed below.

  It is well worth making the short trip to Murano, where the Rio
dei Vetrai is lined with glass-makers and where you can educate
your eye in the two Glass Museums. All the major firms and stores
will make to order anything you like in their range and will pack
and ship anywhere. Remember that Venetian glass is the product
of a highly-skilled and time-consuming craft, and therefore the
authentic product, as opposed to copies of it made in molds, is very
expensive.

  The central showroom on Murano is **CAM** (*IB Piazzale Colonna*
☎739944 [AE] [CB] [◉] [◉] [VISA]), which has a large selection of modern
designs, not all in the best taste, as well as antique copies.

  The aristocrats of Murano glass are **Barovier & Toso**
(*Fondamenta Vetrai 28, Murano* ☎739049), which descends from
the Angelo Barovier who made the famous blue-glass wedding cup
in the Glass Museum. **Nason & Moretti** (*Fondamenta Serenella 12,
Murano* ☎739020) produce exceptionally elegant table glass. **Piero
Toso** (*Toso Vetri d'Arte, Fondamenta Manin 1, Murano* ☎736843)

is an independent craftsman who makes exquisitely simple classical Venetian table glass, copied, if you like, from Old Master paintings.

Back in Venice itself the three most prominent established manufacturers of Venetian glass have stores in Piazza San Marco. They are **Cenedese** (*San Marco 40 and 139* ☎*5225487/5229399*), **Pauly** (*San Marco 76 and 316* ☎*5209899*) and **Salviati** (*San Marco 78 and 110* ☎*5224257*); all take major credit cards. Cenedese and Salviati also have demonstration furnaces in Dorsoduro, near the Salute, and on Murano.

More refined examples are available in Venice from the following:

Amadi
Map 14C2. San Polo 2747, Calle Saoneri ☎*5238089.*
Children love the little shops making and selling tiny glass figures. This one is far above the usual level; the exquisite birds are expensive but nice enough for wedding presents.

Battison
Map 15E4. San Marco 1320, Calle Vallaresso ☎*5230509* AE CB ◈ ◉ VISA
A representative selection, conveniently located near Harry's Bar, of the best (including Nason & Moretti and Barovier & Toso) and the worst.

L'Isola
Map 15E4. San Marco 1468, San Moisè ☎*5231973* AE CB ◈ ◉ VISA
The most attractive of the central glass stores stocks the beautifully restrained work of Carlo Moretti.

Giovanni Moro
Map 15D4. San Marco 1644, Frezzeria ☎*5204362* AE CB ◈ ◉ VISA
This fascinating store is like a museum of antique glass. There are pieces from all over Italy, but the emphasis is on Art Deco from Murano. Don't miss the upstairs rooms where some of the rarest items are kept. Repairs also undertaken in a furnace on the premises.

Siffi
Map 11E8. Castello 4683E, Campo San Zaccaria ☎*5235379.*
Delicately engraved table glass in traditional ornate styles made on Murano by a family of artisans. There are also some reproductions. Siffi will pack and ship anywhere.

Venini
Map 15D5. San Marco 314, Piazzetta dei Leoncini ☎*5224045* AE CB ◈ ◉ VISA
The most innovative of the glass firms, Venini produces heavy modern tableware and architectural lighting.

See also *Jewelry and silver.*

Hair and beauty
There are hairdressers in most of the luxury hotels in Venice and on the Lido. Otherwise, two of the most reliable independent hairdressers, both offering a full range of beauty treatments, are **Carol's** (*San Marco 2422, Calle Larga XXII Marzo* ☎ *5229944/ 5287360* AE) and **Umberto** (*San Marco 5024, Mercerie San Salvador* ☎ *5225589/5221013*).

Jewelry and silver
Under the Republic, Venetian goldsmiths had shops along the Ruga degli Orefici at the Rialto; there you will still find imitations of the thin gold chain, known as *la manina*, for which they were famous. Today the important established jewelers are located around San Marco.

Codognato
Map 15D4. San Marco 1295, Calle Ascensione ☎5225042 AE CB ⓪
⓪ VISA
Codognato sells rare antique pieces as well as modern designs.

Giuseppe Dominici
Map 15D5. San Marco 659-664, Calle Spadaria ☎5223982 AE ⓪ VISA
A good source of old Venetian silver tableware.

Herriz
Map 15E4. San Marco 2381, Via XXII Marzo ☎5204276 AE ⓪ ⓪ VISA
Specialists in Baroque pearls and Art Deco pieces of very high quality.

Manù
Map 15D4. San Marco 1229, Calle del Salvadego (off the Frezzeria)
☎5229294 AE CB ⓪ ⓪ VISA
Antique Murano-glass beads sold separately or strung into charming
necklaces. Stock is authentic, not expensive. Good for presents.

Missiaglia
Map 15D5. Piazza San Marco 125 ☎5224464 AE CB ⓪ ⓪ VISA
The aristocrat of Venetian jewelers will also reset fine stones.

G. Nardi
Map 15D5. Piazza San Marco 69-71 ☎5225733.
Appealing creations in gold and silver worked with precious stones.

Sfriso
Map 14C2. San Polo 2849, Campo San Tomà ☎5223558 AE VISA
Exclusive outlet for the work of Venice's leading modern silversmith, who
will also repair or copy. The cleverly designed key rings, weighted with
reproductions of antique Venetian coins, make desirable, useful souvenirs.

Lace, linen and textiles
Fine lace and sumptuous textiles are as intimately connected with
Venice as glass. The lace island is *Burano* (see *The Venetian
lagoon*). The *Fortuny Museum* displays the famously sensuous
fabrics, which have inspired some modern Venetian textile makers
to rival the master's refined textures and exotic designs.
  You can sometimes find pieces of antique lace and materials in
the antique stores around the Giglio and Fenice. Try **Beppe
Patitucci** (*San Marco 2511B, Campiello de la Feltrina* ☎5236393).

Jesurum
Map 15D5. San Marco 4310, Ponte Canonica ☎5206177 AE CB ⓪
⓪ VISA
Michelangelo Jesurum was one of the people responsible for reviving the lace
industry in the 19thC. His name lives on in the suitably august surroundings
of a converted 12thC church, where you can have your trousseau trimmed
with antique lace or buy household linen.

M
Map 15D4. San Marco 1651, Piscina di Frezzeria ☎5235666 AE CB
⓪ ⓪ VISA
Mirella Spinella's alluring hand-dyed and hand-blocked silk velvets can be
bought by the length or made into turbans, robes, evening bags.

Martinuzzi
Map 15D5. Piazza San Marco 67A ☎5225068 AE CB ⓪ ⓪ VISA
Some of the prettiest hand-embroidered table linen, handkerchiefs and
blouses, as well as lace.

Norelene
Map 14E3. San Marco 2606, Campo San Maurizio ☎5237605.
Imaginative Oriental designs applied to the finest panne velvet or cotton can
be bought by the meter or made into shoes or dresses.

Shopping

V. Trois
Map 14E3. San Marco 2666, Campo San Maurizio ☎5222905/ 5226175.
Furnishing fabrics still made to Fortuny's original designs in 450 different patterns and colors.

Masks

Since the revival of Carnival, masks have become popular souvenirs, but what is made for tourists does not always do justice to a traditional Venetian craft. A good mask-maker is **Emilio Massaro** (*Map 14E2, San Marco 2934, Calle Vetturi* ☎ *5204283*).

Paper

Stores selling printed or marbled bookend papers are now widespread in Venice. The only source of paper hand-printed according to the *carta varese* method is **Legatoria Piazzesi** (*San Marco 2511C, Santa Maria del Giglio* ☎*5221205*), whose stunning range is produced from a vast collection of old blocks. The most delightful of the marbled papers (also marbled silk made into scarves or cushions) are available from **Alberto Valese** (*San Marco 1920, Calle del Teatro and San Marco 3135, Salizada San Samuele* ☎*5200921* AE ◉ ◉ VISA).

Shoes and handbags

Some of the most desirable Italian shoes are made in the Veneto. Alas, they are no longer less expensive in Venice than elsewhere in Europe. There are also plenty of imported status labels, including Gucci, Armani, Ferragamo, Maud Frizon, Vuitton. Cheaper, but still stylish, shoes can be found in the streets near both ends of the Rialto bridge; or, in the center, from **Zecchi** (*Map 15D5, San Marco 300, Merceria* ☎ *5204453* AE CB ◉ ◉ VISA).

Bottega Veneta
Map 15E4. San Marco 1337, Calle Vallaresso ☎5228489 AE CB ◉ ◉ VISA
Shoes and handbags for chic resort life made by a Vicenza firm.

Franz
Map 14E3. San Marco 2765A, Calle del Spezier ☎5285408/5227846 AE ◉ VISA
Custom-made shoes.

Renè
Map 15C5. San Marco 4983, Merceria San Salvador ☎5229766 AE ◉ ◉ VISA
Renè Caovilla is the self-styled 'Fabergé of shoemakers.' His leather shoes and handbags — embroidered, gilded, studded with metal or rhinestones — are, not surprisingly, among the most expensive in the world.

Rolando Segalin
Map 15D4. San Marco 4365, Calle dei Fuseri ☎5222115 AE CB ◉ ◉ VISA
Comfortable, fashionable and ever-lasting custom-made shoes.

Toni
Map 14C2. San Polo 2722, Calle dei Saoneri ☎5287825.
Good leather handbags made on the premises at very reasonable prices.

Vogini
Map 15D4. San Marco 1275A-1301, Calle Ascensione ☎5222573 AE CB ◉ ◉ VISA
A useful, centrally located pair of stores selling a good range of formal and informal handbags. Also wallets, purses, suitcases, umbrellas.

The Venetian lagoon

The excursions described in this section cover the Venetian lagoon, and are followed by a separate section on the Venetian mainland.

Venice lies at the center of a shallow lagoon created by the estuaries of three rivers — the Piave, Brenta and Sile — and protected from the Adriatic by a fragile line of sand bars (*lidi*) which are separated by three openings: the Porto del Lido, Porto di Malamocco and Porto di Chioggia.

All of these precariously balanced elements have been modified and controlled over the centuries by Venetian engineers. The rivers were diverted from the 14thC to prevent the lagoon from silting up. Two of the five natural channels through the *lidi* were blocked to minimize flooding; and in the 18thC the *lidi* were reinforced by the massive Istrian-stone sea walls known as the *murazzi*. The next major intervention will be the installation of movable gates across the *porti*, to be raised against the abnormally high tides which cause flooding in Venice.

The lagoon is 52km (32½ miles) long from the mouth of the river Sile at its north to that of the Brenta at its southern extremity. It covers an area of over 500sq.km (193sq. miles) of which a little more than half is 'dead' (*laguna morta*), that is, covered by water only during high tides. The 'live' lagoon (*laguna viva*) is navigable along the course of underwater channels 10m (32ft) deep, some natural and some excavated by man; they are marked by wooden or concrete piles, known as *bricole*.

For you live like sea birds, with your homes dispersed, like the Cyclades, across the surface of the water. The solidity of the earth on which they rest is secured only by osier and wattle; yet you do not hesitate to oppose so frail a bulwark to the wildness of the sea.

Letter to the maritime officers of Venice
from Cassiodorus, praetorian prefect of the
Emperor Theodoric, AD523.

Apart from Venice itself, there are some 40 islands in the lagoon. About half are abandoned; others are used for such purposes as isolation hospitals, mental homes, prisons or market gardens. The island of San Servolo has recently been established as a training center for craftsmen in the building and restoration trades. Several deserted islands near Venice are destined to be used as sports and recreation centers as well as public parks. Venetians enjoy rowing in the lagoon (see p.190 for information about rowing clubs). And it is very pleasant on a fine day to picnic among the fields and orchards of Le Vignole or Sant'Erasmo (*take water bus 13 from the Fondamenta Nuove*).

The islands described below are the most interesting and accessible. All of them may be reached by public transport; there is also a tourist service for Murano-Burano-Torcello from the Riva degli Schiavoni.

Burano

Map 3D5. 9km (5½ miles) NE of Venice. Population: 5,500. Getting there: Water bus 12 from Fondamenta Nuove takes about 35mins.

Burano is the most cheerful and one of the most populous of the lagoon islands. Its brightly painted houses give it the air of an Italian opera set, while the success of its principal industries — lacemaking, fishing and boatbuilding — account for the modest but manifest well-being of its people.

In the 16thC Burano produced the finest lace in Europe (Philip II of Spain ordered Mary Tudor's bridal trousseau from Burano in 1566). The lace industry died out after the fall of the Republic but was revived in the late 19thC. Much of the inexpensive lace and crochetwork on sale everywhere is in fact made in Hong Kong, but those interested in the traditional lacemaking can visit the **Consorzio dei Merletti**, the Lace School (*Piazza B. Galuppi* ☎730034 ▇▇ *open Mon-Sun 9am-6pm*).

The main street and square, the **Via and Piazza Baldassare Galuppi**, are named after the island's most illustrious son, the composer — subject of Browning's poem *A Toccata of Galuppi's*.

The island possesses one important work of art, G.B. Tiepolo's youthful painting of the *Calvary* (*c.*1725), housed in the 16thC church of San Martino which is entered from Piazza Galuppi.

≈ Via B. Galuppi is lined with fish restaurants. The best is **Da Romano** (*Via B. Galuppi 221* ☎ 730030 ▐▐▐ *closed Tues*), an enormous old-fashioned artists' trattoria. The menu is short and rarely varies. Service is friendly but can be slow on busy days.

Excursion

A boat service from the quay beside San Martino will ferry you to the silent cypress-clad island of **San Francesco del Deserto** ☎5286863, *offering welcome, open 9-11am, 3-5.30pm*), where one cloister of the modest little church survives from the 13thC Franciscan hermitage.

Chioggia
Map 3E4. 25km (16 miles) s of Venice. Population: 53,600. Getting there: By bus, SIAMIC buses leave Piazzale Roma every 30 mins and take about 50 mins; by water, water bus 11 from the Lido (Piazza Santa Maria Elisabetta) takes 1½hrs, with bus connections; during July, Aug a direct service from Riva degli Schiavoni takes 2hrs. A pleasant way to make the journey is to stop off on the way, perhaps for lunch at Malamocco, and again at Pellestrina to see the 'murazzi,' the massive Istrian-stone sea walls built 1744-82, returning by bus in the evening.

Chioggia lies on the s edge of the Venetian lagoon, connected to the mainland by a causeway. It is one of the most active fishing ports in Italy and the most densely populated of the lagoon islands. Its atmosphere is reminiscent of the poorer neighborhoods of Venice — the difference being that it is overrun with cars.

One of the most serious threats ever suffered by the Venetian Republic was the invasion of Chioggia in 1379 by the Genoese who devastated the island before they were eventually cornered by the Venetian fleet.

Sights and places of interest

The porticoed main street, known locally as 'the Piazza,' is the **Corso del Popolo**; it is lined with cafés, restaurants and stores.

At the s end of the Corso is **Piazza Vescovile**, the most scenic part of the island, where a marble balustrade adorned with 18thC statues overlooks the canal. The **Duomo** (1624), which stands in the Piazza Vescovile, was Baldassare Longhena's first important work. It has an imposing interior and, in the chapel to the left of the chancel, a youthful painting of the *Torture of Two Martyrs* by G.B. Tiepolo. Next to the Duomo is the 14thC Gothic church of **San Martino**, now used for temporary exhibitions, which has a polyptych of the *Madonna and Child* (1349) attributed to Paolo Veneziano.

The Corso broadens in front of the Granaio (1322) which bears a *Madonna and Child* by Sansovino on its facade. The fish market, which takes place every morning, is behind the Granaio on the Canale della Vena. The Corso ends at the Piazzetta Vigo, overlooking the harbor; in it stands a Greek marble column carrying the lion of St Mark. A minute's walk to the E, across two bridges, is the church of **San Domenico** which contains Carpaccio's *St Paul* (1520), the artist's last known work.

≋ Absolutely fresh fish is a reliable treat on Chioggia. Most of the restaurants are in the Corso and there is little to choose among them. Two good restaurants are **El Gato** (*Campo Sant' Andrea 653* ☎*401806* ◨ to ◨◨◨ ◭ ◉ ◫ *closed Mon and Jan*), and the **Trattoria Buon Pesce** (*Stradale Ponte Canera* ☎*400861* ◨ *closed Wed and Jan*).

Lido
Map 16. 1.4km (just under 1 mile) SE of Venice. Population: 19,300. Getting there: Water bus 6 or 11 from Riva degli Schiavoni (no.6 leaves every 20mins, takes 15mins) to Piazza Santa Maria Elisabetta; no.11 also goes direct to Malamocco and Alberoni; or water bus 2 from Piazzale Roma or Rialto.

The slim, sandy island which cradles the Venetian lagoon, protecting it against the open sea, was developed about 100yrs ago as a middle-class suburb of Venice and a bathing resort. Although no longer quite as fashionable as the resort evoked by Thomas Mann's *Death in Venice* and Evelyn Waugh's *Brideshead Revisited*, the Lido is still the nearest place to the historic center where you can swim in the sea, ride, or play golf and tennis — with the convenience of transport. It is worth a visit if only for the sake of the return trip at sunset. As the boat rounds the island of San Giorgio Maggiore and enters the inner harbor of San Marco, you understand why it is so often said that the only way to approach Venice is by sea.

The Lido is 12km (7½ miles) long and not more than 1km (½ mile) wide. The most highly developed sections are toward its N end around Piazza Santa Maria Elisabetta, where the boats from Venice arrive, and the Quattro Fontane district where the Excelsior Hotel and the Casino are to be found. Farther S is the little fishing village of **Malamocco**, named after the first capital of the lagoon settlements. At **Alberoni**, the curved southern tip of the island, there are two golf courses (one reserved for clients of Ciga hotels) and good beaches. Beach cabanas may be rented by the day or season from the better hotels, but are outrageously expensive. Fortunately, even the Excelsior will provide you with a changing hut and comfortable deck chair for a reasonable charge.

Event The main annual event is the International Film Festival which has its headquarters at the Palazzo del Cinema next to the Casino (see *Calendar of events* in *Planning*).

Sights and places of interest
Although nobody would visit the Lido for the sake of sightseeing, there is one architectural masterpiece which compels attention. This is the massive Istrian stone **Forte di Sant'Andrea** ☆ (1545-71) designed by Michele Sanmicheli, which guards the main entrance to the lagoon, the Porto di Lido, from the island of Vignole; the fortress can be seen from the NW corner of the Lido at the end of the Riviera San Nicolò. Although the sea has now begun to erode its foundations, this low, five-sided structure, its central block in rusticated Doric order, remains one of the most impressive Venetian buildings.

The nearby 17thC **church of San Nicolò** is of little interest apart from the attractive carved choir stalls (1635) and two fine Veneto-Byzantine capitals left over from the original 11thC church. In Via Cipro is the 14thC Jewish cemetery, burial place of many distinguished Italian Jews.

Architectural buffs will be amused by Giovanni Sardi's fantastical Neo-Byzantine **Hotel Excelsior** (1898-1908) and the pretty **Casa del Farmacista** (1926) by Del Giudice in the Via Sandro Gallo.

147

Hotels

Des Bains 🏨
Map 16D3. Lungomare Marconi 17 ☎5265921 ⑥ 410142 ⫴⫴ 258 rms
🛏 258 ⊞ ⬛ ▆ ▆ AE ⑥ VISA *Closed Nov-Mar.*
This Ciga-owned grand hotel offers luxury in a somewhat melancholy
atmosphere. *Death in Venice*, the book and the movie, were set here.
🔲 ⚓ ⇌ 🐾 ⤴ 🏖 🎿 ⛪ 𝐘 ⊙

Excelsior 🏨 🏛
Map 16F3. Lungomare Marconi 40 ☎5260201 ⑥ 410023 ⫴⫴ 230 rms
🛏 224 ⊞ ⬛ ▆ ▆ AE CB ⑥ ⑥ VISA *Closed Nov-Mar.*
This huge, turreted building in pseudo-Moorish style dates from the turn of
the century when it was one of the great hotels of Europe. Now also part of
the Ciga chain, it has been modernized in a slick way inside. Over half of the
rooms overlook the sea. Some guests complain of impersonal service.
‡ ▢ 🖼 ⚓ ⚓ ⤴ ⇌ 🐾 ⤴ ✓ ⤴ 🎿 𝐘

Quattro Fontane
Map 16E3. Via Quattro Fontane 16 ☎ 5260227/5261938 ⫴⫴ 70 rms
🛏 56 ⬛ ⬛ ▆ *Closed Oct to Apr.*
A friendly, privately-owned hotel near the Casino. The building, in
rustic-cottage style, surrounds a cool, shaded terrace where meals and drinks
are taken in summer.
⬛ 🖼 ⚓ 🐾 🐾 𝐘

Villa Mabàpa
Map 16B2. Riviera San Nicolò 16 ☎5260590 ⑥ 440170 ⫴⫴ to ⫴⫴⫴ 64
rms 🛏 64 ⊞ ⬛ ⬛ ▆ ▆ AE CB ⑥ ⑥ VISA
A stylish little private hotel built in the 1930s on the lagoon side of the Lido
and commanding a fine view of Venice. The best rooms, in a newly built
annex, have balconies and overlook the hotel's pretty garden.
⬛ ‡ ⚓ ▢ 🖼 ⚡ ⚓ ⤴ ⇌ 🐾 🎿 ⛪ 𝐘

Restaurants

It is surprisingly difficult to eat fresh fish *al fresco* in the developed northern
sections of the Lido, although some locals swear by **Belvedere** (*Via Cerigo 2*
☎5260115 ⫴⫴ AE VISA *closed Tues*) which is conveniently located opposite
the main boat stops from Venice.

The best fish restaurants are at the far end of the island near Malamocco
and Alberoni. Even better, catch a ferry across the Porto Malamocco to San
Pietro in Volta where there are several simple, attractive restaurants. **Da
Nane** (☎688100 ⫴⫴ to ⫴⫴⫴ *closed Mon and Jan, Feb*) is the most agreeable.

Nightlife

The **Casino Municipale** (*Lungomare Marconi, near the Excelsior Hotel*
☎5260626) is the summer headquarters of the Venice Casino. Boats go there
direct from the station, Piazzale Roma and San Marco every 30mins after 2pm

Murano ☆

*Map 3D5. 1.2km (³/₄ mile) NE of Venice. Population: 7,700.
Getting there: Water bus 5 or 12 (takes 10mins from
Fondamenta Nuove).*
Glass has been made on Murano since 1291 when the furnaces
were banned from Venice as a precaution against fire. In the
16thC, the great age of Murano glass, the island had 37 glass
factories and a thriving population of 30,000. As one of the few
Venetian export industries, glassmaking was a privileged
occupation; the secrets of the craft were rigorously guarded and
artisans in glass were permitted to marry into the nobility.

Even after Murano lost its monopoly of the manufacture of
crystal glass, its blown-glass mirrors and chandeliers (jointed so
they could be dismantled for export) remained popular throughout

Europe. Today the techniques by which Murano glass is made are hardly a secret — indeed the tourist is assailed from every side with invitations to see it being made — but few non-Venetian artisans have the skill required to achieve the exquisite lightness of the native product.

Murano is built on five islands and is divided roughly in half by its own 'Grand Canal.' The canal is spanned by one bridge, the Ponte Vivarini, named after the 15thC family of artists born here. Water bus 5 stops very near the two main sights.

Sights and places of interest
Museo dell'Arte Vetraria *(Glass Museums)* ☆
Fondamenta Giustinian and Fondamenta Manin ☎ *739586* ■ *Open Mon-Tues, Thurs-Sat 10am-4pm, Sun 9am-12.30pm. Closed Wed.*
The largest collection of Venetian glass in the world, consisting of some 4,000 pieces, is housed in the two glass museums. The late-17thC Palazzo Giustinian is arranged in chronological order with Roman fragments on the ground floor, Renaissance-19thC on the **piano nobile**. The most remarkable and precious object of all is the blue-glass wedding cup decorated in the last quarter of the 15thC by Angelo Barovier with enamelwork portraits and allegorical love scenes; it was the first example of enamelwork applied to glass since antiquity.

20thC glass, including the work of living master glass blowers, is housed separately on the Fondamenta Manin.
Santi Maria e Donato † ★
Campo San Donato. Open 8am-noon, 4-7pm.
The most important church on Murano. Despite a heavy-handed 19thC restoration, it is one of the best surviving examples of Veneto-Byzantine ecclesiastical architecture in the lagoon. The 7thC foundation was rebuilt in the 12thC, when the relics of St Donato were brought to Murano from the Greek island of Kefalonia. The most elaborate part of the brick and terra-cotta exterior is the apse, decorated with dog-tooth and zigzag patterns like those on Santa Fosca on *Torcello*.

The interior, much tampered with over the centuries, has a wonderful **mosaic floor** (1140), fine Veneto-Byzantine capitals, and a 15thC ship's-keel ceiling. The dominating work of art is the mosaic, over the apse, of the *Virgin* against a gold ground (early 13thC). Over the first altar on the left is a polychrome wooden relief of *St Donato* (1310) with painted portraits of donors attributed to Paolo Veneziano.
Other sights
On the other side of the bridge is the church of **San Pietro Martire**, which contains two great altarpieces by Giovanni Bellini: the monumental *Madonna and Child Enthroned Between St Augustine and St Mark who Present the Kneeling Doge Agostini Barbarigo* (1488) and the *Assumption with Saints* (1510-13), against a fine landscape.

⚊ There are plenty of modest fish restaurants on the island. One is Ai Frati (☎*736694* Ⅲ AE ⑤ ⑥ WSA *closed Thurs and Feb*).

Shopping
The main glass factories in Fondamenta dei Vetrai will make glass to order and send it on willingly. For details see *Shopping*.

San Lazzaro degli Armeni
Map 16E1. 1.3km (just under a mile) SE of Venice. Getting there: Water bus 10 or 20 from Riva degli Schiavoni or the Lido. Visits permitted Thurs, Sun 3-5pm.
The Armenian monastery of San Lazzaro, **Monastero Mekhitarista** or Mechitar Monastery (☎*760104; donation expected*) is best known to Anglo-Saxons for its associations with Byron, who learned Armenian here.

The monastery museum contains a large collection of Armenian manuscripts, mementoes of Byron and, on the ceiling of the vestibule, a painting of *Peace and Justice* (*c.*1730) by G.B. Tiepolo.

San Michele
Map 7. 1km (1/2 mile) N of Venice. Cemetery open 8am-4pm. Getting there: Water bus 5 (takes 5mins from Fondamenta Nuove).

The church of **San Michele in Isola** ★ stands on the cemetery island of Venice with its lovely white facade turned away from the city. Begun by Mauro Codussi in 1469 shortly after his arrival in Venice and consecrated in 1477, it was the first Venetian Renaissance church, 'a temple which not only evokes antiquity but actually surpasses it,' in the words of one of the Benedictine monks who commissioned it. It remains one of the most perfect small buildings in Italy.

The facade in crisply rusticated Istrian stone — the building material Codussi introduced to Venice — is in a confidently understated classical style. The hexagonal Emiliani Chapel to the left was added in 1530 by Guglielmo Bergamasco.

By comparison with the harmonious purity of the facade, the interior seems awkwardly proportioned and contains little of special interest apart from the monks' choir screen, decorated with some fine carvings, dividing the vestibule from the rest of the nave.

The **cemetery** was laid out in the early 19thC when the Napoleonic regime banned burial in the city, and was remodeled in the 1870s. It is too small to serve the local population and most Venetians are permitted to rest here for a limited time only. Among the illustrious foreigners buried in the cemetery are Igor Stravinsky, Serge Diaghilev, Ezra Pound and Frederick Rolfe.

Torcello ★
Map 3C5. 10km (61/2 miles) NE of Venice. Population: c.100. Getting there: Water bus 12 from Fondamenta Nuove (takes about 45mins).

Torcello is the mother of Venice. The island was settled between the 5th and 7thC by the first waves of refugees from the Barbarian invasions of Altinum on the mainland. They called it 'little tower' after the tower from which a bishop of Altinum had been shown the way to safety by the stars. It became the most prosperous and populous of the early lagoon communities; but its decline, brought about by the growth of Venice and exacerbated by malaria, was rapid after the 14thC and, since the 18thC, Torcello has been nearly deserted, with a population today of only some 100 people. The main monuments are a 10min walk from the boat stop.

Sights and places of interest
Cathedral (*Santa Maria Assunta*) 🏛 ✝ ★
☎730084 ⬛ *Open 10am-12.30pm, 2-6.30pm; closes 2hrs earlier in winter.*

The cathedral was founded by order of Isaac, Exarch of Ravenna (as the original inscription to the left of the high altar records) in 639, the year after the final sack of Altinum, when the Bishop's Seat was transferred to Torcello. Although substantially rebuilt in the 9th and early 11thC, it retains the character of the early Christian churches in Ravenna on which it was modeled. In front of the entrance can be seen the remains of the 7thC Baptistry.

The **interior**, profoundly moving in its solemn dignity, is divided into three aisles by Greek marble columns bearing 11thC Byzantine capitals. The columns and marble panels of the iconostasis, which carries a series of 15thC paintings, are also 11thC, as is the tessellated marble and mosaic floor. The entire interior facade is covered with a huge mosaic of the *Last Judgment* (12th-13thC) which remains impressive despite a heavy-handed restoration in the 19thC, when some sections were replaced by copies.

In the chancel is the original 7thC altar, discovered during an excavation in 1929; in the curve of the aspe is the slender, solitary figure of the *Madonna* ★ (13thC), one of the outstanding masterpieces of Byzantine mosaic, who stands above a frieze of 12thC *apostles*. The vault mosaic of the *Agnus Dei* in the aspe to the right of the chancel is a 13thC copy of a 6thC mosaic in San Vitale at Ravenna. The mosaics have recently been restored.

Mother and daughter, you behold them both in their widowhood — Torcello and Venice.

Ruskin, *The Stones of Venice*, 1851-53

The little church of **Santa Fosca** which stands next to the cathedral was built in the 11thC by Greek workmen. The arcaded porch which surrounds three sides of the church is a 12thC addition. Although it lacks the dome which was almost certainly intended, the beautifully proportioned interior is a fine early example in the lagoon of the centralized Greek-cross plan.

Museo dell'Estuario

☎ 730761 🎦 *Open Tues-Sun 10.30am-12.30pm, 2-4pm. Closed Mon.*
The museum is opposite the cathedral, in the Palazzo dell'Archivio and the Palazzo del Consiglio, both dating from the 14thC. Founded in 1870, it contains archeological material from Altinum and the lagoon and works from demolished churches on Torcello, as well as the 13thC silver altarpiece from the cathedral.

➥ **Locanda Cipriani**

☎ 730150 ▥▥ 🍽 🅰🅴 *Open mid Mar-Oct Wed-Sun (closed Mon, Tues).*
Like Harry's Bar (see *Restaurants*), of which it is an offspring, the Locanda Cipriani is one of the gastronomic institutions of the Veneto. The food and drinks are familiar from the parent restaurant.

➥ **Osteria Al Ponte del Diavolo** (*Via Chiesa 10/11* ☎730401 ▥▯ ▭ ◼) 🍽 ▦ ◁ 🅰🅴 *closed Thurs, Jan and Feb*) is a pleasant restaurant run by a former employee of the **Locanda Cipriani**.

➥ **Villa 600** (☎730999 ▥▯ 🍽 *closed Wed, Jan*) has a limited choice of simple, honest dishes in a pretty.16thC villa with a sunny terrace.

The mainland

It is still possible to meet Venetians who have never set foot on *terra firma*; and after a few days in Venice one may understand why. Many foreigners share their reluctance ever to leave this iridescent, fragile haven from the cars, factories and pressures of the real world.

Venice is unique and its beauty is matchless. It is also stony, confining, sometimes humid, often overcrowded, and can induce moods of melancholy or restlessness. The day may come when you look at the landscape background of a painting, perhaps by Cima or Bellini, and yearn to be off, just for a day, to follow the path that winds through the Venetian plain along the banks of a silvery river and up into the cool green hills. This is the day to plan an excursion onto the mainland.

No attempt has been made to cover the whole of the Veneto, much less the vast area of N Italy which was once under Venetian dominion. The places listed, with the exception of Verona, may all be visited from Venice within a day. Following the individual alphabetically-listed entries is a suggested tour of Palladio's villas, planned as two separate day trips from Venice.

Where possible, good restaurants have been recommended in or near each town or village mentioned in this section. Hotels have not been included, except in Verona, where an overnight stay is essential if you are to see many of the city's attractions. In addition, three country hotels are recommended at the end of this introduction as an alternative base for seeing Venice.

Mainland

Getting to the mainland

Venice is linked to the major centers to the w, Padua, Vicenza and
Verona, by a good train service and the Milan autostrada A4.
There are also frequent trains, as well as the autostrada A27, for
Treviso, Conegliano and Vittorio Veneto to the N and a one-track
train for Castelfranco and Bassano to the NW. There is also a direct
bus service from Piazzale Roma to the places close to Venice, such
as Malcontenta, Mestre, Mirano and Stra.

Although it is possible to reach most other places in the Veneto
by a combination of train and bus, the most pleasant and
convenient way of exploring the rural areas is by car. Renting a car
would also enable you to combine several of the smaller towns and
villages on a one-day trip.

Art and architecture in the Veneto

The two most challenging day excursions are to Padua — the
university city where the Santo, Donatello's sculptures and
Giotto's frescoes are only the most outstanding attractions — and
Vicenza, the home of Palladian architecture. Verona, the most
prosperous and one of the most attractive cities in northern Italy,
has many historic monuments, stretching in time from the Roman
amphitheater to the Renaissance palaces of Michele Sanmicheli.

Some of the smaller towns and villages are suggested primarily,
although not always exclusively, because of their association with
one great artist or school of artists. To see one of the most magical
of Renaissance paintings, Giorgione's *Madonna and Saints*, you
must visit his native Castelfranco. The hill country around
Conegliano inspired some of Cima da Conegliano's loveliest
landscape backgrounds, and he is represented in its Duomo by a
majestic altarpiece. There are key works by the Bassano family of
painters in the museum of their native Bassano. And a visit to
Possagno, birthplace of the greatest of Neoclassical sculptors,
Antonio Canova, is essential for a full understanding of his genius.

Although there are spectacular medieval walls at Montagnana,
Maróstica and Castelfranco, and castles above Asolo and Este, the
chief architectural glory of the Veneto is its rich heritage of
16th-18thC villas. The most influential of all Italian architects was
Andrea Palladio. All but one of his churches are in Venice; most of
his urban palaces are in Vicenza; and his villas are all in the
Veneto.

The landscape

The most dramatically beautiful area of the Veneto is the northern
part of the province of Belluno, where the Dolomites rise to above
3,000m (10,000ft) and where the fashionable skiing resort of
Cortina is located. In the foothills of the Dolomites are the plateau
of Asiago, Monte Grappa and the plateau of Cansiglio; below are
the gentler hills around Maróstica, Bassano, Asolo and
Conegliano. Other hilly regions are the Monti Bérici s of Vicenza
and the Colli Euganei s of Padua.

Eating on the mainland

Mainland restaurants in general maintain a far higher standard,
and lower prices, than those in Venice. The fish and vegetables are
invariably fresher; there is an immense choice of game, cheeses,
wines and mushrooms which rarely seem to find their way onto
Venetian menus.

It is worth planning a day excursion around a meal at one of the
best country restaurants, which are at Conegliano, Giavera del
Montello, Mel, Mirano and Solighetto. Venetians will often make

the short trip to Mestre or Treviso just for the sake of a meal. And there are more good restaurants at Asolo, Bassano, Padua, Rovigo, Thiene, Vicenza, and, particularly, at Verona.

Hotels on the mainland

Venice in summer is hot, sticky and overcrowded; but summer may be the only season when you are free to visit Venice. One solution to this dilemma is to choose a hotel on the relatively cool and peaceful mainland, near enough to Venice to allow for daily sightseeing expeditions.

Three of the best hotels, described below, are in converted villas, originally built by Venetians who wished to escape from the rigors of their own summer.

Relais El Toula' ▥
Map 3B4. Via Postua 63, 31050 Ponzano, Treviso
☎*(0422)969023/969191* ◉ *433029* ▥▥▥ *10 rms* ▭ *10* ▦ ━ ☲ AE ◉
VISA *Restaurant closed Tues.*

Location: 10km (7 miles) NW of Treviso. This 'Relais de Campagne,' in an elegantly converted old farmhouse surrounded by a spacious park, was opened in 1971 by the clever and fastidious restaurateur Alfredo Beltrame. It is run, with considerable charm, like a private villa — except that not many private villas today could match the quality of the food. All the well-furnished bedrooms overlook the park.
◠ ▢ ⬚ � ≈ ⛱

Villa Cipriani ▥
Map 2B3. Via Canova 298, 31011 Asolo ☎*(0423)55444* ◉ *411060*
▥▥▥ *32 rms* ▭ *32* ▦ ━ ☲ ⬟ ⬚ AE CB ◉ ◉ VISA

The Villa Cipriani at Asolo is one of the few links in the Ciga hotel chain which has retained its old character as well as its polish. It is a wholly delightful and beautifully managed hotel in a 16thC villa, its garden overflowing with roses and flowering shrubs and overlooking a peaceful valley clad in vines and olive trees. There is every luxury, but in an unpretentious and relaxing environment which appeals especially to a faithful British clientele. All the bedrooms are well-appointed and some have private terraces and views over the valley. The restaurant still lives up to the name of Cipriani, famous throughout Italy.
◠ ✻ ₺ ▢ ⬚ �is ⥼ ⛱ ☗

Villa Condulmer
*Map 3C4. Via Zermanese 1, Zerman di Mogliano Veneto, 31021
Treviso* ☎*(041)457100* ▥▥▥ *40 rms* ▭ *40* ▦ ━ ⬚ ⬚ ☲ AE ◉ ◉
VISA *Closed mid-Nov to mid-Mar.*

Only 20mins from Venice and next to an 18-hole golf course, tennis courts and stables, the Villa Condulmer is ideally situated for those who wish to combine a sporting vacation with sightseeing in Venice. The 18thC villa stands in a fine wooded park; but the interior is rather gloomy and the bedroom furnishings bland.
◠ ₺ ⬚ ⁒ ☖ ≈ ⥼ ℘ ⟋ ♞ ⬤ ⛱

Asolo ☆
*Map 2B3. 65km (40miles) NW of Venice. Province of Treviso.
Population: 6,200. Getting there: By train to Treviso or
Bassano del Grappa, then bus; by car, road no.13 to
Treviso, then no.348 to Montebelluna. Asolo is off the
Bassano road, no.248* **i** *Via Regina Cornaro 209* ☎*(0423)
52226.*

Asolo is the jewel of Venetian hill towns. Its arcaded streets and frescoed old houses snuggle beneath the massive fortress, the Rocca, which dominates the Asolean hills. Known as the town 'of a hundred prospects,' it overlooks a cypress- and vine-clad landscape which has been conscientiously defended against industrial developments.

Asolo has not only one of the most elegant of country hotel/restaurants (described below and in the introduction to *The mainland*), but also an atmosphere that positively invites relaxation. There is even a word for it, *asolare*, meaning 'to while away the time pleasantly doing nothing in particular'; the word was coined by the Venetian poet and scholar Cardinal Pietro Bembo (1470-1547). Bembo was the most brilliant guest of that sad figure Caterina Cornaro, deposed Queen of Cyprus, to whom the Venetians gave Asolo as her domain in exile in 1489; she remained here until 1509, when she fled from the advancing Imperial army to Venice, where she died the following year.

The British have traditionally been especially receptive to the charm of Asolo, which today has a distinguished Anglo-Saxon colony. Robert Browning, a frequent visitor, set *Pippa Passes* here and celebrated his love for the place in his last volume of poems, the *Asolando*. Eleanor Duse, another frequent visitor, chose to be buried in Asolo. The travel writer Freya Stark made her home here.

Sights and places of interest

In the spacious main square, **Piazza Maggiore**, are the **Duomo**, in which the best paintings are the *Assumption with Sts Basil and Anthony Abbot* by Lorenzo Lotto and the *Assumption with Sts Anthony Abbot and Steven* by Jacopo Bassano, and the 15thC **Loggia del Capitano**, which houses the **Museo Civico** (▧ *open Tues-Sat summer 9.30am-noon, 4-7pm, winter 9.30am-noon, 3.30-5.30pm; Sun 3-6pm; closed Mon*), containing memorabilia of Asolo's most famous foreign residents, Caterina Cornaro, D'Annunzio and his mistress, the actress Eleanor Duse, and Browning, as well as archeological material, paintings (notably by B. Strozzi) and sculptures by Canova.

Above the piazza in Via Regina Cornaro are the remains of the **Castello**, which was Caterina Cornaro's official residence.

Via Dante leads from Piazza D'Annunzio toward the **Rocca**, a restored medieval fortress with Roman foundations, which commands a magnificent panorama over the Asolean hills.

Robert Browning's son, Pen, and Eleanor Duse are buried in the **cemetery of Sant'Anna**, which is reached by taking Via Canova — no.306 on the left was Eleanor Duse's house — from Piazza D'Annunzio.

Restaurants

Charly's One
Via Roma 55 ☎ *(0423) 52201* ▮▮ ⬚ ⬚ ⬚ ⬚ ⬚ ▦ ⬚ ⬚ ▥ *Closed Fri and Nov.*
A fashionable restaurant in an 18thC villa which emulates the atmosphere of an English club. The style of cooking is a pleasing mixture of Veneto and Ligurian with borrowings from the Cipriani.

Villa Cipriani ▥
Via Canova 298 ☎ *(0423) 55444* ▮▮▮▮ ⬚ ⬚ ▦ ⬚ ⬚ ▥
The hotel and its garden are described in the introduction to *The mainland*. The menu, in the classic Cipriani mode, concentrates on exquisite interpretations of the regional cuisine; the American drinks are faultless, like the service.

⬚ Also recommended is **Due Mori** (*Piazza Eleonora Duse 229* ☎ *(0423) 52256* ▮▯ *to* ▮▮▯ *closed Wed and late July*), a cozy, unpretentious *locanda* centered around an open fire.

Shopping

Pen Browning founded a silk factory and shop, the **Tesseria Asolana** (*in the center* ☎ *(0423) 52062*), which today is owned by Freya Stark's family.

Excursions

Within easy reach of Asolo are **Maser**, 7km (4½ miles) E and **Possagno**, 7km (4½ miles) N.

Bassano del Grappa ☆
*Map 2B2. 76km (47 miles) NW of Venice. Province of Vicenza. Population: 37,000. Getting there: By train, a frequent service from Venice takes 1hr; by car, autostrada A4 to Padua, then road no. 47 **i** Viale delle Fosse 9 ☎ (0424) 24351.*

Bassano is dramatically situated at the mouth of the Brenta valley where the river surges down from the mountains into the plain at the base of Monte Grappa.

It has been a flourishing manufacturing town since the early 15thC when it willingly submitted to Venetian control. It is still a thriving industrial center, best known for its ceramics, wrought iron, reproduction antique furniture and *grappa*.

Bassano was the home of one of the most prominent Renaissance schools of Venetian mainland painting, founded by the Da Ponte family, who called themselves Bassano after their native town, and whose outstanding member, Jacopo (1515/17-92), is magnificently represented in the Museo Civico.

Napoleon defeated the Austrians near Bassano in 1796. Despite serious damage during World Wars I and II, the town retains many of its old arcaded streets, frescoed houses, and Renaissance and Baroque buildings.

Sights and places of interest

The town center is **Piazza Libertà** where the 18thC Neo-Palladian church of **San Giovanni Battista** contains a youthful painting of *St John the Baptist* by G.B. Piazzetta. The complex of houses at no.34, opposite the church, is the **Casa Remondini**. This building was the headquarters of the Remondini printing works, the most famous in 18thC Europe, whose engravings of popular subjects were sold all over the world. To the right of the church is the 16thC **Palazzo del Municipio**.

The adjacent **Piazza Garibaldi**, laid out in the 18thC, is dominated by the **Torre di Ezzelino** which remains from the defensive bastions built in the 13thC by the fierce Ezzelini lords, under whom Bassano was briefly capital of the province of Vicenza. The s side of the square is closed by the flank of the Gothic **church of San Francesco**.

The **Museo Civico ★** (*open Tues-Sat 10am-12.30pm, 2.30-6.30pm, Sun 10am-12.30pm, closed Mon*), housed in the former monastery of San Francesco, is one of the outstanding provincial museums of the Veneto. Essential for works by the Bassano family, it also contains gessos, paintings and some 2,000 **drawings ☆** by Canova, as well as interesting material relating to the Remondini printing works.

In the **Pinacoteca**, notable works by Jacopo Bassano include the *Adoration of the Shepherds*, *Flight into Egypt* ☆ *St Martin*, *St Valentine Baptizing St Lucilla* ☆ and *St Giustina Enthroned with Saints*. There is also a fine collection of 17th and 18thC paintings of which the outstanding work is the dramatic *Refectory of the Monks* ☆ by Alessandro Magnasco.

Below Piazza Libertà you pass through Piazza Monte Vecchio, where the **Casa Michieli-Bonato** bears decorative frescoes by Jacopo Bassano, on the way to **Ponte Coperto** ☆. This charming covered wooden bridge is the emblem of Bassano (and can be seen on the labels of *grappa* bottles). The original bridge (built in 1209) has been frequently replaced — once, in 1569, to a design by Palladio and, most recently, in 1948 after extensive war damage.

Restaurants

The local mushrooms and asparagus are justly famous and widely available in their seasons. Fish from the Brenta and game are also good choices from restaurant menus.

Al Sole 🍴
Via Vittorelli 42 ☎ (0424) 23206 ▢ *to* ▯ 🔳 📧 🔲 *Closed Mon and July.*
A sympathetic, old-fashioned restaurant where the hearty regional cooking is at its best in fall.

Cà 7
Via Cunizza da Romano 4 ☎ *(0424) 25005* ▒ ⟋ AE ⊙ *Closed Sun eve, Mon and third week Aug and first half Nov.*
A restaurant specializing in fresh local produce in an 18thC villa 1.5km (1 mile) to the N of Bassano, on road no.47.

Shopping
The famous Bassano ceramics are on sale everywhere and especially in and around Via Ferracina near the Ponte Coperto. Those at **Costa** (*Via Marchesane 58*) are in better, or at least safer, taste than most.

Belluno ☆
40km (25 miles) N of Conegliano; 106km (66 miles) N of Venice. Provincial capital. Population: 36,500. Getting there: Trains from Venice take 2½hrs; by car, autostrada A27 to Vittorio Veneto, then road no.50 **i** *Piazza dei Martiri 27* ☎ *(0437) 25163.*

Belluno is a fine old mountain town magnificently situated on a high escarpment above the confluence of the Piave and Ardo rivers and near the skiing resorts of the Nevegal. It was a powerful medieval commune but gave itself up willingly to the Venetians in 1404. The Renaissance buildings and arcaded streets in the old section were built during the first centuries of Venetian control.

The best known of the artists born in Belluno are Marco and Sebastiano Ricci, Ippolito Caffi and the sculptor and cabinet-maker, Andrea Brustolon.

Sights and places of interest
The modern town center is the extensive triangle of **Piazza dei Martiri**, named after the four partisans who were hung here by the Nazis in 1944. On its N side are the Neoclassical Palazzo Cappellari della Colomba and the 16thC church of San Rocco.

The hub of the old town, which lies to the s of Piazza dei Martiri, is **Piazza del Duomo** ☆. The 16thC **Duomo**, designed by Tullio Lombardo and partly rebuilt after earthquakes in 1873 and 1936, has an imposing interior with paintings by Andrea Schiavone, Jacopo Bassano and Palma il Giovane. Its splendid Baroque **campanile** (1734), by Filippo Juvara, is worth ascending for the sparkling views from its belfry. On the N side of the Piazza are the handsome Renaissance **Palazzo dei Rettori** ☆ (1491), built as the seat of the Venetian governors, and the 11th-12thC **Torre Civica** which remains from the castle of the medieval rulers of Belluno.

The **Museo Civico** (▒ *open Apr-Oct Tues-Sun 10am-noon, 3.30-6pm, closed Mon*), entered from no.16 Via Duomo, contains works by local and other northern Italian artists, notably two *Madonnas* by Bartolomeo Montagna.

Across **Via Mezzaterra**, the main artery of the old town, is the church of **San Pietro**, rebuilt in 1750. Inside, the *Virgin Annunciate* and *Angel* over the door and the *Sts Peter and Paul* flanking the high altar are by Andrea Schiavone. Over the high altar is Sebastiano Ricci's *Madonna and Child with Sts John and Peter*. The wooden angels over the baldachin of the high altar are by Brustolon, as are the sculptures on the second altars in the right and left nave.

Piazza del Mercato, with an early 15thC fountain at its center, is surrounded by arcaded Renaissance buildings.

To the N of Piazza Vittoria Emanuele II is the 15thC Gothic church of **Santo Stefano** with a Roman sarcophagus embedded in its facade. Inside, the chapel to the right of the chancel has frescoes by Bartolomeo Montagna. The carvings of the altar of this chapel are by Andrea di Foro. Andrea Brustolon carved the candelabra here and in the chapel to the left of the chancel, as well as the *Crucifixion* in the left nave.

▬ **Al Sasso** ♣ (*Via Consiglio 12* ☎ *(0437) 22424, closed Mon, late July*) is a homey restaurant tucked away in the center.
The best restaurant in the area is at *Mel*, 13km (8 miles) SW on the low road for *Feltre*.

The Brenta ☆

The Burchiello water bus, named after the one that plied the
Brenta between Venice and Padua in the 18thC, leaves Venice
from San Marco (Pontile Giardinetti, near the Giardinetti Reali) on
Tues, Thurs and Sat at 9.20am. It stops, all too briefly, at
Malcontenta and *Stra*, and lunch is served on board before
arrival in the late afternoon at *Padua*. The return to Venice is by
bus.

Although many people enjoy the trip for its own sake, the
Burchiello is an expensive and time-consuming way to explore the
Brenta. Those who wish to see the villas along its banks, and
Padua, at their own pace should take a bus from Piazzale Roma —
or a car. The A11 runs along the banks of the Brenta as far as Stra.
It is pleasant to return to Venice in the evening by boat from
Fusina, which was the old port for Venice before the bridge was
built from the mainland. Boats from Fusina take about 30mins.

The Brenta is a mighty river, one of the three that feed the
Venetian lagoon, but its lowest reach, which runs between Stra
and its natural mouth at Fusina, and is known as the Naviglio di
Brenta, has long since been reduced to a safe and sluggish stream.
To prevent it silting up the lagoon so close to Venice, the
Venetians began diverting the Brenta into canals in the 14thC. The
largest of the canals, La Cunetta, which runs s from Stra and
enters the lagoon below Chioggia at Brondolo, was completed in
1896.

In the 16thC, when the mainland finally was securely under
Venetian control the Brenta became a glamorous and busy
waterway, an extension of the Grand Canal, its banks lined with
impressive pleasure villas built for the Venetian nobility.

The most beautiful and important of the villas on the Brenta is
Palladio's **Villa Foscari** at *Malcontenta* and the grandest is the
Villa Pisani at *Stra*. As well as visiting the villas it is worth
stopping at **Mira**, largest and most attractive of the towns on the
Brenta, where Byron wrote the fourth canto of *Childe Harold* in
Palazzo Foscarini, now the post office.

Two fish restaurants at Mira are **Margherita** (*Via Nazionale 312* ☎(041)
420879 ▥ AE ⊕ VISA *closed Mon, Aug*) in a welcoming restored farmhouse;
and **Nalin** (*Via Novissimo 29, Mira* ☎(041) 420083▥ AE ⊕ VISA *closed Sun
eve, Mon and Aug*), on the canal, has a shady courtyard. A more ambitious
restaurant near the Brenta is at *Mirano*.

Castelfranco

*Map 2C3. 45km (28 miles) NW of Venice. Province of Treviso.
Population: 28,100. Getting there: Frequent trains from
Venice take 50mins; by car, road no.13 to Treviso, then
no.53 i Via Garibaldi* ☎(0423) 42651.

Castelfranco was the birthplace of Giorgione, the enigmatic artist
who transformed the course of Venetian painting in the early
16thC, and is chiefly visited for his *Madonna* in the Duomo. It is
today an active commercial center of pleasing character.

Sights and places of interest

The old part of Castelfranco is contained within the well-preserved
Castello ☆ a moated square of brick walls punctuated by five towers, built
in 1199 by Treviso as a defense station against the Paduans.

In the central **Piazza San Liberale** is the Neo-Palladian Duomo (1723-45)
by Francesco Maria Preti, a native of Castelfranco. Giorgione's famous and
controversial *Castelfranco Madonna* ★ is over the altar in the chapel to the
right of the chancel. It represents the Madonna enthroned with a saint who

may be Liberale or Theodore on her left and St Francis on her right, and is usually dated 1505-06. The appeal of this altarpiece is not easy to explain. Its attribution to Giorgione cannot be proved with certainty; it is badly damaged; the figure of St Francis is overpainted; and the composition might well have been rendered awkward by the inconsistent perspective of the floor and throne. . . . Yet for all that it is one of the most magical images in art.

On the sacristy walls and ceiling are detached **fresco fragments** ☆ of foreshortened allegorical figures by Veronese, transferred from the destroyed villa of Soranza.

The **Casa del Giorgione** (◨ *open Sat, Sun 9.30am-12.30pm, 3-6.30pm*) near the Duomo has on the first floor a frieze of chiaroscuro frescoes attributed to Giorgione and contains a museum devoted to him.

In Via Garibaldi, which leads off Piazza San Liberale opposite the Duomo, is Preti's very elegant **Teatro Accademico** (☎*(0423) 42039* ◨ *open Mon-Thurs 9am-12.30pm, 2-6pm; Fri 9am-12.30pm; Sat, Sun on application during the opening hours of the Casa del Giorgione*) with a brick facade and a splendid interior decorated with frescoes and gilded stuccoes.

The 19thC **Villa Revedin-Bolasco** (*Borgo Treviso 46* ☎*(0423) 42112* ▩ *open Tues, Sat and the first Sun of each month, summer 4-7pm, winter 2-5pm*) has a fine park with an open-air theater surrounded by statues by Orazio Marinali.

≋**Barbesin** (*Circonvallazione est* ☎*(0423) 490446* ⬛ ᴬᴱ *closed Thurs, early Jan, Aug*) in an old house outside the gates does superb seasonal vegetables, unusual meat dishes and homemade sweets.

≋ **The Roma Hotel** (*Via Filzi 13* ☎*(0423) 44549* ⬛) has a large, straightforwardly pleasant restaurant.

Otherwise there are excellent restaurants at *Asolo*, *Bassano* or *Treviso*.

Excursions

There are three villas within easy driving distance, two of them important works by Palladio.

The 16thC **Villa Corner-Tiepolo** (▩ *open June-Sept Sat only 3-6pm*), 4km (2½ miles) sw at Sant'Andrea, is decorated with frescoes of the school of Veronese.

The **Villa Cornaro** ☆ (*not open to the public*) is 9km (5½ miles) SE at Piombino Dese. Built *c*.1560-65 it is, with the *Malcontenta* on the *Brenta*, one of the grandest of Palladio's mature designs for a village site. It has a double pedimented portico, Ionic below and Corinthian above, projecting from a central block.

The **Villa Emo** ★ (☎*(0423)487043* ▩ *open Sat, Sun and national holidays summer 3-6pm, winter 2-5pm; closed Easter, Christmas*) is 8km (5 miles) NE at Fanzolo. The villa was built by Palladio in the 1550s for Leonardo Emo who was the first of the wealthy Venetians TO invest extensively in farming. With the Villa Barbaro at *Maser*, it is one of the most complete of Palladio's single-story farming villas, with attached *barchesse* for stabling and storage. The relief in the pediment, of angels carrying the emblem of the Emo family, is by Alessandro Vittoria. The frescoes inside are by G.B. Zelotti.

Conegliano
Map 3B4. 59km (37 miles) N of Venice. Province of Treviso. Population: 35,000. Getting there: A frequent train service takes about an hour; by car, autostrada A4, then A27 ℹ Viale Carducci 16 ☎(0438) 21230.
Conegliano stands above the Venetian plain in a fertile, gently rising landscape familiar to art-lovers from the paintings of its most illustrious son, Cima da Conegliano, and to wine-lovers as the source of some of the most delicious Veneto wines.

Sights and places of interest
In the old town, on the slope of the hill above its flourishing modern commercial and industrial district, the arcaded **Via XX Settembre** is lined with handsome palaces of the 15th-17thC.

At one end is the **Duomo** (14th-15thC), where Cima's majestic *Madonna and Child with Saints and Angels* ☆ (1493) hangs in the apse and, on the right wall of the nave, the other notable native artist, Francesco Beccaruzzi, is represented with the fine *St Francis Receiving the Stigmata* (1545). In the adjacent guildhall (*apply to the sacristan of the Duomo for admission*) the **Sala dei Battuti** is frescoed with *Scenes from the New Testament* by 16thC artists.

Above the Duomo in Via Cima, no.19 is the restored house where Cima was born (☐ *open Sat and Sun winter 4-6pm, summer 5-7pm*).

A pretty road leads up to the **Castelvecchio**, which commands splendid views over the plain and the foothills of the Dolomites. A restored tower of the old *castello* houses a **museum** (☒ *open summer 8am-noon, 3-7pm, winter 9am-noon, 2-3.30pm*) of local history and art.

═══Three pleasant restaurants in the center are the homey **Canon d'Oro** (*Via XX Settembre 129* ☎*(0438) 22171* ▯ ᴬᴱ *closed Sat*); **Al Canton** (*Via Vittorio Emanuele 1* ☎*(0438) 22122* ▥ *closed Sun, Aug*) mainly for fish; and the gastronomically ambitious **Al Salisà** (*Via XX Settembre 2* ☎*(0438) 24288* ▥ ᴬᴱ ⊕ ᵛᴵˢᴬ *closed Tues eve, Wed, Aug*).

═══ **Tre Panoce** ♣
Via Vecchia Trevigiana ☎*(0438)/60071* ▥ ᴬᴱ ⊕ ᵛᴵˢᴬ ⌂ ▤ ⌐ ▤ *closed Mon, Tues lunch, early Jan, Aug.*
An outstanding restaurant in a beautiful and spacious old farmhouse 2km (1¼ miles) to the w of Conegliano. Although the menu changes with the seasons, the soups, risottos and desserts are always worth a journey, as is the *anatra muta all'uva Prosecco.*

═══ And there are many more very good country restaurants to choose from along both wine roads.

Excursions

The **Strada del Vino Bianco** ☆ runs w for 42km (26 miles), as far as Valdobbiadene, through the beautiful vine-clad hills that produce the grapes for Prosecco, Cartizze, and Bianco dei Colli.

The **Strada del Vino Rosso** runs sᴇ for 68km (42 miles) to Oderzo, through the plain to the ɴ of the Piave river where the grapes for Cabernet, Merlot and Raboso are grown.

Este
Map 2E2. 69km (43 miles) sw of Venice. Province of Padua. Population: 18,300. Getting there: By train to Padua, then bus; by car, autostrada A4 to Padua, A13 to Monselice, then road no.10 a few kms w of Monselice ℹ Piazza Maggiore ☎(0429) 3635.
Este is a ceramics-making town at the foot of the Euganean Hills. It was an important center of the Veneto in the Iron Age and is of special interest to archaeologists for the locally-excavated pre-Roman material in its museum. It was the homeland of the Este family, who became Dukes of Ferrara, and of the painter Antonio Zanchi as well as the sculptor Antonio Corradini. Shelley wrote his *Lines Written Among the Euganean Hills* in the Villa De Kunkler behind the castle.

Sights and places of interest

The dominating monument is the vast trapezoidal **Castello**, built in 1339 by the Carraresi lords, which encloses a public garden.

The **Museo Nazionale Atestino** ☆ (☒ *open Tues-Sun summer 9am-1pm, 3-7pm, winter 9am-1pm, 2-5pm; closed Mon*), which occupies a 16thC palace near the entrance to the public garden, is of outstanding interest for the section on the first floor devoted to the pre-Roman Veneto. Cima da Conegliano's *Madonna and Child* (1504) from the church of **Santa Maria delle Consolazioni** is on deposit at the museum.

In Piazza Santa Tecla, the **Duomo**, rebuilt in 1690-1708 after an earthquake, should be visited for G.B. Tiepolo's marvelous *St Teckla Interceding with God the Father to Free the City of the Plague of 1630* ☆ (1759) in the apse, a picture which combines splendor with a moving and tragic expression of the grief of the survivors.

Excursions

The little medieval village of **Arquà Petrarca**, where the poet Petrarch lived from 1370 until his death in 1374, is 7km (4½ miles) NE of Este.

The poet's marble **sarcophagus** (1380), in the main square in front of the church, bears an epitaph composed by himself. **Petrarch's house** (■ *open summer 9am-12.30pm, 2-6.30pm, winter 9.30am-12.30pm, 1.30-4.30pm; ring for admission*), is above the center near Piazzetta San Marco. It retains some original furniture.

Valsanzibio is a 4km (2½ miles) drive farther N into the Euganean Hills. The 17thC Villa Barbarigo has one of the great Baroque water gardens (*open mid-Mar to mid-Nov*) in the Veneto.

■ **La Montanella** (*Via Costa 33* ☎ (0429) 718200 ▥ *closed Tues eve, Wed, Jan to mid-Feb and early Aug*), 1km (less than a mile) above Arquà Petrarca, is a beautifully located restaurant at its best in the fall game season.

Feltre

30km (19 miles) NW of Montebulluna; 88km (55 miles) NW of Venice. Province of Belluno. Population: 22,500. Getting there: By train to Belluno, then bus; by car, road no.13 to Treviso, then no.348.

The old center of Feltre, which stands above a modern commercial and industrial development in the Piave valley, is a remarkably handsome little town. It was rebuilt in the 16thC after its medieval buildings were destroyed by the Imperial armies during the wars of the League of Cambrai.

The native Renaissance painters Morto da Feltre and Pietro Marescalchi executed many of the frescoes which decorate the house facades.

Sights and places of interest

The stepped **Via Mezzaterra** ☆ flanked by steep-roofed, frescoed 16thC houses, climbs through the old town from the 15thC Porta Imperiale. It leads to the strikingly attractive central square, **Piazza Maggiore** ☆ dominated from above by the keep of the medieval **Castello**. In front of the church of **San Rocco** (1599) is a **fountain** (1520) by Tullio Lombardo. The loggia of the **Palazzo Municipio** (1558) is to a design by Palladio.

Via L. Luzzo is lined with Renaissance houses. No.23, just inside the E gate, the Porta Oria, is the **Museo Civico** (■ *open Tues-Fri 10am-noon, Sat, Sun 10am-noon, 4-6pm, closed Mon*) which has an archeological collection and, in its picture gallery, paintings by Venetian and mainland artists.

In Borgo Ruga outside the gate the church of **Ognissanti**, which is unfortunately closed indefinitely, contains Morto da Feltre's masterpiece, a fresco of the *Transfiguration*.

Steps lead to the S gate and the 16thC **Cathedral**. Inside is a fine tomb by Tullio Lombardo, a wooden Byzantine cross (AD542) and Marescalchi's *Madonna della Misericordia*.

■ The outstanding restaurant in the area is at *Mel*, 15km (9½ miles) NE on the low road for *Belluno*.

Giavera del Montello

Map 3B4. 50km (31 miles) N of Venice. Province of Treviso. Getting there: By train to Treviso, then bus; by car, road no.11 to Treviso, no.348 to Montebelluna, then no.248 toward Nervesa della Battaglia.

The pretty stretch of country between the hill of Montello and the Piave river was one of the most fiercely contested battlefields of World War I. Casualties numbering 10,000 are buried in the **Ossuario Monumentale** at Nervesa della Battaglia. The English war cemetery is at **Giavera del Montello,** where the Austrian advance was halted in 1918.

The peacetime pleasures of the Montello include the abundance and variety of the mushrooms which grow on the NE slope of the hill, the local wines — especially Venegazzù and Barchessa Loredan — and the wealth of 15th-18thC villas.

Antica Trattoria Agnoletti ☙
Via Vittoria 121 ☎ *(0422) 876009* ▢ *Closed Mon, Tues and Feb 1-10, July 1-10.*
The mushrooms of the Montello are best eaten at Agnoletti's, a country restaurant which has retained the atmosphere of an 18thC roadhouse. It has an idyllic garden where you can also feast on homemade pasta, young vegetables and local cheeses, under a long pergola hung with vines and jasmine.

Two restaurants at Nervesa delle Battaglia are **La Panoramica** (*Via Ottara Armata 30* ☎ *(0422) 879068* ▢ *to* ▥ *closed Mon, Tues, Jan 10-25, July 1-15*); and **Da Roberta Miron** (*Piazza S. Andrea 26* ☎ *(0422) 879357* ▥ *closed Sun eve, Mon, late Feb, Aug 1-15*).

Malcontenta
Map 3D4. 15km (9½ miles) w of Venice. Province of Venice. Getting there: Frequent buses from Piazzale Roma; by car, road no.11.

The **Villa Foscari** ★ known as the Malcontenta (☎ *969012* ▦ *open May-Oct, Tues, and Sun mornings*) is one of the most impeccably beautiful and influential buildings in the world. Fortunately for visitors it is the closest to Venice of the villas Andrea Palladio built on the mainland.

Palladio designed this villa in the late 1550s for the brothers Alvise and Niccolò Foscari, great-grandsons of the famous Doge Francesco Foscari (who was one of Byron's *Two Foscaris*). The porticoed facade facing the **Brenta** was undoubtedly intended to impress the public with the Foscaris' eminence. Gazing up at the Ionic porch on its high podium, steps tucked away to either side, one might wonder if human beings are welcome in this temple. But the S-facing garden facade (the private side) is, by contrast, one of the happiest, most relaxed of Palladio's creations.

The lofty, beautifully proportioned first-floor *sala* and the four rooms which lead off it are frescoed by Giovanni Battista Zelotti and Giovanni Battista Franco. In one of the smaller rooms there is a fresco of the melancholy lady, La Malcontenta, after whom the villa was supposedly named.

In fact, the more likely derivation is from the *malcontenti*, the political exiles who took refuge in the salt marshes near which the villa was built. The name is in one respect still apt: the salt marshes, cornfields and vineyards which once surrounded the Malcontenta have now been invaded by the gloomy industrial complex of Marghera. But the villa itself is anything but mournful. Carefully restored by its present owner, Count Antonio Foscari, it stands among the factories and oil refineries as a proud monument to a more serene civilization.

Bepi El Ciozoto (*Via Malcanton 8* ☎ *969137* ▥ *closed Mon in winter, 2 weeks in Jan*), is a pleasant fish restaurant very near the villa. Alternative restaurants not too far away are at *Mirano*.

Maróstica
Map 2B2. 82km (51 miles) NW of Venice. Province of Vicenza. Population: 12,400. Getting there: By train to Bassano del Grappa, then bus; by car, autostrada A4 to Thiene, then the Bassano road i *Piazza Castello 7* ☎ *(0424) 72127.*

The crenellated and turreted medieval **ramparts** ★ which march uphill to meet the *castello* of Maróstica are a strikingly dramatic memorial to the despotic lords — the Ezzelini and Scaligeri — who controlled the hills below the plateau of Asiago before the area was taken over by Venice in the 15thC.

Event In Sept (every other year), the *Partita a scacchi* ★ in Piazza Castello, in which a live chess game is played in 14thC costume.

Sights and places of interest

The **Piazza Castello**, which lies in the shadow of the ramparts and the upper castle, is paved with a giant chessboard. At its head is the 14thC **Castello Inferiore**, now the town hall (☒ *open daily*), with a massive, ivy-clad tower and the remains of frescoes in its courtyard.

Above, on the summit of the hill of Pausolino, are the remains of the late 14thC **Castello Superiore**, which commands extensive views over the mountains and the plain below.

⇌ **Al Castello Superiore** (☎(0424) 72110 **Ⅲ** *closed Tues and part of Jan*), is, despite its extraordinary location built into the walls of the upper castle, a rather ordinary restaurant (*closed Mon eve and Tues*). A better choice can be found at *Bassano del Grappa*, 7km (4 miles) to the E.

Maser

Map 2B3. 63km (39 miles) NW of Venice. Province of Treviso. Population: 4,600. Getting there: By train to Montebelluna, then bus; by car, road no.13 to Treviso, then the Montebelluna road (no.348) to Cornuda. Maser is on the way to road no.248.

Just above this farming village at the base of the Asolean hills there stands the most graceful, most complete and best preserved of Palladio's farming villas, the **Villa Barbaro** ★ (☎(0423) 565002 **■** *≫* *open Tues, Sat, Sun and local holidays, summer 3-6pm, winter 2-5pm; closed public holidays*).

The villa was commissioned in *c*.1555 by the brothers Daniele and Marcantonio Barbaro, Venetian patricians who were among the wealthiest and most cultivated of Palladio's patrons. The villa reflects Daniele Barbaro's station in society and his informed taste for classical architecture, but it was also intended to function as a working farm from which he could supervise the cultivation of the land on which his wealth depended. The central block, its porticoed facade bearing Ionic half-columns, is flanked by arcaded wings (*barchese*) which were used for stabling animals and storing farm equipment. The niche statues and the stucco relief in the pediment of the Barbaro emblem, the two-headed eagle, are by Alessandro Vittoria.

Inside, all the rooms on the upper level are decorated with **frescoes** ★ by Paolo Veronese, which are one of the most joyously brilliant decorative schemes in all art, the perfect complement to Palladio's architecture, and the only known instance of collaboration between the two artists. New 'windows' open from the already airy interior onto illusionist country scenes. Startlingly realistic *trompe l'oeil* portraits of the Barbaro family and servants mingle invitingly with an allegorical series of mythological and classical subjects.

Behind the villa is the **nymphaeum**, with stuccoed statues of Greek gods and goddesses by Vittoria. Below is the villa's chapel, the domed **Tempio** ☆ — the only church Palladio built outside Venice — with a freestanding Corinthian temple front and, inside, stuccoed statues by Vittoria. There is also a **carriage museum**, in the wooded park above the villa.

≡ Perhaps the most delightful restaurant in the area is at **Giavera del Montello**, 16km (10 miles) to the E. There are also excellent restaurants at Asolo, 7km (4½ miles) w.

Mel

39km (24 miles) N of Montebelluna; 90km (56 miles) NW of Venice. Province of Belluno. Population: 7,600. Getting there: By train to Belluno, then bus; by car, road no.13 to Treviso, then no.348 to Feltre. Mel is on the low road to Belluno.

Mel is a fine old town halfway between *Belluno* and *Feltre*, which commands views of the Dolomites from a plateau above the Piave river. Its handsome central square, **Piazza Umberto I**, is surrounded by 16th-18thC buildings, one of which is occupied by a remarkable restaurant.

≡ Antica Locanda al Cappello
Piazza Umberto I ☎ (0437) 753651 ⬜ ≡ Closed Mon eve, Tues, 2 weeks in July.
In the frescoed rooms of a 17thC house, once occupied by the Knights of Malta, Giovanni and Liliane De-Zordi serve imaginative country food prepared according to antique recipes. The combinations of textures and of flavors (e.g. pasta with beetroot) are sometimes surprising and always delicious. There is no menu because the proprietors like to vary the daily choice as inspiration and the season move them. Their best dishes include *papardelle, risotti, fesi con salsa di noci, pastin di capriolo*.

Mestre

Map 3C4. 8km (5 miles) NW of Venice. Province of Venice. Population: 150,000. Getting there: Frequent trains and buses take 10mins.

Mestre, which merges with the ugly industrial port of Marghera, is — for tourists at least — the unacceptable face of Venetian capitalism. But it is administered as part of Venice and its population is largely drawn from the historic center.

There is little enough worth looking at apart from the fragments of medieval buildings in the central **Piazza Ferretto**. Still, Mestre is where the money is made, and its restaurants, which cater to the local businessmen and industrialists, maintain a higher standard and give better value than most of those in Venice, which exist to serve the passing tourist trade.

≡ Dall'Amelia
Via Miranese 113 ☎ 913951 ⬜ to ▦ ▬ ≡ ▤ AE ⊙ ⊙ VISA Closed Wed in winter. Open every day in summer.
Conveniently located near the Mestre exit from the main road w (the *tangenziale ovest*) from Venice, this is a large, unpretentious businessmen's restaurant swarming with efficient waiters. There is a tempting display of fresh fish and a superb selection of antipasti; the pasta, risotto, meat and game dishes are also excellent.

≡ Valeriano
Via Col di Lana 14 ☎ 926474 ⬜ ▤ Closed Sun eve, Mon and Aug.
A small, justly popular family-run restaurant near the railroad station. The menu, which changes daily, emphasizes regional cooking. The risottos are especially well-made.

Mirano

Map 3D4. 19km (12 miles) NW of Venice. Province of Venice. Population: 23,500. Getting there: Frequent buses from Piazzale Roma.

Mirano is a lively little town north of the Brenta which is worth visiting for an excellent restaurant and for the pleasant old villas on its outskirts. Two villas open to the public are the **Villa Tiepolo-Grande** (🖾 *open Thurs 3-5pm*) and the **Villa Donà delle Rose** (🖾 *open Mon 2-5pm*).

━━ There are two excellent restaurants and a useful pizzeria in the building complex of yet another pleasure villa, the 18thC **Villa Belvedere** (Via Belvedere 8-10). The best is **El Tinelo** (☎432344 ⅢⅢ AE ⊕ VISA ━ *closed Mon, Tues lunch*), a tiny restaurant (advance booking is essential) that serves Venetian and French dishes of a quality that would not have been scorned by the original noble owners of the villa. **Ai Molini di Sopra** (☎430063 ⅢⅢ AE ⊕ VISA *closed Mon, Tues lunch*), in the old mill, is charming if sometimes over-crowded, and does good shell-fish antipasti and fresh seasonal salads.

Montagnana
Map 2E2. 85km (53 miles) sw of Venice. Province of Padua. Population: 10,000. Getting there: By train to Padua, then bus; by car, autostrada A4 to Monselice, then follow road no.10.

The moated medieval **walls** ★ of Montagnana are among the most impressive and intact in Europe. Built in the 13th-14thC of trachyte blocks and bricks, and punctuated by 24 towers, they enclose the little town in a complete rectangle. There are four gates, of which the most imposing is the western **Porta Legnago**, erected in 1388 at the time that the walls were reinforced by the Carraresi.

Just outside the eastern gate, the 13thC **Porta Padova**, stands the **Villa Pisani** ★ (*c.*1553-55). More of a town house than a villa, it was begun to a design by Palladio but left incomplete. The two orders, Doric below and Ionic above, are divided by a handsome frieze.

In the central square of the town, Piazza Vittorio Emanuele, is the Gothic-Renaissance **Duomo** (1430-1502) which has a classical portico attributed to Sansovino. In the apse, the *Assumption* by Giovanni Buonconsiglio is the largest fresco of its period in the Veneto. Over the high altar is a splendid *Transfiguration* (1555) by Veronese. The **Palazzo del Municipio** in Via Carrarese is to a design by Sanmicheli.

Padua ★
Map 2D3. 37km (23 miles) w of Venice. Provincial capital. Population: 242,000. Getting there: By train, a frequent service takes 30mins; by bus, SIAMIC buses leave Piazzale Roma every 30mins and take 30mins; by water, the Burchiello motor launch leaves Venice Tues, Thurs, Sat at 9.20am May-Sept from Pontile Giardinetto near Piazza San Marco, stopping at villas along the Brenta Canal, and arriving Padua late afternoon — return to Venice by bus (La Smeralda, a similar service, leaves Venice Fri and Sun); by car, take autostrada A4 just after Marghera or, time permitting, drive along the Brenta i station ☎(049) 27767, or Piazzetta Pedrocchi 18 ☎(049) 44711.

When Padua was absorbed into the Venetian empire in 1406 Venice handled its new conquest with respect. Padua was a rich, populous and cultivated market town. Its university, founded in 1222, is the second oldest in Italy after that of Bologna. Its largest church, the Santo, begun in 1232 to enshrine the miracle-working bones of St Anthony, rivaled the Byzantine splendor of Venice's San Marco and was one of the great pilgrimage churches of Europe.

Fifteenth-century Padua became the 'left bank' of Venice, the university city where young Venetians studied law and medicine, and where intellectual and artistic innovation was encouraged in a way that it was not in conservative Venice. While Venetian artists clung tenaciously to Gothic modes of expression, Paduans accepted the challenge of Giotto, whose revolutionary frescoes in the Scrovegni Chapel were painted in the early 14thC, and of Donatello, whose sculptures in the Santo introduced the Florentine classical style to the Veneto in the 1440s.

These Tuscan examples were crucial to the development of the Paduan painter Andrea Mantegna, as was the enthusiasm for classical antiquity of his adoptive father Francesco Squarcione. Mantegna's frescoes in the church of the Eremitani were the first fully realized Renaissance paintings in N Italy and he was the foremost N Italian painter before his Venetian brother-in-law, Giovanni Bellini.

In the 16thC, after Venice had taken the lead in all the arts, Padua remained a stimulating environment for visiting artists. The young Titian's frescoes in the Scuola di Sant'Antonio transformed the course of Venetian narrative painting; and Padua's town gates and the Cornaro Loggia and Odeon, designed by the Veronese painter and architect Giovanni Maria Falconetto, were the first classical buildings in N Italy.

The city is today an active commercial center. Despite severe bomb damage in World War II, it retains a distinctive if charmless character.

Tour of the main sights

The town center is Piazza Cavour, and the ideal start to a visit would be over a drink at the **Caffè Pedrocchi** in the adjacent piazzetta. This handsome Neoclassical building designed by Giuseppe Japelli in 1831 is one of the most famous Italian cafés.

Nearby is the **University** (*Via VIII Febbraio 2* ☎*(049) 651400), open Mon-Fri 10am-12.30pm; guided tours start at 10am, 11am, noon*) where one may visit the oldest **anatomical theater** ☆ in Europe, founded in 1594 by the surgeon Fabricius whose pupils included the Englishman William Harvey. Corpses were dissected here for the benefit of medical students until 1872.

On the other side of the Via VIII Febbraio, beyond the Municipio, the **Palazzo della Ragione** ☆ or law courts (*Piazza delle Erbe* ☎*(049) 661377* ▨ *open Tues-Sat 9.30am-12.30pm, 2.30-5.30pm, Sat, Sun 9.30am-12.30pm, closed Mon*) stands between the fruit and vegetable markets. Known locally as 'Il Salone,' it was built as the tribunal in 1218-19 and rebuilt in 1306. The interior consists of one vast hall covered with 15thC frescoes of religious and astrological subjects and contains an immense **wooden horse** (1466), which is possibly a copy of Donatello's *Gattamelata* statue outside the Santo (see below).

Via Manin leads from the Piazza delle Erbe to the Duomo, rebuilt in the mid-16thC, next to which is the 13thC Romanesque **Baptistry**, its interior entirely covered with important frescoes (1374-76) by Giusto de' Menabuoi.

The Augustinian church of the **Eremitani** (*Piazza Eremitani 9* ☎*(049) 31410, open Apr-Sept Mon-Sat 8.15am-noon, 3.30-6.30pm, Sun 9am-noon, 3.30-7pm; Oct-Mar Mon-Sat 8.15am-noon, 3-5.30pm, Sun 9am-noon, 3-5pm*) is a few minutes' walk away to the N. The church was built in 1276-1306 and reconstructed after bomb damage during World War II. Among the monuments in the simple, plain interior is the tomb of the lawyer Marco Benavides (1546) by the Florentine sculptor Bartolomeo Ammannati. In the Ovetari Chapel, to the right of the high altar, you can pay your respects to the tragic remains of Mantegna's great **frescoes** (1454-57), the first Renaissance paintings executed in the Veneto, shattered by a bomb and pieced together after the war. The most intact are the *Assumption* behind the altar and the *Martyrdom of St Christopher* to the right. On the left wall are the recomposed fragments of the *Martyrdom of St James*.

The **Scrovegni Chapel** (*Corso Garibaldi* ☎*(049) 650845* ▨ *open Apr-Sept*

Padua

1 Caffè Pedrocchi
2 University
3 Municipio
4 Palazzo della Ragione
5 Duomo and Baptistry
6 Eremitani
7 Scrovegni Chapel
8 Donatello's Gattamelata monument
9 Basilica of Sant' Antonio (Il Santo)
10 Scuola del Santo
11 Cornaro Loggia and Odeon
12 Santa Giustina
13 Museo Civico
14 Orto Botanico
15 Santa Sofia
16 San Gaetano
17 Casa degli Specchi

0   100 200 300 m
0   100 200 300 yds

9am-12.30pm, 2.30-5.30pm; Oct-Mar Mon-Sat 9.30am-12.30pm, 1.30-4.30pm, Sun 9.30am-12.30pm) stands behind the Eremitani among the ruins of the **Roman arena**. Inside is the **fresco cycle** ★ with which Giotto laid the foundations of Italian Renaissance painting, demonstrating for the first time his full narrative powers and ability to simulate three-dimensional space. Painted in 1303-5 for Enrico Scrovegni, who built the chapel as an act of atonement for his father's usury and as a plea to the Virgin for forgiveness, the frescoes illustrate the theme of Christian redemption. The cycle begins with the *Expulsion of Joachim* at the top of the right wall nearest the chancel and ends with the *Descent of the Holy Ghost* at the chancel end of the left wall. The lowest bands represent, on the right wall, the *Seven Virtues* and, on the left, the *Seven Vices*. On the entrance wall is the *Last Judgment* with *Scrovegni Offering up the Chapel to the Virgin and his Patron Saints*. Above the chancel is the *Eternal Father Enthroned with Angels*. The statues on the altar of the *Virgin and Child* with two *Angels* are by Giotto's contemporary, Giovanni Pisano.

From the Scrovegni Chapel it is less than 10mins walk to the **Piazza del Santo** at the s end of the town. In front of the Basilica of Sant'Antonio, facing the approach from the Via del Santo, stands Donatello's **monument to the mercenary commander Erasmo Gattamelata** ★ (1443-53), the first and most powerful of Renaissance equestrian statues.

With its seven domes and minaret-like spires, the Basilica of Sant'Antonio, usually called **Il Santo** ★ (*Piazza del Santo* ☎ *(049) 663944, open 6.30am-7pm*), has an even more Oriental appearance than Venice's San Marco. It was begun in 1232 to contain the relics of St Anthony and completed in the mid-14thC. One of the great shrines of western Christendom, it continues to attract votive visits by pilgrims from all over the world.

The **bronze sculptures** ★ on the high altar executed by Donatello and his assistants between 1443-50 were the works of art which introduced the classical style to the Veneto (*ask a custodian to unlock the gates*). Above the *Madonna Enthroned* is *The Crucifixion*, which is surrounded by the *Six Patron*

166

Saints of Padua.

The four reliefs on either side of the *Pietà* depict the *Miracles of St Anthony*. Behind is a *Deposition* in stone. The candelabrum (1507-15) to the left of the altar is the masterpiece of Andrea Briosco, who was known as Il Riccio.

The **Chapel of St Anthony** ★ in the left transept was designed by Il Riccio in 1500 and completed by Falconetto in 1546. St Anthony's green marble tomb behind the altar is the particular focus for the Christian pilgrims' intense devotion. The nine large panels depicting the **Miracles of St Anthony** which line its walls constitute the most important assemblage of 16thC relief sculpture in Italy. The fourth from the left, Jacopo Sansovino's *Miracle of the Maiden Carilla* (1562) has been called by John Pope-Hennessy 'the unchallenged masterpiece of High Renaissance sculpture.' The sixth and seventh (both 1525) are by Tullio Lombardo, the seventh, The *Miracle of the Miser's Heart*, being among his most forceful works. The ninth, the *Miracle of the Newborn Child* (1505), is a severely classical work by Antonio Lombardo.

Just outside the chapel on the right is the monument to the jurisconsult Antonio Roselli (1467), Pietro Lombardo's most important surviving work in Padua.

In the right transept is the **Chapel of St Felix** (1372-77), splendidly decorated with frescoes by Altichieri and Jacopo Avanzo illustrating the *Legend of St James* and other stories.

To the right of the Santo in the **Scuola del Santo** (*open May-Sept 9am-noon, 2.30-6.30pm; Oct-Apr 9am-noon, 2.30-6pm*) are the Oratory of San Giorgio and the Scuola di Sant'Antonio. The 14thC **Oratory** is frescoed inside by Altichieri and assistants. The upper *salone* of the **Scuola di Sant'Antonio** ☆ is frescoed with the most important series of the 16thC paintings in Padua including, most notably, the three earliest documented works by Titian, executed in 1511.

The first and largest, the *Miracle of the Newborn Child*, is a remarkable departure from the conventions of Venetian narrative painting; it was inspired by one of Giotto's frescoes in the Scrovegni Chapel and by the reliefs of the same subject in the Santo by Donatello and Antonio Lombardo. The two other paintings by Titian represent the *Miracle of the Jealous Husband* and the *Miracle of the Restored Foot*.

In a courtyard around the corner from the Santo are the **Cornaro Loggia and Odeon** ☆ (*Via Cesarotti 37* ☎ *(049) 23106* �︎ 🔲 *open Apr-Sept Tues-Sat 9am-12.30pm, 2.30-5.30pm, Sun 9.30am-12.30pm; Oct-Mar Tues-Sun 9.30am-3.30pm; closed Mon*). Designed in 1528-30 by Giovanni Maria Falconetto as settings for theatrical and musical entertainments, these two small buildings were the first in N Italy to emulate the style of the Roman Classical Renaissance. They are decorated inside with delightful 16thC frescoes, stuccoes and statues.

The Via L. Belludi leads from the Santo to the **Prato della Valle**, the elegant moated oval park laid out in 1775 on the site of the Roman theater and adorned with a double ring of 78 statues of illustrious Paduans and honorary Paduans. Next to it is the imposing 16thC church of **Santa Giustina** ☆ whose domes echo those of the Santo. Its vast interior contains numerous 16th and 17th-century works of art, the most notable of these being Veronese's huge paintings of the *Martyrdom of St Justina* (1575) in the apse.

Other sights

The **Museo Civico** (*Piazza del Santo 10* ☎ *(049) 23106/23713)* 🚌 🔲 *on Sun and holidays; open Tues-Sat 9am-1.30pm, Sun 9am-1pm*) has a good collection of Venetian and mainland paintings. The **Orto Botanico** (*Via Orto Botanico 15* ☎ *(049) 656614* 🚌 *open Mar-Oct Mon-Sat 9am-1pm, Sun 10am-1pm; Nov-Feb Mon-Sat 9am-1pm; closed Sun*), between the Santo and Santa Giustina, is the oldest botanical garden in Europe. Two churches of special interest are **Santa Sofia**, in Via Morgagni, the oldest church in Padua, and **San Gaetano**, in Via Altinate, designed by Vincenzo Scamozzi. Other buildings by Falconetto include two of the city gates, **Porta San Giovanni** and **Porta Savonarola**, and the **Casa degli Specchi**, located in Via Vescovado.

🍽 There are plenty of pizzerias, trattorias and cafés in the streets around the Santo.

For a more elaborate meal try **Dotto** (*Via Squarcione 23* ☎ *(049) 25055* ▮▮▮▮ 🆎 🆑 🔘 *closed Sun eve, Mon and late Jan and Aug*), conveniently located between the Duomo and the Palazzo della Ragione, or **Al Falconiere** (*Via Umberto I 31*, ☎*(049) 656544* ▥ AE ⊕ VISA *closed Thurs, Sun lunch and Aug*).

Possagno

Map 2B3. 72km (45 miles) NW of Venice. Province of Treviso. Population: 1,900. Getting there: By train to Bassano del Grappa, then bus; by car, road no.11 to Treviso, then the Montebelluna road (no.348) to Pederobba. Possagno is on the Bassano road.

The farming and brick-making village of Possagno is enfolded in a fertile valley of the Asolean hills below Monte Grappa.

Possagno was the birthplace of Antonio Canova (1757-1822), the son of a local stonecutter who became the leading Neoclassical sculptor and one of the most widely admired and loved public figures in Europe. Stendhal, who was his contemporary, judged him a worthy rival of the ancient Greeks and even of Michelangelo himself. The finished sculptures, which are scattered throughout the museums and private collections of the world, have in our day sometimes been dismissed as chilly, if charming, academic works. He was in fact one of the greatest of all Italian artists, but for a full appreciation of the spontaneous tenderness as well as the polished technique and sophistication of his style you must visit his native Possagno.

Sights and places of interest

Gipsoteca e casa di Antonio Canova ★
In the village center ☎(0423) 54323 ▥ Open summer Tues-Sat 3-6pm, Sun, holidays 3-7pm; winter Tues-Sun 9am-noon, 2-5pm. Closed Mon except holidays.

The Gipsoteca (gallery of plaster models) next to Canova's family house is one of the most elegant and moving small museums in Europe, and the only complete collection of a sculptor's working models (apart from the Thorvaldsen *gipsoteca* in Copenhagen). In its spacious, still, sunlit rooms are assembled nearly all of his *gessos* (plaster models), brought here after his death from his studio in Rome on the initiative of his half-brother and secretary, Monsignor G.B. Sartori, Bishop of Mindo. Sartori also supervised the building of the Gipsoteca (1831-36), to which a new wing was added in 1957.

In the house itself are more models and Canova's paintings — he painted only as a hobby — including 34 temperas of mythological subjects which reveal the endearingly frivolous aspect of the sculptor's complex sexual personality. In the room where Canova was born hangs his portrait painted by Sir Thomas Lawrence during the sculptor's visit to London in 1815.

Tempio di Canova †
▣ Open summer 8am-noon, 2-7pm; winter 8am-noon, 1.30-5pm.

On the rise of the steep hill facing Canova's house is the astonishing present he gave to Possagno at the end of his life when he was a very rich man — a parish church in the shape of the Pantheon with a porch carefully copied from one of those on the Parthenon. This refrigerated synthesis of Greek and Roman classical architecture is one of the most unexpected — and, perhaps, inappropriate — sights in the Veneto. The project was designed with advice from the Neoclassical architect, Antonio Selva; the citizens of Possagno provided the labor. It was started in 1819 and completed in 1830, eight years after Canova's death.

Moving right from the entrance, the second chapel contains Canova's *Pietà*, cast in bronze in 1829. In the fifth chapel is the **tomb of Canova** and his half-brother G.B. Sartori, to a design made by Canova in 1794 for another project. The bust on the right is a self-portrait, that on the left is a portrait of Sartori by Baruzzi. Over the high altar is Canova's painting of the *Deposition and Trinity*.

A custodian will admit you to the spiral staircase which leads to the summit of the cupola, commanding views over the surrounding countryside as far as the Rocca of *Asolo*.

≈≈**Socal** ♣ *(Via Roma 18* ☎*(0423) 544006* ▮❙ *to* ▮▮❙ *closed Oct and Tues except during July, Aug)* is a comfortable 19thC country inn, with rooms, serving healthy old-fashioned local specialties.

Rovigo

Map 2F3. 80km (50 miles) sw of Venice. Provincial capital. Population: 51,800. Getting there: Frequent trains from Venice take 1hr 20mins; by car, autostrada A4 to Padua, then A13 **i** *Corso del Popolo 101* ☎*(0425) 22835.*

Rovigo is the principal town of the Polesine, the strip of Veneto which lies between the lower reaches of the Adige and Po rivers. As a growing commercial center in an exceptionally fertile agricultural area the town has, as you might expect in Italy, a first-rate restaurant. It is also near one of Palladio's most important villas.

The town is particularly worth visiting for the pictures in its art gallery and in the church of the Beata Vergine del Soccorso.

The central square is Piazza Vittorio Emanuele, where no.14, the **Pinacoteca dei Concordi** (⊡ *open Mon-Fri 10am-noon, 4-7pm, Sun 10am-noon, closed Sat)*, is rich in Veneto-school paintings of the 15th-18thC including Giovanni Bellini's *Madonna and Child*; G.B. Pittoni's *St Roch*, G.B. Piazzetta's *St Francis of Paola*, and G.B. Tiepolo's *Portrait of Antonio Riccoboni*. Also noteworthy are Mabuse's *Venus with a Mirror* and Sebastiano Mazzoni's *Death of Cleopatra*.

Via Silvestri leads past the church of San Francesco to Piazza XX Settembre, at the far end of which stands the church of the **Beata Vergine del Soccorso**. Known as La Rotonda (1594-1602), it is an octagonal building by Francesco Zamberlan, with a campanile (1655) by Longhena.

The interior walls are entirely covered with important 17thC pictures illustrating scenes from the life of the Virgin and Venetian governors being presented to the Virgin. The most impressive are those by Francesco Maffei: nos.5, 6, 12 and 14 in the lowest row.

≈≈**Tre Pini**

Viale Porta Po 68 ☎*(0425) 27111* ▮▮▮▮ ≈≈ ▱Ａ̲Ｅ̲ ⊙ ▾ᴵˢᴬ *Closed Sun and Aug.*

This is a gastronomically exceptional restaurant in deceptively modest premises on the southern edge of Rovigo. Fresh local produce is the basis of a cuisine which makes original and sophisticated use of French and Emilian influences. Everything on the menu, which changes with the seasons four times a year, can be confidently recommended. Clients may choose their wines from a carefully selected cellar, but the house wines are also excellent.

Excursion

About 16km (10 miles) sw of Rovigo is the pretty village of **Fratta Polesine**, divided by a canal shaded by umbrella pines and well-endowed with fine villas built by the Venetian nobility in the 16th-18thC. The most beautiful and important is Palladio's **Villa Badoer** ★ (1554-63) (⊡ *open 3.30-7pm; also in morning on Tues 9am-noon mid-Sept to mid-June, Thurs 9am-noon all year around, Sun 10am-noon mid-Apr to Sept)* with a central block in the Ionic order preceded by an imposing balustraded staircase and flanked by graceful curved *barchesse* in the Tuscan order.

Solighetto

Map 3B4. 75km (47 miles) NW of Venice. Province of Treviso. Getting there: By train to Conegliano, then bus; by car, autostrada A27 to Conegliano, then road no.13 to Nervesa della Battaglia. Solighetto is on the road to Follina.

The grandest, and one of the best, of the rural restaurants in the

Province of Treviso is to be found in this hamlet on the Strada del Vino Bianco, the road that runs through the rich white-wine-growing country between Conegliano and Valdobbiadene.

≡ **Da Lino**
Via Brandolini 31 ☎ _(0438) 82150_ ▯▯ AE ⊙ ⊒ ⊜ _Closed Mon and part of July, Christmas._

Da Lino is a favorite restaurant of wealthy local landowners as well as businessmen from Rome and Milan, actors and actresses, and artists. Indeed, the unwitting foreigner may feel he has entered an exclusive country club with a membership restricted to successful Italians. Nor is this the place for those with timid appetites. Everything is conceived on a grand and glossy scale: enormous portions, attentive service, newly done-up 'rustic' decor; all the food, from the delicate antipasti to the fruit and cheeses, is of the highest quality. In late summer and fall, mushroom lovers should try the _piatto del vescovo_.

Stra
Map 2D3. 25km (16 miles) sw _of Venice. Province of Venice. Population: 5,900. Getting there: Frequent buses from Piazzale Roma; by the Burchiello water bus along the Brenta; by car, autostrada A4 or road no.11._

Stra is a pleasant little town at the fork of the Brenta river and its main canal; it is particularly well-endowed with fine villas, notably the **Villa Pisani 'Nazionale'** ☆ (▨ _open Tues-Sun 9am-1.30pm, park open 9am-4pm; closed Mon_).

Although some tastes are offended by the outrageous, Versailles-like grandeur of the Villa Pisani, it must be visited, certainly for the Tiepolo ceiling in the ballroom, but also because, with Ca' Rezzonico in Venice, it is one of the few surviving houses open to the public which convey the style in which the Venetian aristocracy lived on the eve of the fall of the Republic.

The villa was built for the Pisani family to celebrate Alvise Pisani's election as Doge. The original design by Girolamo Frigimelica was elaborated in 1736-56 by Francesco Maria Preti.

Napoleon bought the villa from the Pisanis in 1807 and presented it to his follower and brother-in-law Eugène Beauharnais, whom he had made Viceroy of Italy. Two less sympathetic dictators, Mussolini and Hitler, met here for the first time in 1934.

The **interior apartments** are decorated with paintings by some of the leading 18thC Veneto artists, but the highpoint is G.B. Tiepolo's fresco on the ballroom ceiling of the _Apotheosis of the Pisani family_ ☆ (1762). It represents Venice and the Pisani family surrounded by the Sciences, Arts and Spirits of Peace, watched over by the Madonna while Fame trumpets their glory throughout the world.

After that experience it is time for a stroll in the magnificent **park** ☆ which offers, among other diversions, a maze.

≡ The best restaurants in the vicinity are to be found at _Padua_, on the _Brenta_ and at _Mirano_.

Thiene
Map 2C2. 91km (57 miles) nw _of Venice. Province of Vicenza. Population: 18,600. Getting there: By train to Vicenza, then bus; by car, autostrada A4 to Vicenza, then A31._

Thiene is a textile-producing town below the Asiago plateau which is primarily worth visiting for two great buildings, the Palazzo

Colleoni and the nearby Villa Godi. It is also a pleasant place to stop for lunch on a tour of the Palladian villas N of Vicenza (see *The Villas of Andrea Palladio*, page 184).

The centerpiece of the town — and one of the most romantic buildings on the Venetian mainland — is **Palazzo Porto Colleoni** ☆ (in *Piazza Ferrarin* ☎(0445) 32121 🖼 𝗫 compulsory *15 Mar-31 Oct; open Tues-Sun 9am-noon, 3-6pm; closed Mon*). It was built in the second half of the 15thC on the site of an earlier *castello* and consists of a low central block in the style of a Venetian Gothic palace guarded by a pair of crenellated towers. The style dramatically evokes a period when the desire for architectural grace and grandeur was still checked on the Venetian mainland by the need for security.

The palace is frescoed inside by G.A. Fasolo and G.B. Zelotti and hung with a collection of pictures, including 17thC portraits of horses (the Colleoni were inspectors-general of the Venetian cavalry). In the grounds are a charming chapel contemporary with the palace, and handsome 17thC stables.

🍽 **Roma**
Via Fogazzaro 8 ☎*(0445) 361084* 🔲 *to* ▥ *Closed Thurs, Aug.*
A big, jolly hotel restaurant serving excellent freshly-prepared regional dishes such as *tortelloni*, *gnocchi*, *bigoli* and *baccalà*, from an open kitchen.

Excursion
The Palazzo Porto Colleoni is a particularly grand example of a building type, common in the 15thC Veneto, which influenced Palladio's early villas, notably the **Villa Godi Malinverni** ☆ (🖼 *open mid-Mar-May, Tues, Sat, Sun and hols 2-6pm; June-Aug 3-7pm. For group bookings at other times* ☎*(0445) 860561*) which stands on a hill above Lugo di Vicenza, 8km (5 miles) N of Thiene.

Begun *c.*1539-40 and completed in 1542, the Villa Godi was Palladio's first building. Although the simplicity of its exterior may surprise those who are familiar with the more mature classicizing villas, it contains the germs of many elements he would develop in later patrician villas and anticipates a concern with the interrelationship of architecture and its surrounding landscape that was eventually fulfilled most successfully at *Maser*.

Inside, every room on the *piano nobile* is magnificently decorated with allegorical and mythological **frescoes** ☆ (begun 1552) in architectural settings by Gualtiero Campagnola, G.B. Zelotti and Battista dal Moro. They are among the most attractive and important of the decorative schemes executed in the 16thC Veneto, the earliest examples of landscape frescoes covering the walls of a Palladian villa, and those by Zelotti are probably his masterpieces.

The villa was restored in 1962-63 by Prof Remo Malinverni, whose representative collection of 19thC Italian paintings is displayed in the **picture gallery**. There is an attractively arranged **fossil museum** attached to the villa.

The Italian-style **garden** is adorned with 17thC statues by Girolamo Albanese and Oravio Marinali. There is a restaurant in the detached, colonnaded **barchessa** (dated 1533).

The **Villa Piovene**, an attractive blend of 16th and 18thC Palladian architecture, stands on the hill just above the Villa Godi commanding stunning views of the mountains. Its central block was built by Palladio *c.*1538-40, at the same time as the Villa Godi was begun. The Ionic porch was added rather later, in 1591, and the portal and staircase later still, in the 18thC.

Leave time to wander for an hour or so in the magnificent wooded **park** (🖼 *open 2pm-sunset*), landscaped in the 19thC in the English manner with natural grottoes and a lake.

Treviso ☆
Map 3C4. 30km (19 miles) NW of Venice. Provincial capital. Population: 90,700. Getting there: By train, a frequent service takes 20mins; by car, autostrada A4, then A27 𝒊 Via Toniolo 41 ☎*(0422) 47632.*

171

The bombs released by a tragic error on Treviso at the end of World War II caused severe damage to the most charming of the Venetian mainland suburbs, but did not altogether rob it of its distinctive character. The little town is watered by two rivers, the Sile and Botteniga, and crossed by a network of canals. It preserves many of its arcaded old streets, frescoed houses, and medieval monuments.

Treviso was a loyal subject of Venice from 1384, and the fertile countryside around is still dignified by handsome villas built by the Venetian nobility from the 16th-18thC. A local school of Renaissance painting was founded by the Pennachi family, known as Da Treviso, but the greatest of the native artists was Paris Bordone.

The town has many good restaurants, including one of the most fashionable in the Veneto, and more than enough of cultural interest to occupy half a day's sightseeing.

Tour of the main sights

The historic center is **Piazza dei Signori**, where the scrupulously restored 13thC **Palazzo dei Trecento** 🏛 with a double-branched exterior staircase and 16thC loggia adjoins the **Palazzo del Podestà**, rebuilt in medieval style in the 19thC.

Calmaggiore, the arcaded main street of the old town, leads to the **Duomo**, a 12thC foundation altered and enlarged over the centuries and restored after World War II. The Neoclassical porch was added in 1836. The plain, lugubrious interior contains notable works of art. Over the second altar on the right is an *Adoration of the Shepherds* by Paris Bordone.

A staircase at the top of the right aisle leads to the **Malchiostro Chapel** (which can be entered separately from no.9 Viale Duomo during services). Its chancel is decorated with vigorous **frescoes** ☆ by Pordenone. On the left wall is the *Epiphany* and in the lunette the *Visitation*. On the right wall is *St Liberale* and, in the apse, *Sts Peter and Andrew*. The *Augustus and the Sibyl* in the vault is one of the works that introduced illusionist painting to the Veneto. Over the altar is Titian's *Annunciation* (*c.*1520), recently returned after a painstaking restoration; unfortunately little of the original paint remains.

In the chancel, built by Pietro Lombardo and his sons Tullio and Antonio, is their **monument to Bishop Zanetti** ☆ (1486), one of the great Venetian sepulchral monuments.

At the top of the left aisle, in the vestibule of the 16thC **Chapel of the Sacrament**, is the richly decorated Lombardesque **monument to Bishop Nicolò Franco** (1501).

The Romanesque **Baptistry** to the left of the church and the **campanile** behind survive from the 11th-12thC.

Opposite the Baptistry is **Via Canova**, lined with pretty old houses, some frescoed. No.38 is the 15thC Gothic **Casa Trevigiana** (🔲 *open Tues-Sun 9am-noon, 2-5pm, closed Mon*) occupied by a museum of local history and applied arts — weapons, dolls, armor, wrought iron, musical instruments — mainly of the 16th-19thC. The museum is worth visiting for its atmosphere as well as its undemanding contents.

There are more old houses in the parallel Via Riccati; this leads on to Borgo Cavour, where the **Museo Civico** (🔲 *open Tues-Sat 9am-noon, 2-5pm, Sun 9am-noon, closed Mon*) is located at no.22 on the right. There is an **archeological collection** on the ground floor. The **picture gallery** on the first floor contains a huge collection of works by mainland and Venetian artists, of which the most compelling is the dramatic *Crucifixion* ☆ by Jacopo Bassano in Room XI. Other notable paintings include the detached frescoes of *Scenes from the Life of St Ursula* by Tommaso da Modena and the *Portrait of a Dominican* by Lorenzo Lotto.

A short walk to the s brings you to the enormous 13th-14thC brick Dominican church of **San Nicolò**, which has a severely imposing interior, its colossal pillars frescoed with saints by Tommaso da Modena and other 14thC artists.

In the apse of the **chancel** hangs a *Sacra Conversazione* (1521) begun by Marco Pensaben and finished by Girolamo Savoldo, and on the left wall is the remarkable early 16thC **Onigo monument** ☆ executed soon after the Zanetti monument in the Duomo, by Pietro Lombardo and his sons Tullio and Antonio in collaboration with a painter, probably Lorenzo Lotto, to whom the **frescoes of pages** are attributed.

In the **seminary** next to the church (*ring for entry*) the chapter house contains lively **frescoes of members of the Dominican order** (1352) by Tommaso da Modena.

Restaurants

The best known of the local produce is *radicchio di Treviso*, eaten in a salad or cooked. Look out also for the sausages known as *luganega*, usually cooked with rice, and the slowly-simmered pigeon soup called *sopa coada*.

Alfredo el Toula'

Via Collalto 26 ☎(0422) 540275 ▥ ▤ ☗ ☖ AE ⊕ ▥ *Closed Sun eve, Mon and part of Aug.*

Alfredo's was opened more than 20yrs ago by Alfredo Beltrame, a native of Treviso. It is today one of the famous deluxe restaurants of the Veneto, the original link in a glittering chain which now includes restaurants in Milan, Rome and New York, as well as a small country hotel near Treviso (described in the introduction to *The mainland*). The quality of the food, which ranges adventurously through the great culinary traditions of Europe, remains extraordinary.

Some more sympathetic restaurants are: **All' Antica Torre** (*Via Inferiore 55* ☎(0422) 53694 ▥ AE ⊕ ▥ *closed Sun, Aug*); **Le Beccherie** (*Piazza Ancilotto 10* ☎(0422) 540871 ▥ AE ⊕ ▥ *closed Thurs dinner, Fri, and July*); **Al Bersagliere** (*Via Barberia 21* ☎(0422) 541988 ▥ AE ⊕ ▥ *closed Sun and Aug*); **Carletto** (*Via Bibano 46* ☎(0422) 62955. *Closed Mon and Aug*); and **l'Incontro** (*Largo di Porta Altinia 13* ☎(0422) 547717 ▥ *closed Wed, Thurs lunch and Aug*).

Excursion

10km (6½ miles) to the sw, in the village of **Santa Cristina** near Quinto di Treviso, the church of Santa Cristina has over its high altar one of the two outstanding 16thC paintings in the area (the other being Giorgione's much more famous *Castelfranco Madonna*). This crystalline *Madonna and Child with Sts Peter, Christina, Liberale and Jerome* ★ (1506) was the first and one of the finest altarpieces painted by Lorenzo Lotto.

Verona ★

114km (71 miles) w of Venice. Provincial capital. Population: 271,400. Getting there: By train, a frequent service takes 1½hrs; by car, autostrada A4 just after Marghera **i** *Piazza Bra 10, Galleria Liston* ☎(045) 30086.

Verona is one of the most romantically beautiful of all northern Italian cities. It is also the biggest and most important city in the Veneto after Venice. Dramatically situated on two deep curves of the fast-flowing Adige river below the Monti Lessini, the city's noblest monuments — the Roman amphitheater, the Romanesque church of San Zeno, the Gothic Castelvecchio and the Renaissance walls and palaces built by Michele Sanmicheli — span a period of some 1,500yrs.

From the house facades, often trimmed in dusky red Verona marble, pretty 'Juliet' balconies overlook the animated streets where the elegance of the stores and restaurants testifies to Verona's high level of prosperity. Thanks to its position at an important intersection of commercial traffic, Verona has enjoyed this prosperity throughout its long history.

It would be worth visiting Verona for its restaurants alone; and its grand hotel, the **Due Torri**, is one of the most comfortable and best managed in Italy.

Verona was a flourishing Roman colony from the 1stC BC and in the Middle Ages enjoyed the special favor of the Ostrogoth,

Verona

1 Arche Scaligere
2 Santa Maria Antica
3 Arena
4 Castelvecchio (Museo Civico)
5 Palazzo Bevilacqua
6 Palazzo Canossa
7 Arco dei Gavi
8 Duomo
9 Palazzo Pompei (Natural History Museum)
10 Piazza dei Signori
11 Palazzo del Commune
12 Palazzo dei Tribunali
13 Loggia del Consiglio
14 Palazzo del Governo
15 San Anastasia
16 San Bernardino
17 San Fermo Maggiore
18 San Giorgio in Braida
19 Santa Maria in Organo
20 San Zeno Maggiore
21 Teatro Romano
22 Archaeological Museum
23 Garden of Palazzo Giusti
24 San Giovanni in Valle

Walk 1 ——————
Walk 2 - - - - - - -

* Walk 2 continues along Via Pallone until you turn right into Via del Pontiere. Turn first left and follow the road down to **Juliet's Tomb**. Retrace your steps to Via del Pontiere then turn left. Follow this road as far as Via del Zappatore where you turn right. Continue to the end then turn left into Corso Porta Nuova. Pass through **Porta Nuova**, then follow the road round to the right along Viale Luciano dal Cero, with the **city walls** on your right. After the Zoological Gardens and a large car park, pass through the **Porta Palio** into Stradone Porta Palio. Turn left into Vicolo Lungo San Bernardino and continue as shown on the map below.

Lombard and Frankish emperors. As a free commune from the early 12thC the city was plagued by the domestic rivalries commemorated in the story of _Romeo and Juliet_ (the original version dates from _c._1303).

From 1262-1387 the city was ruled by the Della Scala (or Scaliger) family, under whose rule many of the city's most imposing monuments were built. Verona was annexed by Venice in 1404, and it was under Venetian orders that the city's medieval walls were strengthened by Sanmicheli's innovative fortifications. The city remained under Venetian dominion until the fall of the Republic to Napoleon, whose forces were bravely resisted by the people of Verona during the 'Pasqua Veronese,' at Easter in 1797.

The most famous local painters are Altichiero Altichieri, Pisanello and Paolo Veronese. Interesting artists less well represented outside their native Verona include Domenico Morone and his son Francesco, Girolamo dai Libri, Il Cavazzola, Bonifacio de' Pitati, the brothers Gian Francesco and Giovanni Caroto, and Domenico Brusasorci.

Events In July and Aug, operas are performed in the spectacular setting of the Arena (_i Ente Lirico, Arena di Verona, Piazza Bra 28, 37100 Verona_ ☎(045) 23520 ☎ 480869; _Ticket office: sixth arch of the Arena_ ☎(045) 24660).

In July and Aug, drama festival, with the emphasis on
Shakespeare's plays, in the Teatro Romano.

Sights and places of interest

Ideally, you should allow two days to see Verona, one day to visit the center
and a second day for the peripheral quarters; the map shows two suggested
itineraries which can be followed on foot and which take in all the major
sites. The main parking lots are located in the s of the city, two of them in the
public gardens, either side of Porta Palio. The churches are all very dark, so
take a flashlight if you hope to see the altarpieces.

The hub of the city is **Piazza Bra**, the semi-circular open space dominated
by the massive **Arena** on its NE and bounded on the NW by the **Liston**, lined
with open-air cafés. The traffic-free **Via Mazzini**, the most elegant shopping
street (especially for women's clothes), links the Arena to the medieval center
around **Piazza delle Erbe** and **Piazza dei Signori**.

Arche Scaligere † ★

    Open Tues-Sun 9am-noon, 2.30-6pm (closes 30mins earlier in
winter). Closed Mon.

The cemetery of the Scaligeri rulers behind the E corner of Piazza dei Signori
is enclosed by a 14thC wrought-iron grille in which the ladder (*scala*), the
heraldic emblem of the Scaligeri, is a repeated motif. Over the side doorway
of the Romanesque church of **Santa Maria Antica** is the **tomb of Cangrande I**
(died 1329); the equestrian statue is a copy of the original now in the
Castelvecchio. The most impressive monuments within the enclosure are

the **tomb of Mastino II** (built four years before his death in 1351) and the **tomb of Cansignorio** (begun before his death in 1375), signed by Bonino da Campione.

Arena 🏛 ★
Piazza Bra ☎ *(045) 23204* ▓ *Open Tues-Sun 9am-noon; 2.30-6pm (closes 30mins earlier in winter). When operas are being performed (July, Aug) open 8am-1.30pm. Closed Mon.*

Completed in c.AD30, the Arena is the third largest and one of the best preserved Roman amphitheaters in existence. It consisted originally of four concentric elliptical rings. Of the outermost ring only the four arches, known as the Ala, at the N end survived an earthquake in the 12thC; but all 72 arches of the second ring are intact. The floor space of the interior measures 73 by 44m (80 by 48yds), and the 44 rows of stone benches seat no less than 22,000 spectators.

Gladiatorial performances were banned by the Emperor Honorius in the early 5thC. During the Middle Ages the Arena was used for public executions, in the Renaissance for fairs and tournaments, in the 18th and 19thC for bull-baiting and plays. The first of the regular opera seasons opened in 1913 with a performance of Verdi's *Aida*, still the most spectacular set piece.

Castelvecchio 🏛 ★
☎ *(045) 594734/28817* ▓ *Open July, Aug Tues-Sun 9am-7pm; Sept-June Tues-Sun 9am-noon, 2.30-6pm (closes 30mins earlier in winter). Closed Mon.*

The most prominent medieval civic monument in the city, the Castelvecchio was built in 1345-75 as the residence of Cangrande II and Cansignorio della Scala on what was then the western edge of the city. The two parts of the castle, the military barracks on the city side and the palace or *reggia*, on the other, are separated by a deep ditch and a section of the medieval walls and guarded from the river bank by the *mastio* or castle keep. The three-arched **Ponte Scaligero** ☆ which spans the Adige river behind the castle, was bombed — along with all Verona's bridges — during World War II and reconstructed, partly from original fragments, in 1950-51.

The **Museo Civico** ★ has occupied the Castelvecchio since 1925 and was beautifully reorganized during a major restoration in 1956-64.

On the ground floor a fine collection of 12th to early 15thC **sculpture** is displayed in five rooms of the Napoleonic wing.

The upper floors of the castle provide a wonderfully romantic setting for a large and important collection of 14th-18thC Veronese and other Veneto-school paintings which are arranged in roughly chronological order. Notice especially the following works: Stefano da Verona's *Madonna of the Rosebud*; Pisanello's *Madonna of the Quail*; Mantegna's *Holy Family*; two *Madonnas* by Giovanni Bellini; Crivelli's *Madonna of the Passion*. The **Via Trezza treasure**, a hoard of medieval jewelry rediscovered in 1938, is also displayed here.

The **equestrian statue of Cangrande I** ☆ from his tomb in the Arche Scaligere is displayed on a plinth over the courtyard and can be seen as you cross the bridge to the last rooms of the museum. Don't fail at this point to walk along the battlements which command a stunning view of the river and the Ponte Scaligero.

The final section of the museum in the upper rooms of the Napoleonic wing is devoted to an outstanding collection of 16th-18thC pictures, including Cavazzola's *Passion Scenes* and *Pietà*, Girolamo dai Libri's *Madonna of the Umbrella*, Lotto's *Portrait of a Man*, Veronese's *Bevilacqua Altarpiece*, *Deposition* and early oil sketches of the *Stories of Esther*; Tintoretto's *Adoration of the Shepherds*; Brusasorci's (attributed) *Portrait of Pase Guarienti*, Strozzi's *Portrait of a Man* and the *Expulsion from Eden*; and works by Luca Giordano, Tiepolo and Francesco Guardi.

Corso Cavour ☆
The most interesting street for palace architecture runs from the Roman Porta Borsari to the Castelvecchio and is lined with Gothic, Renaissance and Baroque buildings. The masterpieces are no.19, Sanmicheli's powerful **Palazzo Bevilacqua** ★ (1530) and no.44, his **Palazzo Canossa** ★ (1537). Near the Castelvecchio stands the **Arco dei Gavi**, a reconstruction of a 1stC AD Roman triumphal arch demolished in 1805. A stretch of the original Roman road passes through the arch.

Duomo 🏛 † ☆
The cathedral dates from the 12thC, with 15thC Gothic and Renaissance additions. The w and s **porches**, both 12thC, bear good sculptures and

reliefs. The **campanile** was designed by Sanmicheli. The Gothic interior (very dark, like all Veronese churches) contains a number of important works of art. Over the first altar on the left is Titian's recently restored *Assumption* ☆ (1530), probably painted with the help of his brother Francesco; the central figure of St Peter is especially fine. Over the second altar on the right is Liberale da Verona's strange *Epiphany*. There is a charming *Madonna and Saints* by Caroto in the left aisle. The first three chapels on either side are decorated with architectural frescoes (1503) by Falconetto. The handsome polished marble **enclosure** (1534) of the chancel is by Sanmicheli.

To visit the Romanesque **Baptistry** in the cloister to the left of the church you have to apply to the custodian of the Duomo.

Palazzo Pompei *(Museo Civico di Storia Naturale)*
Lungadige Porta Vittoria 9 ☎ *(045) 24567* 📷 🔲 *on Sun. Open Sat-Thurs 9am-12.30pm, 3.30-6.30pm (3-6pm in winter). Closed Fri.*
One of Sanmicheli's most elegant palaces (1527-30) now houses the Natural History Museum, containing a good collection of fossils, minerals, flora and fauna.

Piazza delle Erbe ★
The lively market square, one of the most picturesque in Italy, is located on the site of the Roman forum next to Piazza dei Signori. The central **fountain**, surmounted by a Roman statue known as *Madonna Verona*, is surrounded by market stalls shaded by a jostling crowd of huge white umbrellas. The square is lined with a pleasing architectural farrago of old houses (some frescoed) and towers.

Piazza dei Signori ★
The Arco della Costa leads from Piazza delle Erbe to the civic center of the medieval city. On the right is the 12thC **Palazzo del Comune** or della Ragione; its Romanesque courtyard has a Gothic external staircase and is surmounted by the 12thC **Torre dei Lamberti** (☎ *(045) 32726* 🔲 *on foot* ▬ *by elevator; closed Mon*), which is worth ascending for a splendid view. Beyond is the **Palazzo dei Tribunali**, with a crenellated tower and a gateway (1530-31) by Sanmicheli. On the opposite side of the piazza is the graceful early Renaissance **Loggia del Consiglio** ☆ built by an unknown architect as the meeting place of the council of citizens. The piazza is closed at the far end by the 13thC **Palazzo del Governo**, originally the residence of the Scaligeri lords (who entertained Giotto and Dante here) with a doorway (1532) by Sanmicheli. Behind this is E end are the **Arche Scaligere**.

Porta Borsari ☆
The best-preserved of the Roman gates, at the NE end of **Corso Cavour**, was probably built during the reign of Emperor Claudius (AD41-54). Its name derives from its use as a toll gate during the Middle Ages.

Porta Palio ☆
The most architecturally powerful of Sanmicheli's city gates, at the end of Stradone Porto Palio, was built in 1542-57. The severely classical external facade has fluted Doric half columns and three rectangular openings surmounted by busts of mythological warriors.

San Anastasia 🏛 ✝ 🔲
The vast Dominican church dominating the inner curve of the Adige river was begun in 1290-1323, possibly by the architect of *Santi Giovanni e Paolo* in Venice, and completed between 1423-81. The unfinished facade has a fine double **portal**. The 15thC **campanile** is one of the tallest in the city.

At the base of the first two columns of the interior the holy-water stoups are borne by curious crouching figures carved in the 16thC. The **Fregoso altar** (completed 1565), the first altar on the right, was singled out for special praise by Vasari. The architecture is by Sanmicheli and the sculptures, which glorify the military career of Jano Fregoso, are by Danese Cattaneo. In the second of the apsidal chapels to the right of the chancel, the large fresco of the *Cavalli Family Presented to the Virgin by Three Saints* (1395) is by Altichiero. In the **Pellegrini Chapel**, to the right of the chancel, the **terra-cotta reliefs** (1435) are important works by Michele da Firenze.

Pisanello's fresco of *St George and the Princess* ★ — one of the most romantic of International Gothic fairy tales — has been removed from the Pellegrini Chapel to the Giusto Chapel off the left transept.

San Bernardino 🏛 🔲
Built in 1451-66 in transitional Gothic-Renaissance style, the church is entered through a frescoed cloister. The church's interior contains interesting 15th-16thC frescoes and paintings, but is chiefly remarkable for Sanmicheli's **Pellegrini Chapel** ☆ (1556) to the right of the chancel.

177

San Fermo Maggiore 🏛 † ☆
The building consists of two superimposed churches, the 11th-12thC
Romanesque lower church and the 13th-14thC Gothic upper church. The
meeting of the two styles can be clearly seen at the apse end.

The aisle-less nave of the **upper church** is decorated with 14thC frescoes
and roofed by a ship's-keel ceiling. Outstanding among the 15th-16thC
paintings and sculptures is the **Brenzoni monument** ★ (1427-39) on the left
wall by the Florentine sculptor Nanni di Bartolo, with a frescoed background
of the _Annunciation_ ★ the earliest surviving major work of Pisanello.

San Giorgio in Braida 🏛 †
The northern outer curve of the Adige river is dominated by the dome and
campanile of San Giorgio in Braida, both designed by Sanmicheli, as is the
Porta San Giorgio in front of the church. The church was begun by an
unknown architect in 1477 and completed with a 17thC facade. The two
outstanding works inside are both by local 16thC painters and both over
altars designed by Sanmicheli: in the apse is Paolo Veronese's _Martyrdom of
St George_ ☆ (1566), painted when the artist returned briefly to Verona from
Venice to marry the daughter of his painting master; and over the fourth altar
on the left is Girolamo dai Libri's calmly spacious _Virgin Enthroned with Sts
Zeno and Lawrence Giustiniani_ ☆

Santa Maria in Organo 🏛 †
The lower facade of the 15thC Gothic church was completed in the 16thC
with a severe marble screen by Sanmicheli. The interior, decorated with
16thC frescoes and paintings, is worth visiting for the superb intarsiaed choir
stalls ☆ (1491-1523) by Giovanni da Verona in the apse and sacristy.

San Zeno Maggiore 🏛 † ☆
One of the most beautiful and moving Romanesque churches in Europe, San
Zeno was founded in the 5thC as the shrine of the first Bishop of Verona, and
assumed its present appearance under the Commune between 1120-1225.
The apse was rebuilt in the 14thC.

The **facade** is flanked by two towers, the tall **campanile** (1045-1178) on
the right and on the left the crenellated tower which is all that remains of the
once-powerful Benedictine monastery. On the **porch**, supported by
endearing marble lions, and on the panels to either side are important 12thC
relief carvings ★ by the masters Niccolò and Guglielmo. In the lunette the
San Zeno Trampling on the Devil symbolizes the establishment of the free
Commune. The vigorous, primitive reliefs on the **bronze doors** ★ (11th-12thC)
illustrate _stories of San Zeno_ and _scenes from the Old and New Testaments._

Entrance is normally through the Romanesque cloister to the left. The
calm, imposing interior is roofed by a ship's-keel ceiling. The raised chancel
is enclosed by a marble balustrade bearing 13thC **statues of Christ and the
Apostles.** The frescoes in the right aisle and chancel date from the
13th-15thC. In the little chapel to the left of the chancel is the early 14thC
painted marble statue of _San Zeno Laughing._ San Zeno's modern tomb is in
the spacious **crypt** beneath the chancel.

Over the high altar, in its original frame, is Mantegna's triptych (1457-59)
of the _Madonna and Child with Sts John the Baptist, Augustin, Lawrence,
Benedict, Peter, Paul, John the Evangelist and Zeno_ ★ the first major
Renaissance painting to be seen in Verona. The figures, displayed in a
Roman loggia against a vivid dark blue sky, stand out as though in crisp
relief. The wheel of fortune, one of the themes of the decorations on the
church facade, appears at the base and foot of the Madonna's throne. The
predella panels are copies of the originals, now in the Paris Louvre.

Teatro Romano _(Roman Theater and Archeological Museum)_
☎_(045) 25360/33974_ 📷 _Open Tues-Sun 9am-noon. 2.30-6pm
(closes 30mins earlier in winter). Closed Mon._
The Roman theater, which backs onto the slope of the hill of St Peter, was
probably built in the late 1stC BC and was excavated between 1834-1914.
Shakespeare's plays are performed here in July and Aug.

The **Archeological Museum** in the former monastery of San Girolamo
behind the theater contains a nicely-presented collection and commands
superb views of the city.

Tomba di Giulietta _(Juliet's Tomb)_
Via del Pontiere, off Via Pallone ☎ _(045) 25361_ 📷 _Open Tues-Sun
9am-noon. 2.30-6pm (closes 30mins earlier in winter). Closed Mon._
Despite the unreliability of the legend that Juliet was buried in the church of
San Francesco al Corso, the complex of buildings around the church cloister
is very evocative. The attached **Museum of Frescoes** has a reconstruction of
a frescoed 16thC music chamber.

Other sights

Those with more leisure might also wish to visit some of the following places of interest: the 18thC garden of **Palazzo Giusti**; the churches of **San Giovanni in Valle** and **Santi Nazaro e Celso**; the **zoo**, which is located around one of the bastions of Sanmicheli's walls in the sw.

Hotels

Aurora ✿
Piazza delle Erbe ☎ *(045) 584717* ▯ *22 rms* ▭ *17* (VISA)
The joy of this modest but clean small hotel is the view from your bedroom of the Piazza delle Erbe.
🏠 ‡ 🖅 ◁ɛ

Colomba d'Oro
Via C. Cattaneo 10 ☎ *(045) 595300* ◐ *480872* ▯▯ *55 rms* ▭ *40* 📧 🖭
🚞 AE ⓪ (VISA)
A comfortable, carefully managed and very central hotel with a reputation for good service. But the decor lacks style.
🏠 ‡ 🖅 👬

Due Torri 🏨
Piazza San Anastasia 4 ☎ *(045) 595044* ◐ *48054* ▯▯▯▯ *100 rms* ▭ *68* 📧
🖭 🚞 AE ⓪ ⓪ (VISA)
An attractive and beautifully managed private hotel rebuilt in 1958 on the site of a Scaliger palace. Ruskin and his wife Effie always stayed here in the 19thC, when the palace was already a hotel.
🏠 ‡ ₺ 🖅 🐾 👬

Restaurants

Arche
Via Arche Scaligere 6 ☎ *(045) 21415* 🍷 AE ⓪ ▯▯ to ▯▯ *Closed Sun, Mon lunch and first three weeks in July.*
A cool, elegant and comfortable fish restaurant next to 'Romeo's House' behind the Arche Scaligere.

12 Apostoli
Corticella San Marco 3 ☎ *(045) 596999* ▯▯▯▯ 📧 AE ⓪ *Closed Sun eve, Mon.*
No longer the best restaurant, but still as pretty as a picture book. The service is good, so are the soups, the *torta di tartufi neri*, *cotolletta dodici Apostoli*, and the desserts.

Il Desco
Via dietro San Sebastiano 7 ☎ *(045) 595358* ▯▯▯▯ AE ⓪ (VISA) *Closed Sun. Open late after opera performances at the Arena.*
The most gastronomically creative and interesting of the restaurants in Verona. Seasonal specialties include *zuppa di porcini in crosta*, *branzino ai carciofi*, *filetto di manzo all'Amarone*.

Nuovo Marconi
Via Fogge 4, by Piazza dei Signori ☎ *(045) 591910/595295* ▯▯ AE ⓪ (VISA) 🚞 🏠 *Closed Sun, Tues eve and two weeks in mid-Aug.*
Deliberately unfussy modern decor and short menu from which you might choose *crepes ai carciofi*; *taglierini verdi con pomodoro, basilico e gamberi*; *seppie nere con polenta*, or *rognoncino all'aceto balsamico*.

Excursion

The hilly country around Verona is one of north Italy's most prolific wine-growing regions (see *The wines of northeast Italy*, pp 187-188). Although the lower slopes of the Valpolicella to the NW have been spoiled by development, the higher reaches are still lovely. Palladio enthusiasts will wish to stop at Santa Sofia di Piedmont where a giant fragment of Palladio's unfinished Villa Sarego (1568-69), his most ambitious and least characteristic design, stands forlornly behind a wine depot.

Vicenza ★

*Map 2C2. 51km (32 miles) w of Venice. Provincial capital
Population: 119,100. Getting there: By train, a frequent
service from Venice takes about 1hr; by car, autostrada A4
just after Marghera i Piazza Matteotti, near Teatro Olimpico
☎(0444) 28944.*

Vicenza is a handsome, prosperous, well-ordered city, which was
the home of Palladianism, the most influential building style in the
history of Western architecture.

Andrea di Pietro della Gondola moved to Vicenza from his
native Padua in 1524 at the age of 16. He worked as an apprentice
stone carver for 14yrs before he met the humanist scholar and
amateur architect Count Giangiorgio Trissino, who gave him his
classical name — Palladio — and the classical education which,
combined with his native genius and long practical experience in
the building trade, enabled him to satisfy so precisely the tastes of
the Vicentine nobility.

When Palladio began his career as an architect Vicenza was at
last recovering from the devastation of the wars of 1509-17. A
discontented outpost of the Venetian Empire since 1404, the city
had sided with the emperor against Venice and had been sacked by
both sides. There had been little incentive or opportunity for
building, and the Renaissance style which was by then flourishing
in Venice and Padua had passed the city by. The Vicentine
aristocracy, a class composed largely of mercenary soldiers who
had no direct political power, was avid for the prestige which
grand classical buildings would confer on their families and their
city.

By his death in 1580 Palladio had designed 11 palaces and public
buildings for Vicenza, as well as numerous villas for Vicentine-
owned country estates. (For a suggested tour of the surviving
Palladian villas see *The villas of Andrea Palladio*.) Although not
one of the Vicentine palaces was more than half finished inside,
their facades transformed the appearance of the city and set the
style, faithfully followed in Vicenza ever since, that gives the city
its homogeneous dignity.

Vicenza is pleasantly situated at the confluence of the rivers
Retrone and Bacchiglione in a fertile plain at the foot of the Monti
Bérici. In the older sections of the city the dialect word *contrà* (or
contrada) is used in place of *via* to indicate a street.

The center of the city is closed to traffic.

Tour of the main sights

The central monument of Vicenza is the **Basilica** ★ *(Piazza dei Signori* 🗖
open Tues-Sat 9.30am-noon, 2.30-5pm, Sun 9am-noon, closed Mon) which
stands between the main square, **Piazza dei Signori**, and the market square,
Piazza delle Erbe. The Basilica, Palladio's first public commission and his
only work executed entirely in stone, is also his masterpiece. It is not actually
a building but a screen wrapped around the 15thC Palazzo della Ragione. It
consists of a double loggia, Doric below and Ionic above, organized by a
flexible system of pillars and arches which conceals the irregular shape of the
Gothic core and creates an impression of thrilling grandeur. From its N
corner, the **Torre di Piazza**, raised in three stages from the 12th to
mid-15thC, shoots upward like a rocket.

On the N side of Piazza dei Signori is Palladio's unfinished **Loggia del
Capitaniato** ☆ (1571-72) begun for a Venetian captain to commemorate the
victory over the Turks at Lepanto.

To the s of Piazza delle Erbe in Via Pigafetta, no.5 is the odd
Gothic-Renaissance **Casa Pigafetta** *(c.*1481), showing a Spanish influence.
Farther s, near the river in Viale Eretenio, is Palladio's earliest and least
striking Vicentine palace, the **Casa Civena** (1540-46).

The Gothic **Duomo** was reconstructed after almost total destruction in

World War II, and is mainly of interest for the fact that its apse and vault were designed by Palladio. Nearby, in Piazza Castello, no.18 is the unfinished **Palazzo Porto-Breganze**; it was designed by Palladio in the 1570s, and its two bays built posthumously by Scamozzi.

From Piazza Castello the **Corso Palladio** ★ — the main street of Vicenza — runs straight across the city. It is lined with fine palaces, the most notable being no.98, the **Palazzo del Commune** (1592) built by Scamozzi and no.147, the 14thC **Palazzo da Schio** in Venetian-Gothic style. At the far end, no.163, the **Casa Cogollo** (built in the 1560s) is known as the Casa del Palladio although its attribution is doubtful.

Facing the river across Piazza Matteotti is Palladio's **Palazzo Chiericati** ☆ (begun in 1551, completed in the 17thC) enveloped by its airy tripartite portico which is surmounted by an Ionic loggia closed at the center. The palace is occupied by the **Museo Civico** ★ *(Piazza Matteotti ☎(0444) 21348 📷 🔲 on holidays; open Tues-Fri 9.30am-noon, 2.30-5pm, Sat 9.30am-noon, Sun 10am-noon, closed Mon)*, which has in its picture gallery on the first floor an outstanding collection of Venetian and mainland Veneto art. The highlights of the collection are: *The Crucifixion* (c.1470) by Hans Memling; *The Madonna and Child Enthroned with Saints* and *The Madonna and Sts Mary Magdalen and Monica* by Bartolomeo Montagna; *The Madonna and Sts Jerome and James* (1489) by Cima da Conegliano; *Lamentation over the Dead Christ* by Giovanni Buonconsiglio; *The Madonna and Child with Saints* (c.1556) by Veronese; *A Miracle of St Augustine* by Tintoretto; *The Governors of Vicenza at the Feet of the Virgin* (1573) by Jacopo Bassano; the *Portrait with Allegories of Alvise Foscarini* by Francesco Maffei; *The Three Ages of Man* by van Dyck; *The Immaculate Virgin* (*c*.1730) by G.B. Tiepolo; *St Francis Receiving the Stigmata* (*c*.1732) by G.B. Tiepolo; *Time Revealing the Truth* (*c*.1744) by G.B. Tiepolo; the six large lunettes by Maffei and Giulio Carpioni.

Across the piazza is the **Teatro Olimpico** ★ (*Piazza Matteotti* ☎(*0444*) *23728* 🎫 🎭 *on holidays; open mid-Mar to mid-Oct Mon-Sat 9.30am-12.30pm, 3-5.20pm, Sun 9.30am-12.15pm; mid-Oct to mid-Mar Mon-Sat 9.30am-12.30pm, 2-4pm, Sun 9.30am-12.15pm*). This was Palladio's last and perhaps his most fascinating work, begun in 1579-80 for the Vicentine Academy. The fixed perspectives of the stage were designed and built by Scamozzi in 1584-85. The toga-clad Roman figures on the proscenium are portraits of the academicians.

Off this end of the Corso Palladio, in the Contrada Santa Corona, is the Dominican church of **Santa Corona** (*open Tues-Sun 9.30am-12.15pm, 3.30-6pm, Mon 3.30-6pm*). Begun in 1261, this church has the earliest Gothic interior in the Veneto and a Renaissance chancel (1489). The Valmarana Chapel to the right of the crypt is to a design (1576) by Palladio. In the third chapel off the right aisle is a painting of the *Adoration of the Magi* (1573) by Veronese. The fifth altarpiece on the left is Giovanni Bellini's late masterpiece, the *Baptism of Christ* ★ (1501) in a magnificent stone frame.

Opposite Santa Corona, no.21 is the Baroque **Palazzo Leoni Montanari**, headquarters of the Banca Cattolica del Veneto. It has a splendid interior courtyard, superb stuccowork and frescoes on its *piano nobile*; it contains paintings by Pietro Longhi and his imitators.

The next turning on the right off the Corso Palladio is Contrada Zanella, where the Baroque church of **Santo Stefano** is to be found. In the left transept is the finest 16thC altarpiece in Vicenza after the Santa Corona Bellini: Palma il Vecchio's *Madonna and Child with Sts George and Lucy* ☆ which rivals the quality of his *Santa Barbara* in *Santa Maria Formosa*, Venice.

In **Contrà Porti** ★ next right off the Corso Palladio, there are three of Palladio's palaces. No 12 is **Palazzo Thiene**. Its Contrà Porti facade is 15thC; the vigorously rusticated **east facade** ☆ (*c*.1545-50) is traditionally attributed to Palladio. Opposite, no.11 is **Palazzo Porto Barbarano** (1570); its ornately stuccoed facade was thrown out of symmetry later in the 16thC by the addition of two bays. No.21, **Palazzo Iseppo da Porto**, whose facade was finished in 1552, shows the influence of Roman palaces designed by Bramante and Raphael.

There are more fine palaces across the 13thC Ponte Pusterla in Contrà San Marco; no.39 is Palladio's **Palazzo Schio-Angaran** (pre-1566). Returning to Corso Palladio, turn right into Corso A. Fogazzaro. No.16, **Palazzo Valmarana** (1565), restored in 1962 after it was damaged in World War II, is one of Palladio's subtlest and most sophisticated designs, well-suited to its location on a narrow street. Beyond, facing Piazza San Lorenzo, is the Baroque **Palazzo Repeta** (1701-11), now the Bank of Italy, by Francesco Muttoni.

The 13thC Franciscan church of **San Lorenzo** has a magnificent splayed **portal** with 14thC sculptures. The Poiana altar, in the right transept, bears notable 15th-16thC reliefs. In the left apse chapel is a detached fresco of the *Beheading of the Baptist* by Bartolomeo Montagna.

🍽 **The Gran Caffè Garibaldi**
Via Cavour 7 ☎*(0444) 544147* ▦ 🍷 ▥ AE CB ◉ ⬡ VISA *Closed Wed and late Jan.*
A big, brightly lit, dignified restaurant in the center overlooking the Basilica. The 'grand café' is on the ground floor.

🍽 **Allo Scudo di Francia**
Contrà Piancoli 4 ☎*(0444) 233368* ▥ AE ◉ VISA *Closed Sun dinner, Mon, Aug and after Christmas.*
Classic Vicentine cooking and authentic antique furniture. The name refers to the days under the Napoleonic regime when this was an inn and rendezvous for the French in Italy.

🍽 **Tre Visi**
Contrà Porti 6 ☎*(0444) 238677* ▥ ▯ AE CB ◉ ⬡ VISA 🍽 *Closed Sun dinner and Mon.*
Terra-cotta-colored walls, beamed ceilings and sympathetic service create a welcoming environment much appreciated by the locals. A short, carefully

considered menu concentrates on Vicentine dishes, such as *ravioli alla Tre Visi* and *baccalà*, as well as some imaginative soups.

Excursion to Monte Bérico, Villa Valmarana and La Rotonda

This excursion is about one hour's walk southward from the center, or take a bus to Monte Bérico from Piazza Duomo.

The Baroque **Basilica of Monte Bérico** (1688-1703) (*open 6.30am-8pm*) which overlooks Vicenza from the hill to the s is reached on foot in 15mins along the steep covered way known as the Portici. In its refectory is the greatest of Veronese's 'Suppers,' the *Supper of St Gregory the Great* ★ (1572), painted only a few months before the better-known *Feast at the House of Levi* in the Venice *Accademia* for which Veronese repeated this composition on a larger scale. In the church, to the right of the high altar, is a moving *Pietà* ☆ (1500), one of Bartolomeo Montagna's best works.

To reach the **Villa Valmarana** 'ai Nani' (☎ *(0444) 21803/43976* ■ (*open mid-Mar to mid-Nov 3-6pm, also Thurs, Sat, Sun 10am-noon*) go back along the Portici and turn right halfway down into the Spianata del Cristo, then right again into Via San Bastiano. The Villa Valmarana is called 'ai Nani' after the statues of dwarfs on its garden wall. The *palazzina* and its *foresteria* (both 1668) are decorated inside with some of the most joyous and elegant **frescoes** ★ in the Veneto by Giambattista Tiepolo and his son Giandomenico.

The pretty Strada Valmarana leads down to **La Rotonda** ★ (■ *open (grounds only) 9am-noon, 3-6pm*), Palladio's most famous villa and the model for numerous later buildings including Chiswick House in England and Marly in France. It was begun before 1570 for Monsignore Paolo Almerico and completed by Scamozzi in 1606 for the Capra family. Unlike Palladio's other villas, which were built for working farms, the Rotonda was conceived as a suburban pleasure palace and *belvedere*, where the owners entertained and enjoyed the views from its four porches. Its plan, a domed circular *salone* enclosed in a cube, is unique among Palladio's finished buildings.

Vittorio Veneto

Map 3A4. 10km (6 miles) N of Conegliano; 70km (44 miles) N of Venice. Province of Treviso. Population: 31,000. Getting there: Frequent trains from Venice 1hr 10mins; by car, autostrada A4, then A27 i Piazza del Popolo ☎(0438) 56804.

Vittorio Veneto is located in the foothills of the Dolomites where the Meschio river tumbles out of its mountain gorge. It consists of two separate towns, Ceneda and Serravalle, which were joined in 1866 on the unification of Italy and named in honor of Victor Emanuel II. The Battle of Vittorio Veneto, which was the decisive battle of World War I on the Italian front, took place from October 24-November 3 1918.

The modern industrial quarter of Ceneda is linked to the old walled town of Serravalle by the Viale della Vittoria, lined with handsome 19thC houses.

Sights and places of interest

Although a short visit may safely be confined to Serravalle, it is worth stopping briefly in the cathedral square of Ceneda, where material relating to the battle of Vittorio Veneto is displayed in the **Museo della Battaglia** (■). The design of the **Loggia Cenedese** (1538) in which the museum is housed is attributed to Sansovino.

Serravalle ☆ itself is a strikingly well-preserved Gothic-Renaissance walled village dramatically situated below the rocky Meschio gorge. Zeffirelli shot parts of his film *Romeo and Juliet* here.

Just inside the southern gate is the Gothic Ospedale Civile. Its **Chapel of San Lorenzo** is decorated inside with 15thC **frescoes** ☆ in the International Gothic style which were uncovered in 1953.

The arcaded **Via Martiri della Libertà** ☆ , lined with 15th and 16thC houses (notice especially nos. 4, 35, 47 and 48), leads to the **Loggia Serravallese** (1462), in which you will find the **Museo del Cenedese** (■), containing archeological material, sculptures, Veneto-school paintings and detached frescoes.

The 18thC **Duomo** (Santa Maria Nova) and its 13th-14thC **campanile** stand on the other side of the river. Over the high altar of the Duomo is Titian's *Virgin in Glory with Sts Andrew and Peter*, largely a studio work of the 1540s.

From Piazza Santa Maria Nova behind the Duomo there is a splendid view of the gorge and the old houses in Via del Battuti on the opposite bank.

🚃 Try the restaurant of the **Hotel Terme** (*Via della Vittoria 4* ☎*(0438) 554345* 💳 💳 *closed Mon*); and there are many good country restaurants in the wine-growing area around *Conegliano*.

Excursion

A beautiful winding road, no.422, climbs 17km (10½ miles) NE to the high **plateau of Cansiglio**, a vacation and winter-sports resort thickly wooded with beech and fir trees, which were once grown for the oars of Venetian galleys.

The villas of Andrea Palladio

Up-to-date information about all villas in the Veneto open to the public can be obtained from the rather sleepy offices of the Ente per le Ville Venete (63 Piazza San Marco, Venice ☎5230783, open Mon-Sat 9am-noon). They will also give advice about visits outside normal opening hours. The province of Vicenza is particularly rich in villas, and the Vicenza tourist board issues useful maps and suggested itineraries of all villas in the province, including Palladio's.

Anyone who has admired the spectacular array of vegetables in Venice's Rialto markets or tasted the best of the wines grown in the vineyards of the Veneto will have guessed that the soil on which such produce is grown is of exceptional quality. But it was not until the 1520s that the Venetian Republic was ready to exploit to the full the agricultural potential of its mainland territories. The Venetian government offered substantial subsidies for reclamation of marshland; and the aristocracy began to build uncastellated villas on their country estates.

Some were rich enough to build and decorate their country houses on a lavish scale; others wanted cheap, practical farmhouses which would nevertheless reflect their status as gentlemen. Either way, the ideal architect was Andrea Palladio, who knew how to build cheaply and quickly and was also thoroughly versed in the newly fashionable architectural vocabulary of ancient and contemporary Roman buildings. Palladio was certainly not the only great 16thC architect employed on the Venetian mainland. Jacopo Sansovino, to name only one other, built a palatial country seat for the Garzoni family which still stands at Pontecasale in the Adige delta. But Palladio was the most prolific, and his villas set a style which was to be imitated or copied by the landed gentry of the western world for more than two centuries after his death.

All 19 of Palladio's surviving villas are in the Veneto, and 18 of them may be easily visited in two day trips from Venice, as outlined here. (His last, the Villa Sarego at Santa Sofia di Piedmont, is more conveniently seen from *Verona*.)

Architectural historians point out that the mature villas fall into two basic types, determined by the nature of their sites. Those in villages or suburbs have two stories and freestanding, pedimented porches. Those on large agricultural estates have a one-storied central block with a temple-fronted facade and attached wings, known as *barchesse*, which were used for dovecotes, stables and for storing farm equipment. The outstanding example of the first type is the *Malcontenta* and of the second *Maser*, both of which are in excellent condition and open to the public. If you see these two villas, as well as the Villa Godi near *Thiene*, and the Rotonda near *Vicenza*, you will have a good impression of his range.

The Villas of Palladio

	Palladio's villas	10	Villa Emo
1	The Rotonda		(at Fanzolo)
2	Villa Chiericati	11	Villa Cornaro (at
	(at Vancimuglio)		Piombino Dese)
3	Villa Thiene	12	The Malcontenta
	(at Quinto)	13	Villa Badoer (at
4	Villa Valmarana		Fratta Polesine)
	(at Lisiera)	14	Villa Pisani
5	Villa Marcello	15	Villa Poiana (at
	(at Bertesina)		Poiana Maggiore)
6	Villa Caldogno	16	Villa Saraceno
7	Villino Cerato (at		(at Finale)
	Mont. Precalcino)	17	Villa Pisani
8	Villa Godi		(at Bagnolo)
	(at Lugo)		
9	Villa Maser		

0 5 10 15 20 km
0   5   10 miles

Nevertheless, for a full appreciation of the flexibility of his style,
you should try to visit some of the other 15 villas. Each is
significantly different from the others. We may all think we know
what is meant by a 'Palladian' villa, but none of Palladio's
innumerable posthumous imitators ever fully matched the sense of
a tirelessly inventive imagination harnessed to deep understanding
of classical buildings that is conveyed by the original models.

The tours

Each of these two tours takes a full day but can only be
accomplished in that time if you travel by car. They are
architectural adventures, which have their disappointments as well
as their rewards. Although the exteriors of all the villas are visible,
not all are open to the public — and not all are worth entering.
Some were never completed, others have been partly rebuilt, a few
are derelict. The plainness of some of the earlier villas will surprise
those who associate the Palladian style with elaborate 18thC
imitations — but so will the beauty of some of the less well known.

The authority on Palladio is James Ackerman and the
information in these notes and the dating of the villas are taken
from his book, *Palladio*.

The villas near Vicenza and to the north
Thiene is a convenient place to stop for lunch.

Take the autostrada A4 to Vicenza, the city which was Palladio's adopted
home. Most of his urban palaces are in Vicenza (but they will have to wait for
another day) and many of the villas nearby were commissioned by Vicentine
patricians. The **Rotonda** ★ on the SE edge of the city and described under
the Vicenza entry is different from all the other villas in that it was conceived
not as a farmhouse but as a *belvedere*. It is, if anything, more impressive from
a distance. There are good views from the *piazzale* of Monte Bérico and from

the Este road, no.247.

Those on a tight schedule who wish to skip the less impressive cluster of villas near Vicenza could now drive straight on to *Thiene* to see the earliest of Palladio's patrician villas and the one that anticipates so many of his future developments.

Otherwise take the old Padua road, no.11, to Vancimuglio where the **Villa Chiericati**, now Casarotto (1554-57) (☎(0444) 559056, *open Sun 8am-noon, 1-6pm*) is worth noting in passing, before getting onto the autostrada A31.

The next three villas are to the NE of Vicenza, near the Vicenza Nord exit of the autostrada A31. At Quinto, the **Villa Thiene** ☆ (pre-1550) is now the town hall. It is only one pavilion of a much larger project which was never realized. It is unstuccoed, but the architectural decoration is carried around all sides, with the more elaborate facade at the back.

The **Villa Valmarana** (*c*.1565-66) at Lisiera stands in a romantic, overgrown garden. It was seriously damaged in the war and the only visible trace of the original building is a *barchessa* at the back.

The **Villa Marcello** (*c*.1540-44) at Bertesina is a privately-owned working farm standing next to a hideous modern church. It is a handsome early work, but its proportions have been changed by the removal of a staircase.

The easiest way to reach Caldogno from Bertesina is to drive through Vicenza and out again on the Thiene road, no.349. The **Villa Caldogno** ☆ (*c*.1560-65) is a grandly impressive building in mournful condition. The facade facing the long garden at the back has rusticated arches and the original staircase. The villa is apparently derelict, but if you peer through the glass of the doors, you will see that the interior is decorated with entertaining 16thC frescoes in a good state of preservation. They are by G.A. Fasolo, G.B. Zelotti and Giulio Carpioni.

Take the road to Dueville and then cross the autostrada to Montecchio Precalcino where the villa in question is not the grand 18thC Palladian Villa Bucchia but the tiny **Villino Cerato** (1540-45)), now a private house. It was built in the early plain style typified by the Villa Godi at Lugo, which is the next stop. The **Villa Godi ★** and nearby **Villa Piovene** are described under *Thiene*. Allow at least half an hour to see them.

From Thiene the road no.248 travels eastward across the beautiful country below the Asiago plateau to *Maróstica*, *Bassano*, *Asolo* and *Maser* (allow a good hour to see the villa at Maser ★).

Now drive S on the Castelfranco road, no.307. The **Villa Emo ★** at Fanzolo and **Villa Cornaro** ☆ at Piombino Dese are described under *Castelfranco*.

The villas in the southern Veneto
There is an excellent restaurant at Rovigo, which is a convenient place to stop for lunch.

One possibility is to start this trip at *Malcontenta*, but, since the latter is so easily reached from Venice by public transport, it is probably better use of a car to take the autostradas A4 and A13 direct to Rovigo.

If it is not yet lunchtime, visit the **Villa Badoer ★** at Fratta Polesine first. One of the most imitated of Palladio's villas, it is described under *Rovigo*.

Now head NW via Lendinara and Badia Polesine to *Montagnana*, where the handsome **Villa Pisani** ☆ stands just outside the old walls.

You now have the choice of carrying straight on to Bagnolo or visiting two minor villas at Poiana Maggiore and Finale. The **Villa Poiana** (1545-50) (*open 3-4pm*) is a relatively simple work in what James Ackerman calls the 'early stripped style.' Near Finale, in the plain below the Monte Bérico and the Euganean Hills, is the uncompleted **Villa Saraceno** (*c*.1560), now a deserted farmhouse.

The last stop is at Bagnolo, in beautiful rural country, for the **Villa Pisani** (1540s-60s; now Ferri) (☎(0444) 831104 *open Wed, Sat 10am-noon, 3-5pm, Sun 2-7pm; also by appointment*). This big, rectangular building on the banks of the Gua river was restored in the 1970s by its present owners. The facade facing the river has a rusticated central block with Doric pilasters.

In the hills around Lonigo, which is on the way to the autostrada for Venice, there are two more villas which make a fitting conclusion to this tour. They are not by Palladio himself, but they are spectacular demonstrations of his influence. Just above Lonigo is the **Rocca Pisani** ☆ (1576), masterpiece of Palladio's close follower Vicenzo Scamozzi, based on the Rotonda.

A few kilometers SE of Lonigo is the majestic Palladian **Villa da Porto** (1714-15) by Francesco Muttoni. It stands above the village of Monticello — a name, as Americans in particular will remember, associated with that ardent follower of Palladio, Thomas Jefferson.

The wines of northeast Italy

You may be reminded that the ancient Romans drank the Rhaetic of Verona's hills and that Petrarch kept a vineyard near Padua, but in a region as geared to wine's future as is the Veneto, historical anecdotes seem hopelessly remote.

Not only is the Veneto Italy's most modern wine region, it is also the most comprehensive in type and, in some years, the most productive. Unlike other heavyweights of Italian wine, though, the Veneto prides itself on style. The region makes more classified wine (*Denominazione di Origine Controllata* or DOC) than any other, Verona's Soave, Bardolino and Valpolicella leading the way; it also exports more wine in bottle.

The Veneto is often linked with its neighbors in NE Italy — Friuli-Venezia Giulia and Trentino-Alto Adige — to form the Tre Venezie, a triumvirate which accounts for a third of all DOC wine produced and which leads the nation in vinicultural research and equipment manufacture (everything from oak barrels to stainless-steel vats and isobaric bottling machines). Italy's leading wine schools are at Conegliano in the Veneto and San Michele all'Adige in Trentino. The world's largest vine nurseries are at Rauscedo in Friuli.

The wines of NE Italy cover the gamut of types, styles and grape varieties, which include the noblest vines of France and Germany. The Veneto's Veronese trio is complemented by delightful bubbly wines and Bordeauxlike reds. Friuli-Venezia Giulia vies with Trentino-Alto Adige for the title of champion of Italian white wine, but both make an appetizing array of red and pink wine as well.

Most wines of the Tre Venezie are made to drink young. For whites and rosés, look for the latest vintage but don't hesitate to try bottles from the excellent years 1986 and 1985. For youthful reds — Bardolino, Valpolicella, Santa Maddalena, Caldaro, most Merlot, Pinot Nero and some Cabernet — look for 1986, and 1985, but don't exclude other years, for some wine-makers excel regularly. For the few big reds for aging — Refosco, Raboso, certain Cabernets and Merlots and composites such as Venegazzù — count on 1985, 1982, 1979, and 1978.

If your visit is confined to Venice, you can find a fair sampling of the Tre Venezie's wines at better-known wine-bars and at restaurants such as Antico Martini, La Regina, Poste Vecie, La Caravella and, of course, the Gritti Palace and Locanda Cipriani, where Hemingway downed his Valpolicella and *grappa*, as well as in nearby Mestre at Dall'Amelia. Venetians have the contagious habit of the *ombra* or *ombretta*, the tiny glass of wine sipped at intervals through the day. Join them at the Enoteca al Volto (*Calle Cavalli, San Marco 4081*), the best place in town to educate your palate. Several towns in the wine-growing area also boast an *enoteca*, or wine library, where the wines can be bought as well as tasted.

Dedicated enophiles will want to visit the wine country, and the first destination would probably be Verona. April is an opportune time, when *Vinitaly*, a national wine fair, provides a chance to sample thousands of Italian wines.

Verona's hilly outskirts are webbed with wine roads. Bardolino is seductive in the spring, when Lake Garda reflects apple blossoms and snow-covered Alps (try Guerrieri-Rizzardi's perfumed red Classico Superiore). Soave is for summer (you probably know Bolla, so sip Pieropan or Anselmi in view of the town's castle). The higher reaches of Valpolicella are inviting in the spring and fall, though the warming robustness of Amarone is for winter evenings (Allegrini, Bertani, Bolla, Le Ragose, Tedeschi, Masi and Giuseppe Quintarelli excel). While in the Verona area, be sure to try the white Bianco di Custoza and Lugana.

Near Vicenza lie three DOC zones. To the N is Breganze, where Maculan leads the way. s is Colli Bérici, where the Merlot and Pinot Nero of Villa dal Ferro-Lazzarini stand out. To the sw is Gambellara, a rival (in quality, not quantity) of Soave. Padua has its Colli Euganei, with a full array of red and white wines.

The Piave, one of Italy's major wine rivers, courses through the alpine foothills of Treviso province and down across the Venetian plain. Wine roads can be followed in both terrains (see the suggested excursions from *Conegliano* in *The mainland*). The hills between Conegliano and Valdobbiadene are famous for Prosecco, which is white, bubbly and has a superior version known as Cartizze. The area produces fine reds and still whites, as well as Champagne-method sparkling wines based on Pinot. Leading producers include Cardinal, Gregoletto, Carpené-Malvolti, Desiderio Bisol, Adamo Canel, Nino Franco and Pino Zardetto. s of the Piave in the hills around Asolo, Venegazzù is a legendary estate with a fine red wine and *spumante*.

The alluvial plains of the eastern Veneto produce notable Merlot and Cabernet and combinations of the two, as well as some pleasant whites.

Some of Italy's best wines come from Friuli's Collio Goriziano and Colli Orientali along the Yugoslav border adjacent to Udine and Gorizia. The style here is flowery and fruity in wines best drunk within a year or two. Tocai Friulano is the popular native, although Pinot Bianco and Grigio, Riesling, Sauvignon and Chardonnay thrive as well.

Friuli actually makes nearly as much red wine as white. Merlot dominates in the Grave and Isonzo DOC zones, where Cabernet and the native Refosco are also well represented. Local tastes run to fresh and fruity in red wines as well, so most are designed to drink in 2-5yrs.

Wine roads lead through Collio, Colli Orientali and Isonzo. Friuli's wines are screened for quality before being admitted to the Enoteca La Serenissima at Gradisca d'Isonzo. A few elite names among the region's many skilled producers include Collavini, Livio Felluga, Schioppetto, Jermann, Abbazia di Rosazzo, Gravner, Doro Princic, and Russiz Superiore.

Mountainous Trentino-Alto Adige is a jewel of Italian winemaking. Vineyards along the Adige river produce exquisite red, white, pink, dry, sweet and sparkling wines.

Alto Adige, the South Tyrol around Bolzano, is noted for perfumed white Sylvaner, Müller Thurgau, Riesling, Pinots and Gewürztraminer from the native Traminer vine. But reds can be nearly as distinguished: Cabernet, Pinot Nero, Santa Maddalena and the popular Caldaro (Kalterersee) and Lagrein. Reputable names to look for include Lageder, Tiefenbrunner, Schwanburg and Bellendorf.

Trentino, the province of Trento, has two fine native reds, Teroldego Rotaliano and Marzemino Schwanburg, and Bellendorf. plus Cabernets, Merlots and Bordeaux-type blends. But the emphasis here is on white wines. Chardonnay is in vogue, but Müller Thurgau, the Pinots and the native Nosiola are also convincing. Top producers are Pojer & Sandri, Zeni, and Foradori. The Champagne-method sparkling wines of Ferrari and a few other producers are nowadays among Italy's most respected *spumanti*.

Biographies

A personal selection of some outstanding Venetian artists: see also
Art and architecture (in *Culture, history and background*)

Bassano, Jacopo da Ponte (c.1510-92)
Painter of powerful and original genre and religious subjects.

Bellini, Giovanni (c.1430-1516)
The most innovative and sensitive painter of his period. His
brother **Gentile** was a narrative painter and portraitist.

Bon (or Buon), Bartolomeo (c.1374-?1467)
The outstanding architectural sculptor before the Lombardos.

Canaletto, Antonio (1697-1768)
Painter of luminous topographical views, mostly sold abroad.

Canova, Antonio (1757-1822)
The first and greatest of Neoclassical sculptors.

Carpaccio, Vittore (c.1460/5-1523/6)
Narrative and religious painter influenced by the Bellinis.

Cima da Conegliano, Giovanni Battista (1459/60-1517/18)
Painter of altarpieces in the manner of Giovanni Bellini.

Codussi, Mauro (c.1440-1504)
The outstanding architect of the early Venetian Renaissance.

Giorgione (1475-1510)
Enigmatic artist who transformed Venetian painting.

Guardi, Francesco (1712-93)
Impressionistic view painter who also collaborated on figure
paintings with his brother **Giovanni Antonio**.

Lombardo family
Pietro *(c.1435-1515)* and his sons **Tullio** *(c.1455-1532)* and
Antonio *(c.1458-?1516)* were the leading sculptor-architects of the
Venetian Renaissance.

Longhena, Baldassare (1598-1682)
The foremost Venetian Baroque architect.

Longhi, Pietro (1702-85)
Prolific painter of spirited scenes from daily life.

Lotto, Lorenzo (c.1480-1556)
Restless, independent religious and portrait painter.

Palladio, Andrea (1508-80)
The most influential northern Italian classical architect.

Palma il Vecchio (Jacopo Negretti) (c.1480-1528)
Giorgionesque painter of buxom blondes. His great-nephew
Palma il Giovane was the leading successor to Tintoretto.

Piazzetta, Giovanni Battista (1683-1754)
Rococo painter and first director of the Accademia.

Sanmicheli, Michele (1484-1559)
Veronese architect and military engineer.

Sansovino, Jacopo (1486-1570)
Florentine-born sculptor and city architect of Venice.

Tiepolo, Giovanni Battista (1696-1770)
The greatest Rococo painter. His son **Giovanni Domenico**
(1727-1804) is best known for his clowns and mountebanks.

Tintoretto, Jacopo Robusti (1518-94)
Dynamic, intense painter; Titian's greatest successor.

Titian (Tiziano Vecelli) (c.1490/90-1576)
The greatest, most worldly 16thC Venetian painter.

Veneziano, Paolo (active 1321-62)
The principal named Venetian Byzantine painter.

Veronese (Paolo Caliari) (1528-88)
The most brilliant decorative painter before Tiepolo.

Vivarini family
15thC painters who settled in Murano.

Sports, leisure, ideas for children

Most outdoor activities in Venice are centered on the Lido, only a few minutes' boat ride away from the historic center. Rowing is the exception, a sport Venice has made its own.

Bicycling
A bicycle ride on the Lido is a favorite Sunday outing for Venetians. Bicycles, tandems and tricycles can be rented from **Giorgio Barbieri** (*5 Via Zara, Lido*).

Flying
The **Aeroclub di Venezia** (*Aeroporto San Nicolò, Lido* ☎760808/761124*) has eight planes and offers, at a price, short tourist flights over Venice. It also runs a flying school.

Golf
There is an 18-hole golf course at **Alberoni** at the s end of the Lido (☎831015).

Horseback riding
The **Venice Riding Club** (*Circolo Ippico Veneziano*) is at **Ca'Bianca** on the Lido (☎765162). It has an indoor riding school and paddock as well as fixed and competition fences and competition horses.

Rowing
Rowing is now the most popular Venetian sport at all social levels. Regattas are held throughout the year, the main event being the **Vogalonga** (see *Calendar of events* in *Planning*). If you want to learn, you can join a rowing club (*società canottieri*). You must know how to swim.

Società Canottieri Francesco Querini
6576a Fondamenta Nuove ☎22039. *Open June-Sept 7am-8pm; Oct-May Tues-Sat 8am-noon, 1-6pm, Sun 8am-1pm (closed Mon)* AE
Being near the more peaceful waters off Fondamenta Nuove, this club is a good choice for beginners. Hourly sessions with an instructor are available to a schedule published in early May.

Sailing
Ciga hotels run a sailing club, the **Excelsior Yacht Club** (*52 Lungomare G. Marconi* ☎761845); it operates from the last Sat/Sun in May, when the beach opens.

Swimming
There are pools on the Lido at the Excelsior Hotel and Hotel des Bains and on the Giudecca at the Cipriani. Nonresidents can buy daily or season tickets, but they are expensive.

   Swimming on the Lido is more salubrious than you might think and can be irresistible in hot weather. The main hotels on the seafront have private beaches and the smaller hotels share one on Lungomare G. Marconi. Changing-tents may usually be rented from the hotels by nonresidents, but for the Excelsior you should reserve well in advance. The public beaches are at San Nicolò and Alberoni at the N and s ends of the Lido.

Tennis
There are tennis courts on the Lido at the larger hotels and at Lungomare D'Annunzio. Two clubs are the **Lido Tennis Club** (*163 Via San Gallo* ☎760954) and the **Tennis Union** (*Via Fausta* ☎968134).

Venice for children
You will find that the everyday water life of the city is a source of endless amusement for small children visiting the area. If they tire of riding on the water buses you can give them a poor man's

gondola ride simply by crossing the Grand Canal on a *traghetto* (see the *Orientation map* in *Planning*); and it is sometimes possible to rent a small motorboat from the boatyards at San Trovaso and on the Rio degli Ognissanti.

Although there are two public parks in Venice, the Giardini Pubblici and the smaller Giardino Papadopoli near Piazzale Roma, Venetian children prefer to play in their local campo or on the Zattere.

Games and bicycle rides are sometimes set up in Campo San Polo and Campo Santa Margherita, and an amusement fair visits the Riva degli Schiavoni.

For young people there is an excellent (but expensive) pre-university course which takes place annually in Feb and Mar. Information can be obtained from John Hall (*36 King's Rd., London SW3 4NB, UK* ☎*(01) 584-7335*).

Cultural activities

Venice has a very active musical life with concerts and recitals in the churches and smaller theaters as well as opera and ballet at the **Fenice**. Concerts and lectures are also given at the larger hotels and at the various learned societies, which include the **Ateneo Veneto, Cini Foundation** and **Istituto Veneto di Scienze, Lettere ed Arti**.

The **Società Italiana Dante Alighieri** offers Italian language courses (*further details from the tourist information office*).

Glossary of art and architecture

Aedicule Niche framed by columns

Ambulatory Aisle running around the E end of a church, usually enclosing an apse or sanctuary

Baldachin Canopy, usually over altar or throne

Basilica Rectangular Roman civic hall; early Christian church of similar structure

Belvedere Building sited primarily to command a fine view

Biforate Of windows, having two opening perforations

Chiaroscuro (Heightened) light and shade effect in painting

Crossing Space in church at intersection of chancel, nave and transepts

Diapered Patterned with a small, repeated design

Grotesque Decoration in paint or stucco mixing human, animal and plant forms

Impasto Paint applied thickly, revealing brush and palette marks

Intarsia Inlay of wood

Lantern Small circular turret with windows all around, crowning a roof or dome

Loggia Gallery or balcony open on at least one side

Lunette Semicircular surface or panel, often painted or carved

Ogival Of a double-curved line, both concave and convex

Piano nobile Main floor of house, usually on first floor

Pietà Representation of the Virgin lamenting over the dead Christ

Polyptych Work of art on several hinged panels

Predella One or more small paintings attached to the bottom of an altarpiece

Putto Plump, naked child, often winged, in work of art

Reredos A screen or wall decoration at the back of an altar

Rustication Masonry cut in massive blocks, separated by deep joints, to give bold texture to a wall or column

Stucco Light, reinforced plaster

Thermal window Semicircular window divided into three lights by two vertical mullions, derived from Roman baths and revived by Palladio in the 16thC

Tondo Circular painting or sculpture

Transept Transverse arms of a cruciform church

Triptych Work of art on three hinged panels

Volute Form of a spiral scroll

SPECIAL INFORMATION

A guide to Italian

This glossary covers the basic language needs of the traveler: for pronunciation, essential vocabulary and simple conversation, finding accommodations, visiting the bank, shopping and using public transport or a car. There is also a menu decoder.

Pronunciation

Most Italian words are pronounced exactly as they are written, with each syllable clearly enunciated. Some letters change their individual sounds, however, when grouped together, as shown below. Double consonants, such as in ca*pp*ello, are strongly pronounced. The letter 'r' is rolled. Stress in Italian nearly always falls on the penultimate syllable. An accent is used when the stress is final (e.g. with città, caffè). The Venetian dialect is really a separate language with its own pungent pronunciation and its own rules of spelling and grammar.

Vowels

a	as the *a* in father; e.g. and*a*re
e	as the *e* in pet; e.g. p*e*zzo, or as the *a* in may; e.g. part*e*
i	as the *i* in machine; e.g. pr*i*mo, or, when followed by another vowel, as the *y* in you; e.g. più, p*i*ove
o	as the *o* in pot; e.g. n*o*tte, or as in v*o*te; e.g. R*o*ma
u	as the *u* in prune; e.g. *u*scita, or, when followed by another vowel, as the letter *w*; e.g. *u*omo, g*u*ida

Consonants/letter groups

c,g	before e,i	soft, as the *ch* in *ch*urch and the *g* in agent; e.g. ba*ci*o, *Gi*no
c,g	before a,o,u	hard, as the *k* in *k*ing and the *g* in get; e.g. *c*amera, *c*osa, *g*atto, *g*uida
ch gh	before e,i	hard, as the *c* or the *g* above; e.g. *chi*esa, al*ghi*
cc	before e,i	soft, as the *ch* in *ch*urch; e.g. fa*cci*o, sals*icce*
gg	before e,i	soft as the *dg* in do*dg*e; e.g. o*gg*etto, o*gg*i
gli		as the *ll* in mi*lli*on; e.g. fi*gli*o
gn		pronounced nasally, as the *n* in *n*ew; e.g. ba*gn*o
qu		as in s*qu*are; e.g. *qu*esto
s	between vowels	soft, as the *z* in ga*z*e; e.g. ri*s*o, ca*s*a
sc	before e, i	as the *sh* in *sh*ift; e.g. *sc*ena, *sc*iopero
z		as the *ts* in ca*ts*; e.g. gra*z*ie, or as the *ds* in bir*ds*; e.g. me*zz*o

N.B. Gender

Gender has been indicated, where necessary, when not apparent from the regular masculine (-o, pl. -i) and feminine (-a, pl. -e) endings.

Reference words

Monday	lunedì	Friday	venerdì
Tuesday	martedì	Saturday	sabato
Wednesday	mercoledì	Sunday	domenica
Thursday	giovedì		

January	gennaio	July	luglio
February	febbraio	August	agosto
March	marzo	September	settembre
April	aprile	October	ottobre
May	maggio	November	novembre
June	giugno	December	dicembre

1 uno	11 undici	21 ventuno
2 due	12 dodici	22 ventidue
3 tre	13 tredici	30 trenta
4 quattro	14 quattordici	40 quaranta
5 cinque	15 quindici	50 cinquanta
6 sei	16 sedici	60 sessanta
7 sette	17 diciassette	70 settanta
8 otto	18 diciotto	80 ottanta
9 nove	19 diciannove	90 novanta
10 dieci	20 venti	100 cento

First primo, -a	Quarter-past . . . . e un quarto
Second secondo, -a	Half-past . . . . e mezzo
Third terzo, -a	Quarter to . . . . meno un quarto
Fourth quarto, -a	
One o'clock l'una	
Six o'clock le sei	

Mr signor(e)	Ladies signore, donne
Mrs signora	Gents signori, uomini
Miss signorina	

Basic communication

Yes sì
No no
Please per favore/per piacere
Thank you grazie
I'm very sorry mi dispiace molto/ mi scusi
Excuse me senta! (to attract attention), permesso! (on bus, train etc.), mi scusi
Not at all/you're welcome prego
Hello ciao (familiar), pronto (on telephone)
Good morning buon giorno
Good afternoon buona sera
Good evening buona sera
Good night buona notte
Goodbye ciao (familiar), arrivederci, addio (final or familiar)
Morning mattino
Afternoon pomeriggio
Evening sera
Night notte (f)
Yesterday ieri
Today oggi
Tomorrow domani
Next week la settimana prossima
Last week la settimana scorsa
. . . days ago . . . . giorni fa
Month mese (m)
Year anno
Here qui
There lì
Big grande
Small piccolo, -a
Hot caldo, -a
Cold freddo, -a
Good buono, -a
Bad cattivo, -a
Beautiful bello, -a
Well bene
Badly male
With con
And e, ed
But ma
Very molto

All tutto, -a
Open aperto
Closed chiuso
Entrance entrata
Exit uscita
Free libero
On the left a sinistra
On the right a destra
Straight ahead diritto
Near vicino
Far lontano
Up su
Down giù
Early presto
Late tardi
Quickly presto
Pleased to meet you. Molto lieto/ piacere.
How are you? Come sta?
Very well, thank you. Benissimo, grazie.
Do you speak English? Parla inglese?
I don't understand. Non capisco.
I don't know. Non lo so.
Please explain. Può spiegare per favore.
Please speak more slowly. Parli più lentamente per favore.
My name is . . . . Mi chiamo . . . .
I am American/English. Sono americano/inglese, -a.
Where is/are . . .? Dov'è/dove si trova/dove sono . . .?
Is there a . . .? C'è un, una . . .?
What? Cosa?
When? Quando?
How much? Quanto?
That's too expensive. È troppo caro.
Expensive caro
Cheap a buon mercato
I would like . . . . Vorrei . . . .
Do you have . . . .? Avete . . . ?
That's fine/OK. Va bene/ benissimo/OK.
What time is it? Che ore sono?
I don't feel well. Non mi sento bene/sto male.

Words and phrases

Accommodations

Making a reservation by letter

Dear Sir/Madam,
Egregio Signore/Signora,
I would like to reserve one double room/double-bedded room/ (with bathroom)—
Vorrei prenotare una camera doppia/matrimoniale/(con bagno)—
—a twin-bedded room, and one single room (with shower)
—una camera con due letti, e una camera singola (con doccia)
for 7 nights from 12 August. We would like bed and breakfast/half board/full
board
per 7 notti dal 12 agosto. Vorremmo una camera con colazione/mezza
pensione/pensione completa
and would prefer rooms with a sea view.
e possibilmente camere con vista sul mare.
Please send me details of your terms with the confirmation
Sarei lieto di ricevere dettagli del prezzo e la conferma.
Yours sincerely,
Cordiali saluti,

Arriving at the hotel

I have a reservation. My name is . . . .
Ho già prenotato. Sono il signor/la signora . . . .
A quiet room with bath/shower/WC/washbasin . . . .
Una camera tranquilla con bagno/doccia/WC/lavandino . . .
. . . .overlooking the sea/park/street/the back.
. . . .con vista sul mare/sul parco/sulla strada/sul retro.
Does the price include breakfast/tax/service?
E'tutto compreso — colazione/tasse/servizio?
This room is too large/small/cold/hot/noisy.
Questa camera è troppo grande/piccola/fredda/calda/rumorosa.
That's too expensive. Have you anything cheaper?
Costa troppo. Avete qualcosa meno caro?

Floor/story piano
Dining room/restaurant sala da pranzo/ristorante(m)
Manager direttore, -trice
Porter portiere
Have you got a room? Avete una camera?
What time is breakfast/dinner? A che ora è la prima colazione/la cena?
Is there a laundry service? C'è il servizio lavanderia?
What time does the hotel close? A che ora chiude l'albergo?
Will I need a key? Avrò bisogno della chiave?
Is there a night porter? C'è un portiere di notte?
I'll be leaving tomorrow morning. Parto domani mattina.
Please give me a call at . . . . Mi può chiamare alle . . . .
Come in! Avanti!

Shopping (La Spesa)

Where is the nearest/a good . . . .? Dov'è il più vicino/la pi
vicina . . . .? Dov'è un buon/una buona . . . .?
Can you help me/show me . . . .? Mi può aiutare/Può mostrarmi . . . .?
I'm just looking. Sto soltanto guardando.
Do you accept credit cards/travelers cheques? Accettate carte di credito/
travelers cheques?
Can you deliver to . . . .? Può consegnare a . . . .?
I'll take it. Lo prendo.
I'll leave it. Lo lascio.
Can I have it tax-free for export? Posso averlo senza tasse per
l'esportazione?
This is faulty. Can I have a replacement/refund? C'è difetto. Me lo
potrebbe cambiare/rimborsare?
I don't want to spend more than . . . . Non voglio spendere più di . . . .
Can I have a stamp for . . . .? Vorrei un francobollo per . . . .?

Words and phrases

Shops

Antique store	negozio di antiquariato	Jeweler	gioielleria
Art gallery	galleria d'arte	Market	mercato
Bakery	panificio, forno	Newsstand	giornalaio, edicola (kiosk)
Bank	banca	Optician	ottico
Beauty parlor	istituto di bellezza	Perfumery	profumeria
Bookstore	libreria	Pharmacy/drugstore	farmacia
Butcher	macelleria	Photographic store	negozio fotografico
Cake shop	pasticceria	Post office	ufficio postale
Clothes store	negozio di abbigliamento, di confezioni	Shoe store	negozio di calzature
Dairy	latteria	Stationers	cartoleria
Delicatessen	salumeria, pizzicheria	Supermarket	supermercato
Fish store	pescheria	Tailor	sarto
Florist	fioraio	Tobacconist	tabaccheria (also sells stamps)
Greengrocer	ortolano, erbivendolo, fruttivendolo	Tourist office	ente del turismo
Grocer	drogheria	Toy store	negozio di giocattoli
Haberdasher	merciaio	Travel agent	agenzia di viaggio
Hairdresser	parrucchiere, -a		

At the bank

I would like to change some dollars/pounds/travelers cheques
Vorrei cambiare dei dollari/delle sterline/dei travelers cheques
What is the exchange rate?
Come'è il cambio?
Can you cash a personal check?
Può cambiare un assegno?
Can I obtain cash with this credit card?
Posso avere soldi in contanti con questa carta di credito?
Do you need to see my passport?
Ha bisogno del mio passaporto?

Some useful goods

Antiseptic cream	crema antisettica	Shampoo	shampoo
Aspirin	aspirina	Shaving cream	crema da barba
Bandages	fasciature	Soap	sapone (m)
Band-Aid	cerotto	Sunburn cream	crema antisolare
Cotton	cotone idrofilo (m)	Sunglasses	occhiali da sole
Diarrhea/upset stomach pills	pillole anti-coliche	Suntan cream/oil	crema/olio solare
Indigestion tablets	pillole per l'indigestione	Tampons	tamponi
		Tissues	fazzoletti di carta
Insect repellant	insettifugo	Toothbrush	spazzolino da denti
Laxative	lassativo	Toothpaste	dentifricio
Sanitary napkins	assorbenti igienici	Travel sickness pills	pillole contro il mal di viaggio

Bra	reggiseno	Shirt	camicia
Coat	cappotto	Shoes	scarpe
Dress	vestito	Skirt	gonna
Jacket	giacca	Stockings/tights	calze/collants
Pants	mutande	Swimsuit	costume da bagno (m)
Pullover	maglione (m)	Trousers	pantaloni

Film	pellicola	Postcard	cartolina
Letter	lettera	Stamp	francobollo
Money order	vaglia	Telegram	telegramma (m)

Motoring

Service station   *stazione di rifornimento (f), distributore (m)*
Fill it up.   *Faccia il pieno, per favore.*
Give me . . . . lire worth.   *Mi dia . . . .lire.*
I would like . . . . liters of gas.   *Vorrei . . . . litri di benzina.*
Can you check the . . . .?   *Può controllare . . . .?*
There is something wrong with the . . . .   *C'è un difetto nel/nella . . . .*

195

Words and phrases

Accelerator	acceleratore(m)	Lights	fanali, fari, luci
Axle	l'asse(m)	Oil	olio
Battery	batteria	Spares	i pezzi di ricambio
Brakes	freni	Spark plugs	le candele
Exhaust	lo scarico, scappamento	Tires	gomme
Fan belt	la cinghia del ventilatore	Water	acqua
Gear box	la scatola del cambio	Windshield	parabrezza (m)

My car won't start. La mia macchina non s'accende.
My car has broken down/has a flat tire. La macchina è guasta/la gomma è forata.
The engine is overheating Il motore si scalda
How long will it take to repair? Quanto tempo ci vorrà per la riparazione?
I need it as soon as possible. Ne ho bisogno il più presto possibile.

Car rental

Where can I rent a car? Dove posso noleggiare una macchina?
Is full/comprehensive insurance included? E'completamente assicurata?
Is it insured for another driver? E'assicurata per un altro guidatore?
Does the price include mileage? Il kilometraggio è compreso?
Unlimited mileage kilometraggio illimitato
Deposit deposito
By what time must I return it? A che ora devo consegnarla?
Can I return it to another depot? Posso riportarla ad un altro deposito?
Is the gas tank full? E pieno il serbatoio?

Road signs

Accendere le luci in galleria	lights on in tunnel	Divieto di sosta	no stopping
Autostrada	highway	Lavori in corso	roadworks ahead
Caduta di massi	falling stones	Passaggio a livello	level crossing
Casello	toll gate	Pedaggio	toll road
Dare la precedenza	yield	Raccordo anulare	beltway
Divieto di accesso, senso vietato	no entry	Rallentare	slow down
		Senso unico	one-way street
Divieto di parcheggio	no parking	Tangenziale	bypass
Divieto di sorpasso	no passing	Tenersi in corsia	keep in lane
		Uscita (autocarri)	exit (for trucks)

Other methods of transport

Aircraft	aeroplano	Train	treno
Airport	aeroporto	Ticket	biglietto
Bus	autobus(m)	Ticket office	biglietteria
Bus stop	fermata	One-way	andata
Ferry	traghetto	Round trip	andata e ritorno
Ferry port	porto	Half fare	metà prezzo
Motorboat	motoscafo	First/second/economy	prima classe/
Water bus	vaporetto		seconda classe/turistico
Station	stazione (f)	Sleeper/couchette	cuccetta

When is the next . . . for . . . ? Quando parte il prossimo . . . per . . . ?
What time does it arrive? A che ora arriva?
What time does the last . . . . for . . . . leave? Quando parte l'ultimo . . . . per . . . ?
Which platform/quay/gate? Quale binario/molo/uscita?
Is this the . . . . for . . . . ? E'questo il . . . . per . . . . ?
Is it direct? Where does it stop? E'diretto? Dove si ferma?
Do I need to change anywhere? Devo cambiare?
Please tell me where to get off. Mi può dire dove devo scendere.
Take me to . . . . Mi vuol portare a
Is there a dining car? C'è un vagone ristorante?

Venetian street names

Calle	street or alleyway
Campo	square, literally field
Campiello	small square
Corte	courtyard, usually a cul-de-sac
Fondamenta	paved walk along one side of a canal
Molo	quay
Piscina	site of a lake or pond
Ponte	bridge

Ramo   branch of a larger street
Rio   any canal within the city except the Grand Canal, Cannaregio Canal
   and Giudecca Canal
Rio terrà   filled-in canal, now a street
Riva   major fondamenta
Ruga   originally a shopping street
Sacca   meeting of two canals or rii
Salizzada   major street of a parish
Sottoportico (or sottoportego)   archway or covered street

Food and drink

Have you a table for . . . .?   Avete un tavolo per . . . .?
I want to reserve a table for . . . . at . . . .   Vorrei prenotare un tavolo
   per . . . alle . . . .
A quiet table.   Un tavolo tranquillo.
A table near the window.   Un tavolo vicino alla finestra.
Could we have another table?   Potremmo spostarci?
I did not order this.   Non ho ordinato questo.
Breakfast/lunch/dinner   prima colazione/pranzo/cena
Bring me another . . . .   Un altro . . . . per favore.
The bill please.   Il conto per favore.
Is service included?   Il servizio è incluso?

Hot caldo		Salt sale (m)	
Cold freddo		Pepper pepe (m)	
Glass bicchiere (m)		Oil olio	
Bottle bottiglia		Vinegar aceto	
Half-bottle mezza bottiglia		Mustard senape (f)	
Beer/lager (draft) birra (alla		Bread pane (m)	
spina)		Butter burro	
Fruit juice succo di frutta		Cheese formaggio	
Mineral water acqua minerale		Milk latte (m)	
Orangeade/lemonade aranciata/		Coffee caffè (m)	
limonata		Tea tè (m)	
Carbonated/noncarbonated gassata/		Chocolate cioccolato	
non gassata		Sugar zucchero	
Flask/carafe fiasco/caraffa		Steak bistecca	
Red wine vino rosso, vine nero		well done ben cotto	
White wine vino bianco		medium medio	
Rosé wine vino rosé		rare al sangue	
Vintage di annata			
Dry secco			
Sweet dolce, amabile			

Menu decoder

Abbacchio baby lamb	Basilico basil
Acciughe anchovies	Bianchetti whitebait
Affettati sliced cold meats	Bianco plain, boiled
Affumicato smoked	Bietola Swiss chard
Aglio garlic	Bigoli spaghetti
Agnello lamb	Bollito misto boiled meats
Agnolotti pasta envelopes	Brace (alla) charcoal grilled
Agro sour	Braciola chop
Albicocche apricots	Branzino sea bass
Amaro bitter	Bresaola dried salt beef
Ananas pineapple	Brodetto fish soup
Anatra/anitra duck	Brodo consommé
Anguilla eel	Burro (al) (cooked in) butter
Animelle sweetbreads	Cacciagione game
Antipasto hors d'oeuvre	Calamaretti baby squid
Aragosta langouste, lobster	Calamari squid
Arancia orange	Cannelloni stuffed pasta tubes
Aringa herring	Cannochie mantis shrimps
Arrosto roast meat	Capitone large conger eel
Arselle baby clams	Cappelletti stuffed pasta hats
Asiago semi-soft cheese	Cappelunghe a shellfish
Asparagi asparagus	Cappe sante scallops
Astaco river crayfish, lobster	Capperi capers
Baccalà dried salt cod	Capriolo venison
Baicoli hard, semi-sweet biscuits	Carciofi artichokes

197

Words and phrases

Carne meat
Carote carrots
Carpa carp
Carpaccio raw lean beef fillet
Carrello (al) from the trolley
Casalingo, -a homemade
Castagne chestnuts
Castrato mutton
Cavolfiore cauliflower
Cavolini di Bruxelles sprouts
Cavolo cabbage
Ceche young eels
Ceci chick peas
Cèfalo gray mullet
Cenci fried pastry twists
Cervella brains
Cervo venison
Cetriolo cucumber
Cicoria chicory
Ciliege cherries
Cima cold stuffed veal
Cinghiale wild boar
Cipolle onions
Cocomero watermelon
Coda di bue oxtail
Coda di rospo angler fish
Coniglio rabbit
Contorno vegetable sidedish
Controfiletto sirloin steak
Cosciotto di agnello leg of lamb
Costata di bue entrecôte steak
Costolette cutlets
Cotto cooked
Cozze mussels
Crema custard, cream soup
Crespolini savory pancakes
Crostacei shellfish
Crudo raw
Dentice species of fish like sea
  bream
Diavola (alla) in a spicy sauce
Dolci desserts, sweets
Espresso small black coffee
Fagiano pheasant
Fagiolini French beans
Faraona guinea fowl
Farcito stuffed
Fatto in casa homemade
Fave broad beans
Fegatini chicken livers
Fegato liver
Fegato alla Veneziana liver cooked
  with onions
Ferri (ai) grilled
Fesa di vitello leg of veal
Fettina slice
Fettuccine thin flat pasta
Fichi figs
Filetto fillet
Finocchio fennel
Focaccia dimpled savory bread
Fontina Gruyère-like cheese
Formaggio cheese
Forno (al) cooked in the oven
Fragole strawberries
Fresco fresh
Frittata omelet
Frittelle fritters
Fritto fried

Frutta fruit
Frutti di mare shellfish
Funghi mushrooms
Gamberetti shrimps
Gamberi big shrimps
Gelato ice cream
Girarrosto (al) spit-roasted
Girello topside of beef
Gnocchi small potato or semolina
  dumplings
Grana Parmesan cheese
Granchio or Granzeola crab
Granita water ice
Graticola (alla) grilled
Griglia (alla) grilled
Indivia endive
Insalata salad
Involtini skewered veal and ham
Lamponi raspberries
Lampreda lamprey
Lasagne baked flat pasta
Lenticchie lentils
Lepre hare
Lesso boiled (meat)
Limone lemon
Lingua di bue ox tongue
Lombata, -ina loin, loin chop
Lonza cured fillet of pork
Luccio pike
Lumache snails
Macedonia di frutta fruit salad
Magro lean
Maiale pork
Mandorle almonds
Manzo beef
Marscapone rich cream cheese
Marmellata jam
Medaglioni rounds of meat
Mela apple
Melagrana pomegranate
Melanzane eggplant
Melone melon
Merlano whiting
Merluzzo cod
Miele honey
Minestra soup
Minestrone vegetable soup
Misto mixed
Moleche soft-shelled crabs
Montasio semi-soft cheese
Mostarda pickle
Nasello hake
Naturale (al) plain
Nocciole hazelnuts
Noce di vitello veal top round
Noci nuts
Nodino di vitello veal chop
Nostrale, nostrano local
Oca goose
Orata gilt-head bream
Osso buco veal knuckle
Ostriche oysters
Paglia e fieno green and white
  tagliatelle
Paillard thin grilled steak
Palombo dogfish
Panino roll
Panna cream
Pappardelle long flat pasta

Parmigiano-Reggiano Parmesan
Pasta e fagioli bean and pasta soup
Pasticcio layered pasta pie
Pasto meal
Patate potatoes
Penne short pasta tubes
Peperoni sweet peppers
Pera pear
Pernice partridge
Pesca peach
Pesce fish
Pesce persico perch
Pesce spada swordfish
Pesciolini small fried fish
Pesto green basil sauce
Petto di pollo chicken breast
Pezzo piece
Piacere according to taste
Piatto del giorno today's dish
Piccante spicy, piquant
Piccata thin escalope
Piccione pigeon
Piselli peas
Polenta cornmeal served boiled or
  boiled and grilled
Polipi baby octopus (squid)
Pollame poultry
Pollo chicken
Polpette meatballs
Polpettone meatloaf
Polpo octopus
Pomodoro tomato
Pompelmo grapefruit
Porchetta roast suckling pig
Prezzemolo parsley
Primizie spring vegetables
Prosciutto ham
Prugne plums
Quaglie quails
Radicchio rosso red bitter lettuce
Ragù meat and tomato sauce
Rane frogs
Ravanelli radishes
Ravioli stuffed pasta squares
Razza skate
Ricci sea urchins
Ricciarelli almond biscuits
Ricotta cheese — similar to cottage
  cheese
Rigatoni ridged pasta tubes
Ripieno stuffed
Risi e bisi pea and rice soup
Riso rice
Risotto savory rice dish
Rognoni kidneys
Romboliscio brill
Rombo maggiore turbot
Rosmarino rosemary
Rospo (pesce rospo) anglerfish
Rucola bitter herb used in salads
Salsa (verde) (green) sauce
Salsiccia sausage
Saltimbocca alla romana veal
  scallops with ham and sage
Salvia sage
Sampiero John Dory
Sarde sardines
Scaloppine scallops
Scampi Dublin Bay shrimps

Scelta (a) of your choice
Scottadito grilled lamb cutlets
Selvaggina game, venison
Semifreddo frozen dessert
Semplice plain
Seppie cuttlefish
Sgombro mackerel
Sogliola sole
Sottaceti pickled vegetables
Spaghetti
  all'amatriciana spaghetti with
    bacon, tomatoes
  alla bolognese with *ragù*
  alla carbonara with bacon, eggs
  alla napoletana with tomato
Spezzatino meat stew
Spiedini skewers, kebabs
Spiedo (allo) on the spit
Spigola sea bass
Spinaci spinach
Squadro monkfish
Stagionato hung, well-aged
Stagione (di) in season
Stoccafisso stockfish
Stracciatella clear egg soup
Stracotto beef in red wine
Stufato braised, stew(ed)
Sugo sugar
Supplì rice croquettes
Susina plum
Tacchino turkey
Tagliatelle thin flat pasta
Tartufi truffles
Tegame (al) fried or baked
Telline cockles
Timballo savory pasta pie
Tinca tench
Tiramisù a rich pudding
Tonno tuna
Tordi thrushes
Torta flan, tart
Tortellini small stuffed pasta
Tost toasted sandwich
Totano squid
Tramezzino sandwich
Trancia slice
Trenette flat, thinnish pasta
Trifolato fried in garlic
Triglia red mullet
Trippa tripe
Trota trout
Turtuffi sea truffles
Uccelletti grilled beef on skewers
Umido (in) stewed
Uova eggs
Uva grapes
Verdure green vegetables
Vitello veal
Vongole clams
Zabaglione egg yolks and Marsala
  whip
Zucca squash
Zuccotto ice cream liqueur cake
Zuppa soup
Zuppa inglese trifle

Index

Individual hotels, restaurants, cafés, shops etc. do not appear in the general index because they are in alphabetical order within their appropriate sections and can be easily located. Streets and squares are listed in the gazetteer.

Page numbers in **bold** type indicate the main entries. Page numbers in *italic* type denote illustrations.

Index

201

Index

Index

Index

Gazetteer of street names

Numbers after street names refer to pages on which streets are mentioned in the text. Map references relate to the maps that follow this gazetteer.

It has not been possible to label every street drawn on the maps, although all major road, squares and canals are indicated. Some unlabeled streets still appear in the gazetteer, however, with a map reference to show their approximate location.

Gazetteer

VENICE

1

LEGEND

City Maps	Area Maps

0   100   200   300m

City Maps

- Major Place of Interest
- Other Important Building
- Built-up Area
- Park
- † † Cemetery
- † † Named Church, Church
- ✡ Synagogue
- ✚ Hospital
- i Information Office
- ✉ Post Office
- ✋ Police Station
- ⚓ Parking Lot
- ● Water Bus Landing Stage
- **10** Adjoining Page No.

Area Maps

- ═◯═ Superhighway (with access point)
- ▬▬ Main Road
- ▬ Secondary Road
- ─ Minor Road
- A4 Road No.
- ─ ─ Ferry
- ▭▬▭ Railway
- ✈ Airport
- ⌂ Monastery, Church
- ∴ Ancient Site, Ruin
- ♜ Castle
- ■ Villa
- •1569 Heights in Meters

VENICE REGION

0   5   10   15Km

1 2   1 2   2 3

A

B

Mandrielle
50bis
Primolano
348
M

S. Marino
Fener
M. Grappa
1775
Pederobba
Possagno
Onigo
Cornud
Asolo
Montec

Asiago
47
Brenta

1356

Chiuppano
Lugo
Maróstica
BASSANO D. GRAPPA
248
Rosa
Rossano
Vèneto
Riese
Breganze
Montécchio
Precalcino
Galliera
Vèneto
Castelfr
Vèn
Thiene
Malo
A31
348
Dueville
Sandrigo
Cittadella
Resana
Piom
Des
Caldogno
53
Lisiera
Bertésina
Brenta
Camposampiero
307
VICENZA
Piazzola s. Br.
A7
Montecchio
Magg.
VILLA ROTONDA
Vancimuglio
Campodà
11
A4
Arcugnano
Vo M. Bèrici
Grisignano
di Zocco
Limena
A4
11
Pte.
Bren
PADOVA
Lonigo
Ponte
di Barb.
**MONAST.
DI PRAGLIA**
247
Bagnolo
Sossano
Abano Terme
16
A13
Le
Cologna
Finale
Montegrotto
Terme
Poiana
Magg.
**Noventa
Vic.**
Battàglia
Terme
Piove
Bovolenta
Montagnana
10
Este
Monsèlice
Conselve
Pontec
Colli Euganei
A13
Ponso
Bagnoli
di Sopra
Merlara
Anguillara-
Vèn.
Adige (Etsch)
Masi
Stanghella
16
Badia
Pol.
499
Lendinara
ROVIGO
443
Trecenta
Fratta Polesine

1 2   2 3

1 2   2 3

A
B

4

— Mestre

B
C

CANALE   PONTE
TRE ARCHI

FONDAMENTA

FONDAMENTA

DI

RIO DI S. GIOBBE

S. GIOBBE

**San
Giobbe**

RIO DELLA CREA

RIO DELLA CREA

B

C

Isola del
Tronchetto

C
D

S

Ferrovia

FE

CANAL

F. DI S. SIMEONE

Stazione
Marittima

CANALE DI S. CHIARA

FOND. DI S. CHIARA

F. CROCE

P. ROMA

GIARDINO
PAPADOPOLI

CAMPO S. ANDREA

S. Andrea

PIAZZALE
ROMA

RIO
NUOVO

Sar
da S

D
E

CANALE

SCOMENZERA

RIO DI S. MARIA MAGGIORE

RIO DELLE BURCHIELLE

RIO TERRA DEI PENSIERI

R.D. CAZZIOLA

RIO

E

S. MARTA

RIO DELL' ARZERE

RIO DI S. MARIA MAGGIORE

RIO BRIATI

F

1 2   2 3

8
Palazzo
Arian

Carmini

RO

CAMPO S.
PIETRO

**San Pietro
di Castello**

E
F

pe

VIALE 24 MAGGIO

*Darsena
di
S. Elena*

F
G

CAMPO
STRINGARI

*CAMPO
SPORTIVO*

→ **Sant' Elena**

G
H

VIALE

VITTORIO

S. ELENA

VENETO

H
I